REVIVE US AGAIN

REVIVE
US AGAIN

THE REAWAKENING OF
AMERICAN FUNDAMENTALISM

Joel A. Carpenter

New York   *Oxford*
Oxford University Press
1997

Oxford University Press

Oxford New York
Athens Auckland Bangkok Bogotá Bombay
Buenos Aires Calcutta Cape Town Dar es Salaam
Delhi Florence Hong Kong Istanbul Karachi
Kuala Lumpur Madras Madrid Melbourne
Mexico City Nairobi Paris Singapore
Taipei Tokyo Toronto Warsaw

and associated companies in
Berlin Ibadan

Copyright © 1997 by Joel A. Carpenter

Published by Oxford University Press, Inc.
198 Madison Avenue, New York, New York 10016

Oxford is a registered trademark of Oxford University Press, Inc.

Library of Congress Cataloging-in-Publication Data
Carpenter, Joel A.
Revive us again: the reawakening of American Fundamentalism
p. cm. Includes bibliographical references and index.
ISBN 0-19-505790-2.
1. Fundamentalism—United States—History—20th century.
2. Fundamentalist churches—United States—History—20th century.
3. United States—Church history—20th century. I. Title.
BT82.2.C37 1997 277.3'082—dc21 97-13227

1 3 5 7 9 8 6 4 2

Printed in the United States of America
on acid-free paper

To Tim, who urged me to start this book

and

to Janis, who encouraged me to finish it.

CONTENTS

ACKNOWLEDGMENTS

This work was many years in the making, and along the way to its conclusion I have been helped by many people. First I must acknowledge the late Timothy L. Smith, who as my graduate mentor encouraged me to study American fundamentalism and guided me through the travails of writing a dissertation on this topic. Tim's great respect for the religious creativity and integrity of ordinary people was a lesson I shall never forget.

I have benefitted more than I can easily reckon from a community of scholars who share my interest in the history of evangelicals in America. George Marsden, Mark Noll, Grant Wacker, Michael Hamilton, Nathan Hatch, the late George Rawlyk, Larry Eskridge, Edith Blumhofer, James Bratt, Harry Stout, D. G. Hart, Richard Hughes, Randall Balmer, Donald Dayton, Virginia Brereton, and Margaret Bendroth have been my conversation partners, advisors and critics through the years. They have read and evaluated various drafts of chapters, and the first four mentioned ploughed through the entire manuscript. I learned a great deal from their comments, even when I did not fully agree with them. This book is stronger, I think, because of their help, but its remaining flaws are solely my responsibility. I am grateful also for the help of some outstanding assistants at the Institute for the Study of American Evangelicals, especially Ron Frank and Carmen Ballou.

Writing the history of popular religious movements has its occupational hazards, as Timothy Smith once warned, notably the need to spend so much time in the dark and musty places where old religious magazines are shelved. The librarians who manage those collections make this burden much lighter, and I am grateful to many more than I can name here for their expertise, kind assistance and companionship. I would be remiss, however, not to mention a few who have been extraordinarily helpful: Walter Osborn of the Moody Bible Institute Library, Thom Morris of Trinity College's Lew Library, Jolene Carlson of Wheaton College's Buswell Library, Conrad Bult and Peter DeKlerk of

Calvin College's Hekman Library, Ferne Weimer and Ken Gill of the Billy Graham Center Library, and Bob Shuster and Paul Erickson of the Archives of the Billy Graham Center. A historian can have no better friends than these highly skilled supporters of good scholarship.

I am also grateful to several administrative assistants for their expertise in preparing manuscripts and communicating with editors and readers through the years: JoAnne Haley at Wheaton College early on in the project, Glory Donovan at The Pew Charitable Trusts through my years there, and now at the very end of the task, Eunice Stegink at Calvin College. Each has been more happy to help and more interested in the project than I had any right to expect. The same is true, I might add, of Craig Noll, who created the index.

I was able to get this book off to a flying start thanks to a grant from the Stewardship Foundation, which allowed me to take a study leave from Wheaton College. My special thanks, then, to George Kovats and C. Davis Weyerhaeuser for their interest, support and patience. During my seven-year sojourn at The Pew Charitable Trusts, its president, Rebecca W. Rimel, graciously allowed me to spend part of my time in the study to work on this book.

There must be some special reward in the hereafter for the patient families of authors. My daughter, Rebecca, and son, Andrew, cannot remember a time when this book was not in the making. I am grateful that they have allowed this project to have some claims on my time and attention. No words can repay the debt of love I owe to my wife, Janis, who always believed that I would complete this project even when I did not. Well, my dear, it is done and you were right, as ever.

PREFACE

Some seventy years ago, the editors of the *Christian Century*, the major voice of liberal Protestantism, pronounced the passing of fundamentalism. "Anybody should be able to see," they declared, that "the whole fundamentalist movement was hollow and artificial," and "wholly lacking in qualities of constructive achievement or survival."[1] Fundamentalism was dying out and soon would be gone from the American religious scene; it was a dysfunctional mutation away from the main thrust of religion's evolutionary progress. While many people today might agree with the Century about the movement's lack of constructive achievements, no one can deny that fundamentalism has survived. Its contemporary heirs are thriving, and present a fairly wide spectrum of belief and orientation, ranging from Bob Jones III to Senator Mark Hatfield. And each group of them—militant, moderate, and revisionist—has found ways to influence American public life. The recent resurgence of these descendents of the older fundamentalism has received a great deal of attention, but very little of this coverage probes deeply into the movement's history and character. Thus for many observers, fundamentalism is a puzzle and its origins are murky. This book is an attempt to remedy that lack of understanding.

Thanks to the work of historians Ernest Sandeen and George Marsden, the origins, early development, and historic significance of fundamentalism are, if not well known, at least available for public consumption. But the questions of how fundamentalism survived its setbacks in the 1920s and adapted itself to changing cultural conditions thereafter have not been carefully explored.[2] Indeed, historians of American religion and culture have almost totally ignored fundamentalism's career between the winding down of its antimodernist crusades in the 1920s and the emergence in the 1950s of what the *Christian Century* called "neo-fundamentalism."

There are good reasons for this lapse of knowledge, notably fundamentalism's retreat from public view and the academic world's distaste for ideas and movements that seem retrograde and obsolete. Yet it is shortsighted to view resurgent evangelicalism in general and militant fundamentalism in particular as the temporary byproducts of cultural strain or as throwbacks to the movements of the 1920s. Ernest Sandeen's important point that fundamentalism has been a "self-conscious, structured, long-lived, dynamic entity"[3] and not merely a mentality or a passing byproduct of modernization suggests that the years between fundamentalism's fall from public respect in the late 1920s and the rise of Billy Graham and the "new evangelicals" in the 1950s should command careful scrutiny.

The first purpose of this book is to bring the fundamentalist movement's career in these hidden years to light, and in the process to provide answers to the riddle of its survival. The key to its solution is the insight that fundamentalists carried several paradoxical tensions, perhaps the most important being their indecision as to whether they were alienated outsiders or quintessential Americans.[4] During the 1930s and 1940s, this tension proved to be creative, allowing fundamentalists to establish their identity, consolidate an institutional network, and rethink their mission to America. Ironically, they were freed by their defeats in the antimodernist controversies to concentrate on these more positive tasks. While they were predicting the world's imminent demise and building a subculture to protect themselves from worldly society, fundamentalists were also retooling their evangelistic techniques and seizing upon inviting cultural trends to mount a renewed public presence. Their goals were time-honored evangelical ones: to bring revival to America and the gospel to the world.

While this book devotes most of its attention to the internal affairs of the fundamentalist movement, it does so with reference to several contexts. As a religious history, it refers to fundamentalists' relationships with other religious groups. Since fundamentalists shared an adversarial or perhaps even symbiotic relationship with liberal mainline Protestantism, this context appears fairly often in the narrative. Frequent reference is also made to the broader constellation of evangelical movements and conservative Protestant traditions (such as pentecostals, holiness Wesleyans, and Southern Baptists) that were neighbors and relatives to fundamentalism in American popular religion. An important part of this story is how some of the fundamentalists came to dream of a grand alliance of evangelicals, and what opportunities and constraints confronted them in that task. Nevertheless, this book can provide only a partial view of the larger evangelical landscape in North America; there are many more kindred stories that must be recovered before the panorama is complete.

Fundamentalists also responded to the changing conditions and moods of American culture more generally. So this book is by necessity an attempt at cultural history. Fundamentalists were in many respects determinedly sectarian and isolated from the American cultural mainstream, but they were also remarkably sensitive to changes in the cultural atmosphere and quite conscious of their reputation. While sincerely trying to flee worldliness, they had a deep yearning to be respected. Although this study avoids the temptation to make fundamentalism a mere byproduct of cultural shifts, it does show the continuing interplay between fundamentalism and American culture.

It is only fair that the reader be made aware of another context. I am intimately acquainted with fundamentalism on both personal and scholarly levels. I was reared a fundamentalist and still am a Christian, albeit of another kind. I am intimately aware of the dangers of writing about something that comes so close to home, but I also recognize that there are advantages to being a participant observer that have been made abundantly clear by the authors of recent ethnic and religious histories. I can only let the reader judge how well I avoid the pitfalls and use the advantage of an insider's knowledge and sensibilities in trying to tell the truth about my own heritage.[5]

Both the religious and nonreligious readers of this book should know one more thing about it. While written from a Christian perspective about the nature and destiny of humans and their history, this work is an exercise in ordinary history. Historical study ordinarily concerns itself with the affairs of this world and seeks to explain them in publicly accessible terms. Its task is to search out the cultural and natural causative factors that have shaped the human story. For religious believers there are supernatural factors in the human drama as well, and these forces ultimately direct its outcome. I write history with the assumption that these spiritual forces are at work in human events, albeit in ways not easily discerned. Not claiming to be an inspired prophet, however, I am largely content to focus on ordinary historical causation, and to defer any interpretation of God's particular role in what has transpired until the day when we shall know more perfectly than is possible here and now.

Perhaps this choice is a reaction against my fundamentalist rearing, for fundamentalists tend to de-emphasize historical causation. They regularly read world events and their role in them from a divine angle of vision, as if they, like the authors of Scripture, are divinely inspired. Yet I hope that I am not reacting in a purely naturalistic direction. My aim is to affirm the classic Christian belief that supernatural and natural perspectives on this world are complementary, since God governs creation through the secondary means of natural law as well as by more direct involvement in its affairs. Thus it is perfectly proper to regard history as the simultaneous outworking of divine, human, and natural causation. Under these terms, the task of understanding "ordinary history" is eminently worthy of a Christian's time and talent. I offer this book in that spirit; it is open to the inspection of both secular-minded and God-worshipping readers with the hope that I have honored my commitments to each community.

This book's mission will be fully achieved if its readers gain a deeper understanding of fundamentalism's continuing role in American life, a historical perspective on the movement's contemporary behavior, an appreciation of the rich diversity within American evangelical Christianity, and a fresh insight on what it means to be religious and to be American. This is a large agenda, and it can be covered only incompletely and suggestively. But if this book accomplishes its simplest and most primary task—to explain what happened to fundamentalism between the demise of its crusades in the 1920s and the rise of Billy Graham—it will move us forward on the larger agenda.

Grand Rapids, Michigan   J. A. C.
February 1997

REVIVE
US AGAIN

INTRODUCTION

This book covers a chapter in the history of the fundamentalist movement that has been little explored, the 1930s and 1940s.[1] This period was, as we shall see, a "classic" era for fundamentalism. Forced by their failed antimodernist crusades to rely on their own institutional network, fundamentalists spent these years developing a distinct religious movement with an ethos and identity that was different from the various denominational heritages of its members. They were, however, not content to remain in sectarian isolation and quietude. Prompted by their revivalist heritage to dream of another great religious awakening in America, they set about to make it happen. The result was, if not a national religious revival, a popular resurgence of fundamentalism and other kinds of evangelicalism after World War II.

In a book that was published in 1959, Edward John Carnell, one of the revisionist heirs of fundamentalism who was leading a conservative theological renaissance, accused his tradition of having become "orthodoxy gone cultic."[2] That theological verdict, however much truth it conveys, does not do justice to fundamentalism's practical achievements as a religious movement. In retreat from public embarrassment, fundamentalists cultivated distinctive religious communities, or "shelter belts" as one person called them, to provide some respite from the gales of modern secularity and a home base from which to launch evangelistic campaigns. Fundamentalism became a way of life with a subculture to sustain its doctrinal distinctives. Those who sought to stretch this religious world or break with it might suffer nearly as much psychic strain as one who tries to abandon a religious cult; indeed, such was the experience of Carnell.[3] But fundamentalism's cultural alienation, sectarian behavior, and intellectual stagnation should not distract us from seeing the movement's important achievement during the 1930s and 1940s. As participants in a popular religious movement, fundamentalists weathered their defeats and humiliation and not only survived but thrived during those decades. They were

3

successful enough in the free market of American popular religion that they began to influence other evangelical movements and traditions. As a result, fundamentalists became the chief organizers of a new evangelical coalition, and were some of the most influential agents in the postwar evangelical resurgence. The recovery of American fundamentalism is an amazing story, and one of most important purposes of this book is to explain how it happened.

Some day it may be possible to begin such a book as this without pausing first to define fundamentalism and locate it within the American religious and social landscape. But fundamentalism, even apart from its popular misuse as a synonym for bigotry, fanaticism or anti-intellectualism, is an elusive term. The problem is that *fundamentalist,* like *puritan,* has become a word of wide usage and immense symbolic power. It has been spoken with derisive loathing and, no doubt, some fear in liberal intellectual circles, for *fundamentalist* evokes images—such as the Scopes "monkey" trial in Dayton, Tennessee in 1925 or, more recently, the widespread demonstrations against abortion—that represent deep and long-standing cultural conflicts in modern America.

The term also connotes a broadly experienced human propensity to defend the "old ways" in religion and society. Millions of modern people see religious traditionalism as the best—indeed the only—way to satisfy their yearning for a "still point" (as T. S. Eliot once put it) in our rapid-paced world. As a result, the term *fundamentalism* now is often used to describe a more universal religious and cultural phenomenon than the American Christian religious movement that arose in the early twentieth century. Fundamentalism has become a generic label for militant religious and cultural conservatism worldwide. It has been used to identify Mormons, Roman Catholics, Jews, Muslims, and Hindus who share some basic traits with the party within American Protestantism that coined the term some seventy years ago.[4]

There is some value in using *fundamentalism* generically. We have much to learn about these varied groups: what they have in common, what sets them off as distinctive, and what their responses to modern life reveal about the struggle to live humanely in today's world. Nevertheless, historians of American religion should reserve the right to define fundamentalism narrowly, for in their field of study the more generic usage obscures more than it illumines. If it is used as a common label for reactionary cultural nativism, it obscures the fact that relatively few religious fundamentalists have followed right-wing radicals. Its usage as an easy tag for a variety of "conservative" religious movements and traditions can create havoc also. In North America especially but also among Protestants elsewhere, many evangelical, revivalistic, millenarian, confessional, and pietistic groups that have some traits in common with the original fundamentalists have arisen. Labelling movements, sects, and traditions such as the pentecostals, Mennonites, Seventh-day Adventists, Missouri Synod Lutherans, Jehovah's Witnesses, Churches of Christ, black Baptists, Mormons, Southern Baptists, and holiness Wesleyans as fundamentalists belittles their great diversity and violates their unique identities. People in these variegated patterns of the American religious kaleidoscope have a clear sense that there are important differences between themselves and the fundamentalists. Using *fundamentalist* generically in a North American setting makes it virtually impossible to appreciate the nuances that shape these groups' internal development and their relations with other Christians.[5]

Thanks to the careful work of historians Ernest R. Sandeen and George M. Marsden, it is possible to give a more precise and historically authentic definition of fundamentalism. Marsden gives this simple definition: fundamentalism is "militantly anti-modernist Protestant evangelicalism."[6] He and Sandeen show, however, that behind this simple denotation is a particular religious persuasion with fairly distinct boundaries that set it apart from other forms of Protestant evangelicalism and conservatism. Sandeen's pathbreaking study, *The Roots of Fundamentalism,* clarified matters considerably by stressing that fundamentalism was rooted in more than a generalized antimodern and antiliberal mentality and that it was also not properly equated simply with evangelical Protestantism. Fundamentalism was a historically new religious movement with distinctive beliefs, notably premillennialism and the verbal inerrancy of the Bible.[7] Marsden's masterful *Fundamentalism and American Culture* enriched and revised Sandeen's thesis. Marsden traced fundamentalism's other important origins: the revivalist tradition, Common Sense realist philosophy (especially as it informed American evangelicals' views of theological and scientific truth), and a non-Wesleyan branch of the holiness movement.

Marsden also insisted that tracking down fundamentalism's religious and intellectual antecedents does not characterize it fully enough. None of these beliefs and concerns made fundamentalism fully distinct from other evangelical movements and traditions. Thus he resurrected the discussion of a fundamentalist *mentality,* and argued that the movement's militant opposition to modernism, both as theology and as cultural secularity, distinguished fundamentalism from other evangelical traditions.[8]

Marsden refined his definition further in a lengthy article on fundamentalism in the *Encyclopedia of the American Religious Experience.* In order to shed more light on what made the fundamentalists distinctive, he compared fundamentalism to two closely related movements that share its roots in nineteenth-century revivalism and also arose to provide religious antidotes to secularizing trends: the holiness Wesleyans and the pentecostals. While these groups emphasized moral and experiential answers to modern secularity's challenge, fundamentalism favored the cognitive and ideological battleground. Although the fundamentalists shared the other two movements' concerns for right living and the power of the Holy Spirit, they cared more about fighting for right doctrine. Perhaps here more than elsewhere, Marsden suggested, fundamentalists displayed their Calvinist bloodlines.[9]

One final definitive trait, which Marsden suggests may be derived from Puritan lineage and a largely middle-class status, is that fundamentalists have felt a strong "trusteeship" for American culture. Much more than holiness or pentecostal evangelicals, fundamentalists have involved themselves in cultural politics. The mythic chords of "Christian America" have played loudly in their

memories, and their periodic public crusades have displayed their determination to regain lost cultural power and influence.[10] Even when fundamentalists
have expressed their alienation toward American cultural trends and advocated
separation from worldly involvement, their words have been more those of
wounded lovers than true outsiders. They have seen themselves as the faithful
remnant, the true American patriots.[11]

So fundamentalism in its broadest sense may be used as a label of a religious
and cultural type, a widespread tendency that has appreared worldwide in a
variety of militant traditionalist movements. But in a North American setting,
and when dealing with the varieties and nuances within Protestant evangelicalism, fundamentalism is best understood as a distinct movement with a particular mixture of beliefs and concerns.

Thanks to Sandeen's and Marsden's contributions, a much clearer picture of
the fundamentalist movement's origins and development emerges. The movement which later was transformed into fundamentalism began in the last quarter of the nineteenth century as an interdenominational revivalist network that
formed around the era's greatest evangelist, Dwight L. Moody. This movement drew most of its constituents from the generally Calvinist wing of American Protestantism: the Baptists, Presbyterians, and Congregationalists. Some
of its early leaders were Adoniram J. Gordon, a Baptist pastor in Boston;
Arthur T. Pierson, a Presbyterian pastor in Philadelphia; Cyrus I. Scofield, a
Congregationalist "Bible prohecy" teacher; and Reuben A. Torrey, a Congregationalist evangelist who was for a time the superintendent of Moody's Bible
institute in Chicago. While fundamentalism has been called a "Bible Belt"
phenomenon of the South and Midwest, its origins and organizational centers
were in the cities of the northeastern quadrant, from Chicago and St. Louis to
Philadelphia and Boston.

The characteristic beliefs and concerns of this movement came to be the
hallmarks of fundamentalism. These included an intense focus on evangelism
as the church's overwhelming priority, the need for a fresh infilling of the
Holy Spirit after conversion in order to live a holy and effective Christian life,
the imminent, premillennial second coming of Christ, and the divine inspiration and absolute authority of the Bible, whose very words were free from
errors. The leaders of this late-nineteenth-century movement knew about the
growth of liberal theology and saw secularizing forces at work in society, but
they did not feel especially defensive about their faith. Their beliefs and concerns still commanded a modicum of respect in American Protestantism, and
they were confident their brand of evangelical Christianity would be vindicated by the results it produced. They busied themselves with building a network of Bible and missionary training schools, Bible conference centers,
domestic and foreign missions agencies, and religious magazines. During the
1880s and 1890s, this movement looked much more like a Calvinistic variation of the Wesleyan holiness movement (which it was, in some important
respects) than an antimodernist crusade.[12]

By the early twentieth century, however, Moody's successors were becoming alarmed at the growth of liberal theology and the erosion of evangelistic commitment in their home denominations. They were also troubled by the increasingly secular spirit that they perceived in American life more generally. Between 1910 and 1915 they published a series of twelve small booklets called *The Fundamentals,* in which a variety of conservative pastors, scholars, and lay leaders criticized liberal theological beliefs, defended cardinal evangelical doctrines, upheld older models of Protestant spirituality, and reaffirmed evangelism's preeminence among the church's tasks. Yet it would take the cultural shocks brought on by World War I to transform these conservative evangelicals into militant fundamentalists. The war-induced sense of cultural peril prompted some harsh quarrels between Protestant liberals and the premillennialist evangelicals who formed the core of nascent fundamentalism. Liberals accused the premillennialists of being disloyal, unpatriotic, and perhaps subversive for denying that World War I was the "war to end all wars" and that an Allied victory would "make the world safe for democracy." The premillennialists replied that it was the liberals and not themselves who were dangerous. Germany's vicious militarism, they alleged, came from the cultural decay that followed from disbelief in the Bible's authority and the acceptance of evolutionary philosophy and ethics. The liberals, their opponents argued, taught these same ideas, so who was the real threat to America? In 1919 this premillennialist party led a coalition of conservative Protestants in forming the World's Christian Fundamentals Association to purge these ideas from the nation's churches and schools.

The resulting antimodernist federation became known as the "fundamentalists," a title coined in 1920 by Curtis Lee Laws, editor of the Baptist paper the *Watchman-Examiner.* After raising some public controversies of major proportions and enjoying some initial success, fundamentalists' attempts to purge evolution from the schools and to drive liberalism from the denominations met with defeat and growing public ridicule. As fundamentalists' reputation declined, their coalitions began to disintegrate. Many of the coalition's respectable conservatives quietly abandoned the cause when its leaders grew more strident and sectarian. The remaining fundamentalists felt increasingly isolated in churchly circles and alienated toward public life. America was turning its back on God, it seemed, and all there was left for a "faithful remnant" to do was to "come out and be separate" from such apostasy.

In the two denominations hardest hit by controversy in the 1920s, the Northern Baptist Convention and the (northern) Presbyterian Church in the U.S.A., separatist movements erupted and produced the General Association of Regular Baptist Churches in 1932, the Presbyterian Church of America (later, Orthodox Presbyterian Church) in 1936, and the Bible Presbyterian Church in 1937. Other "come-outer" congregations became wholly independent or joined loosely organized fellowships such as the Independent Fundamental Churches of America (formed in 1930). Perhaps the greatest number of fundamentalists, however, remained within the older denominations in rather quiescent conservative fellowships. These different responses to controversy fragmented the movement and left enduring resentments. By the early 1930s, the fundamentalist protest had lost any semblance of unity or collective force.

At this point, *fundamentalism* no longer signified a broad federation of conservative cobelligerents. The movement had been pared back to those whose roots, by and large, were in the older, interdenominational, premillennialist, and "Bible school" network. Over the next two decades, the surviving fundamentalist movement would tend its own affairs, nurse its grudges, and prophesy God's impending wrath, yet still hope for revival. The career of this distinctly fundamentalist remnant is the subject of this book.

The above discussion of the fundamentalist movement's origins, distinctive beliefs, and early career should provide a sense of fundamentalism's place and role in the American social and religious landscape, but the task of locating the movement is not quite finished. Since there were a variety of other similar movements and traditions sharing the scene with fundamentalists, and since *fundamentalist, conservative Protestant,* and *evangelical* have often been equated in both scholarly and more general discussion, distinctions between these terms must be clarified. Fundamentalists are evangelicals, but not all evangelicals are fundamentalists. Evangelical Christianity in America has amounted to a vast, varied, and interactive aggregation of at least a dozen different groups that historian Timothy Smith so aptly described as the American evangelical "kaleidoscope," only one segment of which should be labeled as fundamentalist.

The very conservative, creedally strict Missouri Synod Lutherans, for example, made the proclamation of the gospel and opposition to modernism central concerns, but they were also critical of true fundamentalists. They abhorred fundamentalists' emphasis on conversion and deemphasis of the sacraments, their interdenominational latitude, and their views of biblical prophecy. On this last point, the Missourians considered fundamentalists near-heretics.[13] Southern Baptists, to cite another example, were heartily evangelistic and theologically conservative, and they have had fundamentalist agitators in their midst since the 1920s. The denomination's leaders, however, resented fundamentalists' exaltation of premillennialism as a test of orthodoxy while downplaying denominational differences. The real fundamentals of Christian faithfulness, Southern Baptist spokesmen insisted, must include such items as restricted communion, believer's baptism, and denominational loyalty.[14]

Fundamentalists were very closely related in belief, practice, and historic roots to both the Wesleyan holiness movement and the pentecostals. But as is often the case among closely related religious groups, their differences came to be very important. Assemblies of God people and other pentecostals considered themselves to be doctrinally "fundamental," but they insisted that mere fundamentalists were missing the "full gospel," which included such miraculous signs and wonders as speaking in tongues. Fundamentalists, for their part, felt threatened and repelled by such extravagantly emotional outbursts.[15] Holiness Wesleyans, such as those in the Church of the Nazarene, were often outspoken opponents of theological liberalism. Yet they too thought funda-mentalists were missing all that the Father had promised to believers. They taught that God was able and willing to fully cleanse the Christian's heart of the inward moral propensity to sin. Fundamentalists, on the other hand, were usually very serious about the need to defeat sin in their lives and many had experienced a fresh cleansing and empowerment from the Holy Spirit, but they did not believe that they would be totally freed from sinning in this life. They thought that the "entire sanctification" doctrine taught by holiness groups was erroneous and tended to lead Christians to despair.[16]

So it went with other groups of evangelical or conservative Protestants who were by their own recognizance and affiliation something other than funda-mentalist. These many nuances of difference and a relative lack of intergroup fellowship (or even contact, in some cases) characterized the American evan-gelical mosaic of the 1930s and 1940s. Nevertheless, fundamentalism was probably the most broadly influential American evangelical movement in the second third of the twentieth century; its ideas, outlook, and religious "goods and services" penetrated virtually all of the other movements and traditions. How that came about is an important part of this story.

Like all other religious movements and traditions, fundamentalism has occupied a particular place in society and culture and gained much of its shape and thrust from its context. Earlier analyses of fundamentalism made much of the movement's social sources, and in fact tended to reduce it to a passing populist reaction to America's rapid modernization.[17] Such interpretations, argued Ernest Sandeen, do not take fundamentalism seriously as a long-lived, genuinely religious movement that is rooted deeply in nineteenth-century reli-gious ideas and has survived some major public defeats. Fundamentalists' longevity, vitality, and abiding appeal contradict reductionistic treatment, and in fact suggest that for millions of ordinary Americans, this movement has been an adaptive way of living with modernity. Fundamentalism has offered ordinary people of conservative instincts an alternative to liberal faith in hu-man progress, a way of making sense out of the world, exerting some control over their lives, and creating a way of life they can believe in. Fundamentalism was of course historically conditioned; it has been both a product of and an agent in modern America's cultural contexts and contests, but its creators deserve more credit for their success at fashioning and sustaining a genuine religious and cultural tradition.[18]

Nevertheless, the social location of fundamentalism has been an important shaper of its character. Who were the people that formed these fundamental-ist communities, and what were they attempting to do? Only a few studies have sought to answer such questions at the local level, but what they have found is not too surprising. Fundamentalism, like other historic evangelical movements, has tended to attract Anglo-Americans and northern European immigrants of Protestant background who were part of the upwardly aspiring and "respectable" sector of the working class, and of the lower middle class. According to Walter E. Ellis's study of conflicts in Baptist congregations, the fundamentalist factions did not tend to attract either the poorest of people or the most socially and economically secure in the business and professional classes. This latter group more often sought a genteel version of Christianity that would reinforce their cosmopolitan, optimistic outlook and elite perspective. Fundamentalists tended to attract more working-class people and fewer professionals than their less conservative counterparts in the Protestant mainline, even though each side had a significant share of both business owners and lower-status white-collar workers. Notably absent from fundamentalist ranks were professionals of the emerging "knowledge sector" such as lawyers and teachers.[19]

While this fundamentalist social profile does not fit the "disinherited" stereotype often attributed to millenarian and populist movements, it does have fairly distinct outlines. Ellis found, for example, that fundamentalists also tended to be younger and more recently arrived in the community than their moderate-to-liberal opponents. This profile suggests that fundamentalism cut a rather broad swath across American society, including both factory workers and company owners, bank clerks and farmers, workers at skilled trades, and small business owners. Following the American revival tradition, fundamentalism was aimed at a wide spectrum of society with a populist message tailored to be simple and urgent, appealing to popular tastes and sentiments, and claiming universal relevance.[20]

Fundamentalists thus tried to build religious communities that were organized more around broadly shared hopes and memories than around conscious identification with any particular social class. They struggled against the powerful tendencies of modern industrial society to segregate groups of people by occupation, neighborhood, and inherited or ascribed status. One study of Presbyterian congregations in a metropolitan area during the 1940s showed that the moderate and liberal congregations drew most of their constituents from fairly affluent residential areas nearby, whereas fundamentalist congregations attracted constituents from a much broader geographic area and from a greater social range of neighborhoods.[21]

Fundamentalists seemed to be trying to recreate the religious culture of earlier small-town America, where people of different classes had extensive contact. Fundamentalists' ideal of the good society harkened back to the apex of evangelical influence in the mid-nineteenth century.[22] This social ideal, described by Anthony F. C. Wallace as the "Evangelical Christian Capitalism" of the antebellum North during evangelist Charles G. Finney's heyday, aspired to a harmony of interests among classes, socially integrated communities, upward social mobility, a consensus of Protestant moral values, and voluntary cooperation.[23]

An important way of understanding fundamentalism as a social entity, then, is to see the movement's ongoing attempts to preserve these earlier evangelical cultural ideals in the face of rapid social change. Moody's generation tried to resuscitate these ideals during the late nineteenth century by means of urban revivalism.[24] Moody's successors, however, such as William Bell Riley, the talented pastor of First Baptist Church of Minneapolis, saw their status as community leaders and the influence of their evangelical values decrease sharply while a new elite of university-trained secular professionals and liberal clergy gained power and prestige. The religious and cultural modernism that the new "experts" advocated would ruin the nation, Riley believed. Determined not to let America slide into what they perceived to be a spiritual and moral abyss, Riley and his colleagues mounted the fundamentalist crusades of the 1920s.[25]

By the 1930s, however, in the wake of their defeats, all the fundamentalist heirs of Finney and Moody had left was the opportunity to preserve some outposts for evangelical culture by building their own religious communities. Joining the fundamentalists was certainly not for everyone, but the movement's appeal was considerable. Its attraction was not entirely nostalgic, either, since the fundamentalists were remarkably adept at styling themselves as modern, up-to-date, and conversant with trends in popular culture. One indication of their success at translating nineteenth-century ideals into a twentieth-century popular idiom was their movement's allure for many people in ethnic Protestant denominations.[26] Another, as we shall see, would be the rise of one of its sons, Billy Graham, to an unofficial role as evangelist to the nation.

This brief consideration of fundamentalism's place in American religion, society, and cultural politics shows that the fundamentalist–modernist conflict needs to be put in context of the movement's longer career and more abiding concerns. Much as their defeats and public humiliation stung and embittered many of the movement's leaders and stigmatized the rank and file, fundamentalists had not pinned all their sense of identity and purpose onto purging the denominations of liberalism and the schools of evolution. Fundamentalism had deeper roots as an evangelical and pietistic movement, and it would continue its efforts to win souls and nurture believers in Christian spirituality. It also was a millenarian movement, which gave it some ideological leverage on its failed crusades. The movement's teachers of "Bible prophecy" long had been preparing their audiences to accept marginalization as their calling. God's faithful, they prophesied, would be a mere remnant of professing Christians in the last days, a "little flock" that would raise a "testimony to the truth" in the midst of widespread apostasy. Thus fundamentalists could turn the world's rejection into a powerful affirmation of their chosenness.

At the same time, fundamentalists lived with a built-in tension. On the one hand, they had been part of the American evangelical "establishment," and still longed to shape their nation. On the other, they had been treated disrespectfully and felt like outsiders. A sectarian, fortress mentality offered some consolation, but it would prove to be less than fully satisfying. Fundamentalists had been deeply shamed in the battles of the 1920s, but they could not give up on the vision of a Christian America. They found a way out of this impasse in the concept of revival. Overt political campaigns had failed, and the movement bore the wounds of that failure. But a revival could restore fundamentalists' own spirituality, vision, confidence, and power. It could also restore, they believed, evangelical Protestantism's influence in America.

The following chapters, then, pursue these themes in fundamentalism's career from its diaspora out of the American religious mainstream to the early stages of its postwar recovery. They explore the movement's many facets: its sectarian, separatist impulses, the "separated life" ideal it held up to its members, its millenarian world view, its talent for building effective organizations and communicating to a popular audience, and its yearning to restore evangelical Christianity's respectability and cultural influence. Each of these traits influenced fundamentalists' resurgence in the postwar years, and each has contributed to the legacy that the movement's contemporary heirs carry.

1

A THRIVING
POPULAR MOVEMENT

How was fundamentalism faring by the end of the 1920s? That question is more complicated than it first appears, but the common perception has been that it was, as one historian put it, "split and stricken."[1] Many observers would go further and judge that fundamentalism was rapidly declining and would soon die out altogether. Indeed, the movement was in retreat. Without a doubt it had lost influence and respect. Yet fundamentalism remained a viable grassroots religious movement and it prospered as such in the 1930s, in spite of its defeats and disgrace. In order to see fundamentalism in this light, however, we need to know how and where to look for it.

A Dying Crusade?

The first part of that task is to see why fundamentalism's survival and continuing vitality has not been duly acknowledged. The conclusion that fundamentalism was dying by 1930 has been based on a variety of perceptions, notably those formed by the movement's opponents, by fundamentalist leaders themselves, and, more recently, by historians. The major problem was in a sense a definitional one. If fundamentalism was viewed as the organized offensive against liberalism in the denominations and evolution in the schools, then it was a spent force. There was little doubt in the mind of the movement's secular and religous critics; they were certain that fundamentalism was finished. To religious liberals especially, its death seemed imminent. In the wake of the Scopes trial, the *Christian Century* described the fundamentalist movement as "an event now passed," a brief, dysfunctional mutation away from the main line of religious evolution. Theologian H. Richard Niebuhr's article on fundamentalism in the 1931 edition of the *Encyclopedia of the Social Sciences* assumed that the movement was finished, for Niebuhr referred to it exclusively in the past tense.[2] While these diagnoses probably owed much to wishful thinking, secular critics with less at stake in the church fights, such as H. L. Mencken and Walter Lippmann, observed that the movement, if not dead, certainly was no longer a significant force in American thought and culture. Mencken relegated fundamentalists to the "mean streets" of America, "everywhere where learning is too heavy a burden for mortal minds to carry." Lippmann observed that fundamentalists' ideas no longer appealed to "the best brains and the good sense of the modern community."[3]

Fundamentalists themselves often developed a martyr's mentality in the 1930s and spoke as though theirs was a lost cause. Northern Baptist separatist leader Oliver W. Van Osdel, for example, urged his colleagues not to seek the world's acceptance, but to emulate "the rejected Son of God in these days of declension and compromise."[4] A rhetoric of martyrdom, fortified with biblical imagery of persecuted faithful remnants, prevailed in many fundamentalist circles. Such talk was an important device for counteracting the world's scorn and restoring a sense of mission, but it has added to the illusion of fundamentalism's dying.[5]

Historians are also responsible for the myth of fundamentalism's demise. A number of leading American historians have argued that fundamentalism was a momentary reaction to the irresistible tide of America's passage into modern, cosmopolitan secularity. They suggested that the movement had been an obstacle to enlightened and rational public discourse.[6] Consequently, many American history texts ignore fundamentalism and other kinds of evangelical Christianity after 1920. By eliminating fundamentalism from any sustained treatment in the narrative, American historians have betrayed a secular and progressivist bias that, as one critic pointed out, has led them to try to "write Americans beyond their religious backwardness as quickly as possible."[7]

Two recent historians of fundamentalism, Ernest R. Sandeen and George M. Marsden, have argued to the contrary that America's cultural breadth and multiplicity give dissenting movements the space and freedom to survive, and that fundamentalism found a lasting niche for itself in modern America.[8] Their treatments have a rather elegaic tone, however, since they focus on fundamentalism's role as a defender of nineteenth-century religious ideas whose influence and credibility were failing. Sandeen summed up his story as "the decline if not the collapse" of premillennialism as a "valiant nineteenth-century minority view."[9] Marsden likewise insisted that the fundamentalist impulse still carries much force today, but he saw that tendency primarily as a symptom of American evangelicals' loss of intellectual vigor and cultural influence.[10] Following in this vein, Mark Noll's recent commentary on evangelicals and the life of the mind more generally treats fundamentalism as an intellectual disaster.[11]

The dominant story line for fundamentalism's career, then, has been declension and dissolution. Fundamentalists' opponents gave them premature burials or banished them to the outer darkness of cultural marginality; fundamentalists gloried in their tribulations; liberal historians passed fundamentalists off as marginal and vestigial; and even the historians who rehabilitated fundamentalists as worthy of scholarly attention considered them to be the tattered remnant of a once-powerful tradition.

Each of these judgments about fundamentalism's state of health conveys some truth, but the movement's career during the 1930s and 1940s demands a different sort of treatment. *Movement,* indeed, is the operative term, for fundamentalism was not merely a collection of mental or religious proclivities, nor was it simply a defeated party in ecclesiastical politics, nor solely the guardian of spent ideas. It was a comprehensive religious movement with a whole panoply of aims and aspirations. Loss of the respect of intellectual elites does not necessarily mean loss of popular support, and it may actually enhance a group's appeal in some circles. The rhetoric of heroic alienation can also be misinterpreted, for popular movements often ascribe more marginal status to themselves than a realistic assessment would dictate. Indeed, the "outsider" pose was an important tool in shaping fundamentalists' sense of mission for their movement.[12] While it certainly suffered from external defeats and a variety of internal fractures and strains, and contributed few if any fresh and powerful ideas, fundamentalism provided a believable faith and a strong, lively religious community for hundreds of thousands in the 1930s and 1940s. Indeed, the movement's success posed a double irony: while liberal Protestant spokesmen smugly predicted that such "belated forms" of religious life would "gradually be starved out," their own mainline Protestant denominations suffered a severe religious depression during the 1930s. At the same time, the fundamentalists—who talked melodramatically about being a tiny, despised minority—prospered.[13]

It was an odd sort of prosperity, one must admit, for scarcely anyone, fundamentalists included, recognized it at the time. Fundamentalists had been conditioning others and themselves to associate their movement with antimodernist crusading in the nation's public forum. But by 1930 or so, the antievolution crusades and the pressure groups that mounted them had failed, and the once-formidable coalitions of conservatives who were determined to drive modernism from the churches had been split and scattered. So where was fundamentalism to be found? If the answer was, among the "come-outer" sects and fellowships—such as the Union of Regular Baptist Churches of Ontario and Quebec (founded 1927), the Independent Fundamental Churches of America (founded 1930), the General Association of Regular Baptist Churches (founded 1932), the Orthodox Presbyterian Church (founded 1936) or the Bible Presbyterian Church (founded 1937)—then the movement had diminished indeed.

Another common answer has been that fundamentalism revolved around the empires of its most prominent champions, such as William Bell Riley of First Baptist Church in Minneapolis, J. Frank Norris of First Baptist Church in Fort Worth, John Roach Straton of Calvary Baptist Church in New York, and Mark Matthews of Seattle's First Presbyterian Church. The fact that these regional "warlords" were fiercely independent, jealous guardians of their fiefdoms and scarcely able to get along on a personal level, much less continue any cooperative ventures, adds to the impression that fundamentalism was thoroughly fragmented by the 1930s and lacking in any basic cohesion.[14]

Another common way of locating fundamentalism has been by identifying it with the ultra-right-wing fringe of the movement that continued to campaign against evolution and communism. The bizarre words and deeds of this "Old Christian Right" helped to confirm the movement's stereotype as rural, bigoted, and pathological in mindset. If fundamentalism is equated with any of these features, each of which reveals a facet of the movement's character, then it truly was performing its death dance by the 1930s.[15]

The best that fundamentalists could say for themselves was, in the words of the North Carolina Baptist preacher Vance Havner, that "just because the great broadcast chains do not carry our message and because popular periodicals give us no space, it need not be deduced that we are bound for extinction." There were still many "old-fashioned Christians" around, Havner pointed out, who "have not bowed to the modern Baal." It was the age's "moderns" who were frantic self-wounders, not the fundamentalists. Echoing the apostle's words to the Philippian jailer, Havner quipped that fundamentalists would "say to this bewildered age, 'Do thyself no harm, we are all here.'"[16]

But where was "here"? Simply put, fundamentalism in the 1930s and 1940s was not to be found primarily within the broken ranks of the antimodernist crusades, nor was it limited to the small and alienated groups of separatists or the "super-church" empires of some of its chieftains. Fundamentalism was a popular movement and, as such, its strength was not to be measured according to the degree of its organizational unity. Movements commonly have internal variation and tensions. This is not a sign of declension so much as of vitality, for movements, like patches of dandelions, grow and spread when they are agitated. Movements have horizontal, web-like, informal lines of leadership and organization, not vertical, pyramid-like ones. So if we are to see how fundamentalism was doing in the 1930s, we must explore its major network of operations, the grid of institutions bequeathed to it by the revivalistic and premillennial pastors, evangelists, missions leaders, and Bible teachers who had laid the foundations of the movement at the turn of the century. One of the most important developments in fundamentalists' career during the 1930s and 1940s was their growing dependence upon this web of agencies as the channel for their work, the mediator of their message, and the focus of their affiliation and identity. How was this fundamentalist enterprise faring during the 1930s? It was thriving and growing. Its network of institutions was expanding in order to accommodate the movement's demand for trained leaders, popular religious knowledge, and vehicles for evangelism.

Training Leaders

Without a doubt, the most important terminals in the fundamentalist network were its Bible institutes. These schools, which were tightly knit, familial, and religiously intense places, had been founded to train lay volunteers and full-time religious workers such as evangelists, Sunday school superintendents, and foreign missionaries. By the early 1930s there were at least fifty of them, according to one report, that served fundamentalist constituencies.[17] Some, like the Detroit Bible Institute, were little more than evening classes run out of a local church for training Sunday school teachers. But over time, as some of the institutions became well established, they developed into comprehensive centers of religious activity. The largest and most important of the fundamentalist Bible institutes by the early 1930s were the Bible Institute of Los Angeles (known as BIOLA), Gordon College of Theology and Missions in Boston, Moody Bible Institute in Chicago, National Bible Institute in New York City, Northwestern Bible and Missionary Training School in Minneapolis, Nyack Missionary Training Institute (in Nyack-on-the-Hudson, New York), the Philadelphia School of the Bible, and the Bible Institute of Pennsylvania (also in Philadelphia). Two other schools that were founded in the 1920s but were developing rapidly were Columbia Bible College in South Carolina and the Prairie Bible Institute in Three Hills, Alberta. For fundamentalist pastors and parishoners who were weary of the theological tensions they felt with their denominational neighbors and wary of the perspectives emanating from their denominational agencies, Bible schools often became denominational surrogates. These agencies provided educational and other religious services, a support structure for fellowship and inspiration, and opportunities to participate in such "Christian work" as evangelism and foreign missions.[18]

It became standard practice, for example, for these schools to host week-long evangelistic, missionary, or Bible prophecy conferences that were open to the public. Some of the larger schools also had what were known as extension departments. These offices sent out "field representatives" to organize Bible conferences and revival meetings off-site and provide churches with guest preachers.[19] Several institutes operated bookstores or distributing agencies, such as the BIOLA Bookroom, the Approved Books depot and store at the Philadelphia School of the Bible, and Moody's Bible Institute Colportage Association, a very large operation that eventually became Moody Press.[20] These schools' magazines provided communications links with constituents and became important organs of fundamentalist opinion and expression. Some of the more prominent were the *Moody Bible Institute Monthly,* the *King's Business* of BIOLA, the Philadelphia School's *Serving and Waiting, The Pilot* of Minneapolis's Northwestern Bible and Missionary Training School, and Denver Bible Institute's *Grace and Truth.*[21] When radio broadcasting became available in the early 1920s, several Bible institutes saw this medium's potential for education, evangelism, and developing a broader constituency. BIOLA opened its own station, KJS, in 1922, and Moody installed WMBI three years later. Smaller schools, notably the Providence (R.I.) Bible Institute, Columbia Bible College, and Denver Bible Institute, sponsored programs on commercial stations.[22]

In this proliferation of services, the Moody Bible Institute, the largest of these schools, set the pace. No other fundamentalist agency of any kind could match its scope of activity or the reach of its influence during the 1930s and 1940s. The Moody Extension Department held weekend Bible conferences in nearly 500 churches during 1936, which more than doubled its efforts of six years earlier. WMBI and its radio staff were also extending the school's reach. The station's write-in campaigns created listener support networks, and so did the WMBI musical and preaching teams, who accepted invitations to minister in the region's churches on weekends. By 1942 they had visited nearly three hundred different congregations in Illinois, Indiana, Michigan, and Wisconsin. Radio thus played an important role in the Institute's developing a network of fifteen thousand contributors, enrolling an equivalent number of registrants in the Correspondence School, and increasing subscriptions to the *Moody Monthly* by thirteen thousand (to total forty thousand) by 1940.[23]

Other Bible institutes could not match Moody's scale or scope of activity, but they exerted strong regional influence. By the mid-1930s Gordon College of Theology and Missions in Boston, a nondenominational school with strong historic ties to the Northern Baptists, had trained one hundred of the pastors in its metropolitan area and half of all the Baptist pastors in New Hampshire. At one time during the 1930s, according to Gordon's president, every white Baptist pastor in the city of Boston was either a Gordon alumnus, professor or trustee.[24] In Minneapolis the Northwestern Bible and Missionary Training School, directed by William Bell Riley, pastor of the city's First Baptist Church, reported in 1937 that there were seventy-five pastors in the state who were its alumni. With the help of this growing network, Riley was able to build a power bloc and stage a fundamentalist takeover of the state Baptist convention by the late 1940s.[25]

Considering all the activity that Bible schools generated, the influence they wielded through friends and alumni, and the publicity they focused on their own work and on their extended "family," it is hard to avoid the conclusion that these schools functioned much like denominations in the lives of thousands of people. In fact, a reader of the *Moody Bible Institute Monthly* once wrote to complain, "Why don't you publish something on the other denominations once in a while?"[26]

Without a doubt, the Bible school was the dominant fundamentalist educational institution. Fundamentalists' tendency to reduce the church's mission to evangelism and their premillennial urgency to get the job done predisposed them to favor the pragmatic, trade-school approach of Bible school training for their leaders over the more extensive and cosmopolitan approach of college and seminary education. Furthermore, they had been dispossessed of the colleges and seminaries in their home denominations, since liberal theological views now prevailed in those institutions. Thus it was tempting to depend on the Bible institutes to train pastors, even though their founders had not intended them for that purpose. By the 1930s, several of the larger Bible institutes had added a "pastoral course" to their programs.[27]

Fundamentalists also built some theological seminaries of their own. They felt keenly the "loss" of denominational theological schools to the control of their moderate and liberal opponents, and sought to replace them. These new seminaries were less central than the Bible schools to the general fundamentalist enterprise, but they were important incubators of the movement's next generation of leaders.

Baptists contributed the most numbers to fundamentalism's ranks, and they were also the most prolific of the movement's seminary-builders. They were aided in these efforts by Baptist polity, which allowed such agencies to be founded by local initiative and then to seek denominational endorsement at either the state or national level. The first seminary to be established as a conservative evangelical alternative to more liberal institutions was Northern Baptist Theological Seminary, which was founded in Chicago in 1913 as an alternative to the Divinity School of the University of Chicago. Northern enjoyed official denominational recognition, as did Eastern Baptist Theological Seminary (founded 1925) in Philadelphia, a fundamentalist alternative to nearby Crozier. Western Baptist Theological Seminary (founded 1927) in Portland, Oregon, was endorsed by the state's predominantly conservative Baptist convention but not by the Northern Baptist Convention. Another conservative theological outpost for Northern Baptist fundamentalists was Kansas City Baptist Seminary (founded 1902) in Kansas City, Kansas.[28] These new seminaries were an important part of the strategy of Baptist fundamentalists; they hoped by this means to strengthen their place in the Northern Baptist Convention and gradually to reform it by placing more pastors than the liberals. Their final effort in this campaign was the founding in 1944 of California Baptist Theological Seminary in the Los Angeles area.[29]

Demand for seminary education among fundamentalists within the Northern Baptist Convention continued strong throughout the 1930s and 1940s, and these institutions grew steadily. By 1940 Northern had 340 students; Eastern had 287 in 1941; and California had 238 by 1950. Western had over one hundred students by 1951, despite its serving a much smaller constituency. Two Bible schools also evolved seminary degree programs to serve Northern Baptist fundamentalists. Gordon College of Theology and Missions had two such curricular tracks in place by 1931, with ninety-one enrolled, and was on the Northern Baptists' list of approved schools. W. B. Riley's more militant Northwestern Bible and Missionary Training School certainly was not on the approved list, but it had been turning out Baptist pastors nonetheless. In 1935 Northwestern inaugurated a seminary program and enrolled thirty-nine students.[30]

Separatist Baptists were also founding seminaries, most notably the Los Angeles Baptist Seminary in 1927 and the Baptist Bible Seminary in Johnson City, New York, in 1932. In 1940, five years after each had been placed on the approved list of the General Association of Regular Baptist Churches, Los Angeles Baptist had one hundred students enrolled and Baptist Bible had two hundred.[31]

Baptist fundamentalists' theological education shows how influential the Bible school model had become, for each of these seminaries had Bible institute–type components in their programs. While all the seminaries offered some graduate-level theological studies, they also faced the reality of hundreds of eager aspirants for the ministry who were not college graduates. To accommodate them, they devised preparatory undergraduate programs that were either identical to Bible institute courses of study or a combination of Bible school and liberal arts curricula. Many of the students in these seminaries were Bible institute graduates, and they demanded a continuation of typical Bible school–type courses on the English Bible and the practical techniques of ministry.[32]

Fundamentalists did have some purely post-baccalaureate theological seminaries. The three most important of these were independent, but served mostly Presbyterian constituencies in the 1930s and 1940s. The Evangelical Theological College (later Dallas Theological Seminary) was founded in 1926 in Dallas, Texas, by close colleagues of the late C. I. Scofield, the eminent dispensationalist Bible teacher. In its early years Dallas Seminary had many Presbyterians on its faculty and in its student body. It grew at a healthy rate throughout its first twenty-five years to nearly two hundred students in 1950, and became probably the most influential fundamentalist seminary.[33] Another influential independent seminary of Presbyterian heritage was Westminster, founded in Philadelphia by J. Gresham Machen and three other dissident Princeton Seminary professors after Princeton's reorganization in 1929. While it developed informal ties to the Presbyterian Church of America after the latter's founding in 1936, Westminster attracted intellectually aspiring fundamentalists of many varieties in its early years.[34] After Machen died in 1937 and a controversy over eschatology and Christian lifestyle split the separatist Presbyterians later that year, Westminster suffered. It enrolled seventy-two students in 1937 but in 1946 had only about half that many.[35] Nevertheless, its faculty upheld high intellectual standards and produced some valuable scholarship.

The faction that left the Presbyterian Church in America to form the Bible Presbyterian Church also founded Faith Theological Seminary in Wilmington, Delaware, in 1937. Faith Seminary had thirty-five students enrolled by 1940, and it continued to grow. Unlike Westminster, which became more exclusively Calvinist and distanced itself from the mainstream of fundamentalism, Faith built ties to other separatists by including independent Baptist and "Bible church" pastors on its board of trustees and adding J. Oliver Buswell, Jr., former president of Wheaton College, to its faculty.[36]

Seminaries could not carry as much associational freight as Bible institutes, but they served fundamentalism in another fashion. They kept an intellectual spark alive in an otherwise activistic and often anti-intellectual movement. Seminaries provided institutional homes for fundamentalist thought leaders, a few of whom were able to rise above the movement's intellectual stagnation and, in spite of crushing institutional demands and paltry resources, produce some conservative scholarship of lasting merit. These schools also provided a nurturing environment for the coming generation of fundamentalist leaders, some of whom eventually headed up the postwar movement to reform fundamentalism, revive evangelical thought, and restore evangelical Christianity's cultural influence.[37]

Acquiring a college diploma in an evangelical academic setting was not a major priority among fundamentalists in the 1930s and 1940s, but those who sought a Christian liberal arts education encountered problems. Liberal theological perspectives were as pervasive in the colleges of the old-line northern denominations as in the seminaries. These colleges were also following the universities' lead in divorcing theological thought from other forms of learning.[38] Perhaps more disturbing for conservative pastors and parents was the waning of evangelical piety, moral constraints, and religious idealism on these campuses.[39] The Bible institutes responded to this change by offering to fortify young people with a year of biblical and doctrinal studies and spiritual growth before setting out for more secular campuses.[40] Thousands of families chose that route, and in the process they permanently changed the character of these Bible schools, many of which previously had limited admission to adults.[41]

The older evangelical ideal of a liberal arts education still had influence within fundamentalism, however, and a number of institutions were available to serve the movement. In some cases, schools that were founded as Bible or missionary training institutes developed bachelor's degree programs and course offerings in the arts and sciences. That is what was happening at Gordon College in Boston and at Nyack, just north of New York City, during the 1930s. In some other instances, fundamentalists created new schools, such as Bob Jones College, founded by evangelist Bob Jones in Florida in 1926 but relocated in 1933 to Cleveland, Tennessee; William Jennings Bryan University, begun in 1930 in Dayton, Tennessee, as a memorial to the Great Commoner's last stand at the Scopes trial; youth evangelist Percy Crawford's The King's College, which first held classes in 1938 in Belmar, New Jersey; and Westmont College, begun in Los Angeles in 1940.[42] Fundamentalists also attended liberal arts colleges operated by the holiness Wesleyans, such as Taylor University in downstate Indiana and Houghton College in upstate New York; and a few enrolled in conservative Calvinist church-related institutions such as Geneva College in Beaver Falls, Pennsylvania, and Grove City College in another western Pennsylvania town.[43] All told, these conservative colleges prospered during the depression years. A survey of evangelical higher education in 1948 found that the total enrollment of seventy such schools in the United States doubled between 1929 and 1940.[44]

There was only one college of thoroughly fundamentalist pedigree, however, that was neither just half-evolved from Bible school origins nor still waiting for the ink to dry on its charter. That was Wheaton College, in the town of Wheaton, thirty miles west of Chicago. Wheaton had started as a secondary academy under Wesleyan Methodist auspices in the late 1850s, but was reorganized in 1860 by it first president, the Congregationalist reformer and educator Jonathan Blanchard. Wheaton's history to about 1900 was unexceptional for a small midwestern college. But, probably because of its leaders' ties to Dwight L. Moody and his protégés, Wheaton had not become a theologically liberal or an academically and socially secularizing institution like most of its sister colleges. Indeed, the Wheaton of the 1930s and 1940s was something of a throwback to an earlier era, with a pervasively evangelical emphasis and atmosphere, an accent on Christian service, and a strong penchant for training young apologists to defend the faith. J. Oliver Buswell, Jr., who was president of Wheaton from 1926 to 1940, was particularly proud of the school's champion debate teams.[45]

Buswell labored to promote the school far and wide, sending its student musicians, debaters, and athletes on tours during vacations and advertising Wheaton as a "safe school" in all the leading fundamentalist magazines. The president worked hard on Wheaton's academic standing as well. During his administration the college won a high accreditation rating and for three years led all the nation's liberal arts colleges in growth of enrollment. By 1941 Wheaton's 1,100 students, up from about 400 in 1926, made it the largest liberal arts college in Illinois.[46] The school was well on its way toward becoming a "Harvard of the Bible Belt," the foremost fundamentalist college in the nation and a producer of such future leaders as theologians Carl F. H. Henry and Edward John Carnell and evangelist Billy Graham.[47]

Feeding the Multitudes

While educational institutions did much to hold fundamentalism together, form its future leaders, and give expression to its beliefs and concerns, the movement's vitality and cohesion also gained much from its more popularly focused ministries.

At a time when the automobile brought new mobility to the American family and millions motored each summer to popular resorts, fundamentalists were expanding their counterpart to the tourist camp or resort hotel: the summer Bible conference. Although the larger urban congregations and the Bible schools offered week-long and weekend Bible conferences for the faithful's instruction and fellowship during the colder months, there was something more enticing about a conference at an attractive site for a summer vacation. From the Rumney Bible Conference in New Hampshire to the Boardwalk Bible Conference in Atlantic City, from the Montrose Summer Gatherings in the Pennsylvania hills to Winona Lake in northern Indiana, from Ben Lippen in the North Carolina Smokies to Redfeather Lakes in the Colorodo Rockies, and from Mount Hermon in southern California to The Firs in northern Washington state, Bible conferences offered a unique blend of resort-style recreation, the old-fashioned camp meeting, and biblical teaching from leading fundamentalist pulpiteers.[48] Renowned Bible expositors, such as Harry A. Ironside of Chicago's Moody Memorial Church, Paul Rood of the Bible Institute of Los Angeles, or Martin R. DeHaan of the *Radio Bible Class,* spent much of their summers on this circuit. The conferences offered programs for a variety of interests, so one could choose sessions or perhaps even whole weeks that featured missions, young people, the pastorate, Bible studies, the "higher Christian life," prophecy, sacred music, business men or women, or Sunday school teaching.[49] The listings of forthcoming conferences published each spring and summer in the *Moody Bible Institute Monthly* grew steadily larger, as presumably so did the demand. From twenty-seven sites and eighty-eight conference sessions in 1930, the Bible conference roster grew to over two hundred sessions at more than fifty different locations in 1941.[50]

A report in the *Watchman-Examiner* of the Winona Lake Bible Conference in 1941 portrays the character of such meetings. Each summer the whole

Winona Lake community, just a short interurban ride from Chicago, became a religious resort with thousands of people renting cottages and streaming to the Conference Grounds. The account in the *Watchman-Examiner* described the week that capped the 1941 summer schedule, when more than two thousand guests (including some four hundred ministers) and perhaps an equal number of daily visitors, attended the conference. Particicpants listened to as many as six sermons or Bible lectures a day out of the thirteen to fourteen sessions scheduled between seven in the morning and ten in the evening. The men on the platform included such fundamentalist celebrities as William Bell Riley of First Baptist Church, Minneapolis; Harold T. Commons, director of the Association of Baptists for the Evangelization of the Orient; and evangelists J. C. Massee, Ralph E. Neighbour, and J. Hoffman Cohn. The week's coordinator was Billy Sunday's former partner, Homer Rodeheaver, "the leading song director of America."[51] The reporter sensed a comradeship at the conference that crossed denominational boundaries. He was impressed that leaders from many different persuasions "could stand on the same platform and preach the common tenets of the Christian faith while multitudes of believers wept and rejoiced together as if some glorious news had for the first time burst upon their ears."[52] Such events were a powerful force for cementing the bonds of commitment and friendship within the movement.

According to a variety of sources, young people were some of the most avid participants in the conferences. In 1937 the *Sunday School Times* reported an informal poll taken at a small Bible college which showed that all but fifteen of the 150 students had attended a summer conference. Sixty-five first "accepted Christ" or made a recommitment to the Christian life there, and sixty-two claimed that they were in Bible college because of a summer conference experience.[53] Agents of fundamentalist missionary societies also prized opportunities to speak at the conferences, because they found that the young people there were unusually open to a summons to missionary service.[54] As the editor of the *Times* observed, the Bible conference had become "one of the most powerful factors in the spiritual life of the church."[55]

Less easy to gauge but important to mention nonetheless is the role played by fundamentalists' radio broadcasting. The rapidly rising commercial radio industry had become by the 1930s a major source of entertainment in America, and even the Depression could not dampen the broadcasting industry. Between 1930 and 1935 the number of radio sets doubled to over eighteen million.[56] Fundamentalists and other evangelicals were quick to take to the airwaves when commercial broadcasting became available in the early 1920s. Prominent fundamentalist centers such as Calvary Baptist Church in New York and the Bible Institute of Los Angeles were among the first religious insitutions to have their own radio stations. The American revival tradition is filled with examples of evangelicals' early and eager adaptation of new communications technology in the quest to send their message out far and wide, and radio was no exception. A casual, reader-contributed directory in the January 23, 1932 issue of the *Sunday School Times* listed over four hundred programs on eighty different stations.[57]

During the 1930s the major radio networks refused to sell broadcast time to religious groups and instead developed a few "nonsectarian" religious programs in cooperation with mainline Protestant, Roman Catholic, and Jewish national agencies. For a time it seemed as though fundamentalists' and other sectarian groups' access to broadcasting would be severely restricted.[58] Religious programs that offered to pay for air time were too attractive a market for local stations to turn down, however, and hundreds of them sold time to religious broadcasters. As a result, the more entrepreneurial groups dominated the religious programming on the radio. In Chicago, for example, sponsorship of religious broadcasting during the 1930s and early 1940s was overwhelmingly fundamentalist, pentecostal, or otherwise evangelical.[59] As new networks such as the Mutual Broadcasting System and the American Broadcasting Company came into being, they too sold time for religious programs.[60] Indeed, it became clear that paid programs drew the greater share of popular support. One weekly program, Charles E. Fuller's *Old Fashioned Revival Hour,* based in greater Los Angeles and broadcast over the Mutual System, had an estimated audience of fifteen to twenty million by 1939. Fuller's coverage was 152 stations in 1939 and 456 three years later, the largest single release of any prime-time radio broadcast in America.[61] Other programs captured regional and national audiences, most notably Martin R. DeHaan's *Radio Bible Class* from Grand Rapids, Donald Grey Barnhouse's *Bible Study Hour* out of Philadelphia, and the featured programs produced by the Moody Bible Institute's WMBI. Fundamentalists lavished a great deal of effort and pinned many hopes on radio broadcasting, as we shall see. While often billed as evangelistic outreaches to the nation, these programs seemed more successful at providing encouragement, instruction, and a sense of a common cause to their already-born-again listeners. Unlike those who attended the Bible conferences, these "radio friends" rarely if ever saw the broadcasters or each other, but they could tune in to something that was exciting and up-to-date yet adhered to the fundamentals of the faith, and apparently on the vanguard of a new religious advance in the public sphere.

Less ephemeral than radio but still hard to measure in influence was the fundamentalist publishing enterprise. Without a doubt, fundamentalism was a readers' and publishers' movement. It supported a variety of magazine, book, and Sunday school materials publishers, both tiny and substantial. Fundamentalist publishing flourished in part because its readers sought alternatives to what was being offered by the old-line denominations. They had no interest in reading denominationally sponsored magazines, books, and educational materials that endorsed religious and social views they opposed, so they provided a ready market for materials that endorsed their own beliefs.

The lack of Sunday school literature that taught the Bible's contents and the essentials of Christian faith from an evangelical perspective had become a strategic problem for fundamentalists by the 1920s. It did not take long for some publishers to serve their needs. The *Sunday School Times,* a venerable weekly magazine published in Philadelphia, was one important resource. It had long been publishing weekly "lesson helps" to accompany the International Sunday School Lesson Plans, but when the editor, Charles G. Trumbull, converted to a fundamentalist position around 1910, the *Times's* lesson notes followed suit. A similar development occurred in 1934, when Wilbur M. Smith, a fundamentalist Presbyterian pastor in southeastern Pennsylvania, was named the editor of *Peloubet's Select Notes on the International Sunday School Lesson,* a respected and widely circulated series of annual volumes containing lesson notes for the forthcoming year.[62]

Others ventured into the publication of graded Sunday school materials. One prominent enterprise in this field was Gospel Light Publications, founded in 1933 by Henrietta Mears, the director of Christian Education at the Hollywood Presbyterian Church and a former associate of William Bell Riley in Minneapolis. In its first four years, Gospel Light sold a quarter of a million pieces, and by 1940 it was serving over two thousand churches. David C. Cook Publishing, an older independent publisher founded in Chicago in 1875, also catered to conservative evangelicals. So did the All-Bible Graded Series, developed by Clarence H. Benson, head of the Christian Education program at the Moody Bible Institute. This series first appeared in 1934, and less than a decade later it had already published ten million pieces.[63] The fundamentalist market for materials that taught the old-time religion was growing, and presumably so was that of other evangelicals, such as the rapidly expanding Assemblies of God, whose Sunday school rolls tripled in size between 1926 and 1936.[64]

Fundamentalists' book publishing ventures in the 1930s and 1940s were not for the most part the work of substantial commercial firms. The one exception was the company bearing the name of its founder, Fleming H. Revell (who was D. L. Moody's brother-in-law), a major religious publisher with offices in New York and Chicago. More typical was Loizeaux Brothers, a small agency run by a Plymouth Brethren family in the New York area that specialized in books on biblical prophecy. Some prolific authors, such as the itinerant Bible teacher Harry Ironside, circumvented the problem of finding a publisher by setting up their own printing and marketing concerns. Others who had access to magazine publishing put their books out under their journal's imprint. A similar outlet was the press of a Bible institute. Of these, Moody Press was the most substantial. Meanwhile, two publishers in Grand Rapids who had catered to Dutch Reformed constituents, the William B. Eerdmans Publishing Company and the Zondervan Publishing House, were expanding their offerings to a "Yankee" evangelical market during the 1930s.[65] Publishing outlets thus were increasing by the 1940s, but until the explosive growth of evangelical publishing firms after the Second World War, fundamentalists had relatively few regular outlets for their books.

But then the principal media for fundamentalist discourse were not books but magazines. Several substantial magazines emanated from the Bible schools, most notably BIOLA's *The King's Business,* and the *Moody Bible Institute Monthly.* The *Moody Monthly,* with a rapidly growing circulation during the

1930s and 1940s, provided an important editorial platform for the Institute's presidents. It was an important conveyor of information on the movement's trends and events, and a purveyor of its services and goods as well.

There was also a variety of independently published magazines and tabloids that extended the influence of important leaders. Perhaps the most influential in the early 1930s was the *Sunday School Times,* a weekly with a nationwide circulation of some eighty thousand. The *Times* was published in Philadelphia by Charles G. Trumbull, a Presbyterian layman who was a leading "Victorious Life" holiness advocate, and one of the organizers of the World's Christian Fundamentals Association. The *Times* was not a fundamentalist creation. Trumbull's father, Henry Clay Trumbull, had been its editor for a long time before him, and the magazine's origins dated back to 1859. The *Times* was therefore one of the few institutions of "respectable" nineteenth-century Protestantism that fell under fundamentalist control. Its editor's chair gave Trumbull a tremendous amount of influence, which he as a layman was able to wield with impunity during the fundamentalist–modernist controversies. During the early 1930s, after a decade of antimodernist agitation, which Trumbull largely directed at the northern Presbyterians, the *Times* began to commend nondenominational, fundamentalist schools, missions, and evangelistic ministries to its readers for their support. Getting on the *Times*'s endorsement list was a great boon to these organizations; conversely, being removed from it, with editorial explanation appended, was similar to being excommunicated from the movement.[66] For at least a decade beyond Trumbull's death in 1941, the *Sunday School Times* was fundamentalism's paper of record.

Other important independent journals covered religious issues in more depth than the *Times* could, since it devoted most of each issue's pages to Sunday school lesson helps. One of the most influential of these was *Our Hope,* a pocket-sized monthly that had been published out of the New York area since 1894. Its editor was Arno C. Gaebelein, a German immigrant who had been an evangelist in New York's Jewish neighborhoods until about 1900, when he became a full-time author and Bible conference speaker. *Our Hope* never had a circulation of more than about twelve thousand but Gaebelein's talents as a prophetic Bible teacher and dispensational analyst of current events and the state of worldwide Jewry made him an oft-quoted teacher of other fundamentalist leaders.[67] A glossy new monthly called *Revelation* first appeared in 1931; its editor was Donald Grey Barnhouse, the bright, literate, and outspoken fundamentalist pastor of Tenth Presbyterian Church in downtown Philadelphia. *Revelation* was a well-designed, interesting magazine that afforded Barnhouse, who was gaining popularity as a Bible teacher on the East Coast fundamentalist circuit, an outlet for his perspectives on religious and world affairs. As his fame grew, especially through his *Bible Study Hour* radio program, so did his magazine. By 1937 its circulation was over fifteen thousand. Barnhouse was an important voice for nonseparating Presbyterian fundamentalists at a time when militants such as J. Gresham Machen and Carl McIntire were arguing that all consistent conservatives should leave the old denomination.[68] Performing a similar role but more closely focused on Presbyterian affairs were *The Presbyterian,* a century-old weekly, and *Christianity Today,* a monthly begun in 1930; both were published in Philadelphia. Among the Northern Baptists the *Watchman-Examiner,* a venerable weekly published in New York, was the voice of the nonseparating fundamentalists and other conservatives. Curtis Lee Laws, who coined the term *fundamentalist* in the July 1, 1920 issue of the magazine, was its editor until shortly before his death in 1936; his successor, John W. Bradbury, maintained the magazine's moderate fundamentalist perspective.[69]

Fundamentalism's separatist militants had their organs of opinion as well. Toronto's T. T. Shields, pastor of Jarvis Street Baptist Church and leader of the separatist movement in Ontario, disseminated his views within and beyond his own constituency in the *Gospel Witness.*[70] William Bell Riley's efforts at periodical publishing were less constant, but through his *Christian Fundamentals in School and Church* (founded 1918), which merged with the *Christian Fundamentalist* (founded 1927), which in turn merged with his Bible school's magazine, *The Pilot,* in 1932, he was able to keep his views in circulation.[71] Much more successful was Gerald Winrod's *The Defender* (founded 1926), which reached a circulation of sixty thousand by 1934, about the time when the Kansan ultra-right-wing pastor started to be shunned by some of his fundamentalist colleagues because of his anti-Semitism.[72] J. Frank Norris, the fiery separatist Baptist from Fort Worth, Texas, was reaching a circulation of thirty-nine thousand with his paper, *The Fundamentalist,* by 1941.[73] One of his protégés, John R. Rice, began a similar tabloid in 1934, *The Sword of the Lord,* which broadened its reach and influence, if not its views, after Rice moved his base of operations to Wheaton, Illinois, in 1940.[74] New separatist fellowships also established magazines, such as the Regular Baptists' *Baptist Bulletin* and the *Voice* (of the Independent Fundamental Churches of America), but these never developed the spirited editorial voices nor the range of interests that marked the independent journals.

One more kind of magazine made its way to fundamentalist parlors across North America and provided an important link between like-minded people and the ministries they supported. These were the publications of a variety of independent missionary agencies, such as the China Inland Mission's *China's Millions,* the North American editon of which was published in Philadelphia; *Inland Africa,* the magazine of the Africa Inland Mission, located in New York; and the *Missionary Broadcaster,* of the Scandinavian Alliance Mission, which was headquartered in Chicago. Offering more general subject matter, although intently interested in the work of the Sudan Interior Mission in particular, was the *Evangelical Christian,* published in Toronto by Rowland V. Bingham, founder and director of the Sudan Interior Mission.

All told, these magazines connected fundamentalist clergy and laity into networks of ideas and activity that transcended their local congregations, their denominations, and even their nation. One could tell, by the collection of magazines in one's reading corner or in the church library, just where these people's interests and loyalties lay. Were they a separatist Baptist couple from Grand Rapids, Michigan? Then one might see *The Message* (journal of the Association of Baptists for the Evangelization of the Orient), the *Baptist Bulletin,* and perhaps the *Moody Bible Insitute Monthly* (especially if they had attended Moody). A Presbyterian elder from Coatesville, Pennsylvania (near Philadelphia) might want to take the *Sunday School Times, Revelation, China's Millions,* or perhaps the *Moody Bible Institute Monthly* (since his pastor was a Moody alumnus). For a southern Californian pastor of an independent Bible church, it might seem important to keep up with regional happenings and with BIOLA through *The King's Business.* And so it might go, with many variations. Being a fundamentalist was not merely an abstract matter; it meant lin-ing up one's convictions and perspectives with some particular authority or community of belief. It meant being involved with fundamentalist agencies—at least with a fundamentalist congregation. And almost inevitably, such congregations were linked to other congregations, even those from other denominations, by their enlistment in common causes. Fundamentalist periodicals were vitally important links between the local, national, and even international levels of fundamentalist identity and action.

Proclaiming the Gospel

Fundamentalists were activists par excellence in a nation whose most distinctive religious trait has been activism. They pursued their evangelistic mandate by creating a variety of new ministries and sustaining many older ones. Virtually the only limit to what these ministries might do for the gospel's sake was the imagination of their founders. But of all the activities the fundamentalists pursued outside of their own congregations, perhaps the most important to them and the most indicative of their contrasting fortunes with the major Protestant denominations was their foreign missionary work. The missionary enterprise of the Protestant churches had entered the twentieth century with unbounded hope and zeal, but the liberal theological movement had introduced some second thoughts about aggressive evangelizing in other cultures, and this, coupled with inflation, a cooling of popular ardor for overseas crusades, and some explosive controversies over the allegedly liberal character of denominational mission boards added up to a major downturn in missions commitment even before the economic depression set in.[75] The Northern Baptist Convention provides an especially dramatic example of the missions declension in mainline Protestantism. Its overseas staff dwindled from 845 in 1930 to 508 in 1940. In the disastrous year of 1936, the denomination's budget for missions totaled $2.26 million, down 45 percent from 1920. That year no new missionaries went out, and many returned from overseas fields for lack of support.[76]

Some blamed fundamentalism for this sorry state of affairs. Before the fundamentalist–modernist controversies, conservatives and liberals had worked together on denominational boards under a broadly evangelical consensus about the missionary's task. That consensus now was destroyed, the missions community was badly polarized, and conservative constituents had lost confidence in the denominational boards.[77] It is a mistake, however, to infer that fundamentalists were driven to contend with the denominational boards out of sheer dogmatic zeal or desire for denominational control.[78] They were intensely committed to foreign missions, and they were eager to get on with the task of world evangelization. Fundamentalists recoiled from the denominational boards when they found that they could not change the boards' policy of including theological liberals as well as conservatives and social gospel programs as well as evangelization. But fundamentalists' missions interest did not flag. They supported independent "faith" mission societies and founded new denominational agencies. During the mid-1930s fundamentalists contributed about one out of every seven North American Protestant missionaries (about 1,700 of the 12,000 total), and by the early 1950s fundamentalists' portion of the total (5,500 out of 18,500) had doubled.[79]

A few dramatic examples suffice to illustrate the dynamism behind the fundamentalist missionary enterprise. The China Inland Mission (CIM), a nondenominational agency of British origin that became a favorite of North American fundamentalists, experienced remarkable growth during the 1930s. In 1929, just after the antiforeign and anti-Christian campaigns subsided in China, D. E. Hoste, CIM's director, issued a call for two hundred new recruits in two years. He got them, and ninety-two were North Americans who came largely from fundamentalist Bible institutes.[80] But that was just the beginning. Even though China was suffering from internal strife and from Japanese agression, CIM sent out 629 new missionaries between 1930 and 1936, raising its total force to almost 1,400.[81]

Another independent agency, the Sudan Interior Mission (SIM), benefitted immensely from fundamentalists' dissatisfaction with the mainline mission boards and desire to spread the gospel. This society had been founded in 1893 by two Canadians and one American. Its only surviving founder, Rowland V. Bingham, who edited the *Evangelical Christian* and was a revered conference speaker on the "Higher Christian Life" circuit, directed the SIM from offices in Toronto. In 1920 the mission sponsored only 44 missionaries, but by 1945, it had 494 of them in active service. Likewise its income increased from $29,000 in 1917 to $388,000 in 1941.[82] This explosive growth came at a time when "the Sudan," stretching across sub-Saharan Africa from the Niger to the Nile, was either threatened with or (in the case of Ethiopia) engulfed in war.

Not all of the fundamentalist-supported missions fared so famously, but the totals show that these forces were growing briskly. This fact has been overlooked, largely because the fate of the Protestant denominational mission boards has been the main story but also because the fundamentalists' missions are hard to locate. Forty-nine of them appeared on a list of "sound interdenominational missions" in the *Sunday School Times* in 1931, but over half of these did not appear in the report of the International Missionary Council's world survey conducted in 1935–1936.[83] Nevertheless, a closer look at the evidence reveals a thriving, if decentralized, fundamentalist missionary enterprise.

Fundamentalism's missionary fervor also shows through in the way that this enterprise was integrated throughout the movement. Missions were not just a sideline to which local churches absent-mindedly tossed a portion of their discretionary funds. They were a major concern. Bible schools considered the training of missionaries to be one of their major tasks, and they proudly announced how many of their alumni were now in overseas service. By 1933, after twenty years of existence, the two Bible schools in Philadelphia had produced some 150 missionaries. By its twenty-first year in 1944, Columbia Bible College in South Carolina had produced 135. The Northwestern Bible and Missionary Training School in Minneapolis (founded 1902) counted 110 alumni missionaries in 1936, while by 1938 the Bible Institute of Los Angeles (founded 1908) had produced 426, and over 120 in the last decade. The most productive training ground for foreign missionaries, however, was the Moody Bible Institute (founded 1886), the self-proclaimed "West Point of Christian Service." Between 1932 and 1942, at least five hundred MBI alumni became missionaries, which brought the school's total missionary production since its founding to 2,416. In 1936, there were 142 people enrolled in Moody's missions course, and 1,410 Moody alumni were active missionaries. These workers constituted nearly 12 percent of the reported total North American Protestant force.[84]

The faith missions in particular developed many connections with the Bible schools. Retiring missionaries often settled nearby to recruit, encourage, and screen potential candidates. Several schools had interlocking directorates with the mission boards. At one time or another in the 1920s and 1930s, the Philadelphia School of the Bible shared trustees and administrators with four different societies: Africa Inland Mission, China Inland Mission, the Inland South America Missionary Union, and the Central American Mission.[85]

Bible conferences and magazines also promoted the missionary enterprise. Established conference centers might have week-long conferences exclusively focused on missions, while more general conferences would have at least one missionary speaker. Annual missionary conferences in the leading regional "cathedrals" of fundamentalism such as Park Street Church in Boston, the People's Church in Toronto, or the Church of the Open Door in Los Angeles, also publicized the enterprise and afforded recruiting opportunities.[86] Fundamentalist magazines, such as the *Sunday School Times* and the *Moody Bible Institute Monthly*, featured regular missions pages and frequent missions articles and news.

Fundamentalists' primary institutions—their homes, Sunday schools, congregations and local leaders—all served the missions cause as well. Young people received missionary biographies for gifts from friends and relatives. Parents may have dedicated their children as babies—as in the Old Testament story of Hannah and her son, Samuel—to "full-time Christian service." Other exposure and encouragement abounded in the form of Sunday school missions stories and offerings, visiting missionary speakers, and encouraging pastors and pastor's wives. So fundamentalist young people grew up in a subculture that saw evangelism as the church's all-consuming priority and vocational religious careers as the highest calling. Missionaries were the noblest models of all for the life of heroic Christian service; they beckoned devoted, visionary, and adventuresome young people to join them on the front lines of spiritual warfare. The result, once most of the fundamentalist volunteers and supporting churches decided to bypass the older denominational mission boards, was the dramatic growth of a distinctly fundamentalist mission force.[87]

Conclusion

This survey should dispel any doubts about the vitality of fundamentalism in the wake of its public defeats in the 1920s. The movement was thriving; it was developing a complex and widespread institutional network to sustain its activities. Indeed, perhaps the best way to think about the fundamentalist movement and its location in the American social, cultural, and religious landscapes is to remember these interconnections: the ties between people and institutions, the collective interests and concerns being expressed, the mutual involvement in religious projects. These different kinds of fundamentalist activity—education, "conferencing," publishing, radio broadcasting, and evangelization—each connected individuals and congregations to endeavors of a larger scope. Like overlaid map transparencies showing the highways, railroads, waterways, air routes, and communications lines that connect a modern society, each kind of collective undertaking gave fundamentalism another layer of infrastructure as a movement. Fundamentalists surged out of the older institutional structures partly out of protest and alienation, but also because they wished to do many things not possible within mainline Protestantism. Fundamentalists created a host of new agencies and retrofitted many older ones to do their work, and their work prospered.

The success of fundamentalism and other evangelical groups, which also grew very rapidly during the 1930s and 1940s, came at the very time that mainline Protestantism was experiencing decline. Yet there was not a general "religious depression" during the 1930s, as has been supposed, but a crisis mainly among the older or more prestigious denominations. The contrasts in religious fortunes between the two major parties of Anglo-American Protestantism in this period are striking. While fundamentalists' missions and ministries grew, Southern Baptists gained almost 1.5 million members between 1926 and 1940, and the pentecostal denomination the Assemblies of God quadrupled during the same period to total some two hundred thousand members. At the same time, almost every mainline Protestant denomination declined in membership, baptisms, Sunday school enrollments, total receipts, and foreign missions.

Although the mainline Protestants still commanded immense wealth, membership, and cultural prestige, and the evangelicals of various stripes still occupied the margins of public life, a historic shift was beginning. Not only was mainline Protestantism being confronted with its final "disestablishment" in an irreversibly pluralistic nation, but by the 1930s it had reached its apogee as the dominant expression of Protestantism. The mainline was engaged in what would become a long decline, with only a brief respite after the Second World War.[88] Conservative evangelicals, including the fundamentalists but also many others, were perhaps at their lowest point of visibility and respect during the 1930s, but they were thriving and picking up institutional momentum.

By 1950 hints of a changed religious order were beginning to appear. The new pattern in American Christianity has been not so much a challenge to mainline denominations' influence by ascendant conservative denominations as the declining importance of denominations. Like the holiness Wesleyans and pentecostals before them, fundamentalists contributed to the decline of the mainline denominations by promoting dissatisfaction with those bodies' work. Yet fundamentalists were much less prone than the holiness and pentecostal people to solidify their movement around new, break-away denominations. They adopted the parachurch pattern of associational life and, as we have seen, they thrived on it. Instead of compelling its followers to choose between fundamentalism and their home denominations, the movement allowed many to maintain membership in the older denominations while shifting their support to independent ministries. This pattern of forming special-purpose parachurch groups to accomplish religious purposes rather than working through denominational agencies is now increasingly the preference of Catholics and mainline Protestants and as well as conservative evangelicals.[89]

The result, according to sociologist Robert Wuthnow, has been a renewed polarization of American religious life. In their heyday, the mainline denominations were broad enough to include varied viewpoints, mediate differences, and forge the consensus needed to do the church's work. But in the freewheeling world of special purpose religious groups that has grown up since the great Protestant divide in the 1920s, the mainline denominations' power to perform these functions has been seriously weakened, and liberals and conservatives have fewer compelling reasons to resolve their disputes.[90] Ironically, fundamentalists' institution-building in the 1930s and 1940s has become not only the compensatory action of a defeated protest movement, but an important step in the weakening of the American denominational system.

But we are getting ahead of the story. During the 1930s and 1940s, many fundamentalist leaders did indeed feel defeated, and seemed to be trying to compensate for their losses and find their bearings. If the movement's identity was tied up in battling for the "fundamentals" of the faith, what was its purpose when the opponent no longer felt the need to honor the call to come out and fight? Some of the movement's leaders continued their combative posturing, while others focused more intently on evangelizing the neighbors and providing an institutional base for their dispossessed followers. Many felt the need to do both. President James M. Gray of Moody Bible Institute epitomized this complex mood fairly early on when he advised his graduating class of 1922 that they would need to work, like Nehemiah's band, with "a trowel in one hand and . . . a sword in the other."[91]

2

THE SEPARATIST IMPULSE

The fundamentalist network that thrived and grew in the 1930s and 1940s was indeed a trowel-and-sword enterprise, as much an expression of a separatist impulse as a positive drive to "do the Lord's work." Indeed, the two meshed, for most fundamentalists were convinced that they could no longer adequately express their faith and accomplish their calling through their home denominations. Instead they forged a network of religious enterprises that were firmly under their own control. These acts of separation stemmed from the growing estrangement they felt, for it seemed to them that a great gulf had opened up between them and other, more "ordinary" Protestants and Americans more generally. Not long since, they had been a respected evangelical movement within mainline Protestantism, but now they were ideological outcasts whose views no longer were taken seriously in ecclesiastical or secular discourse. Feelings of dispossession and alienation ran strong among fundamentalists, and out of these emotions came much of the energy for creating separate institutions and maintaining an independent identity. As a result, fundamentalists were becoming a distinct religious community by the early 1930s.

By that time it had become clear to many fundamentalists that their ability to gain a respectful hearing in Protestant forums or in the more secular media was coming to an end. For Donald Grey Barnhouse, a young Presbyterian fundamentalist leader from Philadelphia, this new reality hit home fast and hard in 1932. Barnhouse, who was an outspoken opponent of modernism and was gaining a wide following as a Bible expositor and a radio preacher, found that he had provoked his denomination's leaders. In March 1932 he was tried and censured by his presbytery for publicly criticizing the theological views of other Presbyterian ministers. The following fall, his Sunday vespers radio broadcast was taken off the CBS network. It had fallen victim to the Depression and to the network's new policy against accepting paid religious programs. This ruling was meant to silence "sectarian" and "controversial"

33

broadcasters such as fundamentalists. It is not surprising, then, that the editorials in Barnhouse's new magazine, *Revelation,* were filled with gloom. The pastor advised his readers to expect spiteful treatment, for such was the price of being Christ's disciples. Indeed, he argued, "if the world loves us it is because we are not following Christ."[1] Fundamentalists readily turned in those days to the New Testament epistles for comfort and vindication, for biblical admonitions to remain pure and undefiled "in the midst of a crooked and perverse nation" (Eph. 2:15) fit the movement's mood and outlook. Melvin Grove Kyle, the fundamentalist editor of the once-venerated theological journal *Bibliotheca Sacra,* thought that the Apostle Paul's admonition to "Come ye out from among them and be ye separate" (II Cor. 6:17) should indeed be "the program for a devout people" in the days to come.[2]

Fundamentalists' feelings of alienation clearly communicated a great deal of hurt, but the separatist impulse they cultivated actually proved to be a tonic for them as a grassroots movement. Separatism provides a clear point of departure from the established order from which a movement arises. It winnows out the truly committed from the sympathetic hangers-on by making rejection from world a badge of identity. Clearer definition can result from institutional separation as it imposes closure and congruity on a previously indistinct bundle of interests and tendencies.[3] As fundamentalists experienced alienation and set themselves apart from mainline Protestantism, they did in fact gain some coherence as a distinct religious movement. Many denominationally loyal conservatives parted ways with their more militant comrades over the issues of leaving the denomination or forming alternative agencies. In the process, fundamentalism became less of a broad antimodernist persuasion and more of an ideologically compatible and institutionally linked movement.

At the same time, however, the question of how to take a separated stance brought fundamentalists some fierce internal conflicts and fragmentation. From the time of the antimodernist controversies in the 1920s forward, they squabbled over who were allies and who were traitors, under whose leadership the movement should marshall its forces, where the outer boundaries of fellowship and membership should fall, and whether continuing to seek reform within the denominations or considering them a lost cause and withdrawing was the more God-honoring strategy. Lack of consensus on these issues charged the atmosphere within the movement for years to come.

The major complicating factor in these debates was that separatism was at one end of a psychic tug-of-war within the movement's character. Offsetting these feelings of estrangement was a sense of responsibility for the fate of Protestant America. This commitment made it impossible for fundamentalists to release all of the cords of memory and hope that bound them to the nation. But the questions of which connections should remain for the sake of saving America and which should be released for the sake of obedience to a scriptural mandate for separation remained unresolved.

During the 1930s, however, the greater tug was coming from the separatist side. Fundamentalists were in a situation that resembled the dilemma their ancestors, the Puritans, had faced three hundred years earlier. The Puritans had wanted to reform the English church and nation, but they were increasingly disillusioned about ever being able to carry that agenda forward. Some opted for a radical break with church and worldly society rather than compromise their purity. But even those who repudiated separatism, such as John Winthrop, were pushed by the force of events to engage in acts, such as sailing for America, that looked for all the world like separation. So it was with the majority of fundamentalists. They did not go out and found new sects, but found other important ways to act independently of their home denominations and thus became separatists in fact if not in ecclesial form.

Like the Puritans, fundamentalists only gradually developed a sense of alienation. They did not suddenly discover in the 1930s that mainline Protestantism and modern American life were at odds with their convictions. In order to understand the complex sense of marginality that animated fundamentalists in the 1930s, we need to look more closely at the combination of distinctive traits and experiences that fed their growing sense of estrangement.

The Sources of Alienation

Three traits in particular contributed to the transformation of the emerging fundamentalist movement's leaders into estranged dissenters by the 1930s. One of these was the movement's penchant for popularization and populism, which pitted it against the rising cultural authority of the university-trained expert. Another was dispensationalism's prediction that orthodox Christians would become an embattled minority in the last days. The third was the hurt and alienation of once-respected conservatives who were no longer taken seriously.

Popular Appeal versus the New Expertise

As heirs of the American revival tradition, fundamentalists greatly valued being able to reach the masses and to communicate their message in a popularly attractive way. They were, in other words, intensely audience-conscious, market-driven, and concerned to see immediate returns from their efforts. A strong streak of antielitism, coupled with democratic appeals to popular opinion, also ran through the movement.[4] Fundamentalists inherited these values most directly from the evangelistic drive spearheaded by Dwight L. Moody in the last quarter of the nineteenth century.

Moody's partners in this new wave of popular outreach were a group of gifted and respectable urban pastors such as Presbyterians A. T. Pierson of Philadelphia and A. B. Simpson of New York, and Baptists A. J. Gordon of Boston and A. C. Dixon of Baltimore. These ministers mortified their own genteel tastes and values and revamped their congregations to reflect the popular, revivalistic style of the urban evangelists.[5] In order to prepare cadres of religious workers quickly for new evangelistic offensives, they formed Bible and missionary training schools and neglected the life of the mind. Therefore, even though most of these early leaders were well-educated and culturally refined, their movement quickly lost touch with the nation's intellectual currents.[6]

At the same time, an academic revolution was changing the balance of cultural power in America. The modern research universities then emerging were replacing the theistic foundations of earlier intellectual life with naturalistic presuppositions; and educators and scientists, armed with these ideas, were gaining influence as authorities.[7] Liberal ministers, who were becoming their denominations' leaders, readily attached themselves to these educational and scientific elites. Those who founded the fundamentalist movement witnessed this shift in cultural leadership and began to notice that their own status and influence was waning. Probably even more alarming were the ideas and values propounded by the liberal clergy and the new university-trained "experts," especially their attacks on the Bible's divine inspiration and cultural authority and the evolutionary models of moral progress they offered in its place.

The conservative revivalists' convictions were for the most part not fortified with the intellectual discipline needed to confront these new views.[8] They mobilized for an ideological and theological contest, then, with mostly non- or anti-intellectual weapons—such as appeals to popular opinion and populist attacks on elites—and a few older intellectual systems, namely Baconian views of science and Common Sense realist philosophy. When public opinion began to turn against the movement in the aftermath of the Scopes trial, fundamentalism's populist warriors turned increasingly shrill and bitter.

The experience of William Bell Riley, whose active career spanned the 1880s to the 1940s, illustrates how fundamentalism's popular and populist proclivities contributed to its alienation. Born in 1861 and reared in poverty on a Kentucky tobacco farm, Riley scrambled his way upward. He made his way first through Hanover College in southern Indiana and then the Southern Baptist Theological Seminary in Louisville. He served in Baptist churches in Kentucky and downstate Indiana and Illinois; and then, after a short but productive term with a congregation in Chicago, Riley accepted a call to the First Baptist Church of Minneapolis in 1897. Like other revivalists of the Moody era, he sought to transform his congregation, which had been a haven for the city's elites, into a "city temple," a center for popular religious activity. The congregation grew by over 50 percent in the first year of Riley's pastorate, largely on the strength of hundreds of new members recruited from the lower and lower middle classes. On account of these changes, and also because he was an outspoken Bryan Democrat, Riley incurred the wrath of First Baptist's prominent families. After five years of feuding with the old guard, Riley triumphed when his opponents left in 1902 to form a new congregation. That same year Riley founded the Northwestern Bible and Missionary Training School, and throughout the next fifteen years, he was in demand for evangelistic campaigns in other cities. By any conventional measure of his vocation, Riley had become a great success.[9]

Things were happening in America's churches and schools, however, that troubled Riley deeply. Theological modernists seemed to be taking over the

Northern Baptist seminaries and the denominational agencies. And evolution-promulgating professors, such as those at the University of Minnesota, were trying to disabuse students of their traditional Christian beliefs. Riley bristled at the commonly expressed view that these modernists were "progressives" while he and other theological conservatives were "fogies." By about 1909 he was advocating a movement to reassert the conservative evangelical persuasion.[10]

The Menace of Modernism, which Riley published in 1917, shows that by then his concern about modernism, by which he meant both liberal theology and evolutionary naturalism, had turned to genuine alarm. Riley observed that modernism now possessed substantial cultural power, particularly among the educated classes. It was a menace because it attacked the authority of the Bible, the moral foundation of American culture. Because of the modernists' subversive work, Riley warned, a whole generation of educated Americans was on the brink of moral suicide.[11]

This conflict had a deeply personal dimension for Riley. He complained bitterly that modernist ministers in his city had become the lap dogs of the "skeptical" professors at the University of Minnesota. And yet conservative preachers who had by their talent, hard work, and charisma built large urban congregations and won many converts were never invited to speak on that campus. It was doubly galling for him to see his own professional expertise challenged as well. In this "science-mad" age, he protested, professors were looked up to as authorities on all sorts of subjects—even religion—at the expense of pastors, especially those of a conservative stripe.[12]

Never one to back away from a contest, Riley concluded *The Menace of Modernism* with a call for a "confederacy" of "radical conservatives" who would add their voices to debates over religion and public policy.[13] Two years later, Riley led in founding the World's Christian Fundamentals Association (WCFA). During the 1920s he was probably the nation's most prominent fundamentalist. He led the conservative charge repeatedly in the Northern Baptist Convention, preached and lectured far and wide, and held public debates against evolutionists. He took the fight directly to the University of Minnesota, demanding and eventually being granted the right to speak against evolution on campus and then promoting an antievolutionary bill in the state legislature.[14]

Riley's campaigns all came up short, however, by the late 1920s. His last major attempt to pull the Northern Baptist Convention in a conservative direction was voted down decisively in the 1926 annual meeting. The Minnesota state legislature defeated his antievolution bill in 1927 following a massive demonstration (five thousand strong) of the University students' opposition. Attendance dwindled at WCFA meetings, and in 1929 Riley resigned as the organization's president. He had argued for his beliefs in several forums of popular opinion, and the people had spoken—against him.[15]

By the 1930s Riley was an embittered old man. He quarreled with and became estranged from several other eminent fundamentalists, and he wandered ever deeper into the realm of conspiracy theories, including some that were viciously anti-Semitic.[16] His influence was still strong, particularly in his immediate region, where the graduates of his school came to dominate the Baptist state convention.[17] Yet Riley carried about him the redolence of populism gone sour—curdled by his resentment at his diminished prestige. He who had once been a prince of the pulpit and a celebrated Bryanite orator was now considered a pariah and a prime example, according to one young reporter, of profascist attitudes in Depression-era America.[18]

Even though no one bothered to contend against him any more, the old fighter kept on shadow-boxing, smiting his enemies in absentia. He was determined "never to run up the flag of surrender, or even to hint a truce with the enemies of God or His Word."[19] Such aggressive posturing before a congregation of the already-convinced became a hallmark of "fighting fundamentalism," an important ritual reenactment of the movement's purported mission. Frustrated populists such as Riley thus were turning to the more sectarian business of fencing in their flocks and instilling in them a strong sense of "us" and "them."[20]

Prophetic Pessimism

The second factor that pushed fundamentalists toward alienation came from their most distinctive doctrine, dispensational premillennialism. This point of view is as complex as its name is long,[21] and its ideas and outlook shaped fundamentalism in a number of ways. Here it is important to focus on the alienating power of one dispensationalist prediction, "the ruin of the church." What dispensationalists meant by this was that in the years immediately preceding Christ's second coming, deviations from orthodox Christian belief would infect the major branches of Christianity. Thus corrupted, these churches would become the chief promoters of the false religion that was to accompany the rise of a satanically inspired world ruler, the Antichrist.

John Nelson Darby and several other British leaders of the Plymouth Brethren sect had introduced these ideas to Moody's generation in the 1870s. The Brethren urged American revivalists to separate themselves from the mainline denominations and become God's "little flock," whom he would preserve from error in the latter days.[22] The Plymouth Brethren were frustrated in their recruiting efforts, however, because the vast majority of American converts to dispensationalism remained within the denominations. Only one prominent war horse of the dispensational Bible conference circuit, Arno C. Gaebelein, actually practiced ecclesiastical separation; he left the Methodist Episcopal Church in 1899. Apparently it was one thing to believe in the eventual declension of all the churches, but quite another matter to admit that one's denominational colleagues were either dupes or conspirators in the "Great Apostasy." Nevertheless, turn-of-the-century dispensationalists pointed out liberal theological trends and cautioned that these were portents of worse things to come.[23] The "ruin of the church" doctrine was for the time being more a theoretical belief than an operative one.

When the fundamentalist–modernist controversy began to heat up between 1917 and 1920, these views of the church's declension became more important. Ironically, it was the liberals who aroused this dormant dogma. In 1917 several professors of the University of Chicago Divinity School launched an attack against the "premillenarians." They accused the millenarian movement of disloyalty, for its leaders were preaching that the current conflict was not "the war to end all wars," that the kingdom of God would not come through moral progress, and that the social application of the gospel was a waste of time. Such thinking, the Chicago professors argued, was inherently hostile to democratic ideals, unpatriotic in a time of national crisis, and possibly a threat to national security. One of the professors, Shirley Jackson Case, insinuated that the premillenarians might be receiving funding from the enemy.[24]

The dispensationalists leaped to answer this assault. Reuben Torrey, whose Bible Institute of Los Angeles had borne some direct attacks for its premillennialism, turned around the charges of subversive German influence. Torrey maintained that the charge that German agents were providing the funding for "premillennial propaganda" was obviously ridiculous, but "the charge that the destructive criticism that rules in Chicago University" came from German sources was "undeniable."[25] Germany's militarism and barbarity, Torrey argued further, had resulted from that nation's intellectuals' embrace of biblical criticism and evolutionary philosophy. Cultures cut loose from biblical norms could expect to follow Germany's descent into savagery. American university professors and liberal theologians were teaching the same ideas that opened Germany to brutal and godless philosophies. So who were the real traitors?[26]

A different kind of treason also came to mind during these debates, as the heat of contention prompted dispensationalists to go further with their theories about the Great Apostasy than they usually had in the past. They were provoked by the Divinity School's dean, Shailer Mathews, who in an antipremillennial pamphlet, *Will Christ Come Again?*, had denied a literal, personal second coming of Jesus Christ. The true Second Coming, Mathews insisted, was the triumph of the ideals of Jesus in human affairs. To Reuben Torrey, this kind of talk was a pious smokescreen for outright unbelief. Mathews's attack on the literal second coming was clear evidence, Torrey charged, of the apostasy of the church. Mathews's denial echoed the words of the Apostle Peter, who prophesied that "in the last days mockers shall come . . . saying, 'Where is the promise of His coming?'"[27]

Similar conclusions surfaced again in 1919, when fundamentalists responded to the proposed "Interchurch World Movement." This campaign, modeled after wartime fund drives, was to unify and secure financing and volunteers for all the benevolent and missionary agencies of mainline Protestant America. According to one of its promoters, the goal of the Movement was to produce the "religious counterpart to the League of Nations,"[28] but to James M. Gray, dean of the Moody Bible Institute, the League looked ominous. For years Gray had been pointing out that progressives' dreams of world peace tribunals, church unions, and the like, while directed toward noble ends, were foreshadowings of the coming alliance between an apostate world religion and the Antichrist's evil empire.[29] This new Interchurch Movement, he feared, might be something worse than a harbinger. Gray had heard some Interchurch campaign rhetoric that expressed intolerance toward sectarian diversity and talked about "a world league of churches" and "a tremendous new movement, nothing can stop it." Such talk made him shudder. True believers should beware of joining the Movement, he warned, "lest we be found fighting against God."[30]

Both of these episodes show that as the antimodernist controversies began to brew, prophecies about the Great Apostasy seemed increasingly relevant. In the fundamentalists' eyes, their debates with the liberals in these days of world crisis began to take on cosmic proportions. No longer was liberalism simply a tendency to be deplored but generally tolerated. The ruin of the church, long predicted and discussed in dispensational circles, now seemed to be happening before their eyes. Militant conservatives began to suspect that their liberal denominational colleagues had actually gone over to the enemy. The days for polite discussion and giving benefit of the doubt were gone, and the gloves came off.

Such behavior did nothing to enhance intrachurch relations. Obviously the liberals resented being cast as Satan's minions or (perhaps worse) as his dupes, and they fought back. Harry Emerson Fosdick's famous 1922 sermon, "Shall the Fundamentalists Win?" charged that those who would "drive out from the Christian churches all consecrated souls" who did not agree with them on some matters of doctrine were majoring in the "tiddleywinks and peccadillos of religion," and were guilty of an intolerance that was "almost unforgivable."[31] The fundamentalist–modernist conflicts then took off at full steam, and while liberals often made light of the fundamentalists' concerns, the latter were convinced that it was not just differing doctrinal theories but the apostolic faith itself that was at stake. Fundamentalists interpreted these events increasingly in light of the Darbyite prediction of the ruin of the church, and that prophecy proved to be self-fulfilling. The broadly evangelical consensus and mutual trust that had been the foundation for the northern mainline denominations' programs developed some serious cracks under the pressure of the controversies, and fundamentalists thereafter distrusted and felt alienated toward their home denominations, even if they never formally left them.

The Loss of Respectability

The final alienating blow for many fundamentalists who were more moderate in temperament and action than William Bell Riley was the loss of their respectability. This clearly was the case for James M. Gray, the head of the Moody Bible Institute from 1904 to 1934. Gray was a preacher and Bible lecturer of wide acclaim, the author of many books and pamphlets, and a consulting editor for the Scofield Reference Bible (1909). He had served as the rector of a Reformed Episcopal congregation in Boston from 1879 until 1894, when he joined the Institute's resident faculty and its extension staff.[32]

Even though he was preeminently a popular educator, Gray was also a dignified and respectable clergyman. Never one to disparage scholarship, Gray brought leading conservative intellectuals such as President Francis L. Patton and professors Robert Dick Wilson and J. Gresham Machen of Princeton Theological Seminary to speak at the Moody Bible Institute. He told Moody's graduating class of 1928 that he hoped the studious habits they had acquired at the Institute would continue, and that they would always respect higher learning, give it due honor, and make use of its findings in God's service.[33]

From the time he took up the editorship of the Institute's magazine in 1907 to the advent of World War I, Gray devoted much space in it to critiques of liberal religion and of social and political progressivism. While the progressive reformers' work was often beneficial, he thought, it would ultimately fail because it was based on naiveté about human nature and the perfectibility of society.[34] Gray's ideas were by no means those of an isolated crank; he comfortably (and correctly) assumed that his views were congruent with respectable opinion. Gray frequently quoted such eminent conservatives as President William Howard Taft, naval historian Alfred Thayer Mahan, and Nicholas Murray Butler, president of Columbia University. Moreover, Gray heartily supported such mainline Protestant agencies as the YMCA, the Christian Endeavor Union, and the Federal Council of Churches.[35] Gray had every reason to assume that his work and that of the Moody Bible Institute were part of mainline Protestantism.

By the time of the First World War, however, the reputation of Gray's kind of religious conservatism came under fire. One of the first assaults came in 1916 from Professor Harris Franklin Rall of the Garrett Biblical Institute, a Methodist theological seminary in Evanston, Illinois, just a few miles to the north of Moody. In a series of articles in the *Sunday School Journal,* Rall attacked the premillennial beliefs promoted by the nascent fundamentalist movement and particularly its Bible schools. By this time, dispensationalists had grown accustomed to answering their critics' objections, but Rall seemed determined to be unfair. He equated premillennialists' views with those of the Jehovah's Witnesses, accused the premillennialists of holding to crude dictation theories of inspiration, and expressed condescending assumptions about the views of "thoughtful Christians today"—which were opposed, of course, to premillennialists' views. Gray brought on two eminent scholars to answer Rall: professors Charles R. Erdman of Princeton Theological Seminary and W. H. Griffith Thomas of Wycliffe College, University of Toronto.[36]

The assaults on premillennialism from the camps of liberal theology were by no means finished, as we have seen. When barrages began to come from the University of Chicago Divinity School, Gray and his contributors readily answered the critics' fire, but this time Gray felt wounded. It particularly bothered him that the Chicago press had given credibility to these wild charges by repeating them uncritically. Time and again, Gray had marshalled support for his views by quoting the conservative *Chicago Tribune,* but now its editors seemed to pay him very little respect in return.[37]

As is well known, Gray made the Moody Bible Institute and its monthly magazine major champions of the fundamentalist cause in the 1920s. But

Gray seemed to have another agenda in addition to contending for the faith. He was fighting for the Institute's inheritance as a respectable Protestant agency. Convinced that the nation's popular magazines were unfairly sympathetic to the modernists, Gray used the *Monthly* to try to set the record straight. When a contributor to the *Literary Digest* hit very close to home by implying that Dwight L. Moody had considered a certain liberal churchman to be more of a Christian gentleman than Moody's own protégé, Reuben A. Torrey, the *Monthly* printed Torrey's irate reply. In the same issue, evangelist W. E. Biederwolf attacked the *Ladies Home Journal* for favoring modernism in religious affairs. William Jennings Bryan also used the *Monthly*'s pages to respond to the *Chicago Tribune* for misrepresenting and ridiculing his position. It was hardly the first time that Bryan had been maligned in that Republican paper, but now the issue was evolution, not politics.[38] Clearly, Gray and his colleagues felt betrayed by well-bred, middle-class America.

The abuse was beginning to tell on Gray's self-respect, although he resisted the temptation to retaliate with similar tactics. Throughout the 1920s, while the *Monthly* continued to attack modernism, Gray counselled fairness and moderation, urging fundamentalists to contend for the faith with decency and restraint. When the antievolution agitation reached its peak in 1926 and attracted its share of bizarre characters, Gray appealed to the campaigners to use "reason . . . calm logic and . . . statements of fact," and confessed that he thought it wrong to forbid the discussion of evolutionary theory in the classroom. Most of all, he regretted the vulgar level to which the whole discussion had descended.[39]

Nevertheless, Gray and the Institute staff had chosen sides, and their side indulged in some rhetorical street fighting. Once fundamentalists concluded that the other side represented the Great Apostasy, and after they had experienced a few assaults on their integrity, it was easier for them to believe and propagate the worst about their adversaries. Alongside responsible conservative critiques, the *Monthly* printed articles that made some reckless charges. One piece claimed that belief in evolution and modernism would lead to the sins of Sodom, and another suggested that modernist Harry Emerson Fosdick might be demonically inspired.[40] The *Monthly* also fell prey to the social fears afoot in the 1920s. Gray criticized the Ku Klux Klan rather mildly, defended the conviction of Sacco and Vanzetti, supported immigration restriction, warned against the Roman Catholic threat in Al Smith's candidacy, and sympathized with Henry Ford's charge that the *Protocols of the Elders of Zion* documented a Jewish world conspiracy.[41] Thus while the *Monthly* urged fundamentalists to contend for the faith with decency and restraint, it too fell prey to the bitterness that marked the fundamentalist–modernist controversy at its height.

By the late 1920s and early 1930s, then, Gray's outlook had shifted decisively from the more temperate conservatism he had displayed twenty years earlier. Although the *Monthly* had paid relatively little attention to the denominational controversies and Gray had counselled against hasty separation from the mainline churches, he no longer assumed much congruence between his views and those of the nation's religious and political leaders. The Institute was now on the other side of a great divide. The Federal Council of Churches, which Gray had once praised, now regularly drew his fire for its modernism. And in one of its few overtly separatistic acts, the Moody Bible Institute stopped sending delegates to the Student Volunteer Missionary Conventions in 1928. One of the few eminent persons whom the alienated Gray quoted favorably after 1930 was, ironically, Al Smith, who also felt frustrated and marginalized.[42]

By the late 1920s and early 1930s, therefore, even the more moderate fundamentalists were feeling afflicted. As Gray put it, they expected "to be fought, to be spoken against, to be boycotted and picked at," because the "offense of the Cross has not ceased." They should stand firm, he counselled, for the days to come would be "fighting days for us."[43] To be a fundamentalist in the 1930s was to bear the social and psychic burden of an outsider.

Reform or Withdraw?

Even if fundamentalists felt estranged from the mainstream of American life and from their fellow Protestants by the 1930s, the dilemma of their denominational standing still needed solving. Should they stay in their denominations and "strengthen the things which remain" (Rev. 3:2), or come out and be separate, to avoid being implicated in the "evil deeds" of the modernists (II John 11)?

For most fundamentalists, this question did not present itself until the late 1920s or early 1930s, for in the early stages of the controversies, Baptist and Presbyterian militants had hoped to drive the liberals out of power, if not out of the denominations altogether. These hopes were quickly dashed, however, as the Baptist moderate-liberal coalition won key contests at the 1922 Convention and their Presbyterian counterparts were prevailing by the General Assembly of 1925. At this point the fundamentalists seemed forced to adjust their goals. If the modernists could not be purged, then what was to be done?

Leaders of the Fundamentalist Federation in the Northern Baptist Convention judged that it was now time to "play ball" with their opponents rather than wreck so much of the evangelical work that was being accomplished by the Northern Baptist agencies.[44] The strategy of this moderate party of fundamentalists, as it unfolded from the mid-1920s on, was to continue their evangelical witness on the local level; designate funds to support evangelical missionaries through the American Baptist Foreign Mission Society; voice their perspectives through the largest Baptist magazine in the North, the *Watchman-Examiner;* provide an evangelical influence by serving on denominational boards; hold annual preconvention conferences for fellowship and encouragement; and hope for gradual reform as their new seminaries, Northern, Eastern, and Western, trained and placed conservative evangelical pastors and missionaries.[45]

Northern Baptist polity was decentralized enough to allow room for even some of the most militant fundamentalists. During the 1930s and early 1940s, regional fundamentalist champions such as William Bell Riley of Minneapolis, Richard S. Beal of Tuscon, and Albert G. Johnson of Portland, Oregon felt no compelling need to withdraw from the denomination. Riley was a quasi-denominational power unto himself, and his followers eventually captured the Minnesota Baptist Convention. In Arizona and Oregon, the state conventions and local associations were overwhelmingly conservative, so fundamentalists there were not faced with the tensions that nagged their comrades in other places where liberals were more influential. This wing of "Convention" fundamentalism was no less militantly opposed to modernism than the separatist Baptist "come-outers," but its own latent separatist impulses would be aroused during the late 1940s.[46]

Presbyterian fundamentalists had much less room to operate. Presbyterian polity and custom worked against the formation of alternative agencies within the denomination, although extradenominational affiliations were not restricted. Once the "inclusive" party had won its fight to interpret the church's confessions very broadly and had successfully opened Princeton Theological Seminary to a variety of theological views, militant conservatives had neither the means to prosecute their opponents nor a stronghold among the denomination's agencies. Nevertheless, they controlled two influential papers, *The Presbyterian* and (after 1930) *Christianity Today;*[47] and by 1929 they had a new seminary, Westminster, to train orthodox pastors. It is tempting to interpret the founding of Westminster Theological Seminary as the first step toward separation by J. Gresham Machen and his followers, and perhaps that is what it became; but in its first four years, Westminster was clearly an agency for reform, not withdrawal. Although the institution was officially independent, its professors were ministers in the northern Presbyterian church, and its early graduates, such as Carl McIntire and Harold Ockenga, were finding pastorates within the denomination.[48]

In both the northern Presbyterian and Northern Baptist denominations, however, factions developed within fundamentalist ranks and separatist movements emerged. Among the Northern Baptists, the major separatist force was the Baptist Bible Union, which was formed in 1923 by Northern Baptist fundamentalists who were impatient with the Fundamentalist Federation's moderation and by other militant Baptists from Canada and the South. The Bible Union's first directive was to keep on fighting. Northern Baptist radicals William Bell Riley, Robert T. Ketcham, and R. E. Neighbour of Ohio, and John Roach Straton of New York City were incensed that the Federation's more moderate leaders, notably J. C. Massee of Boston and J. Whitcomb Brougher of Los Angeles, would give in so quickly when greater efforts to mobilize the conservative majority in the Convention might bring a fundamentalist victory. They were also repulsed by the idea of cooperating with modernists in the denominational enterprise. This smacked of compromise, and in warfare, compromise with the enemy was treason. The Bible Union demanded nothing less than a thorough purge of the denomination and, failing that, complete withdrawal.[49]

By the late 1920s, after repeated political failures on the floor of the Convention, several state-level Bible Union organizations, such as the Michigan Orthodox Baptist Association and the Southern California Baptist Bible Union, began the process of separation. They were following the example of T. T. Shields of Toronto, who had formed the separatist Union of Regular Baptist Churches of Ontario and Quebec in 1927. In 1932 representatives of various remnants of the Bible Union in the northern United States met in Chicago to form the General Association of Regular Baptist Churches. The Bible Union's leading agitator in Southern Baptist territory, J. Frank Norris of First Baptist Church in Fort Worth, Texas, formed the Fundamentalist Baptist Fellowship in 1931.[50]

Forced to accept the fact that their denomination had embraced theological pluralism, northern Presbyterian fundamentalists also began to divide ranks over the separation question. At first the conservatives' coalition, led by the eminent pulpiteer Clarence Macartney and the formidable apologist, J. Gresham Machen, seemed to hold together well. Macartney served on the board of Westminster Seminary, and he and Machen worked side by side to place Westminster graduates within the church. But when Machen formed the Independent Board of Presbyterian Foreign Missions in 1933, he lost a considerable number of allies, including Macartney, who saw it as a divisive act. And when the General Assembly ruled that the Independent Board was unlawfully constituted and demanded that its members resign or face trial, Machen lost more followers. One who felt compelled to stop fighting was Wilbur M. Smith, a pastor in Coatesville, Pennsylvania, who resigned from the Independent Board rather than drag his presbytery and congregation through further painful disputes. So when Machen left to found the Orthodox Presbyterian Church in 1936, only a small fraction of the original Presbyterian fundamentalist coalition went with him. The following year, in a dispute over premillennialism, polity, and lifestyle, a split in the new church's ranks produced what became in 1938 the Bible Presbyterian Church, led by Carl McIntire of Collingswood, New Jersey, and J. Oliver Buswell, Jr., president of Wheaton College.[51]

In the meantime, hundreds of fundamentalist congregations simply cut themselves loose from any broader affiliation. Some had been Baptists, others came out of Presbyterianism, some had been Dutch Reformed, but quite a few separated from the Congregationalists, the most thoroughly liberal of the major denominations. Longing to establish some links with kindred churches but wary of constituting a new denomination, many of these newly independent congregations joined with free-lance "gospel tabernacles" to form fellowships in the 1920s, including the American Conference of Undenominational Churches, the Eastern Conference of Fundamentalist and Undenominational Churches, and the Central States Fellowship. Pastors representing these three groups in particular came together in 1930 to form the Independent Fundamental Churches of America (IFCA), a nongoverning ministerial association. The major organizer of this venture was William McCarrell, pastor of

First Congregational Church of Cicero (later Cicero Bible Church) in suburban Chicago. McCarrell, an alumnus of the Moody Bible Institute, had just led a number of churches out of the Chicago Congregational Association. Under his leadership the IFCA grew rapidly. By 1935 the organization had a membership of 531 ministers, evangelists, and missionaries, and it grew to over 1,000 by the early 1940s.[52]

The IFCA included a few large churches such as McCarrell's, or M. R. DeHaan's Calvary Undenominational Church in Grand Rapids, but this fellowship seemed most attractive to smaller congregations. Many of the prominent fundamentalist preaching stations in the 1930s—such as the Moody Memorial Church in Chicago, led by Harry A. Ironside; Louis T. Talbot's Church of the Open Door in Los Angeles; or Calvary Baptist Church in New York, whose pastors in the 1930s and 1940s were Will H. Houghton and William Ward Ayer—remained totally independent. With their own newspapers, radio programs, missionaries, youth programs and Bible conferences, they were virtually pocket-sized denominations, separated and sufficient unto themselves.[53]

These acts of separation kept a debate simmering within the broader fundamentalist movement over the proper ecclesiastical stance. Scarcely any fundamentalists would categorically reject the separatist option, for stories abounded of pastors and congregations that had been threatened by heavy-handed denominational officials or so scandalized by their modernist denominational neighbors' deviations from traditional orthodoxy that they felt driven by their consciences to walk out. Pressing the issue further, leaders of the new separatist fellowships, such as the IFCA, the Bible Presbyterian Church, and the General Association of Regular Baptist Churches, argued that ecclesiastical segregation from modernism was required; for them it became a critical test of orthodoxy. How could light fellowship with darkness? How could "two walk together except they be agreed?" (Amos 3:3).

Regular Baptists, for example, were frustrated by the apparent compromise with modernism on the part of the leaders of the Northern Baptist Convention's Fundamentalist Fellowship. Curtis Lee Laws, editor of the *Watchman-Examiner,* actually let liberals publish an occasional word or two; and Earle V. Pierce of Minneapolis served on the board of the theologically inclusive American Baptist Foreign Missions Society and as president of the Convention in 1937. These leaders, the separatists charged, helped legitimize the modernists by going along with the "inclusive policy" that called for liberals and conservatives to work together. Fundamentalists' token presence in denominational offices provided an evangelical veneer under which modernists could hide. The result of Convention fundamentalists' unequal yoking with unbelievers, the separatists charged, would be confusion, complacency, and the eventual spiritual ruin of many evangelical pastors and lay people.[54]

The Regular Baptists were not content to enjoy their separated fellowship and plant new congregations. They saw it as their mission to stir up fundamentalist outrage against Northern Baptist liberalism and recruit as many dissident congregations as possible. Throughout the decade after their founding they mounted a "militant program of publicity," informing Northern Baptist congregations about how bad things really were in the Convention and urging them to join the separatist movement.[55]

Their chief controversialist was Robert T. "Fighting Bob" Ketcham, then pastor of Central Baptist Church in Gary, Indiana. Ketcham published a series of sensational articles and pamphlets called "Facts for Baptists to Face" in which he cited examples of Northern Baptists' placing modernists on the mission field, allowing them to run the denomination's colleges and publications, and pursuing a "deliberate program to land the Baptists of this country completely in the camp of . . . rank Communistic Socialism." Ketcham presented cases, replete with reproduced documents and quotations, of some of the most radical activities of Baptist clergymen in the 1930s. The point of marshalling this evidence, Ketcham wrote, was to show that it was impossible "to bring to pass any adequate correction from within." He implied that anyone who persisted in cooperating with the denomination after finding out these facts was a coward and a compromiser.[56]

Regular Baptist leaders meanwhile argued that it was the sovereign right of any Baptist church to withdraw from the Convention, and they pledged their help to any congregation facing legal obstructions. Ketcham himself spent a great deal of time testifying for come-outers in lawsuits.[57] Scores of Baptist congregations left the Northern Baptist Convention, and the Regular Baptists received many of them. From a tiny sect with some 84 churches and 22,000 members in 1936, the General Association of Regular Baptist Churches grew to 468 member churches twelve years later.[58]

From the perspective of the Convention fundamentalists, however, the Regular Baptists' tactics and motives were disgraceful. John W. Bradbury, editor of the *Watchman-Examiner*, accused the come-outers of practicing "religious racketeering . . . under the cloak of fundamentalism." The separatists were out to wreck the Northern Baptist Convention in order to feed upon the spoils, so who could trust them to give a clear picture of the situation? It made "neither good sense nor good Christianity" to destroy the Northern Baptist Convention, for the majority of its churches were evangelical. Fundamentalists should work instead to strengthen the denomination.[59]

Convention fundamentalists had an unlikely but powerful ally for a time in William Bell Riley. Riley had been a leader in the Baptist Bible Union but opted to stay within the Convention. He stayed, Riley explained, because he simply could not bear to see the liberals inherit a vast denominational enterprise that had been built up by evangelicals.[60] In addition to this pragmatic argument, Riley continued to express hope that the fundamentalists would prevail. Even though the campaigns to oust the liberals had failed, Riley argued that the longer war could be won by placing more pastors and missionaries than the liberals did. "I have learned to labor and wait," Riley advised.[61] Yet if he and other like-minded Northern Baptist fundamentalists who were actually separatists by temperament should experience new frustrations in denominational politics, they might well decide to leave.

Indeed, just weeks before he died in 1947, Riley notified officials that he had to leave the Convention before he departed this world.[62] His decision was an important symbolic blow in a fresh fight that had recently erupted. In 1943 a group of Convention fundamentalists had formed the Conservative Baptist Foreign Mission Society (CBFMS). This action came in response to the appointment of a new general secretary, allegedly a liberal, to head the American Baptist Foreign Mission Society (ABFMS), and its failure to assure conservatives that its standards were evangelical.[63] Hundreds of congregations pledged support for the new venture, which grew rapidly. By January 1947 the CBFMS was working in seven different nations with 114 missionaries under appointment, supported by 1,270 churches and receiving $400,000 a year.[64] Denominational officials judged the CBFMS to be divisive and a damaging source of competition with the ABFMS, and the 1946 Convention ruled against its being allowed denominational status. By 1948 fundamentalist congregations in many states were threatened with a loss of standing if they did not support the denominational boards. Hundreds of them withdrew and formed a new body, the Conservative Baptist Association. The latent separatism among Convention fundamentalists had been provoked, and they organized the Northern Baptist Convention's most serious schism.[65]

The separation question flared up repeatedly throughout the 1930s and 1940s, producing real divisions and lasting resentments among people who not only agreed about the great majority of religious issues but often had been close friends. Two Westminster Seminary classmates, Harold Ockenga and Carl McIntire, for example, developed a bitter rivalry over these issues. Ockenga became Clarence Macartney's assistant pastor in Pittsburgh and, although J. Gresham Machen had preached at Ockenga's ordination, the young pastor sided with Macartney when the latter broke off ties with Machen over the Independent Board of Presbyterian Foreign Missions.

McIntire, on the other hand, stood by Machen and the Independent Board, was tried and suspended by his presbtery, and left the denomination. He remained bitter about his treatment and interpreted his erstwhile colleagues' decision not to separate in the most cynical light. Pastors in comfortable parishes with influential connections had been bought off by the patronage system, he charged.[66]

Thus began a feud that lasted for decades. In 1940 and 1941, Ockenga was involved in forming what would become the National Association of Evangelicals, a broad coalition of Protestant conservatives that included nonseparating fundamentalists from the major denominations. McIntire hastily stole a march on this organization and formed the militantly separatist American Council of Christian Churches in 1941. He lost no time in attacking the NAE, which had elected Ockenga as president, for being soft on separation and thus on modernism and communism. When Ockenga repeatedly denounced "come-outism" during his presidency at the newly founded Fuller Theological Seminary in southern California, McIntire bitterly recalled what separation had cost him and recounted his "betrayal" by William Sanford LaSor, now a

Fuller professor, who had voted for McIntire's suspension from the Presbyterian ministry some dozen years earlier. The hostility carried through the rest of these men's lives.[67]

What Made Separatists and Nonseparatists?

Why did some fundamentalists make ecclesiastical separation a test of faithfulness while others did not? Certainly, no one opposed separatism because of its novelty. Church splits and the creation of new religious bodies have a busy history in North America, largely because of the dissenting heritage of so many of the early settlers and the freedom to reorganize allowed by the separation of church and state. The populist strain in American culture, which has featured a preference for local control and strong dislike for bureaucratic management, also fed into the separatist impulse.[68] In the early days of fundamentalism, the Interchurch World Movement of 1919–1921 touched off widespread opposition and the beginnings of estrangement because overly zealous Northern Baptist state convention officials assigned each congregation a fund-raising quota and used pressure tactics to encourage compliance.[69] Among Southern Baptists, where few if any modernists lurked, J. Frank Norris's separatist movement capitalized on a similar reaction against the denomination's centrally imposed Seventy-Five Million Campaign.[70]

Presbyterians had a much stronger sense of the corporate character of the church, but their record in America (and in Scotland, for that matter) also contained many examples of schism. A frequent ingredient in Presbyterian separatism was the idea, inherited from Calvin, that a true church imposes proper discipline. This could mean, among other things, enforcing doctrinal conformity. As George Marsden put it, conservative Calvinist "Old School" Presbyterians were not often willing to "let sleeping dogmas lie."[71] So as northern Presbyterians moved toward doctrinal pluralism, militant conservatives complained that the denomination was making a mockery of proper discipline and might in fact be losing its status as a true church. After several explicit repudiations in the church courts of their attempts to impose doctrinal conformity, the militants were convinced that the northern Presbyterian church had become apostate and it was time to separate. Thus J. Gresham Machen sighed with relief when his group organized a separatist body. "At last," he said, "a true Presbyterian Church."[72]

The extensive record of separatism in American religious history may help in understanding why that option seemed legitimate in principle, but it does not help distinguish the separatists from the nonseparating fundamentalists. A variety of other factors, then, need to be considered as potential help in sorting out fundamentalism's internal divisions.

Several historians have pointed out that the separatist position drew much support from fundamentalists' widespread pessimism about the future of the church. The dispensationalist doctrinal view, which dominated the movement, predicted the ruin of the church. As we have seen, this belief was one of the key alienating factors in the movement and it carried an explicit mandate for true believers to separate themselves from the coming Great Apostasy. It is noteworthy that with the exceptions of T. T. Shields's separatist movement in Canada and J. Gresham Machen's tiny Old School Calvinist sect, the Orthodox Presbyterian Church, all of the separatist groups were thoroughly dispensationalist. It seemed especially clear in the case of the two Northern Baptist schisms that those fundamentalists who left were predominantly dispensationalists and those who stayed included many who were not.[73]

On the other hand, dispensationalists could be found on both sides of the separation debates. The problem of predicting denominational loyalty on the basis of views of biblical prophecy is especially evident among northern Presbyterians. J. Oliver Buswell, Jr. and Carl McIntire were premillennialists and separatists, but Wilbur M. Smith and Donald Grey Barnhouse were, if anything, even stronger advocates of premillennial and dispensational views yet they did not leave the northern Presbyterian church. An important complicating factor in the Presbyterian conflict was the Machenites' strict adherence to the Westminster Confession and many premillennialists' sense that a looser construction of that creed was necessary if their views of prophecy were not to be judged heretical. Indeed, as the split of Machen's new denomination in 1937 shows, the alliance of these two kinds of militant conservatives was fundamentally unstable.[74]

If dispensationalists could be found on either side of the separation debates, there must have been other important factors prompting separatism. It has often been suggested that separatism attracted people who in other ways felt like outsiders, perhaps because of humble social status, rural or small-town isolation, or relative lack of education. Regular Baptists and J. Frank Norris's Fundamental Baptists appear to have attracted a greater percentage of their congregations from small towns and working-class urban neighborhoods than did nonseparating fundamentalists, but no careful analysis yet sustains these impressions, and some studies show that such a constituency was typical of all fundamentalists and not that different from other white Baptists.[75] Levels of educational attainment and the type of educational experience may provide additional clues, but at present no careful studies exist to demonstrate definitive educational differences between separatists and nonseparating fundamentalists. Bible school education, for example, apparently was important to the entire Baptist fundamentalist movement in the North.[76]

The social backgrounds of fundamentalist leaders reveal no more of a difference between separatists and nonseparatists than does their education. Neither Robert T. Ketcham, an important leader of the Regular Baptists, nor Will H. Houghton, president of Moody Bible Institute who stayed with the Northern Baptists, had much formal education, and both were from humble backgrounds. Both of these traits were in fact still fairly common among Baptist pastors of all persuasions in the 1930s. Harold Ockenga and Carl McIntire both had college and seminary education, as was common for Presbyterian clergy; and Ockenga, the nonseparatist, came from the humbler home. Both "stay-inner" Wilbur M. Smith and "come-outer" J. Gresham Machen were from wealthy families.[77]

Whether or not there were any clear social or educational differences between separatists and nonseparatists during the 1930s, each party eventually perceived the other as having become something different. And to a large extent, they had diverged. For example, while separatists persisted in cultivating Bible-school education, the nonseparatists increasingly sought graduate theological training for their ministers and liberal arts education for their laity. Separatists developed an ethos that scorned the world's praise and its standards of worth, while nonseparatists were more accommodating to middle-class values. Yet this eventual divergence still leaves unanswered the question of whether nuances in social status and cultural values were decisive when separatists and nonseparatists first squared off or whether their opposing stands prompted social differentiation and eventually attracted different clienteles.[78]

The critical catalysts for separatism seemed to be personal factors more than more general patterns of belief or social standing. Leaders' personalities and the contacts and experiences of individual pastors and congregations were the definitive influences on how one might decide whether or not to come out and be separate. Some fundamentalist leaders seemed destined to become separatists by virtue of their personalities. J. Frank Norris, for instance, was a violent person who relished agitation and conflict, and he felt driven to build his own empire. His thirty years' war against the Southern Baptist officials was characterized by a steady stream of character assaults and political maneuverings.[79] By the end of his career, Norris had alienated not only the Convention loyalists but militant allies such as Robert T. Ketcham, John R. Rice, William Bell Riley, and even his former associate pastor, G. Beauchamp Vick. All agreed that Norris was temperamentally unable to be part of any association that he could not dominate.[80] This trait helps explain the highly feudal character of separatist fundamentalism, which is marked more by the empires of regional warlords than by strong networks of cooperation.

For some, the choice to separate came as the result of bitter personal experience. Consider, for example, the case of Robert T. Ketcham. While serving as the pastor of a prospering Northern Baptist congregation in Butler, Pennsylvania, Ketcham was told in 1919 that his church's fund-raising quota for the Interchurch World Movement was $17,000. His congregation refused the assignment and authorized Ketcham to publish an exposé of the Movement's allegedly modernist aims. Soon after his pamphlet came out, Ketcham received a visit from officers of the Pittsburgh Baptist Association. When Ketcham made it clear that he would not retract his pamphlet, one of these callers threatened him, vowing that if Ketcham did not recant and meet his quota, he would never get another pastorate in the Northern Baptist Convention. Ketcham retorted that $17,000 was too much to pay for a Baptist pulpit when he could get a soap box for a dime. At that point another member of the committee grabbed Ketcham's collar, shook him and roared that Ketcham owed God an apology. But Ketcham would not apologize, and this run-in with bullying

note: theology generated in response to resisting organizational power

Baptist officials set his face permanently against the Convention and its "over-lords." Granted, Ketcham was feisty and independent by nature, but here were grounds for separation if ever one had them.[81]

By contrast, another Pennsylvania Baptist pastor, Will Houghton, of New Bethlehem, also published a pamphlet denouncing Northern Baptist modernism. But unlike Ketcham, he had influential friends, notably Reuben A. Torrey, who were able to shield him from denominational pressures. Houghton's career led eventually to the presidency of Moody Bible Institute, and he remained within the Northern Baptist denomination.[82] Meanwhile, Ketcham became the embattled leader of the Regular Baptists. One may well wonder how these two careers might have been different had their early experiences been exchanged.

This comparison of Ketcham and Houghton points to another important factor in the separation dilemma: connections. A fundamentalist pastor's location and personal web of associations seemed to make a great deal of difference in shaping decisions about staying with or walking out of a denomination. Fundamentalist Baptist pastors and congregations in Minnesota, for example, could enjoy the collective security of "Riley's empire," made up of the alumni and friends of the Northwestern Bible School. Because of this influential bloc in the Minnesota state convention of Baptists, very few Minnesota congregations joined the Regular Baptist schism in the 1930s.[83] In a similar vein, young Harold Ockenga found protection and preferment under the care of Clarence Macartney, the leading Presbyterian in Pittsburgh. Carl McIntire, by contrast, continued to tough it out under less favorable circumstances in the towns of southern New Jersey, where both he and Ockenga had begun their ministries.[84] Ketcham once complained to Riley that congregations that were either large and influential or part of a coalition churches could "paddle their own course" without much pressure from the denomination, while smaller, more isolated churches were "constantly under the club" of denominational officials to go along with the program.[85] These more vulnerable churches and their pastors developed a more intense sense of marginality than other fundamentalists and they fed into the separatist movement.[86]

Connections and patronage could also promote separatism if leading pastors chose to pull out. In the Baptist state convention of Oregon, where the leading pastors were fundamentalists, the majority of the Northern Baptist churches joined the Conservative Baptist separation of 1948–1949. In a region where a dynamic fundamentalist empire-builder filled pastorates in preacherless or new congregations with his young protégés, those churches would follow his lead. That was the case with J. Frank Norris's Fundamental Baptist movement in Texas and Oklahoma, where Norris's evangelistic work and that of one of his young lieutenants, John R. Rice, resulted in the growth of anti-Convention Baptist churches throughout the area.[87]

Deciding to join the separatists or to affiliate with those who had decided to stay was often both a highly personal and a connectional matter. It involved a complex and often finely nuanced set of factors—doctrinal, social, temperamental, experiential, environmental and associational—that colored thousands of decisions being made at various times and places throughout these years.

Many people felt compelled to wrestle with the separation question at what was perhaps the most distressing level—their own membership in a local church. In the early 1930s, when the issue had been made fresh and urgent for many because of the controversies in their denominations, laypeople who suspected that their pastors might be modernists agonized over their duty and calling. Wrote one perplexed believer, "Dr. —— used Philippians 3:13,14 and had a long sermon on golf." She was so disturbed by his trivializing the word of God, she confessed, that she "came home from church . . . and wept."[88] Another shocked churchgoer reported that a pastor "referred to the Bible as 'this debris of folklore, myth and tradition.'"[89] Should a church member who believed the fundamental tenets of historic Christianity stay in a church where contrary beliefs were taught? Did the Bible's admonition to "come ye out and be ye separate" (II Cor. 6:17) mean that they should seek fellowship in some other local church?

For many, the easiest thing to do was simply leave quietly and find some other fellowship where the fundamentals of the faith were believed and taught. A pastor from Iowa who taught a rapidly growing weekly Bible class began to receive complaints from other pastors that he was "sheep stealing," even though he had done nothing to recruit new participants out of their home churches. Observed the editors of the *Moody Monthly*, this was a common story. Members of modernist churches, the *Monthly* insisted, were starved for the word of God. "No wonder . . . they leave the churches and denominations in which they were brought up and come out as independents, or fundamentalists, or anything that will mean spiritual life to them and to their children."[90]

The most common counsel that mainstream fundamentalist leaders gave, however, especially if the inquirers were church officers or Sunday School teachers, was for them to stay put, pray for change, and be an influence for orthodoxy. But so many perplexed people reported what they believed were intolerable situations that it was very difficult for leaders who were not out-and-out separatists to offer any hard and fast rule about local church membership. Said the correspondence editor of the *Sunday School Times*, "God graciously allows and even directs a latitude of personal choice and decision in matters of this sort.[91]

Given the relative ease with which one could leave one congregation and join another, these personal decisions to come out and be separate probably were as significant as congregational ones in accounting for the growth of fundamentalist and other evangelical churches.

Separation without the Trouble: The Parachurch Network

Even while the separation debate surged and ebbed through the 1930s and 1940s, many fundamentalists were able to avoid the issue. They were busy developing religious allegiances that had little to do with ecclesiastical structures.

This de facto separatism was made possible by the growing network of independent fundamentalist ministries.

The leaders of these agencies felt caught in the middle of the separation debates. They had nothing directly at stake, since they worked outside of the denominations. But an organization's position on separation had become a critical gauge of its standing within fundamentalism. If the Moody Bible Institute, for example, took a stand for separation from the major denominations, it might please the Bible Presbyterians but alienate denominationally loyal Presbyterians such as Wilbur M. Smith, whose father was a longtime trustee of the Institute. On the other hand, an outright repudiation of separatism—or even too strong an endorsement of staying in a denomination that included modernists—might lose the support of influential alumni such as William McCarrell, the Cicero-based godfather of the IFCA.

So in order to establish some middle ground, many of the parachurch groups developed a mediating position. The correspondence editor of the *Sunday School Times,* to cite one example, suggested that God might be calling some people to come out of impossible situations in order to start new ministries. Others, he mused, might be guided to strengthen the evangelical witness within the older churches. This equivocation would not fully satisfy the separatists, but it seemed to buy independent agencies some peace.[92]

In return, the nondenominational ministries provided a measure of unity to fundamentalism by providing "neutral turf" where both separatists and non-separatists could participate. For denominational fundamentalists, these agencies provided trustworthy channels for their giving and refreshing retreats from their uneasy coexistence with liberals. The separatists benefitted from them as well. Because there were so many theologically fundamentalist agencies performing a variety of ministries, the new separatist denominations did not have to set up a full complement of agencies to serve their constituents. The parachurch network also made it possible for totally independent congregations to enjoy many of the benefits of denominational affiliation with none of the drawbacks. Although fundamentalism was divided over the separation question, the movement retained a loose but effective unity by means of this nonaligned institutional network.

Fundamentalists' involvement with these independent agencies amounted to a de facto separation, however, whether it was acknowledged or not. The easiest option for those who no longer trusted their denominations' leadership was to divert their support and participation to nondenominational ministries. A fundamentalist layperson in Chicago in the 1930s, for example, could attend special meetings at the Moody Memorial Church, support the China Inland Mission, listen to station WMBI, do volunteer work at the Pacific Garden Mission, read the *Sunday School Times,* take the interurban train down to the Winona Lake Bible Conference, and enroll her son in Wheaton College—while remaining a faithful member of the Buena Memorial Presbyterian Church.

At the same time that their supporters were practicing separatism by default, the leaders of these independent agencies thought of themselves as nonsectarian. Rowland V. Bingham, the Canadian head of the Sudan Interior Mission, in stating the broadly nondenominational basis of his agency observed that some of God's "choicest saints" were in denominations other than his own. But his ecumenical welcome had a more critical side as well. Bingham went on to say that too often, one's own denomination might present major hindrances to true Christian fellowship and service, including worldliness, corruptions of doctrine, and even outright apostasy. He had made his mission nondenominational because he believed that in these uncertain times "the lines of fellowship must be drawn horizontally."[93]

Independent agencies were inherently antidenominational in other ways as well. In order to promote support, a ministry's leaders frequently argued or at least implied that it was superior to parallel denominational efforts. In the early days of the independent mission movement, for example, faith mission pioneers such as J. Hudson Taylor and H. Grattan Guinness argued that their missions made more efficient use of funds, cultivated greater spirituality among their missionaries, and were more aggressively evangelistic than the denominational mission societies.[94] Likewise, the pioneers of the Bible school movement asserted that for many ministries, their training was more practical and spiritually bracing than the denominations' preferred college-and-seminary route.[95] And when the fundamentalist–modernist controversies began, independent agencies loudly affirmed their loyalty to the "faith once delivered." In 1920 James M. Gray proclaimed that "in these dark days of apostasy" the Institute was being "leaned upon . . . and turned to by thousands of earnest and sincere Christians all over the world who never were within its walls, but who are seeking for advice, instruction and comfort."[96] Presumably, the multitudes that were turning to Moody and kindred institutions were turning away, in some important respects, from their home denominations.

In fact, fundamentalists were using these agencies to cobble together a loosely connected denominational surrogate. Suggestive evidence of this comes from the *Sunday School Times*. Beginning around 1930 and continuing thereafter, the *Times*'s editors made lists to inform their readers of nondenominational agencies that were available to serve them and to become their channels of ministry. One such list presented "Bible Schools that are True to the Faith," while another gave names and addresses of "Sound Interdenominational Missions." Trumbull and staff generously recommended a variety of "Interdenominational Evangelical Magazines" other than their own and an assortment of evangelistic ministries in North America that were deemed worthy of support. Even the newest kind of religious ministry received endorsement in a "Directory of Evangelical Radio Broadcasts."

The editors of the *Times* never advised readers to drop their involvement with denominational endeavors, and conceded that there were still some worthy denominational enterprises. But the implication throughout was clear: if it was important to endorse these interdenominational agencies as "true to the faith" or "evangelical" or worthy of "full confidence" because they stood for "'the faith once delivered,'" then there must be something fishy about the denominational ones. Trumbull had of course been saying as much for years, since he had been a leading antimodernist agitator. Although he remained a Presbyterian, his primary allegiances were, without a doubt, with the interdenominational fundamentalist network.[97]

The expansion of this cluster of agencies was, then, a manifestation of the separatist impulse, indeed perhaps its most important institutional expression. While in ecclesiastical terms interdenominational fundamentalism was open-ended and free-wheeling, its ideological boundaries were patrolled with a vengeance. If fundamentalists were to have full confidence in these agencies, even the slightest question about their doctrinal integrity must be unacceptable.

So the pleas of Plymouth Brethren leader John Nelson Darby some sixty years earlier for true believers to come away from the "apostasy" of the organized church had finally been heeded, but in a uniquely American way. Some fundamentalists, to be sure, responded to what they believed was apostasy in their home denominations by forming sectarian fellowships such as the Regular Baptists and the Bible Presbyterians. Thousands of others quietly relocated to other congregations. But in America's free-enterprise religious system, where no church had legal favor, denominational loyalty was relatively weak, and many of the major denominations were little more than holding companies of voluntary associations, most fundamentalists became separatists in a much more consumerlike fashion, transferring their support to the nondenominational network of fundamentalist institutions. Recalled Torrey Johnson about his pastorate at the Midwest Bible Church in Chicago during the 1930s, "I was neither a come-outer nor a go-inner. I was just a worker."[98]

So long as fundamentalists felt estranged from the mainstream of American denominationalism and public life more generally, the separatist impulse would remain strong. And the "separation question," since it was not resolved, would arise repeatedly to trouble relationships within the movement and between fundamentalists and their mainline Protestant relatives.

3

SEPARATED FROM
THE WORLD

The most immediate sign and seal of fundamentalists' calling to come away from the world and from worldly Christianity was not their church membership but their commitment to live a "separated life." During the 1930s and 1940s, fundamentalists were developing patterns of devotion and habits of thought that marked them, in both the biblical and ordinary sense of the word, as a peculiar people.

Being a called-out, chosen people, separate from the rest of the world, is an ancient theme in Judaism and Christianity. Both the Old and New Testaments contain repeated admonitions for God's people to set themselves apart in both precept and behavior.[1] Religious history from ancient times to the present is replete with movements that sought to revive and extend biblical patterns of separation. In modern America, faith communities ranging from the Catholic religious orders to the Mormons, the Hasidic Jews, and the Amish have lived out their various understandings of this biblical theme. Evangelicals in early America also insisted on separation from the world, but by the mid-nineteenth century they had assumed such dominant cultural roles that their separatism virtually disappeared, and polite society came to reflect many of their once peculiar values.[2]

As the United States grew more pluralistic in religion and mores and evangelicals' domination of the culture began to wane in the late nineteenth century, Protestant revival movements began to call once again for the separated life. The holiness revivals of the 1870s, 1880s, and 1890s stressed matters of morality—both social and personal. Holiness preachers called for a return to the Wesleys' teaching of a simple, unselfish, and morally disciplined life. Holiness sects began to establish strict behavioral rules that went beyond more typical evangelical standards of modesty, chastity, and temperance. In their attempts to restore primitive Christianity, the more radical holiness communities often imposed regulations on diet, property, and marriage as well. Along with the rules came, virtually by necessity, a turning away from the activities and amusements of the "ordinary" world and a turning inward toward the company of the faithful.[3]

The turn-of-the-century forerunners of the fundamentalist movement had been influenced by the holiness movement to a substantial degree, but they did not develop as strong an urge to be separated from the broader Protestant paths. By the late 1920s and early 1930s, however, fundamentalists' experience had convinced them that their nation was turning away from God, and the call to be an exemplary, called-out people fit their situation. As we have seen, this separatist impulse stimulated the expansion of a complex network of institutions. In this sheltered community of congregations, schools, and other religious agencies, fundamentalist men and women found some rest from the modern world's relentless buffeting of their beliefs. Within these confines, they tried to rear their children according to older evangelical standards of discipline and piety, they cultivated the friendship of people who thought and acted as they did, and they created an array of religious activities that provided alternatives to worldly interests and amusements.

An ideal method for learning more about this "separated life" would be to reconstruct the lived texture of fundamentalism at the congregational level or in its schools, as has been done in some contemporary ethnographic or "participant-observer" studies. Something like this appoach is possible for historians, even from the distant vantage point of more than half a century later. Yet very little closely focused research into the character of these local fellowships has been done to this date.[4] Instead of attempting this sort of reconstructive work, this chapter will instead highlight the ideals and norms that the leaders of the movement taught and cultivated, and provide at least a few glimpses of the movement's lived experience. Common sense warns that gaps exist between what was taught and what was accepted and lived, but there is plenty of evidence to suggest that many made good-faith efforts to practice what was preached.

Peculiar People

The separated life for fundamentalists meant a variety of things, but most visible, of course, was their desire, in the midst of the Jazz Age, to uphold the behavioral standards of nineteenth-century evangelicalism. In addition to abiding by principles of strict sexual chastity and modesty in dress, fundamentalists were to abstain from alcoholic drink, profane or coarse language, social dancing (and dance music), and the theater—including the movies. Using tobacco, playing cards, gambling, and working on Sunday (or even playing too strenuously) were also forbidden. Extremes in fashion and heavy use of cosmetics were considered worldly; the ideal was to look clean-cut and "wholesome." Wrote Shirley Nelson in her excellent novel set in a Bible school like Moody in the 1940s, fundamentalists "simply spurned the world's frenetic search for empty pleasure. They did not smoke or drink or dance or attend the theater or concern themselves unduly with fashions or fads." The novel's major character thought she could always spot a fundamentalist girl on the street, "her face cool and relaxed . . . among the strained and painted, and . . . she could tell the boys too, by a certain clearness in their eyes."[5] Fundamentalists believed, it seemed, that a fair countenance would be the reward for standing, like the prophet Daniel, against the world's debilitating habits.

Perhaps they could identify each other, but compared to bearded and bonneted Mennonites or some pentecostal groups that eschewed neckties and jewelry, fundamentalists would be hard to distinguish from other "ordinary" Americans. Most Protestants probably professed the same norms as the fundamentalists, but these radical conservatives insisted that the mainline churches had grown worldly and were becoming too permissive. There was a time, said Will Houghton, the president of Moody Bible Institute, when Christian people knew what sinful behavior was and avoided it, but now even women brazenly smoked and drank. Profanity "used to be smothered" and adultery "used to be cause for ostracism," but now, "instead of speaking of sin," he complained, pastors "talk of social relationships, and instead of sending for the revivalist they call in the psychologist."[6] The malaise in moral standards was not to be blamed only on the unchurched and the nonevangelicals; many of the "born-again" seemed to be following the world too. An Irish fundamentalist revivalist, J. Edwin Orr, noticed this problem on his tour of the American South in 1935. To his dismay he discovered that "quite a majority of believers go to 'the movies' once a week, as well as other questionable amusements, and the *unpainted* face is more an exception than the rule. The converted Christians behave almost exactly as the non-Christians do—there is no separation." The world may want "good mixers," Orr went on to say, but he agreed with his American fundamentalist friends that "'God wants good separators.'"[7] Fundamentalists championed this separated life, and they molded their institutional network into a close community where such practices would be upheld and enforced.

By the 1930s there were a number of signs that fundamentalists were making their behavioral expectations, which had been largely a matter of community consensus and taken-for-granted practice, into an explicit and energetically enforced code. This was most noticeable in the parachurch agencies, such as Bible schools, colleges, and missions. Such organizations often had simply assumed that evangelical mores would be a natural part of their clients' lives, and few had made formal provisions for codifying them. That began to change, however, as the new public permissiveness of the 1920s and 1930s and fundamentalists' growing alienation from the cultural centers prompted them to find ways to signal and maintain their distinctiveness.

At fundamentalist Bible schools and degree-granting colleges, elaborate codes of student behavior began to appear. According to a historian of the Bible school movement, the early (pre-1930) students at these institutions went largely unregulated. They tended to be adults in their twenties who were highly motivated and already rather athletic in their spiritual and personal discipline. By the 1930s, however, as the average age of the student body dropped at these schools, behavioral codes were put in place, and elaborate systems of monitoring, scheduling, and disciplinary actions developed, under the watchful eyes of the deans of women and men.[8]

At fundamentalist liberal arts colleges, where students tended to be younger and where rules of behavior had been standard features for a long time, officials legally codified the regulations and imposed monitoring systems. At Wheaton College, for example, the 1931 catalog introduced an important change in policy: each student had to sign a formal agreement to abide by the school's "standards of life." The 1939 catalog added that this statement was to be signed every year. The 1944 catalog added the stipulation that the Wheaton "pledge" was in force for its matriculated students year-round, even during summer vacations. The first two changes occurred during the presidency of James Oliver Buswell, Jr., who brought to the school "a more strict approach to student affairs."[9]

Buswell's strictness was not confined to his own campus. At the very time that he was tightening up Wheaton College's behavioral code, Buswell was stirring up a controversy over the "separated life" that eventually fragmented the new separatist denomination he had joined, the Presbyterian Church of America (PCA). Buswell and other militants such as Carl McIntire and Harold S. Laird quickly discovered that they had some serious disagreements with fellow separatists, notably J. Gresham Machen, who were disciples of the Old School Calvinist "Princeton theology." The two main issues in contention were dispensationalism and the "separated life." Carl McIntire seems to have started the fight in the fall of 1936 when he criticized Westminster Theological Seminary in Philadelphia for not requiring its students and faculty to forswear the use of alcohol. The Old School Calvinists, who controlled both Westminster and the PCA, insisted on the principle of Christian liberty, since drinking was not forbidden in the Scriptures.

Buswell saw things differently, to say the least. Like most American evangelicals, he thought that alcoholic beverages were one of the major sources of personal ruin and social evil. In his book *The Christian Life,* which appeared in early 1937, Buswell called on all Christians to abstain and to urge others to quit drinking. Quoting from Habakkuk 2:15 ("'Cursed is he who putteth the bottle to his neighbor's lips'"), Buswell charged that any self-proclaimed champions of orthodoxy who permitted moderate drinking were "guilty of the blood and souls of young men and women."[10] *The Christian Life* provoked a vigorous response from Buswell's opponents, as had his publications defending premillennialism. Within a year, the contending parties split the PCA into two even smaller sects: the Orthodox Presbyterian Church for the Old School Calvinists and the Bible Presbyterian Church for the premillennialist and "separated life" faction of New School heritage. The behavioral code was becoming so important for these fundamentalists' identity that they were willing to depart from their militantly orthodox comrades in order to maintain it. By stiffening their requirements for behavioral conformity, fundamentalists were replicating part of the sectarian pattern of development that had marked the Wesleyan holiness movement several decades earlier. It had become very important, for the identity and coherence of fundamentalism, to be able to tell who was an insider and who was an outsider. The behavioral code was becoming an indispensable tool for boundary-setting.[11]

Behavioral rules were nevertheless only the minimum, outward standards for the fundamentalist community. Along with doctrinal distinctives, such as premillennialism, they formed the basic identifying badges. Fundamentalists were aware that their move to codify their mores ran the risk of being "pharisaical," or strenuously observing behavioral rules and doctrinal orthodoxy while failing to live up to their faith's deeper spiritual and ethical standards. Genuine separation, Donald Grey Barnhouse counseled, was "an attitude of the heart and mind and not a mere withdrawal of the body."[12] So fundamentalist leaders also taught positive norms of belief and activity for the truly separated believer and attempted, through the shared religious life of the movement's institutions, to instill those ideals in their followers.

The basic vehicle for this shared religious life was the fundamentalist congregation, even though "Christian homes," where both parents upheld fundamentalist beliefs and norms, were idealized in sermons and hortatory literature. In such homes, families were to practice daily family prayer and Bible reading, patriarchal rule, firm but tender-hearted rearing of children (including "leading them to the Lord" in conversion and expecting at least a few of them to be called to "full-time Christian service"), and a thoroughgoing enforcement of fundamentalist mores.[13] But even the most resolute and close-knit of such families needed support for their stand against the world that could come only from fellow believers. Furthermore, any given fundamentalist congregation would most likely contain many members who did not have a religious consensus at home. Typically there were a number of members who were single, or were single parents, or were the only ones from their respective families who were "born-again," or who came to church with their children but without their spouses. So it was the congregation, one's "family in the Lord," where commitment to being a "Bible-believing Christian" in an increasingly unappreciative world received its primary boost.[14]

Little comprehensive research into the character of these local church fellowships has been done, but surviving descriptions suggest that in these congregations adherents found forceful religious instruction, a sense of mission, and their closest friendships. These churches sponsored many more activities than the usual Sunday morning and evening services, since church life in fundamentalist (and presumably other conservative Protestant) circles carried more social freight than did mainline Protestant congregations. These extra functions generally included midweek prayer meetings, home or evening Bible classes, missionary societies, boys' and girls' clubs, women's fellowship and men's prayer breakfasts, hospital and jail visitation and street preaching, and the many social gatherings of Sunday school classes and young people's societies.

Congregations also drew on the services of the larger fundamentalist network for auxiliary ministries, such as guest preachers and evangelists, Bible and missionary conferences, radio programs and rallies, Christian business men's or women's groups, youth rallies and outings, and Bible courses—either at a nearby Bible institute, over the radio, or by correspondence.[15]

Those who participated in such activities surrounded themselves with like-minded people and experienced repeated affirmations of their faith. They testified to each other of God's answers to their prayers, heard about the worldwide missionary advance, saw people respond to gospel invitations, and sang reassuring gospel songs such as "I serve a risen Savior, He's in the world today." Twice every Sunday the pastor or a guest preacher would explain the Scriptures, thrash the modernists, warn against worldliness in thought and deed, call the unconverted to saving faith in Christ, or interpret current events in the light of Bible prophecy.[16] Fundamentalist churches covered a great span in size, clientele, and style, ranging from urban "gospel centers" that met in storefronts and converted theaters such as the one founded by the Providence (RI) Bible Institute, to affluent Presbyterian congregations like Stewart MacLennan's in Hollywood, California. There were fundamentalist "cathedrals" of regional and national influence in prestigious center-city locations, such as Park Street Congregational Church next to the Boston Common, as well as many small-town "First Baptists," such as the one in Otsego, Michigan, and ubiquitous "Calvary Baptists" in lower-middle-class urban neighborhoods, such as the one in southeast Grand Rapids. But all had in common an ethos of religious certainty and a clear mission in an uncertain world. Secular intellectuals who believed in an aimlessly evolving universe might look with wistful disbelief at such assurance,[17] but many ordinary Americans found that in such religious communities they could rest their faith, as William Jennings Bryan had put it, on the Rock of Ages rather than on the age of the rocks.

Fundamentalists feared for their young people, however, especially the talented minority who left such supportive communities to go to college. The manager of WMBI, Moody Bible Institute's radio station, reported in the late 1930s that increasing numbers of listeners were requesting information on fundamentalist congregations in Chicago so they could recommend a good church to their college-bound children.[18] Colleges and universities were perhaps the most powerful sources of secular ideology in the nation, and Bible-believing young people who enrolled in them put their faith in jeopardy.[19] In a lecture that evangelist Bob Jones repeated many times as he toured the nation to promote his college, he warned that students at secular or mainline Protestant colleges would become "campus shipwrecks," falling prey to the skepticism of persuasive and authoritative professors and worldly, scoffing peers.[20] A Harvard-educated fundamentalist, Frank E. Gaebelein, who was headmaster of the Stony Brook School for Boys on Long Island, New York, declared that the universities were centers of unbelief where professors and students alike were ignorant of spirituality and crudely misrepresented evangelical faith. Those who accepted the Bible were branded intellectual heretics, he claimed; and the most popular philosophy of life was "a sort of rationalized paganism."[21] Even more threatening to many fundamentalists were the denominational colleges, where evangelical Christianity and a theistic intellectual foundation had once prevailed, but which now were dominated by Protestant liberalism in their religious activities and secular naturalism in their classrooms. On these campuses, fundamentalists alleged, unsuspecting students from traditional evangelical homes were having their beliefs subverted. Parents would do better to send their daughters and sons to the avowedly secular universities, one writer reasoned, rather than expose them to the "pious fraudulence" of a liberal Protestant college.[22] While many fundamentalist young people graduated from such institutions with their faith unshaken, others had both their beliefs and their morals shattered.[23]

In growing numbers, the movement's young people enrolled in Bible schools and liberal arts colleges that promised to fortify them against secular ideologies and lifestyles. A *Moody Monthly* editorial urged those who must attend a state university for professional training to get some "steadying" first at the Moody Bible Institute. Then students could go on to the university well equipped to be "militant" Christians.[24] Wheaton College, to cite another example, advertised itself in the 1930s as a "safe college for young people." Communism and modernism were "conclusively disproven" there, and the faculty taught "conservative social and economic views."[25]

Such schools also aimed to perpetuate the movement's piety by enveloping students in a pervasively evangelical atmosphere. At Wheaton, as was true at other fundamentalist schools, there were student-initiated morning and evening prayer meetings, evangelistic teams, a missionary fellowship and prayer bands for specific mission fields, and yearly campus-wide revival services—all in addition to daily required chapel. Although Wheaton enforced fundamentalist prohibitions against dancing, smoking, drinking, card-playing, and attending the theater, it tried to offer some alternatives. Activities abounded that emphasized "wholesome association and companionship," such as Christian service opportunities, sports, clubs, and literary societies. One alumnus crowed that Wheaton students were proving that college could be fun without "dancing and 'petting'" and that real men did not need "Lucky Strikes or a bottle of Scotch." While others thought that such schools had become extinct, Wheaton reveled in its old-fashionedness.[26]

The separated life for most fundamentalists, however, had to take place out in the "world" more than in the bosom of church and school. This meant going about one's life according to a different outlook, a distinctive morality, or as the fundamentalist saying went, "with eternity's values in view."[27] This-worldly matters were to have lower priority than spiritual matters. Fundamentalists' primary goal in life, they professed, was to pursue the "things of God." Prayer, Bible study, fellowship with other believers, and efforts to convert others were the most prized of life's activities.

This exaltation of religious activities was accompanied by a tendency not to take the affairs of the secular world too seriously—at least on their own terms.

Leaders' discussions of public affairs quickly became attempts to correlate current trends with biblical prophecy or were turned into homilies about spiritual matters. James M. Gray briefly praised the development of the Social Security Administration in 1935, but then he launched into a discourse on "eternal security" that came from knowing Christ as personal savior. In like manner the editor of the *Baptist Evangel* compared the drought on the Great Plains to the spiritual drought in the land and the need for spiritual "showers of blessing."[28]

Such talk frustrated liberal Protestants, who considered the ethical and civic application of their faith to be their foremost duty. Harry Emerson Fosdick may have had fundamentalists' spiritualizing in mind when in his sermon "The Peril of Worshiping Jesus" he argued that too many people would rather put Jesus "up on some high altar, pray to him, sing to him, do anything for him" than do his will in the troubled present age.[29] This criticism, while certainly containing much that is valid, in some ways misses the point. Fundamentalists were being more subversive of the modern world-system than a liberal reformer like Fosdick could comprehend. They were refusing to accept the modern tendency to overpower spiritual consciousness with a matter-of-fact, this-worldly, secular outlook. Fundamentalists may not have developed Christian norms for positive action in business, the arts, learning, civic affairs, and the like, but they consistently subverted the assumption that current events and issues were of ultimate concern.

Fighting Fundamentalists

If fundamentalism had a motto, it would come from verse three of the Epistle of Jude: "Earnestly contend for the faith which was once delivered unto the saints." Fundamentalists were intensely earnest people, and they believed that contending for the old-time faith was central to their mission. Historian George Marsden correctly insists that what finally distinguished fundamentalists from other evangelical or conservative Protestants was their determination to resist modern secularity on an ideological, argumentative level. Militancy was the mark of fundamentalism, and ideological militancy especially. Fundamentalists were, in other words, a contentious lot, and they held up confrontation as one of their principal duties.[30]

By the mid-1930s fundamentalists had relatively few opportunities to contend, face-to-face, with their liberal opponents. The victorious liberals no longer felt compelled to take on fundamentalist provocateurs as serious contenders for power. Maintaining a militant stance against modernism was so important to fundamentalists' sense of identity and purpose, however, that the movement's leaders kept up the rhetorical attacks. They provided their followers with a running argument against Protestant liberalism and cultural secularity. Their magazines and sermons were full of show trials and ritual slayings of their enemies in absentia.

Another common rhetorical theme was the age-old controversy against the world, the flesh, and the devil. Typical was a sermon by E. W. Crowell, a

Baptist pastor from Jackson, Michigan, that began with a text from the prophet Hosea: "the Lord hath a controversy with the inhabitants of the land, because there is no truth, nor mercy, nor knowledge of God in the land. By swearing, and lying, and killing, and stealing, and committing adultery, they break out, and blood toucheth blood. Therefore shall the land mourn" (Hosea 4:1–3). Judging that America lay in the way of onrushing peril, Crowell explained that it was because "immorality is rampant. Sin knows no bounds. Licentiousness is the habit of the hour. The virtues of Christianity are ridiculed and laughed at." Specific sins included the "flooding of our land" with liquor, the "hell-born liquid fire which loosens the passions of sin, lust, desire, licentiousness and every evil work." Mirroring the prophet's speaking of bloodshed were statistics, cited from J. Edgar Hoover and others, proving that America had become "a nation filled with violence." Immorality and lust, Crowell preached, were raging as well; and these he blamed in part on the movie industry, which social scientists said had become a life-molding force for the nation's youth. Crowell charged the "bloated purveyors of commercialized entertainment" with perverting children's character by featuring "nude women, amorous poses," and themes that "flaunt every Christian virtue." Worse, if not yet so influential, were the cascades of "corrupt literature" available at any news stand.

Even the public schools, which had been founded to enable "our young people to know and understand the Word of God," were now permitting the teaching of "a hell-born doctrine of evolution" that "opens the flood-gates of animal passion, and destroys faith in God and His Word" largely through the "devilish doctrine of self-expression," which would throw to the winds such traditional values as temperance and self-restraint. "This teaching is called by the educators 'Psycho-analysis,'" Crowell informed his readers. But "God calls it 'filthy dreaming'" (Jude 8). The inevitable conclusion of such jeremiads was that God had a terrible indictment against the American people and he would punish them for their sins. The remedy was not some new crusade for reform that would only scratch the surface, but individual repentence and born-again, changed hearts.[31]

Not often stated but clearly implied by the setting and audience for these diatribes was that they helped to build and define a gulf between the world and the Lord's own. These sermons might sound as though they were being hurled at the unrepentant, but with the exception of perhaps a few nonbelievers who might be visiting in church, they were preached to the fundamentalist faithful. They were emotionally powerful reminders that the broad path outside the fold "leadeth to destruction," lest any on the inside be tempted to stray. The appeal of making some small accomodations to the world's ways—such as taking a drink now and then in moderation, or attending some nice movies, or joining a lodge along with other upstanding Christians—paled before the ultimate destruction, both temporal and eternal, which the preachers insisted would result from such ostensibly innocent pursuits.[32] Fighting fundamentalism's rhetorical barrages against sin thus helped to fence in the flock and remind the believers of their identity. They were the faithful remnant who had not bowed their knee to the modern Baal.

The fighter's stance became second nature to the fundamentalist movement's leaders, and for the veterans especially, the experience of losing campaigns and respect turned them into reactionaries, pure and simple. Fighting had become a way of life for warlords such as William Bell Riley, who in 1940, at age seventy-nine, published a compilation of accusatory sermons and addresses titled *The Conflict of Christianity with Its Counterfeits.* While Riley purported to take aim at modernism and the rise of a "Red" social gospel, his book does not show any evidence of genuine polemical exchanges with the enemy or any intention of mustering a new crusade. Its major purpose seems to have been to help Riley retain his certification as a red-blooded, militant, fighting fundamentalist. The old warrior was attempting to prove that he was still in fighting trim and would never "run up the flag of surrender, or even . . . hint a truce with the enemies of God or His Word."[33] Aggressiveness was becoming an important badge of fundamentalism, and combative posturing before a congregation of the already-convinced was a way of ritually enacting the movement's emotive trademark, identifying the enemy, proclaiming the party line, and encouraging one's followers to "fight the good fight" (I Tim. 6:12) in their own lives.[34]

Militancy and machismo were part of the movement's mystique. Fundamentalist leaders often bore pugnacious nicknames that seemed more appropriate for boxers than for preachers. J. Frank Norris had earned the epithet "Texas Tornado," while David Otis Fuller of Grand Rapids was known to his friends as "Duke." There were also several "Fighting Bobs," notably Ketcham of the Regular Baptists and Shuler of Trinity Methodist Church in Los Angeles. John R. Rice's aggressive newspaper, *The Sword of the Lord,* evoked the battle cry of Gideon's band of warriors. Even among the more refined, such as Wheaton College's president, J. Oliver Buswell, Jr., aggressiveness was prized. Not only did Buswell encourage the building of winning debate, wrestling, and football teams, but he liked to keep fit by chopping wood. No one was going to accuse him of being a soft-handed liberal.[35]

Fundamentalist pugnacity and ideological militancy could not always be directed toward the enemy on the outside. Once the controversies with the modernists died down, fundamentalists' instincts prompted them to look for infidelity within their own ranks. Like counter-insurgency commandos discharged from active duty, veteran contenders often distrusted even their friends and attacked any idea or person that made strange moves. The annals of fundamentalism are filled with episodes of infighting, nit-picking doctrinal debates, and territorial disputes. It was this state of affairs that led historian Ernest Sandeen to characterize the movement as "split and stricken" by the 1930s.[36]

Fundamentalists' penchant for militancy turned inward in another way as well. Especially among the separatists, for whom the sense of cultural alienation grew deepest, pastors became increasingly authoritarian and at times bullying in their relationships with their congregations. Pastors saw themselves as the Lord's anointed and viewed the world as filled with sinister forces, so the sheep in their fold needed herding. Brow-beating from the pulpit, a common practice in separatist circles, was one of the most obvious indications of this growing dictatorial spirit.

A sermon that John R. Rice delivered at his Fundamentalist Baptist Tabernacle in Dallas on a Sunday night in 1935 exemplifies the accusatory, intimidating thrust of such rhetoric. The topic was dancing, and Brother Rice harangued the crowd, arguing against objections that he imagined would arise to his view that all modern social dancing was evil. Each of his points was punctuated with, "I dare anybody here to deny it," or "you know that it is so," or "brother, whether you like it or not," or "anybody here want to deny it? If so, stand up and do it now," or "I double-dog dare you to stand on your hind feet right now and say it." Then he would pause, as if waiting for someone to challenge him. At one point Rice called the PTA women who sponsored dances at local schools a "bunch of hens that would inflame the minds of boys and girls, who would make prostitutes out of my daughters, who ruin other folks' boys and girls." Since no one in his congregation seemed to feel stung by that, Rice tried calling them out more directly: "If anybody doesn't like that, you can swell up and burst as far as I am concerned. If anybody in this church doesn't like that kind of preaching, . . . you can check out now. . . . I will say right now; under God, I don't have to have your help. Nobody pays you to come to hear me preach. As God is my witness, no man is my boss."[37] By example and by explicit teaching in his publications, Rice taught thousands of fundamentalist pastors how to boss others around.

Another important effect of fundamentalists' contentious, reactionary spirit was that it soured male leaders' attitudes toward women and made them increasingly reluctant to encourage women's partnership in ministry. The changes in outlook and mood that marked the transformation of the more hopeful revivalist movement of Moody's day into embattled fundamentalism by the 1920s included, of course, a growing fear of cultural disintegration. Since nineteenth-century evangelicals had made women and the home the mainstays of Christian civilization, women now seemed to draw a major share of fundamentalists' blame for the demise of Christian America. The widely advertised moral permissiveness of the Flapper Age scandalized fundamentalists and made them shudder about the social consequences. Furthermore, fundamentalists' populist appeals to their faith's (and their own) virility and their gibes at the softness and effeminacy of liberal Protestantism led them to devalue women's contributions to the work of the church.[38] A classic piece of fundamentalist misogyny, *Bobbed Hair, Bossy Wives and Women Preachers*, by John R. Rice, argued that not only had the "modern, masculine, pants-wearing, cigarette-smoking, bobbed-haired woman . . . fallen from her pedestal," but by taking to the pulpit, she was violating "the command of God" against speaking "before mixed audiences . . . ." Rice was convinced that "this sin" was deeply hindering "the work of the gospel of Christ."[39]

Not all fundamentalists shared Rice's belief that women were to be barred from all active teaching and Word-proclaiming roles outside of children's Sunday school and women's Bible classes. Indeed, at the turn of the century, Bible schools trained hundreds of women who served in many capacities in the movement's growing parachurch network: in missionary societies, urban rescue missions, tent-campaign evangelism, houses of healing, Sunday school out-reaches, YWCA-sponsored ministries, Bible and tract society evangelism, and sometimes in regular pulpit ministries. Turn-of-the-century revivalists such as A. B. Simpson, Fredrik Franson, and A. J. Gordon had defended the work of these "prophesying daughters," quoting Peter's sermon at Pentecost as the mandate for women's ministry.[40] But these earlier champions of women's ministry had either accepted the traditional strictures against women's ordina-tion or office-holding or else had avoided the question because of their focus on lay voluntarism. By the 1920s and 1930s, as a defensive, pessimistic, em-battled spirit permeated the movement, fundamentalist leaders began to stress once again the traditional boundaries limiting female leadership.[41]

The fundamentalist movement had become too dependent upon women activists, however, to take them out of service. When the China Inland Mission called for two hundred new missionaries in 1929–1931, sixty-one of the ninety-two North Americans who were recruited were women, even though the Mission had announced its intention to commission a male majority.[42] So it went throughout the fundamentalist movement, especially in its parachurch network. Women found many opportunities to serve as authors and publish-ers, foreign missionaries, and church-planting home missionaries; as directors of vacation Bible schools, public school "release time" religious programs, Sunday schools, and youth ministries, and as itinerant evangelists. The prag-matic need for capable and dedicated religious workers continued to override appeals to constraining principles.[43]

Nevertheless, fundamentalists were moving women out of leadership roles by the 1930s. When the Independent Fundamental Churches of America (IFCA) was formed in 1930 from some preexisting fellowships of nondenom-inational churches and religious workers that included women members, the IFCA's new bylaws explicitly excluded women from membership. Women's representation on mission boards shrank as well, even though women usually constituted the majority on the field. Lucy W. Peabody, a legendary leader of the international missionary movement at the turn of the century, was in-volved in founding an independent fundamentalist board in the 1920s, the Association of Baptists for the Evangelization of the Orient. Peabody was president of the new board for several years, but in 1935 she gave in to pre-vailing prejudice. She resigned her post, in deference, she said, to the principle of "masculine leadership in the church."[44]

At least in its public posture and explicit teaching, fundamentalism had become a male-dominated, macho movement that railed against "effeminate" liberalism and devalued women's service to the church even while continuing to benefit from it. As Margaret Bendroth put it, fundamentalists proclaimed "the continuing need for women's presence in church and society, [but] sought whenever possible to escape it."[45]

It would not be fair to accuse all fundamentalist leaders in the 1930s and 1940s of pugnacious posturing and authoritarian and sexist bullying. There were many whose preaching, demeanor, and relationships with others displayed much more kindness, humility, gentleness, and friendliness. One thinks, for example, of such positive fundamentalists as Charles E. Fuller, the folksy radio preacher of the *Old Fashioned Revival Hour;* J. Elwin Wright, the irenic director of the New England Fellowship; Torrey Johnson, the youthful, upbeat pastor of the Midwest Bible Church in Chicago; and Robert C. McQuilkin, the warm-hearted founder and president of Columbia Bible College. But the spokesmen of this relatively more friendly variety of fundamentalism tolerated the pugilists and dictators and considered them to be important colleagues, even if they did not share all of their attitudes or perspectives. J. Elwin Wright, for example, was an outspoken critic of fundamentalists' contentiousness, but he repeatedly invited two of the movement's leading curmudgeons, William Bell Riley and Bob Jones, to hold forth on the New England Fellowship's Bible conference circuit. An oppositional spirit had become part of fundamentalism's identity, and the movement's leaders and followers alike seemed to condone ferocity, even if they did not all display it.

Bible-believing Christians

Fundamentalists' determination to distance themselves from the secular world's values and view of reality was manifested not only in their militancy but also in their goal of living as "New Testament Christians." In upholding this ideal, they were acting on an impulse—common to many revivalist movements— known as primitivism. Primitivism involves the tendency to blur the distinctions and distance between one's own time and an ideal past. Christian primitivism, according to historian Grant Wacker, refers to "the yearning for pure doctrines, pure beginnings, and pure fulfillments" that only a recovery of the fresh and unspoiled or "primitive" Christianity of the New Testament churches could bring. Modern Christian primitivists drew their models from Scripture in a variety of ways. If the biblical primitivism of the Mennonites echoed the Gospels and the pentecostals lived out the Acts of the Apostles, fundamentalists identified with the Epistles. The apostles' adomonitions to the hard-pressed young churches living in a pagan world resonated powerfully with fundamentalists' experience and temperament.

Fundamentalists' commitment to being New Testament Christians was based on their belief that the Bible communicated God's sure, clear, and unchanging will. They were self-styled "Bible-believing Christians," by which they meant that they upheld the Bible as the verbally inspired, inerrant word of God, as trustworthy in its references to matters of nature and history as in its teaching of religious and moral precepts. This was one of several keystone beliefs upon which fundamentalism rested as both an ideology and a way of life. The supernatural character of Christianity was under attack, fundamentalists believed, so they counterattacked by upholding doctrines that defied modern naturalism and historicism. New Testament Christianity was still available to modern people, fundamentalists insisted, because the Bible spoke timeless truth. Proclaimed Donald Grey Barnhouse, a widely acclaimed Bible expositor, the Christian's Bible was "God's Word for his daily life and needs. It will ever be, for him, his word, rock, lamp, daily milk and meat, besides the Supreme Court from which there is no appeal."[46]

In modern life, however, many educated people had come to doubt that God had spoken any such word. Probably no other issue was so prone to provoke the fundamentalists to throw down the gauntlet than the common suggestion, derived from the field of modern biblical criticism, that the Bible contained errors or did not always, in all of its passages, convey God's timeless truth. Many Protestant leaders had accepted the idea that the Bible's books were culturally conditioned human artifacts and had attempted to revise theories of biblical inspiration and authority to account for these new insights—but not the fundamentalists. To them the critics' claims held such disturbing implications that they did not see how one could accept them and still affirm, with the Apostle Paul, that "all scripture is given by inspiration of God, and is profitable for doctrine, for reproof, for correction, for instruction in righteousness" (II Tim. 3:16). If the Bible was not historically accurate in its accounts and not always written by its purported authors, as Old Testament critics claimed, and if its record of Jesus was colored by the pious elaboration of editors in the early church, as some New Testament critics argued, then how could anyone trust the Scriptures to present a sure word from God? Fundamentalists hammered away at this point, which seemed to carry much force in a culture that still held the Bible in high esteem.[47]

An exalted view of the Bible's divine inspiration, trustworthiness, and authority was neither the creation nor the exclusive property of the fundamentalists. The idea that the Bible was verbally inspired and inerrant, for example, had been taught by most Protestant theologians for several centuries, and had received a new emphasis and clarification over the prior half-century at the hands of the conservative biblical scholars of Princeton Seminary.[48] But in the hands of fundamentalist Bible teachers, biblical inerrancy began to take on an altered character. Earlier Protestant theologians had understood God's governance of the world's operation—and of particular events such as the creation of the Scriptures—to involve his simultaneous employment of natural and supernatural forces.[49] Fundamentalists, however, felt so threatened by the naturalistic bias of modern thought, including biblical criticism, that they stressed the Bible's supernatural character and slighted its humanity. Outside of a few scholarly strongholds such as Westminster Theological Seminary, careful attention to matters of culture, history, and linguistics became rare among fundamentalist scholars of the Bible. Ahistorical and primitivist views of the Bible had virtually free rein during the 1930s and 1940s.[50]

Two important fundamentalist traits contributed to this situation. The first was dispensational premillennialism, the dominant view among fundamentalists of God's plan of salvation through the ages and in the world to come. Dispensationalism was inherently ahistorical because it stressed that each successive age, or dispensation, came to an end and was superceded by another through some dramatic supernatural intervention, such as the flood of Noah's day. "Ordinary" forces, such as natural or human causation, were of little relevance in this scheme.

Dispensationalists encouraged a radically supernaturalist and ahistorical reading of the Bible in another way as well. They claimed that they could pinpoint biblical prophecy's working out in world history. This claim was based on two assumptions: the Bible must be scientifically accurate in matters of detail, and all of its prophetic passages must be intended to be literally fulfilled. Dispensationalists thus dispensed with some old and more historically informed traditions of biblical interpretation that had assigned figurative and contemporary moral and religious meanings to many prophetic passages. By contrast, fundamentalism tended to reduce prophecy to prediction.[51]

The dispensationalists' promise that Bible prophecy would clarify the meaning and direction of modern life may have bemused and irritated biblical scholars, but it certainly had popular appeal. Much of dispensationalism's attractiveness came from the uncanny resemblance of its predictions to the trends of the twentieth century. Prophetic Bible teachers long had been predicting the decline of Christianity's cultural influence, the apparent spread of spiritual deadness within organized Christianity, the rise of world-threatening dictatorships, and, not least, the Jews' persecution and their movement to restore a Jewish state in Palestine.[52] Here was a system that could make sense out of the chaos, that could reassure troubled people that God was still in charge and would intervene again, very soon, in a world that was careening out of control. The distinction between modern times and the Bibles's pages, between ordinary events and the cosmic drama of the books of Daniel and Revelation, thus became blurred, as modern Christians felt that they were "living in the shadow of the Second Coming."[53]

The other major force behind fundamentalists' biblical primitivism was the movement's popular character. Fundamentalism arose more from weekend Bible and missionary conferences than from the centers of theological discourse. Its most influential leaders were evangelists, pastors, and Bible teachers, not scholars. Even though the fundamentalist movement's early (pre-1920) leaders were often well educated, they wrote and spoke to a popular audience. Liberal Christianity had its popularizers as well, but fundamentalist spokesmen seemed much less concerned about imparting scholarly insights to a general audience. Most of them had little contact with the technical work and argumentation of the more conservative biblical critics, who had become quite scarce in North America anyway, and few prominent fundamentalist leaders by the 1930s had the education or the inclination to take on the task of interpreting such work for a popular audience. They were confident of their ability to present the issues in stark and simple laymen's terms.[54]

Thus in fundamentalist leaders' hands the doctrine of biblical authority lost much of its complexity. An earlier generation of conservative scholars had defended biblical authority and inerrancy with a carefully nuanced balancing of the Bible's divine and human character.[55] Such fine distinctions were dropped in the effort to mount a populist defense of the Bible. Fundamentalist defenders made the alternatives seem as clear cut as possible. Either the Bible was God's book or a human creation. Either God was its author or fallible human beings wrote it. The liberals' accusation that fundamentalists taught a "divine dictation" theory of inspiration was uncomfortably close to the mark, for in their desire to defend the Bible's supernatural character fundamentalists seemed to be claiming that the Scriptures were largely untouched by ordinary human existence.[56]

Indeed, their study of the Bible in the 1930s and 1940s reflected this one-sided reverence. In fundamentalist seminaries careful study of the biblical texts continued, but most of the biblical scholars therein rejected the historical-critical method out of hand because of its purportedly naturalistic presuppositions. Few could or would make the case that careful attention to the historical or cultural context in which the Scriptures were written could be done with due reverence to the text's sacredness, and fewer still actually pursued such study. The most sought-after kind of biblical knowledge was the kind provided by the itinerant Bible expositors, such as Harry A. Ironside of Chicago's Moody Church, Donald Grey Barnhouse of Philadelphia's Tenth Presbyterian Church, and Arno C. Gaebelein, editor of *Our Hope,* a New York–based prophecy monthly. Knowledge of the English Bible, especially as interpreted through a dispensational theological grid, spread far and wide among the laity, but biblical scholarship of the highest order languished in fundamentalist circles.[57]

Fundamentalists thus did very little to carry forward a scholarly defense of biblical inspiration and authority. They were intensely interested in dispelling doubts about the Bible that had filtered down to the average person. Did people say that the Bible was unscientific and out of date? Fundamentalists insisted that the Bible was both true to the facts of modern science and relevant to the times. Part of their argument for its timeliness, of course, came from its prophetic passages. Their argument for its truth involved tackling head-on, for a popular audience, the twins of modern doubt, Darwinism and biblical criticism. Fundamentalists insisted that they had the hard facts on their side and that it was their opponents who were unscientific.

Without a doubt, fundamentalists believed that evolution was the prime culprit in the secularization of modern thought and the growth of popular doubt about the Bible's authority, so they summoned their intellectual resources to fight it. As George Marsden and others have made clear, fundamentalism had intellectual roots in early-nineteenth-century inductive empiricism and Scottish Common Sense moral philosophy. To them, evolutionary theory seemed excessively speculative and insufficiently grounded in material evidence. This had been the first line of argumentation that William Bell Riley and the other antievolution debaters of the World's Christian Fundamentals Association had taken in the 1920s.[58]

During the 1930s and 1940s fundamentalists continued to challenge evolution wherever they could assemble an audience. The fact that after the Scopes trial they had trouble getting a hearing outside their own ranks did not deter them, for their antievolutionary arguments were meant to encourage the faithful as much as win a hearing in the larger world. One of their most prolific antievolution champions was Harry Rimmer, a Presbyterian clergyman and amateur scientist. Rimmer delivered thousands of lectures, most of them apparently to student groups, in which he upheld the Bible's scientific accuracy and integrity and ridiculed evolutionists. More scholarly attempts to carry forward this cause languished, however. At Wheaton College in 1935, Dr. L. Allen Higley, professor of chemistry and geology, led the organization of the Religion and Science Association to provide a "united front against the theory of evolution." Its members fell to arguing, however, about the age of the earth and the possibility of harmonizing the Genesis creation account with some aspects of evolutionary theory, so it disbanded the next year.[59]

Rimmer's successor as a popular drawing card was Irwin Moon, a California evangelist whose live demonstrations and movies argued that an all-wise and loving Creator, and not blind chance, was the source and sustainer of the universe. In 1939 Moon was commissioned by the Moody Bible Institute to produce a "Sermons from Science" motion picture series along these themes. By throwing in plenty of crowd-pleasing showmanship, Moon took the rancorous polemical edge off of fundamentalists' scientific arguments without conceding anything to evolution. One of his favorite stunts was to exhibit the properties of electricity by running an electrical charge through his body and letting it arc from his fingertips.[60] It is hard to gauge the effectiveness of such efforts, but fundamentalists found several assets to draw upon that seemed to help them gain a hearing: they were good at popular communications and knew how to play to public opinion; they could speak to a widely held "empiricist folk epistemology"[61] in America that, like fundamentalism, distinguished "hard science" from speculative theorizing; and they understood the public's respect for the Bible. As a result, the fundamentalist-led "creationist" movement has remained vigorous and influential to the present day.[62]

The other major enemy to fundamentalists' biblicism was historical criticism of the Bible, which by the 1930s had prompted many doubts at the popular level about the Bible's divine character and religious authority. Fundamentalists' favorite arguments against the "destructive theories" of biblical criticism in the 1930s came from another historical field that they considered to be more scientific: archaeology. At that time the field of ancient Near Eastern history was blossoming under the leadership of William F. Albright of The Johns Hopkins University. He and other archaeologists were verifying biblical place names, story settings, and other material details that biblical critics believed to be legendary. Albright argued forcefully that some of the assumptions of earlier biblical scholars needed revising, and that recent findings corroborated the Bible's historical accounts.

Even though Albright had no quarrel with biblical criticism per se, he provided powerful ammunition to the fundamentalists. The celebrated archaeologist pointed out, for example, that Old Testament critics' assumptions of linear religious and cultural evolution, rather than genuine historical evidence, had

led them to specious conclusions about biblical texts.[63] One of the fundamentalists' favorite archaeological finds was the new evidence, dating from the
time of Moses, of literacy among the seminomadic tribes of Palestine and
Egypt. This discovery appeared to strike down one of the critical arguments
against Mosaic authorship of the Pentateuch, namely that the Hebrews could
not have been literate at that early date. Fundamentalists exulted that archaeologists' hard evidence, turned up by careful digging, confirmed the Bible's
inerrancy and destroyed the critics' speculative theories.[64]

Other attacks on the critics, while of a more dubious validity, still made for
valuable propaganda. For example, a contributor to the *Sunday School Times* in
1933 eagerly reported the results of a plagiarism case, originating in Canada, in
which an obscure novelist charged that H. G. Wells had plagiarized from her
work for *The Outline of History* (1920). According to the article, the highest
court of appeals in the British Empire had ruled not to allow as evidence the
opinion of a biblical critic regarding the textual sources for Mr. Wells's book.
The author concluded that if such scholarship was inadmissible as evidence in
a court of law, it also lost credibility as the authoritative word about the
Bible.[65] Sometimes ridicule seemed to work as well as argument. Donald Barnhouse once chortled that a renowned biblical critic who was struggling with a
drinking problem "could see the two Isaiahs he had been writing about."[66]

Most fundamentalist laypeople could not articulate all of the arguments
against the evolutionists and higher critics but, fortified with confident rhetoric from the pulpit and in print, they knew they had some champions who
could. The "oppositions of science falsely so called" (I Tim. 6:21) could not
budge their belief that the Bible was "in perfect harmony with the findings of
true science."[67]

These beliefs were far more than empty shibboleths, for their adherents
were defending what had become their way of life. As people of the Book,
fundamentalists made it the identifying totem of their movement. Knowledge
of the Bible was not the only kind of learning they endorsed, but it surely was
the most prized. Thus their training schools for religious workers were Bible
institutes or Bible colleges, where study of the English Bible was everyone's
major. The most popular forms of lay education, fellowship, and entertainment were not revival meetings but Bible conferences featuring eminent Bible
teachers. Theology in the Bible schools became Bible doctrine, in which meta-
physical speculation gave way to the collection and classification of biblical
facts, as in R. A. Torrey's *What the Bible Teaches* (1898), a popular arrangement of Bible verses in topical order that ran through many editions and
printings. Hundreds of independent fundamentalist congregations called themselves Bible churches.[68]

The Bible was a tool as well as an emblem, or in the imagery of spiritual warfare, it was a weapon, a "two-edged sword" (Heb. 4:12). The Word of God
had supernatural power, fundamentalists believed. They rejected the idea that
the Bible had magical properties but insisted that it was God's favored means
of salvation. Not only was it timelessly true and unfailingly authoritative for

one's faith and life, but its very words were used by God to change people. Bible schools stressed the importance of students learning to use the sacred words themselves rather than relying on their own phrases when they preached or did personal counselling.[69] Indeed, in the speech of the more zealous, biblical phrases blended continually into the conversation.[70] Fundamentalists took literally, sometimes to vulgar extremes, the biblical promise that "My word shall not return unto me void" (Isa. 55:11). They printed Bible verses on billboards, jackknife handles, and automobile spare-tire covers. One naturalist wrote them on the tags he tied to Canada geese.[71]

The words of Scripture also became icons for fundamentalists. Bible verses spoke of spiritual reality to believers and reminded them that the sacred realm laid claims on their thoughts and their actions in the here and now.[72] As heirs of the Puritans, fundamentalists avoided the use of images and artifacts in worship or religious architecture, yet the movement's churches and gospel tabernacles often had Bible verses emblazoned high on their walls and balcony facings.[73] A motto plaque or needlepoint sampler with a biblical phrase on it in one's home also functioned much like an icon, crucifix, or phylactery. It was a visual reminder of spiritual truth, a badge of separation, and an act of witness to a culture whose aphorisms and images were increasingly secular. Fundamentalist pastors often urged their parishioners to carry a Bible at all times. It would be with them not only for convenient reference or use in evangelism, but also as a silent testimony to one's faith, much like a Catholic sister's rosary. In even this very personal, literal way, fundamentalists identified themselves as biblical people.[74]

4

SEPARATED UNTO
THE GOSPEL

Fundamentalists taught that living a separated life implied two distinct actions: pulling away from the world and its values, and drawing closer to Jesus Christ to become his disciple. It is common to think about fundamentalism in reference to the first part of this formula—as a separatistic, militantly reactionary, and radically biblicist persuasion. But fundamentalism has had a softer, more experiential side as well, and one cannot have a fully dimensional understanding of the "separated life" without considering it. Fundamentalist piety was dominated by two spiritual experiences: conversion, or the New Birth, as it was often called; and an event subsequent to conversion commonly called entering into the "higher Christian life." These two experiences did much to shape the fundamentalist movement's structure, ethos, and sense of mission.

Born-again Christians

Whereas the Bible was a major source for fundamentalist identity and ideology, the basis of membership in the fundamentalist community was having been "born again."[1] Fundamentalists perpetuated the evangelical tradition of welcoming into full fellowship only those who testified that they had accepted Jesus Christ as their personal savior and were committing their lives to him. This personal relationship with Christ was made possible, fundamentalists insisted, because of his death on the cross to atone for humanity's sins. His death was the once-for-all fulfilment of the Old Testament ritual of blood sacrifice. So the central question for anyone to answer was the one asked by the old gospel song: "Are you washed in the blood of the Lamb?"

Liberal theologians tried to persuade modern Christians to accept less crudely literalistic and legalistic formulations of Christ's redemptive work. Did the Christian God demand blood sacrifices in order to be appeased, like the pagan deities? Liberals thought not; the cross was the emblem of God's selfless love, made manifest in the ministry of Jesus Christ.[2] Fundamentalists would have none of this revisionism; they insisted not only on the ancient Christian doctrine of substitutionary atonement but that it was *blood* atonement. Blood sacrifice may have seemed primitive, magical, and repulsive to modern sensibilities, but to fundamentalists, insistance on this doctrine was both a matter of faithfulness to the Bible's literal teaching and one way to emphasize the costly and supernatural character of redemption. People got *saved*, fundamentalists argued; they did not merely learn to follow the Master's example. Conversion came through Jesus' precious blood; it was a miracle, an answer to prayer, a life-shaking, life-changing experience.[3]

Indeed, conversions were fundamentalists' most powerful experiences of the holy. Even though they had other channels of divine encounter and fellowship, nothing could match the wonder that fundamentalists expressed at the experience of being born again, or in seeing another person come to Christ for salvation. Unlike sacramental Christians, for whom the holy presence of God comes most commonly in the Eucharist, or pentecostals, whose encounters with the Holy Spirit involve a variety of signs and wonders, especially speaking in tongues, fundamentalists have looked to the New Birth to satisfy their yearning for miracles, for signs of God's visitation with them.[4] Fundamentalist preachers regularly gave the invitation for people to step forward and publicly profess Christ as their savior, and many pastors insisted on giving this "altar call" at every service. Their reason for doing this was that it was their evangelistic duty, but this ritual, performed with the musicians softly playing, the congregation singing or praying, and the leader speaking in an almost liturgical cadence, had become the high and holy moment of the fundamentalist church service, the time when miracles happened.[5] For many fundamentalists, the experience of walking the aisle was so inspiring that doing it once was not enough. Surely people might feel encouraged in their faith and be charged with holy joy when others responded to the gospel,[6] but there was nothing like experiencing it personally. Since conversion happened only once, fundamentalists developed ways for born-again Christians to "come forward" more often. By broadening their altar call into an invitation for believers to receive further assurance of their salvation, to dedicate or rededicate their lives to God, to surrender themselves to God's service, or to testify to a "definite call" to a particular field of service, fundamentalists found a way to meet their thirst for holy moments. "Going forward" became a fundamentalist sacrament.[7]

Becoming born again was like receiving one's credentials in fundamentalist circles. It certified one as part of the select company of believers, and it also gave one a commission to do the Lord's work. An important mark of the separated life, then, was giving out a continual testimony of one's faith and seeking to lead others into conversion. Following fundamentalist behavioral standards gave only a mute witness; direct verbal evangelization was the higher expectation. Fundamentalists were urged to use such mundane activities as eating in a restaurant, taking a taxi, train, or streetcar, or chatting on break in the workplace to give out evangelistic tracts or say a few words about their faith. Evangelism was so central a duty for the born-again Christian that some fundamentalists felt guilty if they did not try to give some evangelistic word during even the most casual or fleeting of human contacts. Even a car trip across town might provide the opportunity to lob a few cellophane-wrapped tracts in the direction of the people standing on the corner.[8]

Zeal for evangelism was what gave evangelical Christianity its name, but in fundamentalism, perhaps even more than other twentieth-century evangelical movements, the entire Christian mission was largely reduced to winning converts. Part of this single-mindedness came by default, because most fundamentalists had come to react against other facets of Christian life and work, such as social service and civic reform, as something done by their opponents, the liberal Social Gospelers.[9] Another important reason for focusing narrowly on evangelism was that fundamentalists' dominant theological view, dispensational premillennialism, was culturally pessimistic and weighted priorities toward rescuing as many lost souls as possible before time ran out.[10] But perhaps more important than these factors was fundamentalism's lineage. It was the direct heir, through its Bible schools, missionary agencies, and leading urban pulpits, of the revival campaigns within late-nineteenth-century Protestantism. The leaders of this movement, such as A. J. Gordon, A. B. Simpson and D. L. Moody, certainly wanted to prod complacent churches into new evangelistic outreach, but they did not necessarily see themselves as performing the church's sole function. Over time, however, these soul-winning specialists and their descendents began to create a separate movement. Its vision of the church's mission was becoming narrowly evangelistic even before the fundamentalist–modernist controversies.[11]

By the 1930s, therefore, the evangelistic emphasis overrode virtually every other category of Christian work within fundamentalism. The most common form of postsecondary education in fundamentalist circles was the Bible institute, which was an intensely focused training school for domestic and overseas evangelism.[12] Born-again men and women were forming, in city after city, Fishermen's Clubs, Breakfast Clubs, Christian Business Women's Councils, or Christian Business Men's Committees. These groups may have functioned as channels for fellowship, mutual patronage, and discussion about ethics in the workplace, but their major mandate was to sponsor evangelistic projects. The same was true of children's clubs and young people's organizations under fundamentalist sponsorship. Bringing in newcomers and getting them saved was their primary stated purpose.[13]

Perhaps the most influential institutional product of fundamentalists' evangelistic impulse was the urban gospel tabernacle. Gospel tabernacles used old theater buildings or cheaply constructed auditoriums that resembled (or may have been) the temporary tabernacle structures erected for the urban evangelistic campaigns of D. L. Moody, Sam Jones, and Billy Sunday. The tabernacles featured the entertaining gospel music and sensational preaching styles created by the urban revivalists, but their evangelists did not move on to the next town every four to six weeks. The tabernacles became ongoing evangelistic enter-prises, with revival meetings every week, conducted by the resident evangelist or visiting preachers from the fundamentalist circuit. The master of this new institutional form was evangelist Paul Rader of the Chicago Gospel Tabernacle. While most fundamentalists met in more traditionally organized churches, the tabernacle style and orientation permeated the whole movement. The church was being reduced to a soul-saving station and an armory for mobilizing cadres of lay evangelists.[14]

Fundamentalists' burden to witness to the lost could make them rough on their neighbors and hard on themselves. Some groups invariably took offense at being evangelized. The forays of Moody Bible Institute students into Jewish neighborhoods in Chicago regularly brought down on their heads a cornucopia of verbal and vegetable insults.[15] For the worldly-minded sophisticate, nothing could ruin a good time like an earnest inquiry into the state of one's soul. H. L. Mencken recalled with great distaste the time when his fundamentalist friend, Dr. Howard A. Kelly, the distinguished Johns Hopkins medical professor, took the seat next to his and held him captive with evangelical conversation on the train from Washington to Baltimore. Several times, Mencken said, he had to restrain the urge to jump out of the window to escape.[16]

No doubt Kelly felt compelled to bring spiritual matters into such discus-sions; fundamentalists could carry for years the burden of regret for not hav-ing taken the opportunity to speak about salvation to their acquaintances.[17] Knowing that one might bear some of the responsibility for the eternal state of a friend or colleague could be an inducement to evangelize or, for the more reticent, a motivation to avoid contact with nonbelievers. At any rate, these feelings, if not the acts of evangelizing themselves, could certify one's difference and distance from the rest of humanity. Fundamentalist people came to bear the psychic if not visible marks of separation. Such emotions, one ex-fundamentalist recalled, made it hard for her to feel close to her non-Christian friends.[18]

On the other hand, the common experience of conversion was a powerful bond within the fundamentalist community. Fundamentalist evangelization could seem arrogantly exclusive or imperialistic, but the ideal was to be in-clusive, to bring into warm and intense fellowship anyone who would take the plunge. Indeed, the born-again experience, together with a public testi-mony, baptism, and receiving the "right hand of fellowship," was the initiation into a closely knit tribe. The tie that bound congregations together was not simply their shared ideology but this communal expression of saving faith, which marked one's entry into a new family and the transformation of one's outlook.[19] Fundamentalists' stress on the blood atonement, whatever else it meant, was a theological fencing-in of their most precious possession and central preoccupation with an interpretation that was maximally super-natural, unflinchingly literal, and costly. It also made it possible for some very ordinary people to hold their heads up and identify with one of the Bible's most powerful images: they were part of the book of Revelation's company of the blood-redeemed, and one day they would gather around the throne and acclaim the Lamb (Rev. 7:9–14).

Spirit-filled Christians

The language of postconversion spiritual experience that many fundamentalist students, Bible teachers, and missionaries used in the 1930s and 1940s had a code to it. Terms such as "surrender" or "consecration," and expressions such as "the life of faith," the "Christ life," the "fullness of the Holy Spirit's power," and "proving God" cropped up repeatedly. These terms reflected more than a generically evangelical devotional phraseology; they denoted a particular school of thought and style of piety that had a profound effect on the fundamentalist character.

Consider the testimony of Helen Torrey, the daughter of Presbyterian missionaries to China. Helen was spending the summer of 1935 with her parents in China before returning for her senior year at the boarding school in Pyeng-yang, Korea. She was deeply moved by the devotion she saw among the missionaries and Chinese Christians during a time of great upheaval and suffering, and she began to feel anxious and guilty about not having fully committed her own life to Christ. Then she received a letter from a friend who asked whether she had "surrendered her life to the Lord." This fanned her anxiety into a full-blown spiritual crisis. Not long after, while attending a summer Bible conference, Helen recalled that she surrendered herself to God and then returned to boarding school "really charged up for God." She began to read books such as *Borden of Yale, '09: The Life That Counts* (1926) by Mrs. Howard Taylor and *The Power of Prayer and the Prayer of Power* (1924) by her own grandfather, Reuben A. Torrey. These works inspired her to form a prayer cell with five other girls. Together they prayed and worked for a spiritual revival at their school.

Helen enrolled at Wheaton College in the fall of 1936. The previous spring a revival had swept across the campus after a student stood up in chapel and asked what he and other students should do to receive the fullness of the Holy Spirit's power. Helen must not have seen much of the impact of that revival, however, because she felt the need to start her own small prayer band on campus and remembered feeling bored with chapel most of the time. Like many collegians she felt anxious about her future and her finances, and she was becoming run down physically from the burden of study, work, and worry.

Then Helen learned from her brother, who was living nearby, that the British-based faith mission, the Worldwide Evangelization Crusade,[20] was holding meetings in Chicago. She attended and heard a slant on the Christian faith she had not heard before, "the life of faith." She knew about the faith missions' emphasis on trusting God for one's material provision, but here were people who taught a more comprehensive life of total trust in God. As she listened, Helen felt compelled to choose between continuing her worrisome search for security or trusting God for everything. It was like "hanging on to a little branch" above a great abyss, she recalled. Finally, she decided to "let go and let God do with me what he would, trust him to provide, and go where he wanted me to go," without visible means of support—starting with getting through college. After that decision, she said, she felt like a changed person, and came back to campus eager to tell everyone what she had found.[21]

What Helen had discovered was in fact a pervasive, formative movement that had by then permeated North American fundamentalism. Commonly called the "Victorious Christian Life" or the "Higher Christian Life" or simply the "Keswick" movement, this persuasion was the particular branch of the larger holiness movement that had proven especially attractive to the Baptist, Congregationalist, and Presbyterian evangelicals of Helen's grandfather's generation who laid the foundations for fundamentalism.[22]

This movement drew some of its ideas directly from the American holiness movement, but its most immediate source was a British mutation of the American holiness campaign called the "Keswick" movement, named after a holiness conference begun in 1875 in Keswick, England. Keswick teaching, like the broader holiness movement emanating from American Methodism, emphasized that the key to a more holy and effective Christian life was a postconversion experience in which one yielded fully to God. In most holiness teaching this act of surrender and consecration of will would result in a "baptism of the Holy Ghost" and lead to "entire sanctification," or the eradication of one's propensity to sin. Keswick teachers modified this belief somewhat to make it more compatible with Reformed doctrines of sanctification by stressing that what this fresh anointing of the Holy Spirit brought was deeper communion with God, more power to do his will, and the active suppression—but *not* the annihilation—of the urge to sin. This higher plane of Christian living, then, came to those who surrendered all claims to their lives and entrusted themselves totally to God's care and direction.[23]

By the time of the fundamentalist–modernist controversies, Keswick holiness teaching was thoroughly integrated into the fundamentalist network of Bible schools, summer conferences, and faith missions. Although these beliefs had been accepted and widely disseminated by D. L. Moody's associates in the late nineteenth century, the movement's foremost twentieth-century promoter was Charles G. Trumbull. He was converted to the doctrine in 1910, and in 1913 helped to found the "America's Keswick" conference center in southern New Jersey. Trumbull also established the Victorious Life Council to sponsor speakers and conferences across the country, and he promoted the larger movement and its views in the *Sunday School Times*. Other leading speakers on the Higher Life circuit were Trumbull's protégé, Robert C. McQuilkin, who was the president of the Columbia Bible College, and Rowland V. Bingham, the director of the Sudan Interior Mission, editor of the *Evangelical Christian,* and founder of "Canadian Keswick" in northern Ontario.[24] By the 1930s Keswick holiness teaching had become the most prominent model of the "separated life's" spiritual dimension, and it pervaded the popular biographies of the time, such as *Borden of Yale* (1926), *Hudson Taylor's Spiritual Secret*

(1932), *The Triumph of John and Betty Stam* (1935) by the prolific Mary Guinness ("Mrs. Howard") Taylor of the China Inland Mission, and the several memoirs of Amy Carmichael, the British missionary to India's temple children. Keswick's pervasiveness in fundamentalist circles is by now fairly well known, but its impact has been largely taken for granted. It is important to stress how important this "surrendered life" ideal was to the fundamentalist ethos.

The first thing to notice is that the "life of faith" taught at Keswick was at the very heart of the fundamentalists' missionary impulse. Not only did the "surrendered life" ethos permeate the independent faith missions such as the Sudan Interior Mission, the China Inland Mission, and the Africa Inland Mission, but the very act of fully surrendering one's will and all claims to one's life seemed to fundamentalists to point to the missions field. Running through the Higher Life movement was the idea that yielding oneself brought not only victory over sin and closer communion with God but also the power to serve him effectively. The fifth and final day of the English Keswick Convention was customarily given over to the topic of service; highest on the agenda was foreign missions. North American Bible and Higher Life conferences repeated this pattern and featured missionary speakers who found ways to recruit for their cause while teaching the "life of faith."[25]

Responding to the call to missions, therefore, seemed to many to be the sign and seal of their full surrender. Because the missionary vocation was considered to demand the most radical self-denial and devotion to the evangelical cause, volunteering for missionary service seemed a sure indication that one was a fully consecrated, Spirit-filled Christian. After "giving [her] life to Jesus" at the New Jersey Keswick summer conference in 1925 and entering into the "victorious life," collegian Betty Scott wrote her parents that she was "willing to be an old-maid missionary, . . . all my life, if God wants me to."[26]

Ruth Sundquist, a Moody Bible Institute student in the early 1940s, encountered the missionary call in terms that virtually equated it with being a serious Christian. While attending a conference at the nearby Moody Church, she heard the missionary speaker ask young people to come forward and offer themselves to go to the field, even if they did not yet have a call. Up to then, Ruth recalled, "I thought I was a committed Christian." But now she had her doubts because she didn't feel "willing to go forward." The speaker persisted, in what was by then a time-honored tactic; he said, as Ruth recalled, "'If you aren't willing to go, ask the Lord to make you willing to go.'" And then he pressed further: "'If you aren't willing to do that, ask him to make you willing to be willing to pray that prayer.'" Said Ruth, "that's about where I had to start!"[27]

The sincerity of one's commitment to Christ often was reduced, then, to an acquiescence to at least the possibility of accepting a missionary call. Did you trust fully in God? Were you fully surrendered to his will? Was the life which you were now living in fact being lived through the indwelling Christ? If so, then you would be willing to go anywhere, do anything. And what most needed doing? As the modern American missionary martyr William Borden put it, "If ten men are carrying a log, nine of them on the little end and one at the heavy end, and you want to help, which end will you lift . . . ?"[28] Thus the holiness ideal of "my utmost for His highest"[29] helped fuel fundamentalists' drive to evangelize the "regions beyond."

For many fundamentalist missionaries, and thousands of other who entered "other fields of service" on the home front, the "surrendered life" began in a Bible institute. These schools were familial, religiously and emotionally intense places designed to foster spiritual growth and commitment to the cause while providing an alternative "safe house" environment in the midst of the world. Prayer, hymn-singing, and devotional meetings were the way of life, and outbreaks of revival were fairly frequent. Student publications were filled with the exalted language of service and heroic spiritual aspirations.[30]

Enthusiasm for missions was palpable at these schools. Student-organized missionary prayer bands met regularly to discuss news from their respective chosen fields and to pray for missionaries there. Returned missionaries on faculty and staff offered valuable advice, encouragement, and personal models. Missionary speakers were regular fare in chapel and week-long conferences. Students eagerly testified to their calls to specific fields, announced their appointments to missions, or disclosed their departure dates. Missionary maps and Bible verses on missions themes frequently decorated the walls, and some schools displayed such "trophies of grace" as cast-off idols or fetishes and photographs of smiling, born-again native people. Remarked an observer of daily life at the Prairie Bible Institute in Alberta, "they ate, drank, studied, slept, and sang missions morning, noon, and night."[31]

The gritty daily routine of Bible school life gave students plenty of opportunities to learn the discipline of self-forgetting service and a radical trust in God's provision. "Practical Christian work" assignments such as street preaching, singing at jails and rescue missions, or door-to-door calling in tough ethnic neighborhoods could prompt students to reach beyond themselves to meet such challenges. Exhausting weeks of classes, service assignments, and menial jobs to earn room and board—then learning to make do with old clothes and worn shoes—could also provide laboratory experience in the "life of faith."[32]

The potent combination of Keswick piety and missionary idealism, brought together in the hothouse environment of the Bible schools, made North American fundamentalism a leading recruiter of twentieth-century missionaries. At one point in the mid-1930s, the active missionary alumni of the Moody Bible Institute alone—some 1,400 all told—amounted to 12.5 percent of the total count of North American Protestant missionaries.[33]

Without this infusion of "surrendered life" piety and its byproduct of missionary zeal, fundamentalism might have turned out different. Had not the "surrendered life" ideal helped many fundamentalists to accentuate the positive, evangelistic side of their tradition, the movement might have become preoccupied with the bad-tempered ecclesiastical debates over separatism. Faith missions leaders were generally moderate to "progressive" along the spectrum of attitudes within fundamentalism toward relations with other

Christians. They implemented, within a conservative evangelical doctrinal consensus, interdenominational cooperation and fellowship on their own staffs, and in the 1940s they were among the organizers of such conservative ecumenical ventures as the National Association of Evangelicals and the rejuvenated World Evangelical Fellowship.[34]

The situation at Wheaton College in the 1930s and early 1940s bears this out. According to several observers, Wheaton's third president, J. Oliver Buswell, Jr. (1926–1940), was supportive of missions, but when he became increasingly involved in the separatist wing of fundamentalist Presbyterianism, missions took a back seat to contending for the faith.[35] The atmosphere changed considerably after Buswell was fired in 1940 and V. Raymond Edman, a former missionary to Ecuador with the Christian and Missionary Alliance, assumed the school's presidency. An avid promoter of missions and missionary spirituality, Edman frequently used episodes from the life of J. Hudson Taylor, founder of the China Inland Mission, in his chapel talks; and he personally counselled students in their pursuit of the surrendered life.[36]

As a result, Wheaton was fairly pulsating with missionary piety and enthusiasm and committed to nonseparating fundamentalism's goals of bringing revival to America and the gospel to the world. Edman's support for the Youth for Christ movement in the mid-1940s showed that Wheaton was throwing its support behind the more positive wing of fundamentalism; the Wheaton chapter of the Student Foreign Missions Fellowship, a conservative evangelical alternative to the fading Student Volunteer Movement, involved one hundred students. Fortified with the missionary zeal of returning veterans and a campus revival, one fourth of Wheaton's graduating class of 1950 found its way to the mission field. This rapid rise in the numbers of new recruits after the Second World War was a movement-wide phenomenon; and the higher life–faith missions ethos, if the situation at Wheaton was typical, lent it shape and thrust.[37]

Keswick piety was not always an irenic influence. One of the mysteries of the fundamentalist faith is the apparent contradiction between its militancy and its pietism. It is difficult to understand how fundamentalist contentiousness and separatism could be supported by the sweetly pious, rather quiescent style of the Higher Life movement. The paradox of Charles G. Trumbull, who was at once the leading American apostle of the Victorious Life and one of the most formidable power brokers of American fundamentalism, is an important case in point.

Trumbull taught, on the one hand, that God could give those who were fully surrendered to his will a life that was "brand new, fresh from the hands of God," and marked by love for one's enemy: "a positive outgoing of love, so that you would do anything for him"; and patience: "taking 'all that is coming to you' with a smile"; and self-control—all by means of the Holy Spirit's power.[38] On the other hand, few equalled Trumbull's ability to stir up trouble as a watchdog for the fundamentalist faith. Trumbull was not the meanest of fundamentalists by any stretch of the imagination, but his testimony to having gained victory over all known sin loses credibility in the face of his actions. He

labelled the Presbyterian Board of Foreign Missions "modernistic," he relentlessly attacked fellow evangelical and holiness advocate E. Stanley Jones for his
alleged apostasy, and his assault on John MacInnis, a fellow fundamentalist,
resulted in MacInnis's being hounded from the presidency of BIOLA and the
near-collapse of that school. How do we account for this discrepancy?[39]

It was more than simple hypocrisy. Keswick perfectionism, for all of its sweet
demeanor, could prompt people to be very hard on themselves in their quest
for holiness. And once they felt they had entered the "higher Christian life"
they could be extremely judgmental toward more ordinary Christians.[40] Assurance of his personal spiritual victory apparently gave Trumbull a similar certainty of his doctrinal and ethical rectitude and helped justify his merciless
attacks on those whose views differed from his own. The surrendered life's perfectionist ideals could be twisted to support the sanctimonious debates over
doctrinal details and the personal rivalries that marked so much of fundamentalism's internal affairs.[41]

Perfectionism also could turn community life into an emotional pressure
cooker. Earnest young people might be directed by their counsellors at church
or in Bible school to see the inevitable friction in their personal relationships as
evidence of insufficient surrender. The same might be told them about the
conflicts many felt between their natural desires and abilities and their "call" to
a particular field of service.[42] At its worst, "surrendered life" teaching could be
twisted to provide those who held power with a self-righteous cover for their
meanness and a tool for manipulating their followers into submission.

No discussion of the "surrendered life" movement is complete with mention of one more positive influence it brought American fundamentalism. A
generation of fundamentalist young people who were reared in a prosaic, doc-
trinaire, and aesthetically starved environment were refreshed and delighted by
the devotional works of Isobel Kuhn, Amy Carmichael, and A. W. Tozer, to
cite three of the most prominent examples. These authors conveyed visions of
love, truth, beauty, and holiness with considerable literary artistry.[43] Perhaps
the most influential of the lot was Tozer of the Christian and Missionary
Alliance, a studious editor and pastor in Chicago who was nothing less than a
modern evangelical prophet and mystic. Tozer's jabs at fundamentalists for
their spiritual dryness and his impassioned pleas for Christians to encounter
their God in all of his majesty have lost little of their power over the years.[44]

A Shelter in a Time of Storm

What are we to conclude, after two chapters' worth of explorations into the
"separated life?" Although it was practiced with varying degrees of intensity
and completeness, the fundamentalist separated life ideal became widely used
as a model of what it meant to be a serious Christian in modern America. It
was the identifying core of what had become a religious subculture. Fundamentalist religious communities were growing to resemble ethnic communities, George Marsden noted, because they played a mediating role for many

thousands with roots in the rural and small-town Protestant culture of earlier America who now found themselves in the largely foreign culture of a new urban nation.[45] Fundamentalists, like immigrants or other religious outsiders, wanted to make good in modern America, but they did not feel at home in it, for the controversies of the 1920s showed them that other Americans—even some from their own denominations—thought they were pretty strange. Thus it became vital for their survival to build what sociologist Peter Berger has called "plausibility structures"—institutions, relationships, and an ethos that could shelter them from opposing views and practices and reinforce their own way of living.[46] Claimed one fundamentalist editor, this alternative Christian community provided a "shelter belt" for God's people. Much as the bands of trees that had been planted around midwestern prairie farms protected the land from wind storms, fundamentalist churches, schools, and myriad other agencies screened the faithful from the threatening blasts of modern life.[47]

Fundamentalist separatism was not total, however; the separated life did not utterly seal people off from ordinary existence. There were no attempts, other than promoting "full time Christian work" as a vocational choice, to provide comprehensive alternatives to the residential and economic structures of the larger world. Fundamentalists assumed that most people in their movement would live in ordinary neighborhoods and work in "secular" occupations, so comparisons to Catholic monasteries, sectarian communes, Jewish ghettoes, and Amish farming communities are at best misleading. Fundamentalists were supposed to be in the world but not of it. Their networks were to be "halfway houses," providing respite from the world's trials and temptations, not total escape. Fundamentalist institutions were to operate by the separated life's varying norms—"eternity's values"—and thus encourage and refuel the faithful as they tried to live out these values in mainstream society. In sum, while fundamentalist leaders strove to keep their people and their agencies pure, they never ceased insisting that the separated life should not become monastic or "segregated," as one writer warned. Christians should not become exclusively "shelter belt" people; their duty was always to go out into the storm to rescue the lost.[48]

Nevertheless, the temptation was strong to limit one's more intimate associations to the like-minded, and to provide fundamentalist alternatives for the ordinary world's activities. Summer Bible conferences offered sanctified substitutes for vacations at regular summer resorts. Youth clubs were evangelical answers to Scouting and the "Y"s. The same was true of the evangelistic clubs for men and women over against Kiwanis or the Union League. Adult Sunday school class socials replaced bridge parties, and Sunday evenings at the gospel tabernacle could be as entertaining as a night at the movies. In places where the movement was particularly strong, grade school academies, Bible institutes, colleges and seminaries, and job opportunities in parachurch agencies could extend the sheltering effect across much of one's life. Complained one of the movement's journalists in the early 1950s, Bible-believers could easily become wrapped up in an "evangelical cellophane" that effectively prevented them from ministering to the larger world.[49]

The fundamentalism under this wrapper was not the classic "faith once delivered" that its creators had claimed, either. It was in many respects a crabbed and parochial mutation of Protestant orthodoxy. The "postfundamentalist" conservative theologian Edward John Carnell, who was raised a fundamentalist, wrote in the late 1950s that he objected especially to its unloving doctrinal "pharisaism," which cut off any fellowship with other Christians who disagreed on points of doctrine. Moreover, he complained, the movement's legalism was positively tyrannical.[50] Fundamentalism had become like a cult in that it was bounded and operated according to "mores and symbols of its own devising" rather than by the gospel and Christ's commandments for the church—especially to live in love and unity.[51] The gospel had been warped, Carnell complained, into "Believe on the Lord Jesus Christ, don't smoke, don't go to movies, . . . and you will be saved."[52] Fundamentalism was a parochial religious world of "small talk" and petty minds; it was much too confining for "younger men . . . who have taken time to get a decent education," who longed for "authentic conversation on historic themes" and "fellowship with the church universal."[53] Fundamentalists may have found a means of surviving in modern America, but some of their heirs wondered how much of this legacy was worth preserving.

It is hard not to sympathize with these postfundamentalist critics, but in making judgments about the separated life it is important to note two points that they overlooked. The first is that any religious movement or tradition, whether it is trying to do something new or restore something old, is by necessity "cultic." It must devise "mores and symbols" to live by, and these, by their very nature as human fabrications, reflect the circumstances of their makers. Fundamentalism's "separated life" alienated some of the movement's freer spirits and called out for correction to others who were able to see that it could not be equated with apostolic Christianity. But the same is true of the "new evangelical" movement that fundamentalism's reformers devised. All Christian communities are profoundly shaped by their cultural situation, and revisionists who chide a prior generation for not seeing its own foibles and limitations should know that some day their descendants will say the same of them. Fundamentalism, like so many other historic Christian communities, committed the pardonable sin of presuming its own centrality and timelessness. But this very presumption was one of the ingredients that gave it vitality and staying power.

The postfundamentalist reformers also did not understand a corollary point: their yearning to make some greater contribution than what fundamentalism would allow was in fact a product of the subculture they wanted to broaden. Fundamentalism was often intellectually lame, provincial, petty, mean-spirited, stultifying, and manipulative, but it could be enabling and energizing as well, and by the 1940s it had produced a restive and visionary younger generation. As a popular movement, fundamentalism was a way of life that was largely created, controlled, and propagated by ordinary people. They might have had little chance to be leaders or to express their creativity in the larger world, but in this smaller realm, they had opportunities. The movement's strategy of opposition to the world around them had not, in most cases, descended all the way to pointless negativism. Fundamentalists had their own ideals of goodness, their own visions of duty and opportunity. They were able to create close-knit and supportive fellowships, they had plenty of outlets for inventiveness and entrepreneurial expansion, and they enjoyed life-changing religious experiences that came to them in forms and language they had fashioned. For some who found themselves in these environs, fundamentalism did not fully satisfy, and they either accepted its foibles, sought to reform it, or found the way out. Yet for millions of people, fundamentalism was a satisfying way of life that, within limits, could stretch and grow as their needs changed. Fundamentalism has been, as historian R. Laurence Moore put it, not so much a species of "deviation" in American religious life, but one important way in which "average Americans invested their lives with meaning."[54]

5

A WINDOW ON
THE WORLD

The "meaning" with which fundamentalists invested their lives was colored with distinctive—some might say peculiar—views of history, the church, current affairs, and the future. Fundamentalism's world view was deeply shaded by its understanding of the world's ultimate fate, the end of all things toward which history and contemporary events were leading. Indeed, we have already seen how dispensationalism, the dominant belief system about history and destiny among fundamentalists, influenced the movement's ecclesiastical separatism, its views about the Bible, and its understanding of the church's mission. This supernatural panorama was instrumental in forming fundamentalists' outlook on more public affairs as well, and for that reason it deserves some focused attention.

In the last days, the dispensational Bible teachers told their audiences, the institutional church would become apostate. As a result, Christianity's positive influence on society would wane, and immorality, crime, and religious and political oppression would increase. Natural catastrophes such as earthquakes and floods would abound, wars would proliferate, and bloodthirsty dictators would arise. As the pace of evil quickened, those who placed their hope in human progress would come to despair. Only those whose hope was built on Christ and his promises would persevere. At some point, the exact timing of which would be impossible to predict, Christ would return to take all of his faithful followers out of the world in a supernatural event called the "Secret Rapture."

Meanwhile, God's other chosen people, the Jews, would be at center stage in world affairs. Facing murderous persecution, the Jews would flee to Palestine to reestablish their nation. On another front, a satanically inspired world dictator whom the Bible variously named the Beast or the Antichrist would link up with an apostate, unified world church, reunite the Roman Empire, and establish tyrannical religious and political control over much of the world. At first he would sign a protective pact with the Jewish state in Palestine, but later he would turn on the Jews. During a seven-year period after the Secret Rapture called the Great Tribulation, many Jews would convert and suffer martyrdom for their faith in Jesus as Messiah. Palestine would become the scene of the world's last great battle, as Antichrist's last remaining rivals, the godless hordes of the North (the Russians and their allies, many thought) clashed with the vast assembled forces of the Antichrist on the plains of Armageddon. At that point Christ would return with the armies of heaven to rescue the Jews, slay all the godless forces, and establish the millennial kingdom. Christ would rule from the restored throne of David, and holiness, justice, peace, and prosperity would prevail on earth for a thousand years.[1] After that, many surmised, Satan would rebel one last time and be defeated forever. Then God would usher in his eternal reign over a new heaven and a new earth.

So according to fundamentalist Bible teachers, terrible times were descending upon the world, and the progression of evil was quickening. Only Christ's second coming could redeem and restore humanity and the creation. God was bringing this age to an end, and while the mainstream churches were being drugged into lethargy by the false teaching of modernism, Bible-believing Christians had an urgent mission to bring the gospel to as many as possible, entreating them to "flee from the wrath to come" (Luke 3:7).

During the years of the Great Depression and the coming of the Second World War, these apocalyptic visions gained fresh plausibility, as did fundamentalists' "state of emergency" view of the church's mission. Fundamentalists' sense of being separated from the world thus carried with it a belief that they were destined to be God's faithful remnant as the world hurtled toward its doom. This outlook provided a dramatic, mythic backdrop for their stance toward the rest of the world. Already predisposed to feel alienated from American culture, fundamentalists drew confirmation of that stance from their views of history, current events, and the future. In this sense, dispensationalism functioned as an intensifier of the fundamentalist outlook, a "wild card," as it were, that fortified and gave biblical sanction to the feelings pervading the movement.

Getting the News in Advance

Fundamentalists did not have to invent apocalyptic scenarios, for they were living through some very disturbing times. In the midst of the great economic and political convulsions of the 1930s and 1940s, it seemed to a great many people as though world civilization was hurtling out of control. Even in middle America people found the simple and familiar aspects of their daily existence altered by the grim facts of the Depression. Sociologists Robert and Helen Lynd reported that "for the first time in their lives, many Middletown people have awakened from a sense of being at home in a familiar world to the shock of living . . . in a universe dangerously too big and blindly out of hand."[2] Political instability in Europe and Asia raised disturbing questions. Could it happen here? Were American democracy and capitalism at a dead end? Should the nation seek radically new alternatives? While intellectuals wrestled with these questions in the 1930s, many others searched for security; they longed for lasting values by which to guide their lives.[3]

Escape into a "separated life" offered a potentially attractive package of security, values and community, but most fundamentalists found it difficult to be total isolationists from current affairs. They continued to "earnestly contend for the faith once delivered" in order to convince themselves, if not others, of their faith's relevance. In this vein they were very much the alter egos of their more liberal Protestant kin. Both sensed that conventional Protestantism was losing its influence. "In the old days people went to preachers for consolation, information and inspiration," one Middletown pastor complained. "They still come to us for consolation, but go to newspapers for information and inspiration."[4] Fundamentalist leaders aimed to provide all three, for they sensed that they would lose out to modernity, to the newspapers, if they lost touch with public life.

Fundamentalists insisted that their position was not fanatical but sober and realistic. Like their Marxist contemporaries, fundamentalist leaders reinforced their beliefs by interpreting current events in light of what they knew about the future, and the news often seemed to fit fundamentalists' predictions. While the secular press was straining to interpret the outbreak of the Second World War in 1939, Donald Barnhouse confided to his readers that those "who know the general lines of Bible prophecy" were not at all surprised or confused, because the Old Testament prophet Ezekiel knew more about current events than did the *Saturday Evening Post*.[5]

Barnhouse provides a good example of the way that fundamentalist leaders interpreted the world to their constituents. In the tradition of millenarian journalism as pioneered by A. J. Gordon's *Watchword* magazine in the 1880s and continued since then by Arno C. Gaebelein's *Our Hope,* Barnhouse's monthly, begun in 1931, was called *Revelation,* and was organized to provide a dispensationally informed commentary on contemporary religious and cultural trends. Dispensational perspectives informed its editorial pages and its feature articles, and provided the interpretive leverage for Barnhouse's regular column, "Tomorrow: Current Events in the Light of Bible Prophecy." Barnhouse stressed that the biblical prophecies of the Antichrist, the Great Tribulation, and the battle of Armageddon were not being fulfilled at present; they were all to take place at some future date. Then why study current events in light of these biblical prophecies?

Barnhouse answered by using an analogy: the passage of historical time was like the playing out of a great bolt of cloth from a stamping machine that produced an ever-changing pattern. Looking at the prior progression of the pattern is the study of history. Looking at the pattern just as it comes out of the machine is called journalism, or the study of current events. But no one can know just what will come out next; we can only guess, based on prior patterns. This is the rightful business, Barnhouse said, of historians, statesmen, and contemporary commentators. But the prophetic interpreter's business was different.

The Bible contains "a full-width sample of the cloth that is to come from the machine at a certain time." It is impossible to know whether that section is coming out after another mile or after only a few more inches. Therefore it was foolish, Barnhouse thought, "to identify current events with the positive and actual fulfillment of Bible prophecy." The prophetic commentator's role was more modest; all one could do was "show the direction of the flow, and note the tendency of movements in light of the full outline which we hold in our hands."[6]

Fundamentalist interpreters were mistaken fairly often when they tried to divine the prophetic meaning of particular events, but their errors did not seem to matter all that much. Their audience still drew assurance from the larger implications of prophecy. All is not chaos; history is leading somewhere. Even though the horrific and confusing state of world affairs will get worse before it can get better, it will get better—through the personal intervention of Jesus Christ.

Fundamentalists had inherited their interest in signs of the world's end from their forbears in the late nineteenth century. During this earlier period, however, dispensationalists' predictions—that a godless horde from Russia would storm the plains of Armageddon, that the nations once under the Roman Empire would reunify, that international Jewry would reestablish the nation of Israel in Palestine, and that all of the mainline churches would apostatize— seemed implausible, to say the least. By the early 1900s, however, dispensationalist Bible teachers were more successful in tying these themes to current trends, such as the rise of socialism and nihilism in Russia, the emergence of a Zionist movement, religious liberals' visions of a globally unified "new type of Christianity," and political liberals' dreams of world peace conferences and global federations. Even the American government's increasing powers of regulation seemed to them to fit a new and portentous pattern.[7]

World War I and its aftermath gave dispensational commentators a major boost in plausibility and encouraged them to step up their efforts. Two events of the war led dispensationalists to interpret world affairs with new excitement. First, when General Allenby's British and Arab forces captured Jerusalem from the Turks in 1917 and the British government issued the Balfour Declaration, pledging a national home for the Jews in Palestine, dispensationalists' expectations for the Zionist movement were confirmed. The Bolshevik Revolution seemed to confirm the Bible teachers' predictions that Russia would become a great and evil power in the last days. The prophetic commentator's role was well established by the 1920s, therefore, and the events of the ensuing dozen or so years conspired to encourage their efforts.[8]

Benito Mussolini's rise to power in Italy provoked a new wave of millenarian speculation. During Moody Bible Institute's Founder's Week in 1929 an Australian Bible teacher described how the Italian dictator mirrored the dispensationalist picture of the coming Antichrist: he called for the revival of the Roman Empire, he dubbed himself the "Man of Destiny" and "superman incarnate," and he seemed to be setting up a semipagan state while working out a rapprochement with the Vatican. Though concluding that *Il Duce* was probably not the Antichrist, the speaker thought Mussolini was preparing the way for "the Roman prince," the "Man of Sin," who he was sure already lived somewhere in the world.[9]

The *Sunday School Times* published an interview which the dictator granted to missionaries Ralph and Edith Norton in 1932. Mussolini tantalizingly avoided their questions about resurrecting the Empire but expressed great interest, as one might expect, in their suggestion that the Bible predicted it.[10] Linking Bible prophecy to current events attracted tremendous attention. In late 1935 and early 1936 the *Sunday School Times* ran a special series of articles on the fulfillment of prophecy and accompanied these pieces with a special subscription campaign. In two months the magazine had twenty thousand new subscribers.[11]

Adolf Hitler's Nazi regime in Germany soon appeared a greater threat to world peace than did Italian fascism, and this posed a problem for dispensationalists. They had long supposed that the main political actors in the end times would be Russia and a revived Roman Empire. Accordingly, their estimate of Germany's place in the scenario varied. Either Italy would eventually dominate the Axis, or the Germans would fall under the Soviet Union's domination. Louis S. Bauman of Long Beach, California, probably the most prolific of the current Bible prophecy teachers, insisted that "the Master-mind of Europe today is not in Berlin," nor in Moscow, Paris, or London, but "in Rome," an assessment that would have seemed odd to most secular commentators.[12]

Adolf Hitler attracted dispensationalists' attention chiefly because of his religious and racial outrages and for the ways in which he manifested the "dictator spirit," which they believed to be a harbinger of the Antichrist. Confused at first by conflicting reports coming out of Germany about the true state of affairs, most fundamentalist leaders—with a few notable exceptions—saw the Nazi menace quite clearly and somewhat earlier, perhaps, than most Americans. As early as March 1933, Donald Barnhouse warned of Hitler's evil designs on the Jews and noted his threats to all who opposed his plan to control a unified state church purged of "Hebraic" elements. The Philadelphia pastor visited the eminent German Reformed theologian, Karl Barth, in Zurich and listened sympathetically as Barth exclaimed: "We are face to face with a vigorous paganism, and we are fighting for our very life. What we are seeing today in Germany is the end of Christianity." Barnhouse also visited the leading dissident German pastor, Martin Niemoeller, in 1935 and 1937, and gave *Revelation* readers eyewitness accounts of the state of German affairs. The prophetic implications of Nazism were clear, Barnhouse wrote; the "dictator spirit" was sweeping the nations, and "we may be in the same position . . . before many years have passed."[13]

Indeed, Bible Teachers worried that the totalitarian spirit was showing up in the policies of the New Deal as well. Bauman, Barnhouse, and others thought that the Blue Eagle emblem the New Dealers devised for the National Recovery Administration reflected a global trend toward rallying the masses behind insignia, a development foretold in Revelation 13. The Antichrist would establish the "mark of the beast," which all must display on their hands and foreheads in order to engage in commerce.[14] Many were convinced that the New Deal was moving in a dictatorial direction in substance as well as symbol. James M. Gray wrote that although the Roosevelt Administration was sincere in its desire to revive the economy, its unprecedented use of state power was "preparing people for what is coming later . . . the big dictator, the superman, the lawless one."[15]

To the outsider looking in, fundamentalists' interpretation of current events "in the light of Bible prophecy" might seem fanciful, to say the least. And as two recent scholars of premillennialism have made clear, fundamentalist prophetic diviners were almost invariably wrong when they succumbed to the temptation to make specific predictions.[16] But there was a certain uncanny resemblance between their scenario of the end-times and the way that things seemed to be headed in the 1930s. Even H. L. Mencken seemed to think so. In a fit of pique at the respectable liberal clergy's ideas about current events, Mencken reminded them that "the New Testament offers precise and elaborate specifications of the events preceding the inevitable end of the world, and that a fair reading of them must lead any rational man to conclude that those events are now upon us. If the Bible is really the Word of God . . . then it is as plain as day that the human race is on its last legs."[17] So even if dispensationalist soothsayers missed the mark now and then, their overall scheme was resilient, and it bore a certain plausibility in their day. What if Mussolini turned out not to be a world-conquering mastermind? Some day the old Roman Empire *would* be resurrected by a superman, so Mussolini and other dictators were forerunners, preparing the masses to accept the real Antichrist when he appeared. The times did seem apocalyptic; without too great a stretch of one's imagination the era's personalities and events could be made out to be "rehearsals," as one commentator put it, of the Apocalypse.[18]

Fundamentalist spokesmen were eager to show that their predictions of the world's doom were matched by the fears of important, highly regarded people. Charles G. Trumbull, for example, quoted Walter Lippmann: "'The signs are multiplying that the stage is set for an event of world-wide importance and of unpredictable consequences.'" Then he cited an English lord, Robert Cecil: "'I read the papers with increasing uneasiness. I believe we are headed straight for one of the greatest disasters that has ever come upon mankind.'" And finally, he summoned the words of the former British prime minister, Lloyd George: "'I cannot say what is going to happen to the world. I am alarmed. I will go so far as to say I am frightened at what will happen.'"[19]

In contrast to these expressions of fear and confusion on the part of those who were wise in the world's eyes, fundamentalists could answer with confidence; they knew the signs of the times. Their constant sifting of events into prophetic categories assured them that they understood what was happening to the world. It was exhilarating to be able to put turbulent and confusing events together in a coherent pattern, and their studies reinforced fundamentalists' sense of their own significance. They were "in the know;" they could read the patterns on the cloth of history. In his memoirs of intellectual life in the 1930s, literary critic Malcolm Cowley said that he and many of his friends converted to Marxism because it promised solutions to the present mess and gave them a hopeful "long view." They followed events at home and abroad eagerly, always considering how the news portended the coming revolution. Like the Left, the fundamentalists were confident that they could "get the news in advance."[20]

"Come, Lord Jesus": Vindication and Deliverance

Implied in fundamentalists' certainty that they possessed the "sure word of prophecy" (II Pet. 1:19) was a corollary conviction: in the end, their cause and their beliefs would be vindicated. Their marginalized status and the ridicule to which they were subjected caused fundamentalists psychic pain, but their prophetic perspective allowed them to turn the tables. They took satisfaction from their rivals' confusion and dismay and expected that God would settle accounts with the high and mighty of this world.

The salty North Carolina preacher Vance Havner said that there was a "crumb of comfort" to be had in the screaming headlines of the day's newspapers. "Some are beginning to discover that the faith of our fathers is not the back-number proposition some sophomore smart alecks thought it was." While prophetic teachers had once been regarded as "crepe-hangers" who had "missed the bus," it was now tempting, he admitted, to "pat ourselves on the back with an 'I-told-you-so' attitude." Havner felt cheered by the thought that he was "on the winning side." It might seem sometimes that "this world is running the show," but "God had the first word and He'll have the last."[21]

Fundamentalists took grim satisfaction from the perplexity of contemporary intellectual and religious leaders. Louis Bauman recalled that "for many years our modernistic intelligentsia . . . has amused itself with self-flattery, spending most of its time in boasting of man's high attainments upon the earth, his high degree of civilization, his great advancement." When Bible teachers pointed out the "prophecies of coming human failure and consequent judgments," they were ridiculed and called the bearers of "'old witches' tales.'" But now, Bauman observed, "these intellectuals are talking in whispers—whispers of fear!" In a gentler vein, James M. Gray noted that "about the only hopeful people we meet nowadays are the premillenarians." Gray recalled that "there was a time when they were complained of on every hand as being pessimistic. But now the tables are turned."[22]

The perplexity and suffering of people throughout the world were great in the 1930s and 1940s, and one would have hoped to have seen a measure of compassion from the prophetic diviners. Glimpses of broken-hearted pity appeared now and then, but more common was a detached mood, akin to staring out the window on the world's pain. As war raged across Europe in 1940, Louis Bauman noted that "the forces are now operating in the world for the fulfillment of the prophetic picture with marvelous exactness."[23] It would be a distortion, however, to suggest that fundamentalists were able to remain emotionally distant in all respects from the suffering of their age. They too experienced fear and anxiety in those troubling times; they too were looking for a way out of the economic and international turmoil. In Christ's promise to come again, rescue his saints, and return in full force to establish his messianic kingdom, fundamentalists believed they had found a way out.[24]

Charles Trumbull, editor of the *Sunday School Times,* gave a great deal of attention to the subject, both in the articles he solicited for his magazine and in his own writings. The chief curse of the current day was fear, said Trumbull. The world was "being shaken to its foundations, civilization is tottering," and "'men's hearts failing them for fear.'" Even Christian people "who have not been prepared for the epoch in which we are now living" were "bewildered" and "terrified." The world situation looked utterly hopeless if one sought salvation from the hands of human wisdom, governments, or "even the professing Christian Church, in which apostasy has made such tragic and increasing inroads." But there was hope indeed if people looked instead to "'the glorious appearing of the great God and our Saviour Jesus Christ.'"[25]

While both he and others might have succumbed on occasion to the temptation to feel detached, even smug, about the fate of the unbelieving world, Trumbull seemed to realize that "true believers" were not exempt from the pain. It was one thing to heed the biblical admonitions to remain diligent and watchful, but Trumbull yearned, he said, for some "softer promises" to "slip under the load and ease sore, chafed, and aching shoulders." Future deliverance and rewards for steadfastness were fine, but he was looking for some "balm for us here and now." Probably nothing ate away people's peace of mind more than the fear of war, he said. Living under such threats, how could one keep from "dying, while we live, with a fretting leprosy?" Trumbull also worried about the growth of communism. It had invaded China, captured Mexico, and begun to "filter through" into the United States. The "thought of what lies ahead" was enough to make "the stoutest heart among us" quail.[26]

The litany continued, citing natural disasters "and that strange, incredibly cruel ogre known as 'The Depression'." Trumbull told of devoted Christians who had become deranged—victims of the "alarming increase of mental collapse." He also felt the "burden of our churches, such as "the coldness of those who have avouched Christ, . . . the travesty on his honor and his Word" in liberal churches, and "wild fanaticism" breaking out among some of the fundamentalists.[27] What was worse, making it virtually impossible to live in a "quiet cloister of peace," was the invasion of "our very home . . . by the Spirit of Lawlessness." It was one thing to sit back and nod while the "prophetical Scriptures" were applied to the sins of the day's young people, "but when the sword strikes this home and this heart, we fall back in dumb horror on the sand of our own impotence." Like another broken-hearted parent, the Psalmist, Trumbull said, "we are ready to cry out, 'All thy waves and thy billows are gone over me.'"[28]

Preaching the Second Coming was therefore not merely a way of telling off those who scoffed at them. Fundamentalists shared in the era's anxiety, so the promise that the world's turmoil was in fact the labor pains of a new age was for them, as for Christians in history's other troubled times, a comfort. As Trumbull phrased it, they could "listen once more, through the storm, through the stress of anguish and tears, and hear his sweet Word of comfort . . . 'Be ye not troubled,' but, 'Look up, and lift up your heads; for your redemption draweth nigh.'"[29]

The Time of Jacob's Trouble

The most astonishing sign of the times for fundamentalists, and the one which they were most ready to explain in prophetic terms, was the rise of anti-Semitism and the widespread persecution of the Jews. "Israel's" fate was thought to be the center of human events in the last days. The Hebrew prophets' visions of their people's return to the Holy Land and their restoration as a nation, dispensationalists believed, would be literally fulfilled. But before and after their arrival in the Promised Land, the Jews were to undergo horrific persecution, what dispensationalists called "the time of Jacob's trouble" (Jer. 30:7). According to Louis Bauman, all other prophetic omens paled before this one; the current wave of anti-Semitic persecution demanded the intervention of Christ, he insisted, because God promised to deliver his people. "Let there be no mistake," Bauman insisted, "the present travail of Israel is the surest possible token that . . . David's Son is about to mount His white charger and ride across Armageddon's field."[30]

This focus of prophetic attention on "Israel" played a formative role in shaping fundamentalists' attitudes toward the Jews, but these attitudes were complex and ambivalent. At times, as historian Timothy Weber has pointed out, it was hard to tell whether fundamentalists were the Jews' best friends or worst enemies. Certainly there were many expressions of affection and respect. Many fundamentalists felt prompted to express feelings of sympathy and spiritual kinship with the Jewish community. Their hope of Christ's imminent return paralleled the hope of Orthodox Jews for the coming of the Messiah, and fundamentalists' belief in the restoration of Israel in Palestine generated sympathy for Zionism. Indeed, an early leader of the fundamentalist movement, W. E. Blackstone, was an active supporter of the Zionist movement.[31]

Another product of fundamentalists' professed love for the Jews was their sense of duty to present the gospel "to the Jew first," as the Apostle Paul had put it (Rom. 1:16). By the early twentieth century, every major city in the United States with a substantial Jewish population had missions to the Jewish people, and dispensationalists were usually the sponsors.[32] Some of the larger Bible institutes offered special courses of study in "Jewish Evangelism," with introductory courses in the Talmud and rabbinical theology, Jewish history, and Yiddish, such as those taught at the Moody Bible Institute in the 1920s and 1930s by Solomon Birnbaum.[33]

Fundamentalists never reckoned with the cultural violence that such conversion attempts threatened to bring the Jews. The Bible school students and home missionaries kept going into the Jewish neighborhoods and presenting their message, which made them the targets for insults, eggs, and spoiled fruit as they passed out their Yiddish tracts and Hebrew New Testaments. The only explanation they could muster for their rough reception was that it reflected a prophetic, centuries-long hardening of Jewish hearts that began at the original rejection of Jesus.[34]

In spite of Jews' resistance to such proselytizing, there was a substantial "Hebrew Christian" movement by the early 1930s. Organizations such as Joseph Cohn's American Board of Missions to the Jews and Jacob Gartenhaus's Hebrew Christian Alliance were thriving. The latter group claimed to represent some twenty thousand Jews in the United States who had "openly accepted Jesus as their personal Messiah."[35] Despite the threatening presence of such groups, genuine friendship between Jews and fundamentalist groups persisted. An eager interest in Zionism was often the common link. In Kansas City, Missouri, for example, the president of the local Zionist movement presented a Regular Baptist congregation with a Star of David flag, which was prominently displayed in the sanctuary.[36]

Despite these ties to Jewish people, fundamentalists found it difficult to rise above common prejudice. Even their praise of the Jewish people partook of the familiar stereotypes: Jews were unusually ambitious, intelligent, and adept at making money.[37] But more to the point, fundamentalists' dispensational theology could fortify their suspicion as well as their affection toward the Jews. According to the prophetic Bible teachers, Jesus had offered to establish the Messianic kingdom during his earthly ministry, but the Jewish leaders of his day, for the most part, refused his offer. Their rejection necessitated a delay in his reign as Messiah. As a result, the dispensational teachers emphasized, the Jews had brought judgment on themselves. For centuries God had allowed them to be harried about the earth, and many of them had become apostate and had fallen prey to false messianic schemes, including, many surmised, modern-day communism.[38]

Yet there were alternate emphases as well. As anti-Semitism became more virulent in the 1930s, a number of prominent dispensationalists, and most notably Louis Bauman, emphasized that the ravings of Satan during earth's last days would be directed most intensely at God's chosen people. Rather than blaming the Jews for their own victimization, Bauman and others emphasized the demonic elements behind the current persecution and the surety of divine rescue from this "time of Jacob's trouble."[39]

These complex and conflicting beliefs help to explain the confusion which fundamentalist pundits experienced in trying to trace out fulfillments of prophecy in the contemporary affairs of world Jewry, and the mixed messages they sent out concerning the Jews' plight. In the early days of Hitler's regime, for example, fundamentalists leaders had trouble knowing what to believe about the Jews' situation. In 1933 and 1934 the *Moody Bible Institute Monthly* printed letters from German pastors who alleged that the "social democratic and communistic press" had fabricated reports of racist oppression. Editor James Gray seemed inclined to agree, but Solomon Birnbaum, head of Moody's Jewish Missions Department, rejected these reports. He insisted that all Jews, not just the radicals, were being persecuted, and he pleaded with his fellow fundamentalists to protest such savagery.[40]

In the ensuing years, several fundamentalist leaders began to speak out against anti-Semitism. Prophecy savants Donald Barnhouse and Louis Bauman and several Hebrew Christian organizations led the charge, reporting the persecution of world Jewry, especially in Nazi Germany, and denouncing the anti-Semitic propaganda that was gaining a hearing in the United States, even within their own movement. They warned that nations and individuals who persecuted the Jews would be punished, as had the Pharaoh of the Exodus and the Persian courtier Haman, who plotted against Esther and Mordecai. Some predicted an awful demise for Hitler, often likening him to Haman, who was executed by means of his own provisions for genocide.[41]

Yet some fundamentalist leaders were slow to repudiate anti-Semitic views. William Bell Riley, for example, protested that he did not believe in racial persecution and that he did believe that the Jews were still God's chosen people, but he insisted that rulers had a right to silence subversives. Not only did Riley believe that Jews as a group had become too powerful in Germany, but he suspected them of sedition in America as well. Nonbelieving Jews in the United States, he claimed, were "the most vicious atheists and the most intolerable Communists I have met."[42] How could someone who was professedly pro-Zionist entertain such outrageous views? Riley and other prominent fundamentalists such as Arno C. Gaebelein, a former missionary to Jews and pro-Zionist editor of the prophecy-oriented monthly, *Our Hope,* apparently had been persuaded that nonbelieving Jews in particular were prominent in a communist world conspiracy.[43] Their dispensationalist views greatly enhanced fundamentalists' propensity to look for great conspiracies behind human affairs. And the Jews, whom they thought would have a central role in the end-times, were easily linked to such theories. What is surprising, then, is not that some fundamentalist leaders held such views, but that only a minority of them did.

Robert Ross's study of Protestant journalism's coverage of the Holocaust shows that fundamentalists were the best informed of any American Protestants on the Jews' situation in Europe. Unlike the liberal Protestant spokesmen of the *Christian Century,* to cite one example, most fundamentalist leaders expressed a great deal of interest and concern.[44] Yet for all of the attention they received in print, the Jewish people held a rather low priority on fundamentalists' agenda. The many expressions of sympathy and outrage produced very little positive action. There were a few gestures of solidarity against anti-Semitism, such as a rally of Gentiles and Jews at the Hebrew Christian Alliance's annual conference at the Moody Memorial Church in 1936. There were some refugee relief efforts as well, most of it mobilized by the Jewish missionary boards, and at least one clandestine effort early in the war by American missionaries in Belgium and Portugal to help Jewish fugitives escape the Nazis.[45] But one looks in vain for any further action on behalf of persecuted Jewry.

So were fundamentalists the Jews' best friends or their worst enemies? In the final analysis, perhaps they were neither. The Jewish people had a curious place in fundamentalists' worldview. They were sharers in God's promises of salvation, but theirs would be an earthly redemption, while the Gentile believers were raptured off to heaven. So the Jews would be the primary actors in a doomsday the Christians would escape. For most fundamentalists, "the time of Jacob's trouble" was a portent of things to come, rather than an evil to be resisted. Sympathy mingled with suspicion in fundamentalists' perceptions of the Jews, but in the end, both were offered with a measure of detachment.

The Mark of the Beast: Social and Political Alienation

From the standpoint of America's activist, problem-solving culture, such detachment was a problem. Fundamentalists might draw consolation, vindication, and relevance from their dispensationalist views, but to outside observers the movement's alienation and passivity were more obvious. Since the Progressive Era, critics of the movement had charged that it was fundamentally disloyal to the Christian ethic and unpatriotic because it spurned the nation's reforming spirit.[46] Little had changed by 1936, when the Federal Council of Churches proclaimed that Christians were called to redeem the current age, and pointedly warned against the "impotent fatalism" that was lurking about the margins of church life.[47]

There was a great deal of truth to such criticisms, for the dispensationalist scenario pointed to the worsening of world affairs and suggested that efforts to bring about social improvement would ultimately fail. Fundamentalists expected to see the degeneration of civilization in the last days, and they claimed that it was illusory to think, as many liberal Protestants did, that the Kingdom of God was to be advanced by social reform. When World War II broke out in 1939, and *Time* magazine charged the churches with failure for not halting "Christendom's" march to war, Charles Trumbull countered that the churches' failure was rather in *attempting* to halt the march to war. "Christ never commissioned his Church to put an end to wars or convert the world," Trumbull lectured. "Christ called his Church to *evangelize* the world . . . and 'to take out of them a people for his name.'"[48] The establishment of God's kingdom on earth, dispensationalists insisted, was a promise to the Jews to be fulfilled by Christ's second coming and millennial reign. Therefore the Christian church was called to save souls, not reform society.

Dispensationalists tended to be suspicious of social reform campaigns. During the high tide of the Progressive movement, prophetic savants criticized the reformers' hopes of conquering the world's ills in the present age. In their darker moods, dispensationalists suggested that progressives' drive for governmental solutions was preparing the world for the reign of Antichrist. Progressivism marked the honest efforts of well-meaning people, but they were fundamentally mistaken about God's plan for the ages. Their efforts showed an unwitting movement toward the dictatorial spirit that would dominate the end-times.[49]

Predictably, fundamentalists looked askance at the New Deal's ventures into economic and social planning. Echoing the Lynds' observation that middle Americans in the 1930s were confused and dismayed by the strange times they were encountering, a correspondent of the *Sunday School Times* wrote in 1934 that she had seen her neighbor out in his field doing a crop survey in order to get cash for *not* planting corn. She tartly remarked that even her sow had been warned by the government not to be too prolific, "though half the world goes hungry." These were strange times, she said, when all had to be economists. She feared that the collar of "submission to a controlled economy" was already in place, for "strange forces" were moving, "not only in our own land but throughout the world."[50]

Dispensationalists had a good idea of where those forces were leading. The "present world movement," the editor of *Bibliotheca Sacra* judged, was "progressing away from democracy or republicanism toward dictatorial centralized power." Some of the actions of the New Dealers were strikingly similar to those prophesied as part of the Antichrist's regime, fundamentalists thought. The National Recovery Administration's Blue Eagle insignia aroused a great deal of speculation. One man wrote to the *New York Times* in 1933 that he "found this today in Revelation, 13th chapter, 16–17: 'And he causeth all, both small and great, rich and poor, free and bond, to receive a mark in their right hand, or in their foreheads: And that no man might buy and sell, save he that had the mark.'" This passage about the mark of the Beast was "arresting," he thought, given the current circumstances.[51] Here was another "rehearsal," another measure to prepare people to accept the Antichrist's regime when it came along.[52] The prophetic trend was clear; fundamentalists saw the great historic stamping machine introducing into the current social and political fabric patterns that bore a striking resemblance to what lay ahead. Preconditioned by their political instincts toward individualism and populist antielitism, it was relatively easy for fundamentalists to see Beastlike tendencies in New Deal economic planning and to remain alienated from the public arena. James M. Gray's call for serene detachment was fairly typical: "Whatever comes, the saints can remain undisturbed, for 'He is their refuge and their portion in the land of the living.'"[53]

The Great Conspiracy

This was the milder version of the fundamentalist response to current affairs in the 1930s. As has been well documented, dispensationalism could support a more extreme point of view. Not only was history displaying certain trends that would eventually unfold into the Apocalypse; but Satan was conspiring to bring about the apostasy of the church, the rise of the Antichrist and a revived Roman Empire, the growth of a great godless confederacy out of Russia, and the persecution of the Jews.

Conspiratorial thinking thus was a natural temptation for fundamentalists, who drew on strains found in earlier movements and traditions, notably the anti-Masonic "slave power conspiracy" myths of abolitionism and the Populists' indictments of international financiers, which often carried overtones of anti-Semitism.[54] These patterns of perception were seared into the movement's identity during the late stages of World War I and the 1920s. As fundamentalists experienced increasing conflict with their modernist counterparts in the church, they were reminded of the prophesied Great Apostasy. They also saw what appeared to be the fulfillment of prophecy in the Bolshevik Revolution. And in the cultural conflicts of the 1920s, fundamentalists became convinced that shadowy forces were working to undermine Christian America. Why had their crusade failed? Probably because they were fighting against secret, sinister forces, such as the ones identified in dispensational theology.[55]

This turn of mind comes through clearly in a report of the first annual convention, in late 1926, of The Defenders, the fundamentalist organization led by Gerald B. Winrod of Wichita, Kansas. Over a year had passed since the Scopes Trial, but still the audience wept as they heard a Victrola recording of the late William Jennings Bryan preaching on the Virgin Birth. Then William Bell Riley arose to preach. He slashed away at modernism, "Sovietism," and evolution in the schools. These threats were all connected, he insisted. The "near-universal" recognition of evolution in schoolbooks and "their rather general tendency toward atheism" was no accident, but the "work of some great organization with a sinister purpose."[56]

Of course, fundamentalists were not the only anxious Americans in the 1920s. One of the most famous examples of the fear of subversion at that time was Henry Ford's dalliance with anti-Semitism. Beginning in May of 1920, Ford published a two-year series of articles on the "Jewish problem" in his newspaper, the *Dearborn Independent*. Later collected into a four-volume text, *The International Jew*, these pieces purported to reveal a master conspiracy, led by Zionists, to undermine the American republic and dominate world affairs. The primary documentary source for this "exposé" was *The Protocols of the Elders of Zion*, a fabrication of Russian origin that purported to be the proceedings of a cabal of international Jewish leaders. It was these Elders who had stimulated the growth of alcoholism and pornography. They had popularized the doctrines of Nietzsche, Marx, and Darwin. They encouraged government corruption, incited wars, and were directing the courses of both international capitalism and revolutionary socialism.[57] Ford's promoters circulated several hundred thousand copies of *The International Jew*, and apparently won private praise from some influential leaders. The book became an embarrassment for Ford, and in response to the outcry it raised in the Jewish community, Ford repudiated the book and apologized in 1927. Nevertheless, *The International Jew* became the standard text for conspiracy theorists and anti-Semites during the next decade.[58]

Fundamentalist leaders were, for the most part, a bit put off by Ford's diatribes, but they were fascinated by the *Protocols*. This document seemed to correlate rather closely with the prophecies of the Antichrist. So in response to Ford's articles, some of the leading spokesmen of the movement, including the editors of *The King's Business, Our Hope,* and the *Moody Bible Institute Monthly,* vouched for the plausibility of the *Protocols.* The conspiracies detailed therein were consistent with Bible prophecy, these leaders observed. They agreed that multitudes of Jews were in fact in the process of forsaking their biblical heritage, and these apostates, several asserted, were fully capable of such scheming.[59] The *Protocols* received relatively little attention throughout the rest of the decade, however. Fundamentalists were so fully occupied by their disputes with modernists and evolutionists that they did not have the time to ruminate about conspiracies.

By the early 1930s this conspiratorial specter had returned, and for many fundamentalists, as for other American conservatives, it was "international communism." The Depression brought new life to radicalism in America, and there were numerous examples for the industrious Red-baiter to cite. In 1931, the editors of the *Moody Bible Institute Monthly* published a four-part series on "The Red Menace," tracing the purported role of American radicals in Stalin's plan for class war in the United States.[60] Thanks to Henry Ford, fundamentalist leaders had access to a conspiracy theory that both fit their dispensational scenario and gave credence to fears of communist subversion. If they had expressed some doubts earlier about the *Protocols'* authenticity, the social and political upheavals of the 1930s prompted a number of the movement's more prominent preachers to see a new and frightening fit between older conspiracy theories, the *Protocols,* current events, and Bible prophecy.

One of the most important promoters of such theories was Arno C. Gaebelein, the scholarly Bible teacher and editor of *Our Hope,* a prophecy-centered monthly. Gaebelein had become a scholar of Yiddish and Hebrew sacred literature while he operated a mission in New York's Lower East Side from 1891 to 1899. Since then he had worked full time as a dispensational author, journalist, and itinerant Bible teacher, and his opinion commanded great respect among fundamentalists.[61] Gaebelein presented his arguments and evidence for a great world conspiracy in a 1933 publication, *The Conflict of the Ages.* In it Gaebelein traced the growth of the "spirit of lawlessness"—from ancient Babylon through the Masonic orders, to Adam Weishaupt and the Bavarian Illuminati, to Rousseau and then Robespierre, and on through Karl Marx to the Bolshevik Revolution. This conspiracy had several aims: to overthrow legitimate government, the rule of law, and private property; to destroy national loyalty, traditional morals, and family life; and to crush the Christian religion. With the *Protocols* to fortify him, Gaebelein presented copious evidence, much of which seemed to have come from the Red-baiting literature of the day, to argue that Jews dominated Bolshevism and kindred radical movements worldwide. The current headquarters of the conspiracy was Moscow, but its tentacles were everywhere—even in the New Deal.[62]

Gaebelein's book received very favorable notice in the fundamentalist press, and it was joined by at least two other "exposés" of similar character by notable leaders in the movement, Gerald Winrod's *The Hidden Hand—The Protocols and the Coming Superman* (1932), and William Bell Riley's *The Protocols and Communism* (1934). For a time it looked as though this conspiratorial, anti-Semitic outlook would prevail in fundamentalist circles. Important leaders who were considered to be paragons of sanity and restraint, such as the venerable James M. Gray of the Moody Bible Institute, thought that the *Protocols,* even if some day proven a forgery, contained a revealing reflection of Satan's prophesied role in the last days.[63]

Gray and others were challenged on this point, however. In late 1933, the *Hebrew Christian Alliance Quarterly,* which represented many fundamentalist Jewish mission agencies and claimed a large national constituency of born-again Jews, charged that prominent fundamentalist leaders, including the editors of the *Moody Bible Institute Monthly,* the *Sunday School Times,* and *Revelation,* were tolerating anti-Semitism. The chief evidence for this charge was the editors' refusal to denounce the *Protocols* and their frequent treatment of this forgery as a valid source of prophetic insight.[64] Predictably, editors Gray, Trumbull, and Barnhouse were disturbed by these accusations. Trumbull claimed that the authorship of the *Protocols* was a question about which Christians could "honestly differ." Gray cited articles from the *Quarterly* itself that interpreted the *Protocols* the same way the *Moody Monthly* had. And Barnhouse replied that while he was "inclined to agree" that the *Protocols* were a forgery, he insisted that the "events of history have paralleled the Protocol policy in a remarkable way." Nevertheless, each reaffirmed their love of the Jewish people, drew distinctions between the "right-thinking, high-minded" majority of Jews and the corruption they perceived among "de-Judaized" Jews, and deplored anti-Semitism.[65]

As Timothy Weber points out, these leaders were deeply embarrassed because they truly did think of themselves as pro-Zionist and sympathetic to the Jews. The *Protocols* had become a liability, and they stopped citing the document.[66] Barnhouse told his readers that since the Swiss courts had definitively ruled the *Protocols* to be a hoax, continued quotation from them was "futile if not slanderous." Louis Bauman and another prominent Californian prophetic teacher, Keith Brooks, similarly denounced the *Protocols.* Brooks eventually gathered the signatures of sixty prominent fundamentalist leaders who agreed with him.[67]

Another group of fundamentalist leaders would not relinquish this conspiracy theory. The *Protocols* debate marked their point of no return as they wandered ever deeper into the realm of the far Right. In response to his critics, William Bell Riley insisted that the *Protocols* were authentic and claimed that Jewish conspirators were out to get him. Riley was so convinced of his position that contrary evidence and the scolding of his peers only persuaded him that the plot was broader than he had thought.[68] Gerald Winrod, the evangelist and publicist from Wichita, was probably the most notorious fundamentalist leader to join the far Right, thanks to his campaign for the Senate in 1936 and his trial as a Nazi sympathizer during the "Brown Scare" of the 1940s. Winrod professed no ill will toward Jews as a group, but he insisted that the prophetic facts pointed to a monstrous conspiracy on the part of apostate Jews. He accused the New Dealers of being a party to that plot, as were the Soviets; and he repeatedly praised Hitler for saving Germany from Jewish radicals.[69]

By the late 1930s, however, Winrod's and Riley's views on such matters were far from the norm among fundamentalist leaders. Even militant separatists such as J. Frank Norris were among those who signed Keith Brooks's statement deploring anti-Semitism. Likewise, the militant Regular Baptist leader David Otis Fuller of Grand Rapids preached a rousing sermon against Hitler and anti-Semitism to warm up his congregation for Joseph Cohn's annual visit on behalf of his Jewish mission.[70] What was at issue here was fundamentalists' sense of their relationship to the Jews. Most leaders considered themselves to be friends of the Jews who were concerned for their well-being and ultimately their salvation. They believed that the Jews were God's chosen people, the heirs of every promise recorded in the Old Testament, and under a divine protection which would bring their enemies to destruction. The last thing that most fundamentalist leaders wanted was to be called anti-Semites.

Yet they struggled with the deep ambivalence of their own position. At the same time that they stressed the Jews' chosenness, they also taught that the race was under judgment for rejecting Jesus' offer to establish the Messianic kingdom. So did anti-Semitism stem from Satan's hatred of the Lord's anointed or was it because of the race's own malefactions? Fundamentalist leaders never seemed to resolve this dilemma. Nevertheless, it was important to them to be considered friends of the Jews and not their enemies.[71]

The *Protocols* episode was largely forgotten by the mid-1940s, and the founding of the state of Israel in 1948 caused great jubilation and millennial expectancy in the dispensationalist camp. Since that time the movement has been staunchly pro-Israel. Fundamentalists' dalliance with the *Protocols* was more than a matter of being fooled once, however; it shows the suggestive power of dispensationalism as a support for conspiratorial thinking. In more recent decades the dispensational scenario has kept fundamentalists busy looking for plots of prophetic proportions behind world affairs, eyeing with great suspicion the rise of the United Nations, the Common Market, and, of course, the World Council of Churches. International communism remained at the top of their list of conspirators in the Cold War era. It is important to remember, as historian Leo Ribuffo put it, that "not all bigots were fundamentalists, and not all fundamentalists were bigots."[72] But with dispensationalism heightening their feelings of marginality and alienation and lending credence to conspiratorial thinking, fundamentalist leaders have entertained vicious ideas more than once.

A Plain Person's Religious Realism

The dispensationalist outlook fortified another viewpoint as well, one that might take the contemporary reader by surprise. Dispensationalism helped fundamentalists develop a critical perspective over against the cultural optimism that has dominated American public life. Even during the high tide of Progressivism in the 1910s, prophetic Bible teachers were saying that Americans' faith in human progress was fundamentally misguided; the world was not getting better. World War I was never for them the war to end all wars or the war to make the world safe for democracy. Liberal and radical dreams of remaking society and humanity never seduced them. While the first four decades of the twentieth century marked the progressive disillusionment of many western intellectuals, fundamentalist leaders, who had held none of these illusions in the first place, tried to delve behind the symptoms of modern civilization's crises and expose its deeper flaws.

Like many others in the 1930s, fundamentalists interpreted the depression as a day of reckoning for America. Sages have said this age marked the "Triumph of Man," wrote the editor of the Alliance Weekly, but the "machinery of which they proudly boasted" had "gotten out of control." People were searching for a way out, he observed, but few had the courage to admit that they had no hope.[73] The economic crisis was no mere temporary setback, warned the *Sunday School Times* editor in 1933. Only willfully ignorant and complacent observers, he argued, could deny the implications of World War I and the Depression. Not only was humanity a failure; it was being judged for its sins.

The coming of World War II generated another wave of fundamentalist criticism aimed at modern values. The Nazi blitzkrieg, observed Will Houghton in the summer of 1940, was a "great mechanical monster" created by evolutionary and materialistic concepts of progress.[74] A year later, during the season of college and university commencements, Houghton called these ceremonies a "grim . . . gathering of the impotent." The universities had produced the techniques and ideologies of destruction, and they owed the world a great apology for their "fat-headed conceit."[75] Once hooted down for such appraisals, fundamentalists now found they were in good company, as the *Sunday School Times* editor discovered when he read a review of Jacques Barzun's *Darwin, Marx, Wagner* (1941), a history of the ideas that were producing the bitter fruit of totalitarianism. Fundamentalists had been warning what would happen if modern civilization embraced godless ideologies, commented the editor. Now the world had been "set on fire" by the ideas of these "enemies of God."[76]

This critical perspective was, in effect, a plain person's parallel to the "realism" of the neo-orthodox ideological movement that sought to temper the cultural optimism of liberal Protestantism. Fundamentalists' interest in prophecy helped them identify some of the deepest flaws in American life. Fundamentalists agreed with neo-orthodox critics Karl Barth and Reinhold Niebuhr on at least one point: liberalism's faith in progress was naive and unfounded. Amidst economic depression, the rise of demonic tyrannies, and the growing threat of war, fundamentalists' earnest contentions sounded genuinely prophetic at times.

In other ways, however, fundamentalists couldn't have been more different from the neo-orthodox prophets, who held no brief for standing by in passive detachment. Sherwood Eddy, Reinhold Niebuhr, and others sought strategies to identify with the poor and to intervene in the fight against totalitarianism, even though they were convinced that their efforts were bound to be flawed.[77] Fundamentalists were also "realists," but their reading of the Bible and the times gave them very little motivation, if any, to "go out and crusade for political righteousness," as Donald Barnhouse put it.[78]

In retrospect, it is hard to see how fundamentalists could have developed an activist impulse in the 1930s and 1940s. Their forays into cultural politics in the 1920s had ended in defeat and ridicule. Their view of history and the future gave them no mandate to be reformers. And their marginal status gave them little hope of access to the nation's corridors of power. Social and political activism is dependent upon a sense of efficacy, the judgment that one can make a difference. Fundamentalists had little reason to believe that their voices could be heard in the arenas of public affairs in the 1930s, so it seemed practical for them to steer clear of such activity.

Liberal intellectuals have been exasperated with fundamentalists and other grassroots religious movements because they have so often opted for apolitical detachment or for a politics of reaction and resentment. But "regret is no substitute for historical analysis," as R. Laurence Moore so aptly puts it. Frustration with ordinary Americans' choices in belief and practice should not lead intellectuals to write these people off as a dysfunctional fringe led by demagogues. Fundamentalist leaders represented multitudes of citizens; the vast majority of these chieftains were decent and honorable; and their views were congruent with those of middle America. If some of their beliefs are fanciful and even reprehensible, they are also not all that unusual.[79] If for the sake of argument one can set aside the bizarre assertions of conspiracy and the propensity to become entangled in unsavory speculation about the Jewish people, fundamentalists' perspective on the past century has been fairly realistic. Will Houghton's tart observation that the airplane "has made it possible to be robbed at dinner time in New York and shot at midnight in Chicago" sounds as true today as it did over fifty years ago.[80] The world has not gotten better. On this point, history has proven the fundamentalists right and their opponents mistaken.[81]

Because of the "realism" that it offered, the dispensationalist outlook provided an effective way for the ordinary people who became fundamentalists to handle their personal discontent. Fundamentalists could set aside those frustrating aspects of modern life that they had little hope of controlling or even influencing and concentrate on those things that they thought they could manage, such as saving the spiritually lost and building supportive religious communities. Dispensationalism gave fundamentalists a view of the world that made sense out of their alienation and gave them a positive purpose.

Conclusion

Even though dispensational views profoundly informed fundamentalists' outlook, the result was different from that of earlier millenarian movements. Unlike the movements that erupted in medieval and early modern Europe, there were no fanatical self-identifications with the Lord's avenging host. Unlike the founder of the Mormons, no leading fundamentalist claimed to be the Almighty's prophet and revelator. Unlike the founder of the Shakers, none claimed to be united with the Godhead itself.[82] By comparison, twentieth-century fundamentalists followed a much more restrained, rationally argued form of millenarianism.[83]

If the dispensational outlook did not usually lend itself to fanaticism, it surely did add intensity. It fired fundamentalists' single-mindedness for evangelism and sharpened their desire to be found "spotless" in personal behavior at the Lord's return. The prospect of Jesus coming again at any moment, like a "thief in the night" (II Pet. 3:10), was a powerful prompting to live with "eternity's values in view," as fundamentalists put it.[84] Still, most seemed to find some equilibrium between their visions of the future and the demands of living from day to day. The anxious man who wrote to the *Sunday School Times* to ask how to make out his will in case of the rapture probably was exceptionally intense in his expectation.[85] The "any moment" rapture theory had its own built-in protection against fanaticism; since it held that "no man knoweth the day nor the hour" when Christ would return, one had to get on with one's life. The ideal was not dropping out of society but living as "heavenly minute men," wrote Donald Barnhouse. Believers should pursue their mundane tasks but remain ready "to leave it all for the greater work that lies ahead."[86]

Like more radical millenarians, fundamentalists were energized by the great and dazzling, larger-than-life drama they saw unfolding before them. It captured their imagination, reassuring them that the often frustrating and unattractive business of following the old-time religion in the modern world would be vindicated one day; God was still in control and he would reward those who remained faithful. Nevertheless, fundamentalists did not see themselves as key players in these end-times scenarios. They would be spectators, raptured off the scene before the prophesied events really began in full force. Their temptation was not toward the fanaticism that might come from identifying with God's prophets or avenging hosts so much it was toward social and political passivity.

Another important part of dispensationalism's charm for fundamentalists was the intellectual stimulation it provided. Learning "dispensational truth" and applying it to current events afforded the pleasure of piecing together a great puzzle. Figuring out God's plan for the ages with the help of a Scofield Reference Bible, some colorful charts, and detailed outlines and commentaries could give one satisfaction that everything fit together; it was all part of God's plan. For those whose marginality stemmed to a great extent from the lack of respect they received in intellectual circles, it was vindicating to be "in the know" when the world's experts seemed confounded. This inducement to self-study and the elevation of self-taught popular teachers provided fundamentalists with the satisfying experience of cutting down the world's arrogant intellectuals, who so ridiculed and despised born-again Christians.

Fundamentalists also drew fresh meaning for their own predicament from their millenarian views. Why were they, who were God's faithful followers, and the truest and most loyal Americans, being so despised and afflicted? It was all part of God's plan. There would be a millennium. But things had to get worse before they got better. Like their Puritan forebears, then, fundamentalists believed that such treatment was inevitable, that it was in fact a sign that they were God's vanguard in a great cosmic battle against Satan and his minions. The dispensational outlook not only helped fundamentalists understand that God was still in control and on their side; it justified their contentiousness and cultural alienation.[87]

In the end, however, what fundamentalists derived most from their dispensational views was simple comfort and encouragement. There was a solution to the world's chaos. The faithful's suffering would end, and they would be vindicated. God would deliver them, and Satan would be defeated. Some of them now living might not even experience death before Jesus came for them. This was the "blessed hope" with which God comforted them.

6

WILL REVIVAL COME?

Given fundamentalists' preoccupation with the "signs of the times" in the 1930s and their expectation that the world was going to continue to grow worse until Jesus returned, the last thing one would expect to hear from them was that they anticipated another great and general revival of born-again Christianity. But the record is clear: repeatedly, and with growing intensity, fundamentalists called for and looked longingly toward a spiritual quickening in the churches and a great religious awakening in their land. Fundamentalist leaders held out both hopes—of rapture and revival—with little sense of contradiction.

Witness, for example, the editorial comments of Donald Barnhouse during the depths of the Depression in 1932. Barnhouse noted that stores were taking out looting insurance because they feared riots and revolution among the unemployed. He also stated that biblical prophecy pointed to an imminent Second Coming. And yet, he observed, many Christian leaders believed that a "great spiritual awakening" might come soon. So which would it be: revolution, rapture, or revival? While he thought that any one of these events, or perhaps a combination of them, could descend at any moment, Barnhouse said he was hoping to see a revival, "like unto the movement that swept England under the Wesleys and Whitefield."[1]

When Will Houghton surveyed public affairs late in 1938, he came to similar conclusions: "It has been a bad year for democracy." War with Hitler looked inevitable, and even in America, many seemed to be turning to fascism. Houghton sensed that this creeping "dictator spirit" was foreshadowing the rise of the Antichrist, so he concluded that the year's end was bringing everyone "a year nearer the coming of the Lord." Yet he stressed that the future also might bring "the dissolution—apart from revival—of the type of government established by our fathers." The only recourse, he believed, was for America to come "back to the Bible" through another Great Awakening.[2]

110

These views were not anomalous, but they do stand in stark contrast to the many predictions of an inevitable, irreversible, and imminent doom that emanated from the fundamentalists' camps during the 1930s. It is difficult to see how fundamentalist leaders could seriously entertain thoughts of launching a national revival. Given the depth of their alienation, one might expect that fundamentalists would have been content to consign America to perdition and build a religious ghetto in which to await the Second Coming. But many fundamentalists allowed millenarian logic to give way to some more basic and powerful impulses. At the same time it was generating a separatist movement, fundamentalism was also producing a circle of like-minded leaders who set out to bring revival to America and their message to the world.

One simply cannot understand the recovery of fundamentalism as a national public force without exploring this crashing contradiction in fundamentalist ideology, what George Marsden called the "paradox of revivalist fundamentalism."[3] At the same time they predicted the imminent arrival of the cataclysmic end-times, fundamentalists yearned for another Great Awakening that would revive the church's integrity and power, restore the culture's religious character, and bring back national prosperity. Apparently unable to live with the millenarian reasoning that pointed to the irreversible declension of America along with the rest of the world, fundamentalists tempered their "hope of his appearing," as they called it, with yearning for revival, and they increased their efforts to bring one about.

From Alienation to Hope

As we have seen, fundamentalists' outlook in the 1930s was profoundly colored by the conviction that the last days of the present age were at hand. What were the prospects for the "true church," then, in these times of decline and apostasy? Fundamentalists believed that God would continue to use his "faithful remnant" to witness to the truth and gather out of the world a "people for His name" (Acts 15:14). Until Jesus came for them at the Rapture, Bible-believing Christians were to win the lost, heed the signs of the times, keep themselves pure from error, and expose and condemn false religion. This outlook seemed to offer little promise for any reversal of the growing apostasy in organized Christianity and the increasing grip of the "mystery of iniquity" (II Thess. 2:7) on the larger world.[4] A venerable Bible teacher was asked in the 1930s why none of the current leaders seemed to match the stature of the evangelical giants of his generation. The sage replied that the prophetic Bible teachers had been raised up by God to give a final witness to the truth before the end of the age. He expected no revival before the Lord's return.[5]

Such lamentations about the sorry state of the church and the world abounded, but they were only one facet of the movement's outlook in the 1930s. Consider "A Call to Prayer for Revival," issued in 1932 by a Chicago organization called the Great Commission Prayer League. Acknowledging that the "end of this age" was fast approaching, when the world would see the "'distress of nations'" and "'men's hearts failing them for fear,'" (Luke 21:25, 26) the writer insisted that it "still might please God to send revival."[6] During prosperous times, explained the editor of the *Moody Monthly,* people forget God. But when dark days come, as they surely had in those days of economic depression, people begin to examine their lives.[7] Misfortune had brought widespread repentance and revival in the past, fundamentalist leaders believed. Many cited the Prayer Meeting Revival of 1857, when economic and political distress had prompted widespread turning to God. In other words, the worst of times could, in God's economy, become the best of times.[8]

Indeed, a number of prominent fundamentalists, in their efforts to discern the tenor of the times, thought that they heard some sweeter notes than one might think possible, given their millenarian frame of mind. "Surely," said one leader, using a quaint Old Testament metaphor, "there is 'the sound of a going in the tops of the mulberry trees,' and we should be crying out to God to break forth with mighty power" to revive the church.[9] Others were more definite in their hopes. J. Elwin Wright, a lay evangelist from New England, refused to let the nation's economic woes dampen his expectation of an imminent revival. "There has never been a time in my memory," he wrote in late 1931, "when every condition seemed so favorable" for a sweeping revival.[10]

Given the firm grip that dispensationalism and its expectations of growing apostasy had on fundamentalists, these hopes had to be reconciled with the predictions of an imminent apocalypse. Was revival still possible in these "last days"? Nearly everyone who called for a great awakening addressed this question. An Irish evangelist, J. Edwin Orr, expressed his exasperation with Americans who claimed that "a Revival is impossible before the Lord comes." Orr argued that while the Bible did indeed predict apostasy, "every period of apostasy has been paralleled by a period of intense witness." Apostasy and spiritual renewal would coincide, like the wheat and the tares of Jesus' parable. Orr insisted that "the truest preparation for the coming of Christ is a quickening in the Body of Christ." Furthermore, he argued, the Bible predicted a "latter rain" before God's final harvest (James 5:7); there would be a great revival just preceding the Second Coming.[11]

Orr's explanation ran contrary to the standard dispensational interpretation, which held that the "latter rain" prophecies were promises of blessing to the Jews that would be fulfilled after the rapture of the church.[12] Nevertheless, not one eminent fundamentalist publicly denied the possibility of another great revival. Harry Ironside, pastor of the Moody Memorial Church and perhaps the preeminent dispensationalist spokesman of his day, declared that "if there is world-wide brokenness of spirit . . . , God will delight to do some mighty work before the coming again of His blessed Son."[13] Indeed, the dispensational system was flexible enough in theory to allow for some temporary reprieves in the downward spiral toward Armageddon. The "church age" was in fact not a true dispensation, but what some prophecy teachers called the "Great Parenthesis," in which God's prophetic countdown was placed on hold for an indefinite period. Jesus could come tomorrow; then again, his appearing might be a generation away.[14]

Some fundamentalists had to struggle with their millenarian instincts, however, in order to expect and seek another revival. Revivalist Armin Gesswein confessed that for some time his belief in "the growing apostasy" paralyzed his "faith for the Lord to send Holy Ghost revivals." Then he came to see the matter in a different light. Instead of asking whether the prophetic countdown would allow another revival, he began to ask whether he believed that the Holy Spirit was still active in the world.[15] Gesswein was not alone in his struggle. Other revival advocates seemed to equate pessimism about revival with paralyzing doubts about the Spirit's power, and they vehemently denounced such hopelessness. Indeed, their newfound fervency for revival suggests that they were trying to exorcise their earlier despair.[16] But why did fundamentalists so fervently want, expect, and promote revival at this particular time, the 1930s and early 1940s? In order to answer this question, we need to probe deeper into their ideas about revival.

The Cure for Spiritual Infirmity

Fundamentalists' hope for revival was an old and powerful part of their legacy as American evangelicals. Revival heirlooms from the mid-nineteenth century abounded in the movement, especially a bountiful store of lore and literature. Among the many books on revival, one overshadowed all others; it was Charles G. Finney's *Lectures on Revivals of Religion* (1835).[17] Following Finney, most fundamentalist revival promoters started with a simple definition of revival. It was, said J. Edwin Orr, "a time of extraordinary religious awakening." Borrowing also from Finney the idea that revivals are prompted by hard times, when spiritual and material well-being are at a low ebb, Orr insisted that revival could begin only when the church repented of its sins and sought spiritual recovery.[18] Other steps followed, the revivalists taught: repentance led to a new desire for revival, which led to fervent and persistent prayer for revival; then came the revival, giving Christians and their churches a new sense of restoration, healing, and empowerment. The final step was a great and general awakening, in which the churches would cause this revival to break out in society and result in a surge of religious interest and social reformation.[19]

At first glance, these formulas seemed as least as old as Finney's *Lectures*. But there were some strikingly different elements as well. Like their second most influential revival tutor, Jonathan Edwards, the fundamentalist awakeners insisted that revivals were extraordinary events, that in them the Spirit of God moved in surprising and miraculous ways. Finney's stress on God's use of natural and humanly devised means to promote revivals seemed to have become less attractive. The problem, as several revival advocates saw it, was that revivalism had been corrupted in many American churches. Complained Edwin Orr, the word revival had come to mean "eight days of meetings for a membership drive—generally arranged for August." Such meetings had become so mechanical and lacking in extraordinary results that they were making a mockery of the whole idea. By contrast, when a student-initiated revival broke out at Wheaton College in the spring of 1936, President Buswell thought it was utterly authentic because it occurred "quite independent of human instruments."[20]

These yearnings for something more earth-shaking than the annual evangelistic campaign, something downright "Pentecostal," as some referred to it, indicated that by the 1930s a number of the movement's leaders sensed a spiritual dryness in their midst. Fundamentalism was one of the more ideological and rationally oriented of the modern evangelical movements, and it seems to have been vulnerable to this kind of malaise. Many fundamentalists had become rather conservative about religious emotions. They often expressed disapproval of the emotional intensity of their holiness and pentecostal cousins. Even during the most sacred moment in fundamentalist church services, when people responded to the invitation to come forward and find assurance of their salvation, they were often counselled to avoid gauging their standing with God by how they felt. Faith was rather a matter of giving rational assent to God's promise of salvation.[21]

Fundamentalism was not without its emotional satisfactions. The miracle of conversion was still deeply moving for the observer or the spiritual counsellor as well as for the one experiencing it, even if their feelings were somewhat suppressed. Fundamentalists also felt encouraged when their champions scourged modernism and defended the fundamentals of supernatural Christianity.[22] They felt affirmed and vindicated when their dispensational Bible teachers found prophetic trends in current events. But this ideological emphasis seemed to some leaders to have produced a cool and arid spirit within the movement. People needed something more deeply satisfying than a rational acceptance of their faith and intellectual defenses of it. Compared to the profundity of feeling that their respective modes of spirituality afforded the sacramentalists, the holiness Wesleyans, and especially the pentecostals, fundamentalists' spiritual fare could seem rather plain.[23] So at the same time that fundamentalist leaders were deploring the "tongues speakers'" emotional extravagance and credulous claims of miracles, many in their movement were longing to have their souls rekindled "with fire from above," as the old gospel song put it.

Expressions of spiritual thirst surfaced often in the revivalists' laments and calls for repentance. Vance Havner, one of the most acute internal critics of fundamentalism, confessed that "too much orthodoxy is correct and sound but . . . it does not glow and burn, it does not stir the wells of the heart, it has lost its hallelujah, it is too much like a catechism and not enough like a camp meeting."[24] Although Havner himself was a celebrity on the Bible conference circuit, he deplored the passivity and complacency that an overabundance of Bible lectures seemed to produce. He complained that thousands "go from meeting to meeting . . . absorbing information like sponges, but not really doing anything about it after they hear it."[25] Ernest M. Wadsworth, head of the Great Commission Prayer League in Chicago, saw no lack of exertion in the movement, but he wondered whether there was any unction behind it. "A revival is something more than an increase of religious activity," he sighed. People "want something supernatural," he insisted, "they crave a movement that can be called in very truth a work of God."[26]

The desire for "something supernatural" prompted fundamentalist leaders to revive some of their inherited beliefs about the power of the Holy Spirit. The forebears of fundamentalism in Moody's day had been preoccupied with the work of the Spirit in the life of the Christian. Under the influence of the larger holiness movement, Moody and every other notable leader of his circle came to believe that God intended for them to gain victory over spiritual ineffectiveness as they surrendered themselves to him and then received fresh anointings, infillings, or, as some were convinced, the baptism of the Holy Spirit.[27] Fundamentalists shared this holiness ancestry with pentecostals, but perhaps as a reaction against pentecostalism, their interest in the power of the Holy Spirit seemed to have slackened considerably by the 1920s. Nevertheless, the Higher Christian Life advocates in the movement's faith missions and Bible schools kept this particular brand of piety alive within the movement.[28] As complaints about spiritual coldness and ineffective ministry arose alongside calls for revival, holiness teaching made a comeback within fundamentalism during the late 1930s and early 1940s.

The operative word in these renewed discussions of the Holy Spirit and revival was power. This emphasis was not new, but it seems fair to suggest that fundamentalists' alienated stance in the 1930s made it all the more attractive. Not only did fundamentalists feel lacking in personal spiritual fulfillment and effectiveness, they felt impotent in American life more generally. So they sought spiritual channels for regaining a measure of confidence in their own efficacy. Was spiritual power—resulting in victorious Christian living, refreshed and vibrant churches, missionary expansion, and a great harvest of souls—still available in secular modern America? Feeling like outcasts in the land their ancestors had once spiritually dominated, fundamentalists wanted to believe that they could be empowered yet again.

The history of revivalism gave them hope. As the self-proclaimed heirs of the Anglo-American revival tradition traced back to Jonathan Edwards, George Whitefield, and the Wesleys, fundamentalists could see a sine-wave pattern of declension and revival that encouraged them to look for relief. Histories of revivals proliferated in the 1930s and early 1940s, and more often than not, the authors stated their hopes that, as one put it, "the recounting of these times of blessing [will] encourage us to believe that once again God is waiting to visit his church with a new outpouring of the Holy Spirit."[29] Revival histories usually began, if not with the Old Testament,[30] then by recalling the eighteenth-century awakenings in Great Britain and America, then perhaps the great southern revival of 1800–1805, certainly Finney's remarkable campaigns in the 1820s and 1830s, the 1857–1858 "Prayer Meeting Revival," Moody's urban crusades in the 1870s and 1880s, and the Welsh revival of 1903–1905.[31] The implication was clear: since revivals had graced every generation in modern memory, present-day believers could hope for one in their own time.

The revival that fundamentalist awakeners seemed to find most compelling and suggestive was the Prayer Meeting Revival of the mid-nineteenth century. This awakening, as one author after another pointed out, came in an era of deep economic, political, and spiritual malaise. Its initial setting was urban, commercial, and middle-class, it spread along modern networks of communication, and its purported result was the widespread restoration of religious commitment and moral resolve in a time of deep national crisis.[32] This recognizably modern setting spoke to fundamentalists of their own predicament and longings. As one author put it, "this story of what God did more than three-quarters of a century ago ought mightily to arouse all who are aware of our loss of the supernatural."[33] Something miraculous could happen even in this secular age. The world of Jack Benny, Lucky Strikes and Texaco, with its urban landscapes dominated by billboards, trolley lines, and skyscrapers, could be induced to acknowledge God's presence and authority. Pining for new spiritual power and for vindication in a land that had been parched by the dry winds of modernity, fundamentalists were encouraged to expect showers of blessing. Years of ridicule and ostracism would seem worth it all when the realm of the spirit invaded the mundane world in which they lived.

Revivalism as Cultural Politics

The hope of such an invasion was exceedingly attractive to fundamentalists for reasons that transcended personal reassurance or fresh strength and legitimacy for their group. The history of revivals promised these blessings and one more as well: the reformation of society. Fundamentalists' favorite biblical promise concerning revival came from II Chronicles 7:14, in which the Lord told King Solomon: "If my people, which are called by my name, shall humble themselves, and pray, and seek my face, and turn from their wicked ways; then will I hear from heaven, and will forgive their sin, and will heal their land." During years of religious declension, economic depression, drought and political upheaval, fundamentalist leaders eagerly latched onto this promise for national healing. In the six decades since Finney's death, they and other evangelicals had been stripped of their dominance in American culture. Another Great Awakening in America would not only vindicate their stand for Christian spirituality but do much to reinstate America's lost evangelical character. The bitter defeats of their attempts in the 1920s to reverse the decline of "Christian America" had soured them on overtly political crusades, and the cataclysmic upheavals of the 1930s pointed toward an imminent Second Coming. But for the most part, fundamentalist leaders were not content to occupy the margins of American life. Haunted by the "Christian America" of their memory and imagination, fundamentalists could not shake the proprietary responsibility they felt for their nation's character. "God has a stake in the nation," Will Houghton declared, and because they believed this to be true, fundamentalists still felt called to be its guardians.[34] Seemingly against all millenarian logic, they held out hope for the healing of their land through the restoration of an evangelical moral consensus. Reform crusades had failed, but perhaps that was because revival was God's way of bringing reform.

Indeed, a revivalistic understanding of public responsibility was basic to fundamentalists' sense of mission. This older strain of evangelical cultural duty competed with the rhetoric of alienation in fundamentalists' comments on current affairs. A sense of God's stake in the nation was part of fundamentalists' inheritance from the Puritans. Fundamentalist leaders essentially agreed with John Winthrop, the founding governor of Massachusetts Bay Colony, who declared that "it is of the nature and essence of every society to be knitt together by some Covenant, either expressed or implyed."[35] Such a covenant, which entailed promises made to one another for the common welfare and promises made to God to live according to his laws, was thought by many to be the foundation of American public life.

This covenantal basis for Christians' civic responsibility had been reshaped over the years by American pluralism and by the eventual separation of church and state. The Puritans' theocratic ideas of "godly rule" were thus converted by their nineteenth-century descendants, whether Unitarian or evangelical, into a concern for the moral discipline and "godly character" of the nation's citizens, which was thought necessary for the Republic's health. The values of individual freedom, respect for law, and voluntary approaches to social betterment drove this "neo-Puritan" tradition, and although it certainly experienced opposition, it became the dominant cultural and political force in the antebellum North.[36]

For evangelical Protestants, who represented the nation's most influential religious persuasion by the mid-nineteenth century, the chief engine of social reform (in its Northern version) or social preservation (in the South) was the revival. Revivals would change people's hearts, and with this new motivation they would voluntarily organize and engage in activity for the common good. Even though evangelicals were not averse to political solutions, their more natural inclination was to pursue the reformation of manners, morals, and even social structures through the religiously founded special-purpose societies that sprang up in the wake of revivals. Thus an "evangelical Whig" tradition emerged, which by means of revivalism and voluntary reform sought to provide the virtuous political culture that would keep the American republic true to its covenant.[37]

Revivalism and social reform had become somewhat more independent of each other by the late nineteenth century, but the linkages were still evident on either side of the growing divide in Protestant circles. Religious and political liberals still used revivalist rhetoric and techniques to promote the Progressive movement's agenda, while conservative revivalists such as Dwight L. Moody still saw their soul-saving urban campaigns as means to shore up the character of "Christian America." Moody did much to shape the outlook that would pervade fundamentalism. On the one hand, he claimed that he looked "on this world as a wrecked vessel. God has given me a life-boat, and said to me, 'Moody, save all you can.'"[38] Yet Moody was no advocate of avoiding one's temporal duties. During the McKinley-Bryan presidential contest, he chided a fellow evangelist who said that he had no political outlook because his citizenship was in heaven. "Better get it down to earth for the next sixty days," Moody told him.[39] Still, Moody believed that revivalism was a more powerful engine for social renewal, and his urban campaigns were aimed at achieving such results.[40]

Fundamentalists continually chastised progressives, Social Gospelers, and New Dealers for seeking to redeem America through social engineering, and these criticisms were often coupled with millenarian maxims about the ultimate hopelessness of human reform efforts. This rhetoric has sometimes led historians to think that fundamentalists were apolitical. They were nothing of the sort, if one thinks of politics in broader terms as contests for cultural power and influence. Tempted as they might have been by the 1930s to give up on reform efforts and retreat to their religious subculture to await the Rapture, fundamentalists were haunted by the idea that God still had a special claim on their nation and that they still had a responsible social role to play. The memory of a day when America was a much more evangelical place possessed them as well, and the history of revivals suggested that another of these manifestations of God's power could restore much of their lost influence. Issue-oriented public campaigns had failed in the wake of the Scopes trial, but perhaps the revival was the more powerful weapon for cultural warfare.

The most commonly expressed political trait in fundamentalist thinking was what one might call revivalist individualism, which stressed that the regeneration of individuals was the surest way to bring lasting reform. As for the issue of the imminent Second Coming, fundamentalist leaders most often agreed with Moody's notion of dual citizenship: Christians' double duty was to save souls out of this world and to help people get along in the world—"holding the fort," as it were—until Jesus returned.[41] Thus in 1935 the editors of the *Moody Monthly* announced their determination to comment frequently on public affairs and especially, they said, to warn against socialism, fascism, and communism. Their working philosophy, they said, was "the individualism that forms the warp and woof of the Bible and gives meaning to the Cross of Christ."[42] A genuine reformation of society, they insisted, was possible only through the transformation of individuals.

Political progressives and their partners in clerical garb, the Social Gospellers, may have been well-meaning, but they were greatly confused, fundamentalist leaders insisted. They were trying to institute the Kingdom of God on earth, yet the Kingdom was not God's program for this age but for the next. In this age, one spokesman argued, "The whole mission of the Church is to be summed up in the word 'witness.'" When the church took up "social righteousness" and neglected its evangelistic task, too often the result was the freedom-crushing union of church and state and the moral decay of society. Preachers did the most social good when they preached the gospel of individual redemption.[43]

That might seem like counsel for detachment from politics. And indeed, quite a few fundamentalists followed only Moody's "lifeboat" call while ignoring his other call to "hold the fort." But the genius of the revival tradition for these disillusioned crusaders was that it promised its adherents tremendous power for social transformation if they would simply stick to the task of evangelization.[44] There were varying shades of interest in political and social reform measures within fundamentalism,[45] but the underlying issue for all of them was not what one proposed to do about "the *evils* of sin," as Toronto preacher Oswald J. Smith put it, but about sin itself. "My Lord can make drunkards sober," he preached. "He can make harlots pure. Yes, and He can make the rich generous, and employers just. He can transform the dwellers of slums into respectable citizens. . . . He can save His people from their sins."[46] So for fundamentalists, the God-ordained means for social uplift was the gospel of personal redemption by which individuals would be transformed, one by one.[47]

Revivalism, moreover, promised to touch off a process that might be faster and more sweeping, a Great Awakening, which would achieve personal and social transformation on a truly national scale. Revivalism was a potent weapon in the war for America's soul, indeed the only one that fundamentalists fully trusted. Perhaps the reason for their political failures in the 1920s, some speculated, was that revival was the only means of cultural regeneration that God still deigned to use. So fundamentalist promoters of revival in the 1930s and 1940s hammered away with II Chronicles 7:14. If Christians would humble themselves, confess their sins, and pray, revival would be on its way, and the resulting Great Awakening would restore God's blessing to America—and God's people to their rightful influence.[48]

Their revivalist heritage, then, suggested to fundamentalists that they had another chance to take the offensive. The histories of revivals suggested a cyclical pattern of religious and cultural boom and bust, and by the reckoning of a number of fundamentalist revival teachers in the 1930s and 1940s, things were bad enough for them to start looking for signs of the start of something good.[49] Quoting Finney, one recalled that "a 'Revival of Religion' presupposes a declension."[50] Just when things seemed so hopeless they could scarcely get worse, that was the time to pray, work for revival, and expect to see one soon. This pattern offered fundamentalists a way to convert the negative force of their defeats and marginalization into a positive source of energy for a reversal of fortunes. Fundamentalists' revival theories provided a way for them to choose hope over despair and to aim at something they believed was more positive: the restoration of a Christian America.

Mobilizing for a Revival

As these hopes began to flicker and flare during the 1930s and early 1940s, a complex and varied movement for revival began to stir within the ranks of fundamentalism. By the late 1940s this trend would merge with parallel drives among other evangelicals and result in a major pan-evangelical resurgence that captured national attention. In the late 1920s and early 1930s, however, when a small number of revival advocates began their work, they were almost invisible. As time went on, however, they stimulated growing interest and expectation within fundamentalism, and their agitation eventually helped to create a great groundswell of expectation and activity.

One of the most remarkable of these behind-the-scenes revival promoters was Grace Winona Woods, who, with her husband, Dr. Henry M. Woods, served with the southern Presbyterian mission in China. During the early 1920s, the Woodses were involved in the Bible Union of China, an antimodernist organization that attracted some two thousand expatriate members, or about 30 percent of the missionaries in China. Dr. Woods was especially active in the movement; among his contributions was *The Bible Encyclopedia for the Chinese Church* (1925), the fruit of several years of compiling, editing, and translating. This project was part of the Bible Union's program to counteract theological liberalism in China by making conservative literature more accessible.[51]

But for Grace Woods, something else happened while she and her husband were in China that was more important than defending the fundamentals of the faith. On New Year's Day 1924 in Shanghai, the Woodses took part in a day of prayer and fasting with a band of Christian leaders, notably D. E. Hoste, general director of the China Inland Mission; evangelist Ruth Paxson, the former U.S.A. Secretary of the YWCA; and several Chinese Christians, notably the evangelist Dr. Dora Yu. They prayed for worldwide revival, formed a "World Wide Revival Prayer Movement," and were given spiritual assurance that a sign was on the way. The next year, they were swept up in what seemed to Grace Woods to be a remarkable and spontaneous revival in the churches of Shanghai.

In 1926, after the Woodses returned to the United States and settled in Ventnor, New Jersey, Grace Woods began a new ministry. She compiled and published a book, *The Half Can Never Be Told* (1927), which combined a short account of the "Prayer Meeting Revival" of 1857–1858 with a narrative of the 1925 Shanghai revival. She sent out thousands of copies to missionaries around the globe and to the leading evangelicals of the English-speaking world. She was able to attract the interest and support of the editors of two major evangelical papers, the *Sunday School Times* of Philadelphia and the *Life of Faith,* published in London. With these journals' publicity and endorsement, demand for her book grew. All told, over two hundred thousand copies of the little book were circulated.

This was just the beginning, for it provided Woods with a worldwide network of readers, correspondents, and supporters for the World Wide Revival Prayer Movement. Prompted by this overwhelming expression of interest, she began to produce a series of prayer letters and a number of additional books on revival during the 1930s and early 1940s. The point of all of this, Woods made clear, was to encourage Christians worldwide to fast and pray for revival, to spread the news of local revivals, and to point to signs of an impending worldwide awakening. It was a remarkable exercise in generating enthusiasm, expectations, and support for revival efforts, made ironic by the fact that Grace Woods and her circle believed that human agency would play a subordinate role, at most, in the coming world revival.[52]

Other enterprises similar to the World Wide Revival Prayer Movement sprang to life. Ernest M. Wadsworth's Great Commission Prayer League, with offices in Chicago, was one such agency. It produced leaflets, booklets, news-letters, and conferences—all to promote prayer for revival. Another similar agency was the Million Testaments Campaign, out of Philadelphia, headed by George T. B. Davis, a veteran revivalist who had been at the Woodses' New Year's prayer meeting in Shanghai in 1924. The Million Testaments Campaign, as one might guess, specialized in distributing Scripture portions, but it also sent out thousands of pledge cards urging prayers for revival.[53] The premise was that revival would come as God's answer to persistent prayer, but it is clear that these efforts in themselves did a great deal to mobilize people and resources.

While these materials made their way to hundreds of thousands of readers, the revival message circulated in more personal form as well. A variety of eminent pastors, evangelists, and other leaders who edited magazines or ran Bible schools were calling for revival, but one in particular made it the most important part of his ministry. He was J. Edwin Orr, a young evangelist from Northern Ireland. In an astonishing feat, Orr made evangelistic and revival-teaching tours of Great Britain, the Middle East, northern Europe, Canada, Australia and New Zealand, the United States, China, and South Africa; and he published small books that recounted his experiences on each of these excursions—all within about five years in the mid-1930s. Orr urged his audiences to distinguish between the routinized evangelistic campaigns that passed for revivals and the real thing, which was an extraordinary outpouring of spiritual fullness and power. Everywhere he went, Orr exposed Christians' worldliness and taught that for a true revival to take place, the church must first repent. Orr was well received throughout the United States, and apparently he helped to prompt local student awakenings at Wheaton College, Columbia Bible College, and elsewhere in 1936.[54] Eventually, the demand for his leadership in revival conferences and prayer retreats would bring him to Los Angeles in 1948 to organize small bands for prayer on a citywide basis. These meetings were designed to prepare for the fall 1949 evangelistic campaign of a young preacher named Billy Graham.[55]

But that is getting ahead of the story. During the 1930s and 1940s, Orr and other revival advocates were building networks of interest and support for revival. Their networking was critical because even though the fundamentalist movement was thriving on the local level during these years and producing, in the aggregate, an amazing amount of religious activity, it did so in isolated local pockets. Ministers and lay activists alike knew little about their movement's national scope. A number of fundamentalist leaders made it their business to help their constituents see the larger pattern of their movement's activity across the continent and to draw encouragement from it. Donald Grey Barnhouse of Philadelphia, one of the better-traveled fundamentalist leaders, boldly announced in 1934 that the revival had already begun. He cited the more than one thousand students enrolled in Bible institutes in Philadelphia, the "Spirit-led young people" who dominated the city's Christian Endeavor societies, and the many "witnesses to the truth" broadcasting on the nation's radio waves. He noted further that some one thousand congregations now belonged to J. Elwin Wright's New England Fellowship and that evangelical foreign mission boards were meeting budgets and sending out new missionaries in spite of the depression. The reason many more did not know that a revival was occurring, he explained, was that they were isolated from the "fellowship of revival" in communities where "the apostasy" was dominant.[56]

Elwin Wright had been working to counter this problem for a number of years, and in addition to the array of conferences, cooperative ministries and publications his New England Fellowship was producing, he hoped to encourage his constituents to envision another Great Awakening for New England. In order to build morale and visibly display collective strength, Wright planned a massive "Bible Demonstration Day" rally in 1935. Thought foolish to reserve Boston Garden for such an event, Wright was gratified when a stadium-filling sixteen thousand people showed up. This meeting helped cement new friendships among area evangelical leaders and bolstered the courage of those who, Wright said, "had been under the mistaken impression that 'only I am left.'"[57]

Chicago was a center for revivalistic hopes and enterprises, and there in 1930 a vigorous laymen's movement arose. It was called the Christian Business Men's Committees, the first chapter of which was formed in 1930 by C. B. Hedstrom, a businessman and a member of a Swedish Evangelical Covenant congregation on the city's north side. Hedstrom and other born-again businessmen who worked in the office canyons of Chicago's "Loop" business district organized their "CBMC" for fellowship and to take on some evangelistic projects.

This model spread gradually at first, then began to accelerate by the early 1940s, thanks in part to the enthusiastic promotion of the evangelist Paul W. Rood of Chicago, who succeeded W. B. Riley as president of the World's Christian Fundamentals Association. Rood took the CBMC idea with him to California when he began an affiliation with BIOLA in the mid-1930s, and he convinced leading fundamentalist businessmen in West Coast cities to form new committees. From 5 committees in 1938 the CBMC grew at such an explosive rate during the 1940s that it reported 75 committees in operation by 1944 and 162 by 1947. These groups took on increasingly ambitious evangelistic projects, expanding from their customary lunch-break services in downtown theaters to sponsor weekly radio shows, youth rallies, and servicemen's centers during the war. By the mid-1940s, the CBMCs were beginning to organize citywide evangelistic meetings, the scale of which had not been seen since Billy Sunday was at his peak.[58] Was this the prelude to revival? Many were beginning to wonder. Wrote the ever hopeful Elwin Wright after a coast-to-coast tour in 1945, America was "more ripe for revival than I have ever seen it."[59]

Conclusion

The fact that Wright seems to have said something like this every year after 1930 is not nearly so important as the fundamentalist revival movement's growing expectancy and increasing momentum. For fundamentalists, who had endured so much ridicule and seemed so intent on forecasting the imminent doom of civilization, these expressions of hope for revival were both paradoxical and a self-fulfilling prophecy. Even though the revival theorists kept insisting that the revival, in order to be authentic, had to be humanly inexplicable, they did not discourage the activists from mobilizing. The result was a revival of revivalism, even if the mythic Great Awakening the revival promoters envisioned always seemed to escape their grasp. What fundamentalists did hear was a continual "sound of a going" that kept them expectant and active and prevented them from descending into inert despair. They could be revived and America could be saved. Whether it was by fire from above or by the heat generated from their own ardent efforts, fundamentalists felt rekindled.

The Founders. Orbiting around C.I. Scofield, the chief luminary of the World Conference on Christian Fundamentals held in Philadelphia in 1919, are the movement's early leaders, notably William Bell Riley (8), Reuben A. Torrey (4), James M. Gray (5), and Paul Rader (6).

The Separatists. Robert T. Ketcham (*upper left*), the Regular Baptists' tenacious advocate; Carl McIntire (*upper right*) whose ouster from the Presbyterian Church (USA) meant holding church in a tent for a while; and J. Frank Norris (*bottom*), who built tandem ministries in Fort Worth and Detroit.

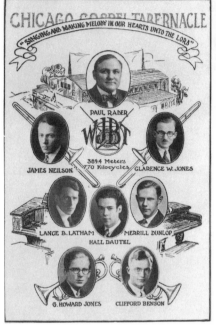

The Radio Style. Broadcast programs gave the movement new appeal and a broader audience. *Right:* Paul Rader's Chicago Gospel Tabernacle; *top:* The Old Fashioned Revival Hour, with Charles and Grace Fuller; *bottom:* The Radio Ensemble of the New England Fellowship.

New Urban Leadership. *Left*, Will H. Houghton, president of the Moody Bible Institute, (*below*).

OPPOSITE PAGE:
Above, Harold John Ockenga of Park Street Church, Boston; and *below,* William Ward Ayer of Calvary Baptist Church, New York.

Park Street
Church

and Its
Pastor

Harold John
Ockenga

Women in Ministry. *Top*, Elizabeth M. Evans (*center*) of the New England Fellowship; *lower left*, Grace W. Woods of the World-Wide Revival Prayer Movement; *lower right*, Grace Payton Fuller of the Old Fashioned Revival Hour.

Officers

Harold J. Ockenga
President

Leslie R. Marston
First Vice-President

Herbert J. Taylor
Treasurer

Members of the Executive Committee

John W. Bradbury

J. Roswell Flower

Harry J. Hager

Kenneth S. Keyes

Stephen W. Paine

T. Roland Philips

J. Elwin Wright
Field Secretary

An Evangelical United Front. First officers of the National Association of Evangelicals; their denominational affiliations were Congregationalist (Ockenga Wright), Free Methodist (Marston), Methodist (Taylor), Northern Baptist (Bradbury), Assemblies of God (Flower), Reformed Church of America (Hager), southern Presbyterian (Keyes), Wesleyan Methodist (Paine), northern Presbyterian (Philips).

The New Evangelicalism. President Harold Ockenga (*left*) points out a new vista for the founders of Fuller Theological Seminary (*left to right*): Charles Fuller, Everett Harrison, Harold Lindsell, Wilbur Smith, Arnold Grunigen, and Carl Henry.

OPPOSITE PAGE:
Geared to the times. *Top*, Youth ministry leaders Jack Wyrtzen (*upper right*) and Torrey Johnson (*center*). Notable among Youth for Christ's International's council members were, (*below, in front row*, Cliff Barrows and T.W. Wilson (*second and third from left*), who joined Billy Graham's team; *in middle row*, Johnson (*fourth from left*) and Charles Templeton of Toronto (*second from right*); *in back row*, Bob Evans (*left*), who founded Greater Europe Mission, Bob Pierce (*fourth from left*) who founded World Vision, and Billy Graham (*fourth from right*). *Bottom*: Youth rally evangelist Merv Rosell, of Minneapolis.

Revival in Our Time: Youth rally headliners, most notably Billy Graham, began holding extended campaigns. Graham's crusade in Los Angeles in the fall of 1949 attracted national media attention and fueled speculation that revival was breaking out.

7

TUNING IN THE GOSPEL

From a vantage point outside fundamentalism, by the 1930s the likelihood that a revival would sweep across America seemed remote. After decades of mass evangelism, reform crusades, and millennial rhetoric, Americans no longer seemed all that interested in being saved. When Billy Sunday went to his reward in 1935, it looked like the passing of an era. Sunday had been America's leading urban evangelist before and during World War I, but his career had declined precipitously since then, and citywide evangelism had fallen on hard times. Increasing populations of non-Protestants in the nation's cities limited these crusades' potential audience. The campaigns also had to compete with the movies, sports, automobile trips, and radio shows for people's attention. Rifts in Protestant ranks caused by the fundamentalist–modernist controversy and a reaction against the excesses of revivalists made unified Protestant support for evangelistic crusades impossible.[1]

Even in the nation's strongholds of born-again Christianity, its smaller cities and towns, whole-community revivalism seemed to be on its last legs. A Muncie, Indiana, minister said that the "business-class" churches were "slowly giving up the revival idea," and observed that a citywide meeting held in the spring of 1930 "almost died on our hands."[2] Sociologists Robert and Helen Lynd wrote of the situation in Muncie that "if the number of revivals is any index of religious interest," there had been "a marked recession."[3]

Were revivals becoming extinct? Yes, declared the *Christian Century*'s theologically liberal editors; Billy Sunday was "the last of his line." Sunday's frenetic style suggested to them both the death dance of revivalism and, they ventured further, the "desperate and hopeless condition of the evangelical type of piety."[4] They counseled their readers not to expect another Great Awakening at least of the evangelical type. Nevertheless, out beyond the horizon of the *Century*'s vision, something new was stirring. Fired with a powerful yearning to bring revival to America, fundamentalists and other evangelicals were

124

fashioning a contemporary religious style by making extensive use of the popular arts and the mass media: advertising, popular music and entertainment, broadcast journalism, and radio broadcasting itself. They were retooling revivalism, and the story of their efforts is critical for understanding how fundamentalists regained the jaded public's attention and began their return from the margins of American public life.

New Measures:
Revivalism and Innovative Communications

It might seem natural to assume that fundamentalists' doctrinal and moral conservatism would cause them to be "old fogies" in every facet of their religious work. Indeed, some leaders tried to give that impression. Said the salty southern preacher Vance Havner, "we do not expect to make a hit with the times." For him, a refusal to "crowd the show windows of modern publicity" was a matter of principle. "We are not cheapening the goods to draw the rush," he said.[5] Yet one of the paradoxes of fundamentalism is that this militantly antimodernist movement eagerly assimilated the latest techniques of mass communication—and beyond that, the idiom and format of popular entertainment—in order to propagate their old-time faith.[6]

With some historical perspective, however, the combination of evangelical faith, mass media, and a finely tuned popular style is not surprising at all. Fundamentalists were the heirs of a two-centuries-old revival tradition that had always relied on mass communications to generate public interest and translate the gospel into a popular idiom. As Harry S. Stout's biography of George Whitefield makes clear, the Great Awakening's leading revivalist was shockingly innovative in his use of theatrical techniques in his preaching, and the results were just as dramatic.[7]

Nathan Hatch's study of popular Christianity in the age of Jefferson and Jackson shows that evangelical religious movements were at the cutting edge of the democratic mass culture then being formed. Religious journals proliferated by the hundreds, and cheap tracts and pamphlets circulated in hundreds of thousands of copies, as did visual aids such as the Millerites' prophetic charts. These were all frontline weapons, Hatch argues, in various groups' "crusades for broadcasting the truth."[8] Preaching to the masses, successfully tested in Wesley's and Whitefield's day, became much more explicitly aimed at popular taste and folk culture in the hands of Lorenzo Dow, Peter Cartwright, and other camp meeting evangelists, who used theatrics, irreverent jingles, jokes and wordplay, stinging invective, and plenty of homespun stories to reach their audiences. This was also the age of "hymnodic revolution," Hatch argues, when waves of new religious music accompanied the growth of the Baptists and Methodists, the embrace of Christianity in the slave quarters, and the rise of new movements such as the Mormons and the Adventists. With heartfelt, down-to-earth lyrics and infectious tunes, gospel music outpaced traditional hymnody, spreading out of the churches into everyday life.[9]

What new measures others had put into the hands of ordinary people, Charles G. Finney, the era's most prominent evangelist, polished and presented to middle-class congregations. New techniques and expressions "are necessary from time to time to awaken attention and bring the gospel to bear upon the public mind," Finney explained. Public acceptance was the proper gauge of their effectiveness. "The results justify my methods," Finney argued. "Show me the fruits of your ministry, and if they so far exceed mine as to give me evidence that you have found a more excellent way, I will adopt your view."[10] Finney admired the aggressive promotion of the politicians and urged it on the more respectable and conservative churches of his day. "The object of our measures," he insisted, "is to gain attention and you *must* have something new."[11]

Popular appeal was already the norm for revivalism by the time that the businessman from Chicago, Dwight L. Moody, took to religious enterprise full-time in the 1870s. Moody brought to urban mass evangelism the sales and managerial techniques that were transforming the American economy.[12] Moody and his soloist, Ira Sankey, also updated evangelism's idiom through their sentimental stories and gospel ballads, calling the weary sinner who had lost his or her way in urban America to accept the tender Savior's invitation to "come home."[13]

Fundamentalism developed to a great extent out of Moody's passion to save the lost souls of urban America, and the movement inherited his flexible, pragmatic approach. Whether straightforward and sentimental like Moody and Sankey or more formal and intellectual like their protégé, Reuben A. Torrey, or sensational and vaudevillian like Billy Sunday, fundamentalists made the revival style and ethic integral to their movement. Even though fundamentalists praised the separated life, their tendency to withdraw from the world was qualified by their urgent desire to tell the world about Jesus. They felt compelled to frame their message in a way that would capture popular interest and address common concerns. By the 1930s, the Moody-Sunday idiom seems to have become stale and outmoded, but in the hands of some creative local practitioners, revivalism was undergoing extensive remodeling.

Paul Rader and the Rise of Radio Revivalism

One of the most innovative and broadly influential of the fundamentalist revivalists was Paul Rader, who directed the Chicago Gospel Tabernacle from 1922 to 1933. Rader was a convert to the doctrinal fundamentalism and the holiness and healing emphases of the Christian and Missionary Alliance after an unlikely pilgrimage. He had been a cowboy, a college instructor and football coach, a boxer, a liberal Congregationalist minister, and a Wall Street oil fields speculator before encountering the Almighty in a turbulent conversion. After a few years as an itinerant evangelist, Rader landed at the Moody Memorial Church in Chicago in 1915. He brought new vitality to that congregation but he earned the resentment of its lay board members because of his emphasis on perennial revival and the frequent absences required by his presidency of the Christian and Missionary Alliance. So Rader left Chicago in 1921, only to return the following year for a six-week evangelistic campaign in a large, steel-framed tabernacle on the North Side. That summer sojourn turned into a long-term ministry, however, as the tabernacle was winterized and organized as the Chicago Gospel Tabernacle. The Tabernacle resembled a local congregation, but it had no permanent membership and featured the evangelists, musicians, and renowned urban pastors of the fundamentalist movement, much like a local theater on the vaudeville circuit.[14]

Rader did not fit in well with the fundamentalist establishment in Chicago. Apparently there were lingering resentments over his departure from and competition with the Moody Church, and doctrinal displeasure over the Tabernacle's hosting pentecostal revivalists such as Aimee Semple McPherson and F. F. Bosworth. None of this seemed to hurt Rader's popularity. Going to the "Tab" on Sunday afternoons became a favorite evangelical pastime in Chicago, "like going to the ballpark," one regular attender reminisced.[15]

Rader attracted some of the area's most talented gospel musicians and evangelists to his staff, including R. J. Oliver, a former Salvation Army musician. Oliver led the Tabernacle band in varied programs of hymns, gospel choruses, semiclassical pieces, and Sousa marches. Special pageants and cantatas also brought out great crowds. The 1932 Christmas special *Let There Be Light* drew a total attendance of forty thousand. Keyboard stylists and composers Merrill Dunlop and Hall Dautell were important members of the creative team, and so was a group of younger assistants: Lance Latham, Howard Ferrin, Clarence Jones, and R. J. Oliver's son, Richard Weber Oliver. Rader was the master organizer of this creative staff and an encouraging mentor. Together, he and his young evangelists made the Tabernacle thrive.[16]

By the late 1920s, the Chicago Gospel Tabernacle was becoming a multifaceted religious enterprise. The Tabernacle Publishing Company printed Rader's tracts and books and *Tabernacle Hymns,* which was adopted by hundreds of congregations nationwide. The Tabernacle developed a Lake Michigan resort just south of Muskegon, Michigan, into the Maranatha Bible Conference and a children's camp. Back home, the Tabernacle featured clubs and programs for children and teenagers, a professionally designed magazine entitled the *World Wide Christian Courier,* and a foreign missionary society bearing the same name. This was not crusade revivalism huddling down into decline and irrelevancy, but a vigorous cluster of ministries that inspired and entertained the region's fundamentalists and generated new ideas and techniques for gearing the gospel to the times.[17]

Just before Rader's initial campaign at the Tabernacle in 1922, he had the opportunity to broadcast several programs over the new radio station, WBU, owned by Chicago's mayor, William H. Thompson. Apparently this experiment convinced Rader that radio was a powerful medium for proclaiming his message. For the next three years, he and his staff took time slots on several stations. Then in 1925, Rader struck a deal with Mayor Thompson's new station, WHT, to broadcast an all-day Sunday program, *The National Radio Chapel.* The program found a large and wide audience, stretching to the East Coast and far into western Canada. By the late 1920s, the Tabernacle received up to three thousand letters every week from listeners and enough funds to keep the program on the air.[18] A foray into national network broadcasting on CBS in 1930 proved to be too expensive for listeners to sustain in a depressed economy, and Rader cancelled the arrangement after only a few months. Nevertheless, Rader managed to keep his programs on the air over prominent Chicago stations during the rest of his tenure at the Tabernacle, and they enjoyed massive interest. In response to listeners' requests, the Tabernacle sent out over a quarter of a million pamphlets and printed sermons in 1932. This response was far heavier, by contrast, than the number of requests being received by the Federal Council of Churches for its preaching series over the entire NBC network.[19]

In addition to being a powerful communications tool, radio was at the cutting edge of popular culture. Being "on the air" added a new timeliness and notoriety to any enterprise. The Tabernacle services gained a new eventfulness, for they were being broadcast live to all of "Chicagoland" and far beyond. By participating in the service, whether in person or at home next to the radio, the audience became part of a large and potent endeavor.[20] Rader and his protégés sensed that radio demanded a fresh religious style. Known as a lively and sensational preacher, Rader noticeably modulated his presentation when in the studio. Imagining his audience sitting in their living rooms or around their breakfast tables, Rader tried to chat with them in an intimate, friend-to-friend way. A radio critic for the *Chicago Tribune* remarked that Rader was a very effective announcer—informal, pleasant, humorous and friendly.[21]

Tabernacle music became radio-tailored as well. Gospel songs had to have a message that was simple and patently obvious, a lively tempo, or a stirring melody, and they had to do their work within one or two verses. Thus pianist Merrill Dunlop's lively chorus:

> My sins are blotted out, I know,
> My sins are blotted out, I know.
> They are buried in the depths of the deepest sea;
> My sins are blotted out, I know.

Paul Rader's "Only Believe," a perennial gospel favorite, was of this same type, even if often sung slowly and reverently:

> Only believe, Only believe,
> All things are possible, only believe;
> Only believe, Only believe,
> All things are possible—only believe.

Like radio jingles, the gospel choruses being composed by the Tabernacle musicians had to be easy to memorize, with catchy melodies and rhythms that almost sang themselves, so that people would find themselves humming and singing them again and again.[22]

Live radio's insatiable appetite for new material and a variety of formats kept the Tabernacle staff busy inventing programs. A *Request Hour* featured musicians playing hymns requested by callers; the *Sunshine Hour* brought comforting thoughts and Bible verses to shut-ins; the *Shepherd Hour* featured skits, songs, and stories for youngsters; and the *Radio Rangers* and the *Aerial Girls* were radio-driven youth clubs. The sign-off program was the *Back Home Hour*, a quiet mingling of hymns with spiritual thoughts presented by Rader himself. In 1930 Rader ventured into daily broadcasting with the early morning *Breakfast Brigade*. Recalled several of Rader's associates, these were hectic but exciting years, when their energy and inventive talents were stretched to the limit.[23]

In the Tabernacle's creative cauldron, the mixture of radio-inspired innovation and missionary vision produced a new ministry, created by one of Rader's assistants, Clarence Jones. In the summer of 1927 Jones got the idea of developing a missionary radio station in South America that would reach the entire continent. Jones received permission to establish a station near Quito, Ecuador, and by 1932 missionary radio station HCJB was on the air.[24] The story of station HCJB is one of many instances of new ministries. A second generation of leaders was rising, and these younger fundamentalists, while no less conservative in doctrine than their elders, were much less interested in prolonging the fundamentalist–modernist controversy. Rather, they were finding fresh ways to present the gospel to their age. A new wave of creativity was rising in the fundamentalist movement, and it was attuned to the new idioms of urban popular culture. The critical medium for this restyling was radio broadcasting.[25]

Cornering the Religious Radio Market

During the Rader years, radio broadcasting became a strong trend within fundamentalism. Only a year after Rader began broadcasting in Chicago, John Roach Straton, the fiery "fundamentalist pope" of New York, had a station installed at Calvary Baptist Church in midtown Manhattan. That same year, 1923, the Bible Institute of Los Angeles (BIOLA) developed its own station, despite the misgivings of BIOLA's founder, T. C. Horton, and its eminent dean, Reuben A. Torrey. The airwaves, these two argued, were the realm of Satan, whom the Bible called "the prince of the power of the air" (Eph. 2:2). But the station went in, and it prospered. Other fundamentalist centers saw radio's religious potential and developed their own radio programs. Among them were J. Frank Norris's mammoth First Baptist Church of Fort Worth, Texas, the Berachah Church of Philadelphia, and the Moody Bible Institute. Moody began broadcasting in 1925 and founded its own station, WMBI, the following year. The first fundamentalist program on national network radio began in late 1928, when Donald Grey Barnhouse of Philadelphia's Tenth Presbyterian Church began a weekly Bible study program on CBS.[26]

Other evangelicals were taking to the airwaves as well. Two of the most remarkable of the scores of religious radio stations that appeared in the mid-1920s were KFUO of St. Louis, the home of Dr. Walter Maier's *Lutheran Hour,* and station KFSG in Los Angeles, which broadcast from Angelus Temple, the home base of pentecostal evangelist Aimee Semple McPherson. Maier's dramatic biblical preaching won him an enormous audience over national networks, while Sister Aimee's radio station was reported to have attracted the second-largest listening audience in Los Angeles.[27]

By the early 1930s radio broadcasting had become a force of tested success within the narrower confines of fundamentalism. In May of 1931, the *Sunday School Times* published another of its lists, this one of radio programs that in the editors' estimation were "sound and Scriptural." Over one hundred different broadcasts by seventy different ministries comprised the list, though McPherson's was not included. An update the following year showed over four hundred programs on eighty stations. Although many were simply broadcasts of church services, others were specially prepared programs that attracted large and loyal audiences. A reader's poll conducted by the *Kansas City Star* in 1932 reported that the most popular program in the area was the *Morning Bible Hour,* taught by Dr. Walter L. Wilson of the city's Central Bible Church. Wilson had outpolled such popular syndicated broadcasts as *Amos and Andy, The Seth Parker Hour,* and the *Lucky Strike* program.[28]

Fundamentalists' and other evangelicals' expanding radio operations were riding a popular wave of immense proportions, for the commercial radio industry was becoming a major source of entertainment in America and even the Depression could not dampen its growth. Between 1930 and 1935 the number of radio sets doubled, numbering over 18 million and reaching 60 percent of American homes. By 1939 the number would more than double again to 44 million, which meant a coverage of 86 percent of all American households. Unlike British radio, which remained subject to the British Broadcasting Corporation's arbiters of propriety, American radio followed popular tastes.[29]

Fundamentalists, who were used to appealing to a mass audience, quickly adapted to the radio style. Taking his cue from an emerging broadcasting species, Percy Crawford of the *Young People's Church of the Air* emulated the urgent, rapid-fire speaking style of the radio news reporter. Some adopted a more conversational style, finding that for many, radio was an intimate home companion. The *Sunshine Hour,* broadcast from Rhode Island in early 1930, featured "musings at the microphone" by one of Paul Rader's former assistants, Howard Ferrin, whose musicians warmly welcomed listeners to his "fireside bright with cheer." Other programs projected a family feeling. From Chicago came "Uncle" John Meredith's *Family Altar League* and WMBI's *Morning Glory Club* for children, featuring "Aunt Theresa" and "the cousins." Still others projected a folksy familiarity, notably Dr. Walter Wilson, the "beloved physician" of Kansas City, Dr. Martin R. DeHaan, a former country doctor and Dutch Reformed minister from Grand Rapids who hosted the *Radio Bible Class,* and the regulars on the Rev. Josiah Hogg's broadcast, the *Country Church of Hollywood.*[30]

Radio seemed especially attractive to fundamentalists. These marginalized populists felt shut out of the main channels of discussion in American life, but radio enabled them to take their message straight to the people. Radio reached into homes, automobiles, and even bars and pool halls. Anyone could tune in. Denominational barriers seemed irrelevant, and so did the question of whether one belonged to a "respectable" denomination or some "sect" of recent vintage. Fundamentalists and other religious outsiders got their hearing on the radio, where they could compete for public recognition, legitimacy—and ultimately, influence.[31]

From radio's early days onward, the industry's leaders tried to constrain populist broadcasting. Citing the crowding of radio frequencies, the poor quality of some stations' signals, and the use of public airwaves for special interest groups' "propaganda," the Federal Radio Commission began to regulate broadcasting in the late 1920s. Evangelical stations were faced with forced mergers or time-sharing agreements with commercial stations, or with the high cost of meeting new standards of technical quality. Combined with officials' dislike for "sectarian" religion and their predisposition not to renew such stations' licenses, these new obstacles forced many religious stations off the air. The representative bodies of mainline American religion played a prominent role in these efforts to limit evangelical broadcasting. Concerned that "belated forms of denominational organization" (Harry Emerson Fosdick's euphemism for "sects and cults") would gain a respectability that they did not deserve, the Federal Council of Churches and other national religious associations persuaded the Columbia Broadcasting System and the National Broadcasting Corporation to cease the sale of network radio slots for religious programs. Instead, the networks would give free time to the more established religious alliances for their "nonsectarian" programs.[32]

These exclusionary tactics proved to be a blessing in disguise for fundamentalists and other evangelicals, for it forced them to work hard at producing popularly appealing programs and building loyal audiences. In lieu of access to the national commercial networks, they developed informal syndicates by purchasing time slots from scores of local stations. One study pointed out that religious broadcasting on Chicago stations during 1932 totalled 290 quarter hours weekly, and 246 of those slots carried "sectarian" programming. Of the seventy-seven religious broadcasts each week in Chicago in 1941, 25 were sponsored by fundamentalists, while only 3 carried the banner of liberal Protestantism.[33] When new networks such as the Mutual Broadcasting System and the American Broadcasting Company came into being, they found that paying religious programs helped them build revenues and develop loyal audiences. By the early 1940s, Mutual derived roughly a quarter of its revenues from paid religious broadcasts.[34]

Building the Networks for a Revival

Fundamentalists found a variety of uses for this new medium, and over the decade of the 1930s a clear pattern emerged. Radio was helpful for building up local preaching posts such as the Chicago Gospel Tabernacle, and also for consolidating regional fellowships and national constituencies. As it stimulated new confidence, more outreach activities, and a fresh religious style, radio was helping to bring about a revival of revivalism.

One lively fundamentalist institution in southern New England, the Providence Bible Institute, shows radio-charged regional organizing in action. In 1925 the backers of a struggling Bible institute in the small town of Dudley, Massachusetts, south of Worcester, invited Paul Rader to become the school's president. Much to their surprise, Rader accepted, but he placed the actual administration of the school in the hands of his protégé, Howard W. Ferrin. After graduating from Northwestern University and the Moody Bible Institute, Ferrin had assisted Rader at the Chicago Gospel Tabernacle. With Rader's blessing, he had founded another preaching station across town, the South Side Tabernacle. Ferrin had been trained to do urban ministry, not rural, so when he came to the Dudley Bible Institute he followed the pattern he learned from Rader. He began a radio program over station WEAN in nearby Providence, Rhode Island, renamed the school's newsletter *The Announcer,* and convinced another Rader assistant, Richard Weber Oliver, a gifted pianist and composer, to join him. Their radio publicity for the rural school soon began to bring results. At the annual campus visitation day in 1928, they hosted a crowd of more than 1,200.[35]

Ferrin was encouraged to move forward with plans for expansion. He relocated the school in Providence and began holding evangelistic services with his Radio Carollers in the Elks Auditorium in the heart of downtown. Ferrin was convinced, he told his supporters in 1929, that the greatest religious problem of the present age was "reaching the city masses for Christ." The church, unfortunately, was too often "content with her old oxcart methods." Modern times demanded modern technology, so what the church needed was to adapt to the automobile age and then "step on the gas."[36]

Ferrin had already shifted his program into high gear. By early 1930 the evangelistic meetings at the Elks Auditorium had evolved into the Providence Gospel Center, located in an old Congregational church building. The Center sponsored organizations for all ages including the *Girl Guides* and *Radio Rangers* clubs for young people. Until his untimely death in 1930, Richard Weber Oliver coordinated these programs and led student "gospel teams" on evangelistic tours to outlying communities. Sometime later the Providence Bible Institute began sponsoring its own summer Bible conference at Old Orchard, Maine. In the spring of 1935 the school hosted the first of its annual conferences for pastors and lay workers, and in 1938 Ferrin inaugurated a young people's conference at the Institute and a prophetic and missionary conference on Cape Cod.[37]

All of this activity was promoted through an expanding radio ministry. By late 1937 the *Mountain Top Hour* was carried on eleven stations, broadcasting from Boston, Providence, and other New England cities, as well as from New York City and Rochester, New York. Using this network, Ferrin developed links between his radio audience and the Institute's more traditional outreach efforts. Radio listeners who wrote in were sent publications and supportive churches hosted the Institute's traveling gospel music teams. Ferrin also began an annual "New England Radio Rally" in 1931, promising to those who came the chance to participate in a live broadcast. By 1933 the rally was being held in the Boston Arena, featuring a choir of two thousand, the Salvation Army Band, and Ferrin as the speaker. Over ten thousand packed the auditorium, and hundreds were turned away. It is no wonder that the Providence Bible Institute grew steadily, from only 45 students when Ferrin moved it to Providence in 1930 to 80 by 1935, 116 in 1940, and 258 in 1945. Meanwhile, new evening and extension programs were expanding rapidly.[38]

Ferrin was following what would become a standard pattern for a successful fundamentalist ministry: programs aimed at young people, a strong emphasis on lay Bible training, an array of off-site programs, evangelistic outreach, and radio broadcasts to attract and sustain the support of a growing constituency. These were the major ingredients of fundamentalism's growth and increasing confidence.

No other fundamentalist institution learned all of these lessons so well or carried them out on so grand a scale as the Moody Bible Institute of Chicago. The Institute had been the center of a national fundamentalist constituency for decades, and already had powerful resources at its disposal. The respective enrollments of the Institute's day and evening schools averaged about 1,100 and 1,400 in the 1930s, and its Correspondence School enrolled another 14,000 each year. The Extension Department retained over a dozen evangelists and Bible teachers who supplied vacant pulpits and staffed hundreds of conferences and evangelistic meetings each year. The Institute's Colportage Association, founded in 1894 to print and distribute evangelical tracts and books, enjoyed explosive growth in the depression years. By its fortieth anniversary in 1934 it had published over 57 million pieces of literature. During the early 1940s the Association, renamed the Moody Press, would publish around ten million pieces each year. The *Moody Bible Institute Monthly,* official organ of the Institute and opinion shaper for the whole movement, grew from an average paid circulation of twenty-eight thousand in 1933 to over fifty thousand in 1942.[39]

Moody Bible Institute's early and sustained commitment to radio broadcasting was one of the most powerful drivers of this expansion. Started as an experiment in 1926 by Vice President Henry C. Crowell, by the spring of 1927 WMBI was on the air thirty-two hours a week. It broadcast a variety of programs, including the Institute's chapels, special meetings and conferences, a weekly *Radio School of the Bible,* the *Family Altar League* with "Uncle" John Meredith, the *KYB [Know Your Bible] Club* for children, gospel music by staff and student ensembles and guest artists, and a question-and-answer period.[40]

Listeners in the Chicago area, the upper Midwest, and scattered across the continent eagerly responded to and participated in WMBI's programs. Between 1928 and 1930 enrollment in the *Radio School of the Bible* grew to over 1,900, and a new children's program, the *Morning Glory Club,* secured a membership of two thousand in its first few weeks. Over twenty thousand letters came to WMBI in 1930 in response to one program or another. Representatives of seventy-one congregations participated in the broadcasts in some way that year, whether as guest speakers or musicians on one of the five regular and eighteen occasional foreign language programs, such as the *Bohemian Hour,* or in broadcasts of their own Sunday services. The Announcers Trio broadcast new gospel songs composed by station manager Wendell P. Loveless and other Institute musicians, and then recorded an assortment of them on Victor Records. The station's development through the 1930s shows a kaleidoscopic progression of new programs, new personalities, and rapid growth. By 1940 the number of regular weekly broadcast hours had grown from forty-nine to ninety-four; the *KYB Club* had enrolled over 17,500 members; and the *Radio School of the Bible* had 11,500 registrants.[41]

At a time when people were relying more and more on radio to keep in touch with the world, WMBI kept its listeners in touch with the Chicago area's growing fundamentalist network. By inviting the participation of area pastors, evangelists, and musicians and publicizing local religious events, WMBI became an important consolidator of local evangelism and a medium for experiments. For example, WMBI cooperated with the emerging Christian Business Men's Committee by broadcasting the Committee's noonday evangelistic services in a downtown theater. The station also pioneered a number of youth-oriented programs such as the *Teen-age Bible Study Class,* begun in 1936, and the *WMBI Crusade for High School Men,* in 1938. WMBI's staff responded to a growing number of invitations to hold services in area churches. Visits by radio personalities such as Wendell Loveless and the Announcer Trio soon numbered in the hundreds. In a dozen years the broadcasting staff logged 723 meetings in nearly 300 different churches in the upper Midwest, including 206 in Illinois and 115 in the city of Chicago. Here was an interdenominational network, plugged in, as it were, to both the Institute and its message.[42]

Moody Bible Institute's president during these expansive years was Will H. Houghton, the eloquent Baptist preacher from New York who had succeeded James M. Gray in the fall of 1934. Houghton arrived at Moody dreaming of a Great Awakening. Soon after he started there he called for a day of prayer at the Institute, and then he revealed his plans for a great two-year campaign: an Institute Jubilee celebration in 1936 and a D. L. Moody Centenary in 1937. His aims for these promotions, Houghton stated, were a "new realization of the value of evangelism" and a "new desire for world-wide revival."[43]

Summoning all of its promotional resources to honor the memory of Mr. Moody, the Institute launched a mammoth effort. Institute agents persuaded over eight hundred congregations in North America and Great Britain to schedule D. L. Moody commemorative Bible teaching and evangelistic services in 1937, at which attendance totaled over four hundred thousand. Some 2,300 churches held a special "Moody Day" service, and an Institute-sponsored rally at the Chicago Coliseum attracted a crowd of fifteen thousand. Houghton was encouraged, and he felt led to launch a nationwide evangelistic crusade by means of a radio program, *Let's Go Back to the Bible.* It was broadcast over eleven major urban stations of the Mutual Network in the fall and winter of 1938 and 1939. Houghton preached a series of twenty-six sermons warning the nation of its spiritual desolation and calling on Americans to repent and turn to Christ. These messages were published in a book that Houghton had sent to mayors of major cities, business leaders, governors, members of Congress, and the White House. The Institute received forty thousand letters in response to the series, and Houghton determined to try a second round of broadcasts the following winter. America was ripe for revival, he believed, and he asked supporters everywhere to pray that God would bring the nation to its knees.[44]

Over the next decade, the Moody Bible Institute would continue to invest its considerable promotional resources in the cause of national revival. Nearly every editorial page of the *Moody Monthly* would devote space and urgent rhetoric to the subject. The Institute's extension evangelists and literature outreaches would focus on evangelism, especially in the booming military camps and war industry towns.[45] But at the cutting edge was WMBI, which had emerged as the powerhouse of evangelical radio. During 1940, in the wake of its *Back to the Bible* chain broadcasts, WMBI produced a new series of transcribed programs, *Miracles and Melodies*. Each program featured music by students and staff, including bass soloist George Beverly Shea, and included testimonies and brief gospel messages. That fall, the programs were heard on sixty-seven stations across America. By early 1942 the program was being broadcast from 187 different stations in forty-five states, Canada, Latin America (via Clarence Jones's station in Ecuador) and China.[46] Radio was the hot new medium, and through it fundamentalists were encouraged to find ways to attract national attention.

Fundamentalist Celebrities

At Moody's annual national meeting, the Founder's Week Conference in February 1942, the theme was "America's God-Given Opportunity for Revival Today."[47] Featured among the speakers was Charles E. Fuller, the radio host of the *Old Fashioned Revival Hour*, a program carried by more than 450 stations over the Mutual Broadcasting System. Fuller had been a celebrity in fundamentalist circles for some time, but his sudden rise to national fame as a revival preacher made him especially appropriate for this conference. More than any other fundamentalist radio venture, the *Old Fashioned Revival Hour* showed fundamentalists that they could attract broad popular interest and also showed them how to do it.[48]

One of the keys, it seemed, was to be clean-cut and middle American, without any trace of Elmer Gantry slickness. That surely was true of the Fullers. Charles Fuller was the son of a prosperous orange grower in southern California and a graduate of nearby Pomona College. His wife and broadcast partner, Grace Payton Fuller, was the cultured, college-educated daughter of a physician. Even with their upper-middle-class rearing, the Fullers had an open, friendly manner and they presented themselves as ordinary folk. Charles had been ordained in 1925 by a Baptist group, but he and Grace seemed more like laypersons. After a short stint as a mining engineer in northern California, Charles had settled in Orange County, joined a local fertilizer firm, and eventually became a dealer in orange groves and other real estate. Although he was raised in a devout home, Fuller said he was converted in 1916 during Paul Rader's evangelistic meetings at BIOLA's Church of the Open Door.

Fired with fresh enthusiasm for "the Lord's work," Fuller founded a Bible class at his home church in Placentia, and in 1919 he began to take courses at BIOLA. He graduated in 1921 and became the president and evangelist of the Orange County Christian Endeavor while supporting himself with his real estate business. Fuller's Bible class grew and eventually took on a life of its own. It parted ways with its host church, Placentia Presbyterian, in 1924, and in the next year became an independent fundamentalist congregation, Calvary Church, with Fuller as its pastor. Calvary Church rapidly became an important point on the southern California fundamentalist circuit.[49]

Radio broadcasting gradually absorbed Fuller's interest. His first regular program seems to have been a Bible class over BIOLA's station KTBI in 1924. After a particularly compelling experience with radio preaching at a midwestern Bible conference in 1929, Fuller began a weekly broadcast of Calvary Church's evening services. In 1931 Fuller launched a program called *The Pilgrim's Hour* on a seven-station CBS hookup reaching from San Diego to Seattle, but it was halted after two months when CBS began to exclude paid religious broadcasting. This incident began a period of severe testing for the Fuller family. They suffered some major financial crises with the onset of the Depression, and a life-threatening illness attacked their only child, Dan. But Charles decided to resign his pastorate and give full attention to radio ministry. By 1935 he was conducting four weekly broadcasts over the powerful KNX station in Hollywood. With KNX's range, these programs were heard far up the Pacific coast, into the Southwest, and at some points in the Rockies.

Fuller did some of his most strategic work off the air, in the realm of promotion and organization. In 1933 he established the Gospel Broadcasting Association, a not-for-profit corporation. This move separated the Fullers' religious work from their commercial ventures and provided a way for them to be held accountable and prove their honesty through publicly audited accounts at a time when radio preachers began to encounter criticism for operating "rackets."[50] Starting with a mailing list of only sixty, the Fullers published a newsletter, *Heart to Heart Talks,* in which they presented inspiring thoughts they had gleaned from here and there, "spiritual" comments on current events, and news of the broadcast. They gave readers behind-the-microphone glimpses of the program, announced new ventures, and solicited prayers and financial support. In the early years these constituents were much like an extended congregation. When the Fullers came visiting, there would be get-togethers, often over a potluck supper.[51] The list of "friends" of the broadcast who received *Heart to Heart Talks* grew rapidly, however, for the newsletter was offered free of charge over the air. By 1940 it was going out to a mailing list of sixty-five thousand.[52] In this publication the Fullers discussed the program's recurring financial crises during the slower summer months and the formidable cost of expanding to new stations. But always their first request was for prayer, for the Fullers keenly felt the need for spiritual intervention. They were certain that the difficulties they experienced were the opposition of the "prince of the power of the air."[53]

In 1936, when CBS acquired station KNX, Charles Fuller had to find a new outlet. A temporary solution was to transcribe the *Radio Revival Hour* for distribution to a number of stations—in California, the Pacific Northwest, Montana, New Mexico, and as far east as Iowa. More people could hear the program now, but Fuller needed increased support to cover the added expenses. So he held rallies and live broadcasts in the cities where the program was on new stations: Portland, Seattle, Boise, Salt Lake City, and Albuquerque.

In early 1937 the new Mutual Broadcasting System offered Fuller a prime-time broadcast slot. Paying network fees and competing with commercial programs was a daunting challenge, but Fuller felt the opportunity was God-sent, and he was determined to meet it. He hired Rudy Albers, a talented radio business and production expert, and upgraded the program's musical talent to meet network standards. From another Los Angeles radio preacher Fuller recruited the Goose Creek Gospel Quartet and their pianist, Rudy Atwood. The quartet's smooth renditions of old-fashioned gospel hymns and Atwood's bright and lively keyboard embellishments added a hint of contemporary styling to program. By November 1937, the *Radio Revival Hour* was heard on prime time Sunday evenings on eighty-eight Mutual stations from coast to coast. A month later the program took on what became its enduring name— the *Old Fashioned Revival Hour.*

Fuller's rapid expansion into national network radio brought with it some breathtaking financial and demographic challenges. The network time slot cost $4,500 a week at the start and the price escalated from there as Mutual added new stations. The Fullers' pleas for their listeners to pray, promote the program to their friends, and make donations became more frequent and insistent.[54] The Fullers also repeated the "radio rallies" promotional strategy that had worked so well for them earlier. The program travelled first to Des Moines, where it was hosted by a local cooperative of "fundamental churches." Then the entourage went to Chicago, where it was sponsored by the Christian Business Men's Committee. In Detroit Fuller preached to an audience of fourteen thousand at the Olympia Arena on Good Friday 1938; then he returned to Chicago, where he addressed forty thousand at an Easter sunrise service held in Soldier Field. The next year the program was required to expand to 152 stations, so the Fullers scheduled meetings in Amarillo, Grand Rapids, Boston, New York, Philadelphia, and Washington, D.C. At Mechanics Hall in Boston, Fuller preached to a capacity audience of eight thousand; at his next stop, New York, two great crowds filled consecutive meetings at Carnegie Hall.

The people who came to these rallies or tuned into the broadcast encountered a familiar religious style. The program "signed on" with the choir singing an old-fashioned gospel song, "Jesus Saves," a favorite of Fuller's because its expansive lyrics ("spread the tidings all around," "shout salvation full and free," "give the winds a mighty voice . . . let the nations now rejoice") spoke of his purpose for being on the air. Typically the choir would then sing some other old favorites, such as "There's Power in the Blood," or "Beulah Land." These were interspersed with similar numbers by the quartet. There were no surprises here (other than Atwood's piano riffs), for this was the stuff of the common-denominator, evangelical Christianity that had existed since the days of Moody and Sankey. And yet this traditional fare had tremendous drawing power, for it evoked childhood memories and familiar church-service settings for millions of listeners nationwide, as the Fullers' mail attested.[55]

These letters, in fact, provided one of the program's most popular and compelling features. During each broadcast, Grace would read selections from the mail. With perfect diction and a sweet, motherly voice, she shared these expressions of hope, comfort, sacred memory, and conversion. Prisoners testified to saving grace and a transformed outlook, troubled young men and women told of suicides averted, impoverished, abandoned mothers spoke of renewed strength and comfort, and lonely families out on the prairies greeted their dear friends, the Fullers. Some letters came on perfumed stationery, some on smudged paper bags. Thousands wrote every week: New Yorkers, Oklahomans, black sharecroppers, white coal miners, a Chippewa evangelist from northern Ontario, a "college man" in Virginia, a missionary on the shores of East Africa's Lake Albert, a Londoner enduring the Blitz, and increasingly, soldiers and sailors in Europe and the Pacific. Mrs. Fuller always had a half-dozen of the more "precious" of these epistles to read on the air.[56]

Charles Fuller's preaching had a little less of the common touch than his wife's letter-reading. His sermons seemed to be aimed at evangelical or fundamentalist Christians who had substantial prior knowledge of the Bible. Sometimes he would delve into rather arcane discussions, such as dispensationalist typology in the Old Testament. And yet, without fail, Fuller ended his sermon with a simple plea for his listeners "out there in radio land" to repent of their sinfulness and accept Jesus as their savior, while the choir softly sang a hymn of invitation. Many thousands professed conversion through his preaching. In 1940, when Fuller addressed the annual Southern Baptist convention, the pastor who introduced him asked how many delegates had new members who had professed conversion while listening to the Fullers. About two thirds of them raised their hands.[57]

So what was the appeal of the *Old Fashioned Revival Hour?* Part of its charm must have been its intimacy. The Fullers, Rudy, and the quartet were like family, and they came into millions of homes at one of the most commonly observed family hours, Sunday evening. They did not sound like high-voltage haranguers but rather like trusted friends, and the listeners' letters attested to this sense of familiarity. The program also seemed to strike a common chord of religious memory. The gospel songs and revival style of the program were the inheritance of the majority of American Protestants. Even if much of mainline Protestantism was moving to more formal, less evangelistic worship services, the childhood memories of both churched and unchurched were infused with the older revivalism. Evangelical Christianity had become a folk religion in America, and the *Old Fashioned Revival Hour* tapped that deep vein in the nation's memory. A Washington columnist wrote that in days when war and crime seemed to dominate the news he found it "restful to hear an old-fashioned preacher preach old-time religion in the good old-fashioned way."[58] Likewise the first chronicler of the Fullers' ministry, J. Elwin Wright, believed that the program was helping America "re-discover something of which it had lost sight."[59] In those dark early days of the Second World War, many kinds of cultural rediscovery were going on in America, and apparently this included old-time religion. In 1942 and 1943 the *Old Fashioned Revival Hour* had the largest audience in national network radio. It surpassed even the most popular shows, such as Bob Hope's and the *Ford Symphony Hour*. By 1944, the program's listening audience was estimated at twenty million.[60]

Conclusion: Back to Center Stage

The Fullers had become famous, and in an unguarded moment Charles Fuller revealed his delight. In May 1939, during one of his radio rallies at New York's Carnegie Hall, Fuller stepped to the microphone before a packed house. He looked around at the great old auditorium, smiled, and said, "When a singer gets to sing in Carnegie Hall he feels that he has arrived. Now here I am in Carnegie Hall, and I don't want to lose my opportunity to sing." So he launched into an old gospel hymn: "What can wash away my sins? Nothing but the blood of Jesus."[61] Charles Fuller had arrived indeed. He enjoyed his celebrity for a moment, and there, in one of the temples of high culture, he did something that was just a little subversive. He sang the gospel.

For the larger public, this moment did not exist. Fuller's Carnegie Hall debut was not the kind of news that the *New York Times* deemed fit to print. Yet the radio preacher's national fame was the pride and joy of the fundamentalist movement. If there was one thing that fundamentalists and other "sectarian" evangelicals lacked—and yearned for—it was respect in the public eye.[62] The *Old Fashioned Revival Hour* provided them with at least a taste of it, and showed them how to use the popular media to regain some visibility and legitimacy. Virtually shut out of the more intellectual channels of discourse, fundamentalists and other evangelicals were learning how to get the public's attention through more populist media. Their yearning to be known—and respected—was being revived and rewarded, and it would become one of the most powerful propellants of the postwar evangelical resurgence.[63]

Fundamentalists' revival impulse ran deeper than the yearning to recover their own cultural standing, however. It was driven by the classic evangelical desire to share the gospel with the neighbors, the nation, and the world, and radio was proving to be a powerful tool for extending the reach of their message. Local groups, such as "fundamentalist fellowships" of churches or Christian Business Men's Committees, were venturing out into cooperative evangelism and dreaming once again of a national religious revival. For them, Charles and Grace Fuller's incredible drawing power—whether in Des Moines, Detroit, or even New York and Boston—was a stunning example of radio's potential to stir religious interest. These radio rallies drew crowds the likes of which had not been seen since Aimee Semple McPherson's heyday. Perhaps radio was the key, the "new measure" that would become the vehicle for another Great Awakening.

For Charles Fuller and other radio preachers, their work had another important, probably unintentional effect. Rather than preaching mostly to the already converted in like-minded churches, they sensed that their audience—both Christians and nonbelievers—was much broader than their own tradition. They felt compelled to adopt a more common-denominator message. Despite Charles Fuller's occasional lapses into doctrinal obscurity, the overall character of the program was classically American evangelical but nonsectarian. Other national leaders, such as Will Houghton at the Moody Bible Institute, also began to recognize the need to move out into broader realms. If they were to bring a revival to America, they would have to cooperate with Bible-believing Christians beyond their ordinary circles of fellowship. The whole mosaic of evangelical traditions—both outside of and within mainline Protestantism itself—would have to put aside internal differences for the sake of successful mass evangelism and a unified voice in the public arena. Radio alone could not finesse the problem of evangelicals' marginality. A new evangelical coalition had to be forged if the born-again were to regain a place for themselves somewhere nearer the cultural center. Houghton and others were beginning to envision a movement to make pan-evangelical cooperation a reality. That development is a remarkable story in itself, one that is indispensable for understanding the scope—and the limits—of the postwar evangelical resurgence.

8

AN EVANGELICAL
UNITED FRONT

On April 7, 1942, J. Elwin Wright, the director of the New England Fellowship, stood to speak before an audience of about two hundred at the Coronado Hotel in St. Louis, Missouri. Wright had addressed a full house at the Boston Garden when Charles Fuller came to town, and he had spoken to more people, no doubt, on snowy Sunday evenings in New England. Still, he must have felt a special thrill as he addressed these delegates and observers at the "National Conference for United Action among Evangelicals." They had come from all over the country and from thirty-four denominations, many at Wright's personal invitation, to make decisions that, according to another conference speaker, might "affect the whole future course of evangelical Christianity in America."[1]

Thus began the National Association of Evangelicals, which was formally constituted the following year at a convention in Chicago. The National Association's mission was to provide a united voice and a cooperative clearing house for conservative Protestants. Some of the delegates at the St. Louis meeting, like Wright himself, were members of denominations already represented by the Federal Council of the Churches of Christ.[2] Others were from religious groups, large and tiny, that were neither represented by the Federal Council nor wished to be. Together they encompassed much of the American evangelical mosaic. Perhaps the strongest contingent were the Baptists, Presbyterians, and independents of the fundamentalist movement, but the audience also included officials from Wesleyan holiness groups, pentecostals, Southern Baptists and southern Presbyterians, the Christian Church (Disciples of Christ), the Lutheran Church–Missouri Synod, the Mennonite Brethren and other "peace church" groups, and several European ethnic denominations such as the Scandinavian Evangelical Free and Evangelical Covenant churches, and the Dutch Reformed and Christian Reformed churches.[3] Not all of the denominations represented at the meeting joined the NAE, but that is an important part of the story as well, for a new evangelical coalition was in the making, the scope and boundaries of which owed much to the reach—and limits—of fundamentalism's vision, influence, and convening power. Indeed, the story of the NAE reveals a great deal about the changes occurring within three spheres of religious action: fundamentalism itself, the larger arena of evangelical movements and traditions, and American Protestantism in general.

There are several ways to begin the story of the National Association of Evangelicals. One is to recall the Evangelical Alliance of the nineteenth century, its virtual absorption and replacement by the Federal Council of Churches, and conservative evangelicals' sense of being disenfranchised. Another would be to speak of fundamentalists' earlier attempts to build a national coalition of conservative Protestants in the 1920s, notably the World's Christian Fundamentals Association. By 1930 the WCFA had ceased to attract a broad representation of evangelicals and had become little more than an annual Bible conference.[4] Both of these approaches reveal important continuities with earlier visions for united evangelical action, but they do not account for the NAE. Because these narratives downplay the importance of a more direct inspiration for the NAE, the New England Fellowship, they miss the heart of the story. One simply cannot understand the NAE without exploring its surprising roots in New England.[5]

From the Margins Toward the Center

The most common image of Protestantism in New England is the prim Congregationalism of the region's white clapboard churches. The New England Fellowship was not that, by any stretch of the imagination. It had started out, in fact, as a holiness and pentecostal movement, founded by J. Elwin Wright's father, Joel Wright. The elder Wright was a dealer in farms and woodlots and a preacher, who served among the Free Will Baptists in New Hampshire and Vermont in the 1880s. After studying the writings of John Wesley, Joel Wright converted to the holiness movement, joining the Free Methodists in 1892 and four years later leaving denominational work altogether. He bought a tent, became a travelling evangelist, and began sponsoring other evangelists as well. This growing movement was formally organized in 1897 as the First Fruit Harvesters Association, an independent fellowship devoted to winning souls and teaching radical holiness in New England. Supported in part by Wright's real estate business, the Harvesters fanned out from their base in the village of Rumney, New Hampshire, to hold revival meetings and organize new churches, then invited their constituents back to Rumney each summer for camp meetings and Bible conferences. Like many holiness groups in the early twentieth century, the Harvesters became pentecostals, and devoted themselves to planting the pentecostal faith in their region. By 1924 the Association reported that its affiliates totalled thirty-seven chapels and twenty-four other small groups.[6]

Standing aloof from other Christians was becoming the norm for pentecostal groups, and it appeared that the Harvesters were taking that course. But when J. Elwin Wright accepted his father's mantle in 1924, he soon grew dissatisfied with the Harvesters' sectarian emphasis. His father's original purpose, Wright believed, had been to unite evangelicals in spreading the gospel. What had happened instead (in that recurring irony of American revivalism) was that a movement founded on a vision of primitive Christian unity was becoming just another sect. Wright advocated a nonsectarian stance for the Harvesters. Christians from all denominations should be invited to attend their conferences; a variety of evangelical speakers should participate; and the Harvesters should help existing congregations rather than form new ones. Despite some dissent, these terms were accepted, and the Harvesters began a remarkable new phase of growth and influence.[7]

For the first five years under Elwin Wright's leadership, change came rather slowly. The summer meetings at Rumney continued, and the evangelistic bands still traversed northern New England. There were signs, however, of the expansion and broadening to come. One of the most striking was an experiment in Florida. Back in 1923 Wright had taken a team of Harvesters with him to Orlando, Florida, to evangelize the tourist camps while he explored the real estate market. Still working this region five winters later, Wright moved his evangelism from the camps on Orlando's outskirts to the Municipal Auditorium downtown. A series of meetings there featured the veteran fundamentalist campaigner, R. A. Torrey, and Torrey's protégé, Will H. Houghton, the pastor of the four-thousand-member Baptist Tabernacle in Atlanta. Wright was yearning to reach the very center of society as well as the margins, and he sensed that fundamentalism, oddly enough, had a broader appeal than his own tradition.[8]

The real breakthrough for the Harvesters, however, came during a five-day summer conference at Rumney in 1929. Invitations went out to the pastors of nearly every denomination in New England to come hear the fundamentalist champion, William Bell Riley. Several hundred pastors attended, and before long they had "their arms around each other, tears coursing down their faces as they realized that not too far from them was the pastor of another denomination who really loved the Lord and His Word." That event sealed Wright's call to promote cooperation for revival in New England, and it showed that he was looking to fundamentalism to provide the common denominator. Wright urged his colleagues to pray fervently for revival, develop a "burning love for the souls of men," avoid sectarian prejudices, be willing both to "bear reproach" and "bear with each other," and try new methods. In real estate Wright had learned to "cut the red tape of precedent and explore new fields," he said, and evangelical churches must do the same.[9]

Wright's strategy succeeded handsomely. In 1930 and 1931 alone the Association added over five hundred cooperating pastors. Renaming itself the New England Fellowship in 1931, the organization expanded its activities and soon thereafter transferred its headquarters from Rumney to downtown Boston. By 1935 the Fellowship was sponsoring fifty-two evangelistic campaigns, over seven hundred special services and short conferences, four summer conferences and a Bible study circuit that held 240 services in 35 cities and towns. Other innovative ministries included camping programs for girls and boys at

Rumney, an outreach to rural school children directed by Wright's talented associate, Elizabeth Evans, the Surrendered Life League for teens and young adults, Fishermen's Gospel Teams for businessmen, and a radio program. "The work is growing so fast," Wright wrote in midsummer 1936, "that we find it hard to keep up with it." Perhaps the crowning events of the Fellowship's rapid development were two massive rallies: a live broadcast in 1939 of the *Old Fashioned Revival Hour* from Mechanics Hall in Boston, and a repeat performance in 1941, this time at the Boston Garden. After years of working at the margins, the Fellowship had brought born-again religion to New England's main arena.[10]

Organizing a National Association

As the stars of the Bible conference circuit came to speak at Rumney, many were astonished by the breadth of evangelical involvement in the NEF and by the great scope of its cooperative work. All kinds of evangelical Protestants were welcome, from New England's denominational mainline—Congregationalists, Episcopalians, Methodists, and Baptists—to the holiness and pentecostal groups such as the Church of the Nazarene, the Salvation Army, and the Assemblies of God. People from independent gospel tabernacles participated, as did Advent Christian and Christian and Missionary Alliance congregations, and the scattered ethnic churches of the United Presbyterian, Christian Reformed, Evangelical Covenant, and Evangelical Free denominations. The vision behind this cooperation was essentially Elwin Wright's. Although he had been reared on the sectarian fringe of American Protestantism, Wright had not been content to stay there. Attracted to the broader reach of fundamentalist revivalism, Wright joined that movement's most influential church in New England, Park Street Congregational, in Boston. But Wright was not willing to break off fellowship with his "disreputable" holiness and pentecostal friends. Under his leadership, the New England Fellowship encompassed a wide spectrum of backgrounds and beliefs. There was not any other group like it in the nation.[11]

In 1937, Wright and the Fellowship Radio Ensemble mounted a coast-to-coast tour. Everywhere they ministered, leaders yearned for cooperation and fellowship like that enjoyed in New England. Wright also heard many complaints about "hyper-critical and intolerant fundamentalists." He predicted that in the next decade a united effort among the more irenic and cooperative evangelicals would bring a national revival. With this vision in mind, Wright asked the advice of some national leaders such as William Ward Ayer, pastor of New York's Calvary Baptist Church; Charles E. Fuller of the *Old Fashioned Revival Hour;* and Will Houghton, now the president of the Moody Bible Institute. They all encouraged him to pursue his dream of evangelical cooperation nationwide and, in 1939, with a mandate from the Fellowship board, he did.[12]

One of Wright's contacts, an executive with the Africa Inland Mission named Ralph T. Davis, circulated a letter in December 1940 proposing a national committee to represent evangelicals in Washington. Davis's immediate concern was the effect of the military draft on missionary candidates, but the larger need he saw was to end the Federal Council of Churches' exclusive representation of Protestants' public concerns. Government's increasing powers of regulation made advocacy necessary, he warned. Davis's missive was favorably received. Will Houghton, for example, wrote to Davis that even though "a thousand critical problems" would hamper any attempt to organize evangelicals, the "real dangers" that threatened them should prompt evangelicals to "lay aside their differences."[13]

At least one of these "critical problems" lay close at hand. Early in 1940, the leaders of two small fundamentalist groups, the Bible Presbyterian Church and the Bible Protestant Church, had decided to do something about the Federal Council's left-liberal political pronouncements and its monopoly over Protestantism's public representation. This group's chief organizer was Carl McIntire, the radio-preaching pastor of the Bible Presbyterian Church in Collingswood, New Jersey. In the fall of 1940, both denominations formed committees to establish a national council of conservative Protestants, and in the summer of 1941, a constitution was drafted. This document was circulated to four hundred conservative Protestant leaders, who were asked to lend their names to a "sponsoring committee." Among those who responded favorably was Will Houghton.[14]

When Elwin Wright learned of this plan in September 1941, he urged McIntire to wait until the group of leaders whom he and Davis were convening could respond. McIntire and his colleagues were meeting just then in New York to establish their council, and they decided to go ahead anyway. They announced the formation of the American Council of Christian Churches, "sponsored by a national committee of prominent Fundamentalists," and designed to be "the voice of evangelical Christians." Charging that the Federal Council spoke only for the "Modernist wing of American Protestantism," the founders of the American Council stated that their aim was to cause a "revolutionary realignment in American Protestantism." It would have been hard for Elwin Wright and his colleagues to imagine a worse scenario. They knew that despite the American Council's grand rhetoric about realignments, McIntire's group simply did not have the national standing to convene a broad alliance. It was a matter of the tail trying to wag the dog, as Donald Barnhouse later remarked.[15]

The second, more serious problem was the American Council founders' position in denominational politics. They considered the mainline Protestant denominations to be irredeemably apostate, but evangelical Protestants were not agreed on this issue. Some were definitely "come outers," having formed new denominations such as the Church of the Nazarene (founded 1908) or the General Association of Regular Baptist Churches (founded 1932). Others belonged to large conservative denominations that had never joined the Federal Council, most notably the Southern Baptists. There were also denominations that were both mainline Protestant and largely conservative or evangelical, such as the Reformed Church of America and the Evangelical United Brethren. The "separation" issue loomed largest, however, for moderate fundamentalist leaders such as Harold Ockenga, Donald Barnhouse, and John W. Bradbury (the editor of the Baptist *Watchman-Examiner*), who had stayed within the mainline denominations. Because come-outers such as Carl McIntire had been vilifying them as compromisers, these leaders found the separatist agenda especially offensive. Barnhouse said that the American Council's plan for a nonstop attack on mainline Protestantism reminded him of a salesman who wanted to sell a man a bill of goods, but started off by insulting the man's wife.[16]

Although taken aback by the American Council's head start, the Wright-Davis group was determined to move forward. First they tried to negotiate. They invited McIntire and two other American Council leaders to a meeting with Wright and Davis hosted by Will Houghton at the Moody Bible Institute. Also attending were Stephen Paine, president of Houghton College, V. Raymond Edman, president of Wheaton College, Harry Ironside of the Moody Memorial Church, and Charles E. Fuller of the *Old Fashioned Revival Hour*. Each side stated its position and plan, and each invited the other to join with them.[17] It soon became clear that the leaders of the American Council would not alter its express purpose of opposing the Federal Council or its membership rules, which gave voting membership only to separatist denominations. These rules virtually shut out nonseparatists such as Houghton and Wright and leaders of independent ministries such as Fuller. So the Wright-Davis group declined to merge into the American Council. They then voted to proceed with their own plans.[18]

Those plans were to canvass evangelical leaders nationwide and issue a call for a national convention in St. Louis during April 1942. A "Temporary Committee for United Action among Evangelicals" was named with Davis as its secretary/treasurer. This group met several times in New York during the winter of 1941–1942 to prepare for the St. Louis conference.[19] Their first item of business was to gain the support of a great cross section of evangelical leaders. Striking out from New York on January 10, Wright toured the South and Midwest for ten days. He met with southern Presbyterian leaders in Charlotte, North Carolina; regional Southern Baptist leaders in Atlanta; various religious leaders in Chattanooga; Southern Baptist denominational executives in Nashville; and both Baptists and Presbyterians in Memphis. In St. Louis, Wright met with the great Lutheran radio preacher, Dr. Walter A. Maier, who warned of the Missouri Synod's probable refusal. In Louisville, another Southern Baptist stronghold, Wright got the editorial endorsement of the influential *Western Recorder* but a more cautious response from President J. R. Sampey of the Southern Baptist Theological Seminary. At one last stop, in Milwaukee, Wright found the Wisconsin Evangelical Lutheran Synod's position to be "noncooperative." After reporting to the committee in New York on January 19, Wright set out again. Before the conference in St. Louis that April, he would visit thirty-four states on similar missions.[20]

Ralph Davis then wrote to Wright's contacts to express the committee's aims and to ask them to sign a call for the St. Louis meeting. This new movement was to be cooperative and inclusive but definitely evangelical, the letter stated; it was not to be confused with any "previously formed group" (i.e., the

American Council); and its aim was to be positive, not belligerent. The call posed a number of organizational needs: a united front to represent issues to the government, a "clearing house" of evangelical programs and campaigns nationwide, and a unified evangelical voice in opposition to the "forces of unbelief."[21] These efforts produced a call that was signed by 147 evangelical leaders from all regions and a wide variety of denominations and agencies. Among them were many well-known fundamentalists, but also leading Southern Baptists, several prominent southern Presbyterians, a United Presbyterian theologian, two eminent preachers in the Evangelical Covenant Church, Assemblies of God officials, a Regular Baptist leader, officials from both the Pilgrim Holiness Church and the Christian and Missionary Alliance, a prominent Methodist businessman and philanthropist, and a senior missionary statesman of the Reformed Church of America.[22]

The Wright-Davis group's welcome into some of these circles was dampened, however, by denominational leaders' hesitation about signing on with some sort of "quack movement." Had the NAE organizers been able to work unhindered on the conservative Protestant denominational front, they might have been able to allay some of these suspicions. The leaders of the American Council, however, would not afford them that chance. Even before the St. Louis meeting, they were trying to discourage the signers of the call from attending the conference. The Temporary Committee was put on the defensive. Davis hastily sent out letters to explain his group's relationship to the American Council and to keep the signers of the call on board. The Temporary Committee came to St. Louis prepared for trouble. The American Council people would be there, promoting their cause and probably trying to discredit the conveners. Wright's group came equipped with plans for controlling the meeting, ready to handle any subversive moves.[23]

The National Association of Evangelicals Is Born

Despite these fears, the meeting got off to an impressive start. Wright addressed the group first and presented an overview of the process that had led to the convention. He was followed by Harold John Ockenga, the scholarly young pastor of Park Street Church in Boston. Ockenga's address was a sweeping jeremiad. America was in peril, he warned, because of the "disintegration of Christianity" and the ensuing "break-up of the moral fiber of the American people." The government had effected a "managerial revolution" that was destroying free enterprise and "secularism" was flooding the nation. Yet when things looked darkest, God would use his faithful remnant to bring a revival. Evangelicals had been faithful, Ockenga argued, but they were scattered, and they needed to organize. This meeting, therefore, could be the vanguard of a great movement to bring a revival and inaugurate "a new era in evangelical Christianity."[24]

The other memorable address came from the Wesleyan Methodist educator, Stephen W. Paine, who urged the group to avoid attacking those whose doctrinal views differed from their own, and to seek unity on a simple evangelical basis. Paine closed with a pointed message to the separatist brethren. He urged them to "shun a spirit of controversy and opposition to existing organizations, even when we question their orthodoxy." Yet he also warned the rest that it would be hypocritical "if we who believe we ought to shun contention should be found contending with those who announce that we ought to maintain a spirit of controversy." Unfortunately, Paine's words proved to be prophetic.[25]

The business sessions of the conference commenced the first afternoon, and so did the fireworks. The agenda was an open discussion about founding an evangelical association, but it also included a time set aside to hear from "representatives of the organizations existing for similar purposes." McIntire and his supporters were already working the convention. They were distributing a pamphlet implying that the Wright-Davis group had made "attacks" upon their organization. Apparently, the conference organizers decided that they had heard enough from the agitators. When a motion was raised to hear from Carl McIntire on the work of the American Council, a floor debate erupted. When at last McIntire was permitted to take the rostrum, he was interrupted after only five minutes by a motion calling for an end to all further consideration of the American Council. After another lengthy debate, the motion passed. The next day, however, Wright apologized to McIntire and offered him thirty minutes of speaking time. McIntire made an eloquent plea for the separatist cause. No sooner had he finished when a flurry of motions and amendments again ensued, but in the end a motion to form a new organization prevailed by a wide margin. The rest of the sessions apparently proceeded without incident, and the delegates ended their business with an agreement to hold a constitutional convention in Chicago the following year. They named an executive committee, with Harold Ockenga as interim president, to lay plans for the organization, and enlisted a "Committee of Twenty-five" to provide endorsements. The conference then closed with a sermon by the Southern Baptist spellbinder, Robert G. Lee of Memphis.[26]

The leaders of the nascent organization quickly began planning for the constitutional convention and promoting it nationwide. They held forty-two rallies in twenty-six states across the country during the intervening year. As a result, thirty-four district committees were formed to advance the new association. This organizing paid off, for some six hundred delegates and observers convened in Chicago on May 3–6, 1943 to establish the National Association of Evangelicals. Once again, Elwin Wright and Harold Ockenga set the tone. Wright discussed his organizing efforts and his hopes for the new association, and he spoke of some very concrete needs that he and others were already addressing. He had led an attempt to stave off a proposed recommendation by the National Association of Broadcasters that would disallow paid religious broadcasting, and he had lobbied congressmen to counter a move to exclude all nonunion (including volunteer religious) musicians from radio. These instances proved, Wright insisted, that the NAE was needed for public advocacy.[27]

Wright's greatest desire for the NAE, however, was that it would steer a true religious course. On one side, he saw the spiritual shoals of modernism, and on the other, the rocks of negative and fractious fundamentalism. Wright challenged the assembly to renounce "the continued fragmentizing of the church" and to "heal the wounded spirits" of those who had been battered by "a narrow and bigoted leadership." What was ultimately at stake, Wright believed, was the opportunity to stir up another great awakening. He hoped that the NAE's "new spirit of cooperation" would make it possible once more to organize community-wide revival campaigns which would "sweep across our land like mighty showers of spiritual refreshing."[28]

Harold Ockenga came next to the rostrum, and his presidential oration, "Christ for America," was a sweeping jeremiad like his speech the year before, but expanded to global dimensions. Like Wright, Ockenga had been travelling widely, and what he saw in wartime America deeply convinced him, he said, that "the United States of America has been assigned a destiny comparable to that of ancient Israel." At the heart of the republic's fate he saw a missionary mandate: America was called to evangelize the world, but the nation had failed to discharge its duty. Meanwhile, the West had become disillusioned with the liberal doctrines of human goodness and perfectibility, and many had turned to the ideologies of fascism and communism, to the modern gods of "blood, power, sex, money, hunger, strong men, and strong weapons." As a result, a terrible war was now engulfing the globe. The current war had a purpose, however; it was showing the nations that they had a choice to make. One path led back "to the Dark Ages of heathendom," but the other road led to the "rescue of western civilization by a . . . revival of evangelical Christianity." Ockenga was hopeful that the trial of war would promote a fresh tide of "common sense, faith [and] vision." A revival was in the offing, Ockenga believed, and he challenged the delegates to become the vanguard for the reconstruction of society's foundations.[29]

Bolstered by such inspiration, the convention tackled the business at hand. Membership and proportional representation was offered to denominations, regional associations, local churches, a variety of other religious agencies, and even to individuals. Affiliation was not made contingent in any way upon one's relationship to the Federal Council, and a simple, nonsectarian statement of faith was approved. The one other major piece of business accomplished at the Chicago meeting was the election of officers. Harold Ockenga was reelected as the president. A Free Methodist bishop, Leslie R. Marston, became first vice president; a Southern Baptist layman from Memphis, John W. McCall, was voted second vice president; a Philadelphia Presbyterian attorney, J. Willison Smith, was elected secretary; and a Methodist business executive from Chicago, Herbert J. Taylor, was picked to be treasurer. The larger boards and committees also showed a careful pattern of balancing to include members from mainline northern denominations, Southern Baptists and southern Presbyterians, and the mosaic of smaller evangelical groups: Reformed and Presbyterians, Wesleyan holiness denominations, pentecostals, Mennonites, and Scandinavian free evangelical churches. There were few significant groups or persuasions within the white American evangelical mosaic that were not somehow represented.[30]

From this beginning the National Association of Evangelicals grew to become a significant source of evangelical action. By 1948 the organization had eighteen small denominations as members, a number of regional bodies of larger denominations, and scores of single congregations. It operated eleven regional offices and sponsored a number of local chapters. The NAE had little success, however, in convincing the larger denominations whose members sat on its committees to become members. In five years it had enrolled somewhat less than a million members out of a potential constituency of some fifteen million who had delegates or observers at the Chicago convention.[31] Still, the NAE's influence exceeded the sum of its membership rolls, for it had either founded or inspired a variety of collaborative ventures, including the National Religious Broadcasters, the Evangelical Theological Society, the Evangelical Press Association, and the Evangelical Foreign Missions Association. The NAE was a convener, catalyst, and confidence-builder, proving that great things could be done by collective effort. It eclipsed the American Council almost immediately, and managed to withstand repeated attacks from the right flank. Ockenga dismissed the separatist critics with an old Gypsy proverb: "The dogs bark, but the caravan moves on."[32]

The Emergence of "Evangelicals"

Forming a caravan such as the NAE and driving it across the American religious landscape was bound to have an environmental impact. One of the most important effects was on fundamentalism. Since the fundamentalist–modernist controversies of the 1920s, the strains caused by the "separation" issue had been mitigated by fundamentalism's nondenominational network of ministries. With both the NAE and the American Council competing for fundamentalists' support, the separation debate heated up once again. The separatists were not able to hold up the NAE entourage, but they were able to frustrate it. The chief hinderer was Carl McIntire, who had emerged as the separatists' most formidable spokesman. McIntire had not been nationally prominent before this controversy, but some of the NAE's leaders were well acquainted with him. During the strife surrounding J. Gresham Machen's movement to found Westminster Seminary and the Independent Board of Presbyterian Foreign Missions a decade earlier, McIntire had been in the thick of the fight. He was eventually tried and suspended from the Presbyterian ministry and his congregation lost its building. McIntire had reason, then, to deeply resent those who "sat comfortably at home" instead of challenging the "forces of apostasy." Personal bitterness, ambition, and rivalry certainly played a role in McIntire's attacks, but for the separatists, this was spiritual warfare, and reluctance to confront the liberal forces was treason.[33]

The last thing that the NAE's leaders wanted was to get into a "back alley scrap," as Ockenga termed it, with the separatists.[34] Yet they found themselves being cornered, with no easy way out. For all the rhetoric about organizing on a positive basis, the NAE obviously was a conservative alternative to the

Federal Council. This posture could not be softened without causing some conservatives to doubt the NAE's integrity. On the other hand, the more time that was devoted to contending with either the Federal Council or the separatists, the more the NAE would look like a narrowly fundamentalist outfit and lose its attraction to many other evangelicals. So NAE leaders were forced to fend off McIntire's punches while holding back their own. Carl McIntire had plenty of experience in ecclesiastical street fighting, and he and his separatist confederates went to work right after the St. Louis meeting, using rhetoric sure to elicit furrowed brows in fundamentalist circles. The *Christian Beacon* repeatedly scolded the NAE for not taking "a definite stand" against the modernism of the Federal Council. The results, the critics charged, were "confusion," "compromise," and "appeasement."[35]

Harold Ockenga replied that the NAE's "positive doctrine and deeds" clearly set it apart from the modernists. The NAE's agenda was not contentious but evangelical, with the ultimate goal of "a national revival." Militant fundamentalists should have learned their lesson, an editorial in *United Evangelical Action* argued. For all of their "bitterness, rancor, carping and ranting," they had "not won any major victories against modernism." The cure for the church's modernistic infection was not more fighting but a revival. Elwin Wright tried to take the rhetorical high ground by identifying with the Apostle Paul's ability to rejoice even when Christ is preached "out of contention" (Phil. 1:16). He admonished his supporters to avoid the temptation to unnecessarily inflame the situation, for the new movement had "no time for fruitless bickering." This was in fact a bit of sanctimonious sneak punching, which provided more than enough provocation to keep the separatists fighting. Indeed, one of the most damning charges McIntire and his colleagues brought against the NAE was that it would not "fight the enemies of the Lord Jesus Christ" in the Federal Council but was contending instead against true blue fundamentalists, whose only offense was exposing "the sin . . . of the Federal Council." Who was the enemy, anyway?[36]

The separatists also put pressure on fundamentalist leaders to stay away from the NAE for fear of alienating some of their constituents. Immediately after the St. Louis meeting, Ralph Davis reported that a leader of Christian businessmen's groups in New York had refused to share his mailing lists. The man had apologized but said that he was getting into "hot water" for cooperating. Davis himself was vulnerable, and McIntire wasted no time in going after him, editorializing in the summer of 1942 that Davis's involvement in the NAE had "already affected the attitude of some" toward the Africa Inland Mission. McIntire came as an "observer" to the NAE's 1943 Chicago convention, where he saw President Edman of Wheaton College. Was he a delegate or an observer? Many would be very concerned, McIntire opined, to know where Wheaton stood on the NAE. McIntire also noted that Will Houghton was not attending, even though the meeting was in his home town. Moody's vice president, Henry C. Crowell, did attend, but he pointedly announced that he was not an official delegate.[37]

Faced with this sort of intimidation, a number of important fundamental-ist leaders and agencies backed away from the NAE. Ralph Davis, for one, retreated from the leaders' circle. Throughout President Edman's tenure, Wheaton College did not join the NAE. Dallas Theological Seminary did not join, either, even though its president, Lewis Sperry Chafer, had signed the call to the St. Louis meeting, contributed a written endorsement to its published proceedings, and blessed the NAE in the school's theological journal.[38] Perhaps the most important fundamentalist leader to back away was Will Houghton. He had endorsed the American Council at first, but then he signed the call for the St. Louis meeting. From that point on, however, he avoided both organizations. So did the Moody Bible Institute. A few editorials in the *Moody Monthly* criticizing fundamentalists' inability to work together was as close as the school's leaders came to addressing the issue.[39] With McIntire and com-pany putting the pressure on, and with constituents, employees, and even their trustees divided over which camp to favor, the major fundamentalist ministries and their leaders could not afford to take a position. McIntire noticed, with a measure of satisfaction, how many groups "had taken the hands-off policy."[40]

Elwin Wright expressed deep frustration at this whole turn of events. Evan-gelical unity was "the paramount issue of this generation," he believed, but because of the separatists, many were sitting "on the sidelines."[41] Yet the argu-ment over the NAE's ecclesiastical stance was opening up a fault line in fun-damentalism between the militants and the moderates. As a result of this controversy, militants felt even more estranged from their moderate counter-parts. The moderates, by contrast, were prompted by the attacks from within fundamentalist circles to identify even more strongly with the new evangelical coalition developing around the NAE. Indeed, a new sense of identity was being formed. The most important ecclesiastical issue of the day, proclaimed the editor of *United Evangelical Action*, was the "growing chasm" between "militant fundamentalism" on the one side and on the other a group which, he said, "we will designate as evangelicals, for the sake of distinction."[42] This differentiation would not be sharp and clear for at least another decade, since the terms "fundamentalist" and "evangelical" continued to be used more or less interchangeably. With the formation of the NAE, however, the embryo of a distinction was taking shape. It was tied to the idea that "evangelicals" were a coalition with a positive purpose, and that they were to be differentiated from militant fundamentalism.[43] Increasingly, the "evangelicals" would become a recognizable entity, a new cluster of players on American religion's field.

A Changing Religious Economy

For a long time yet, no one outside of conservative Protestant circles would recognize the need to distinguish between evangelicals and fundamentalists. From the vantage point of mainline Protestantism they were all antiecumeni-cal sectarians. Indeed, the fight with the American Council had pushed the NAE in a more sectarian direction. In their efforts to carve out a more defensible position against the separatists, the NAE's leaders felt compelled to attack the Federal Council. Elwin Wright published a series of critical "exposés" of the ecumencial movement in *United Evangelical Action* during late 1942 and early 1943. He did this, he said, in response to questions about where the NAE stood. Thereafter, other NAE leaders opened fire on ecumenical Protestantism.[44] Also in response to the American Council's badgering, the NAE changed its bylaws in 1944 to preclude a denomination's taking out dual membership in both the Federal Council and the NAE.[45] The NAE thus was caught in a contradiction. While its leaders tried to convince various audiences that it was a legitimate, broadly based Protestant organization, they were attacking the ecumenical movement and demanding that denominations choose between the NAE and the Federal Council. The NAE's leaders claimed that they rejected separatism as a governing principle and that their organization existed to pursue positive goals, but from a mainline Protestant perspective, the distinction between the American Council's separatism and the NAE's independency did not constitute much of a difference. The *Christian Century's* initial judgment that the founding of the NAE was giving "sectarianism [a] new lease on life" seemed largely just.[46]

By contrast, the mainline Protestants' ecumenical movement seemed to be the wave of the future. As mainline leaders laid plans for a religious reconstruction of the postwar world, their dreams of an inclusive church seemed within their grasp. So the NAE looked like a retrograde effort, an embarrassing reminder that the "belated forms of denominational organization" had not yet been "starved out," as Harry Emerson Fosdick had predicted. Still, the NAE hardly seemed to be worth more than an occasional critical comment. The Federal Council and the constellation of ecumenical endeavors surrounding it could continue to act as though they represented the only Protestants who mattered.[47]

Nevertheless, the NAE (and to a lesser extent the American Council) gave witness to an important reality, to Protestantism's enduring diversity and competitiveness. These "sectarian" organizations pointed out that as much as the mainline might sing, "We are not divided; all one body we," those who would not march alongside them were great in number also, if not in stature. In the free religious marketplace of American society, new religious movements have found ways to wrest a significant market share from older, more respectable bodies that have been less responsive to the changing religious economy. This phenomenon, which marked the rise of the Baptists and Methodists in the nineteenth century, was recurring in the twentieth century. Populist evangelical movements were challenging the mainline's claim to be the sole legitimate representative of Protestantism. While the American Council soon faded, the NAE endured as the symbolic location of a second opinion within American Protestantism. The NAE gave a measure of legitimacy to a new generation of upstart sects.[48]

In addition to representing a new wave of religious entrepreneurship and competition, the NAE was the sign of a new organizational trend. A major structural change was beginning within American religion, in which the denominational pattern of religious organization would decrease in importance. Unlike the Federal Council and even the American Council, the NAE was not a council of churches. It had member denominations but also offered other classes of membership. Congregations, individuals and independent ministries of a wide variety—schools, missions, publishing houses, radio programs, businessmen's fellowships—were eligible to affiliate. For some of the NAE's constituents—notably the Wesleyan holiness, pentecostal, and Dutch Reformed churches—this feature was not terribly important. For them as well as for mainline Protestants, denominations were still the usual way of organizing for ministry beyond the local church.

For the fundamentalists, however, the NAE's provision for individual and parachurch memberships was vitally important. Unlike other popular religious movements that eventually organized new denominations, fundamentalism continued as a network linked by independent, special-purpose agencies. These agencies enabled many if not most fundamentalists to avoid the disturbing issue of ecclesiastical separation but still divert their primary loyalties and financial support away from the mainline denominations. The NAE's founders implicitly recognized this parachurch pattern of organization and tried to accommodate it. And when some fundamentalists shied away from membership, the NAE developed and spun off a number of special-purpose "trade associations" for mission societies, publishers, and religious broadcasters that served NAE members and nonmembers alike. Thus the NAE was able to salvage its role as the convener and encourager of a national evangelical coalition. Although NAE leaders were frustrated with their failure to obtain formal endorsements and memberships from key groups, the broader evangelical coalition the NAE had inspired still won the participation of these groups.

For the Federal Council, the most important sign of its public influence was the sum of its denominations' membership statistics. While both the American Council and the NAE tried to play the same numbers game, the actual influence of the NAE came not so much from formal membership as from the networks into which it was connecting. Fundamentalism's weblike organizational structure, linked by parachurch ministries, endured, expanded, and exported itself to other evangelicals. In the postwar years, other groups such as the pentecostals would experience a gradual weakening of their denominationalism and a growing reliance on the parachurch pattern of religious organization. Indeed, as sociologist Robert Wuthnow shows, this pattern is now surpassing denominationalism as the dominant structure of American religion. Even while it was relatively small and only partially successful in formally uniting evangelicals, the NAE was a harbinger of things to come.[49]

Fundamentalism and the New Evangelical Coalition

One of those emerging trends was a new religious alignment that was beginning to be known as "the evangelicals." Before the NAE was formed, this coalition simply did not exist, perhaps with the exception of the New England

Fellowship. Revivalist, pietist, or doctrinally conservative Protestants—ranging from pentecostals to Presbyterians to Mennonites—were thriving, in great variety and number, both outside of and within the mainline denominations. Yet the many traditions and movements in this mosaic had little or no sense of belonging to some greater entity. Transdenominational fellowship and collaboration was a rarity. The vision of the NAE's founders—that these disparate religious subcultures could somehow be mobilized as a cooperative force—was adventurous indeed. That they would fail to unite all evangelicals under one banner seems in retrospect a foregone conclusion. That they succeeded to a modest extent in their formal organizational goals and convinced many that there was such a thing as evangelicalism were major feats of religious imagination and statesmanship.

One of the oddities of this feat, at least on the surface, is that fundamentalists provided the initial vision and leadership for "united evangelical action." Fundamentalist ecumenism seems like a contradiction in terms, but it was the major shaping force behind the formation of the NAE. Fundamentalists' desire to be "all things to all men" (I Cor. 9:22) for the sake of furthering the Christian message was in fact part of a "paradoxical tension," as George Marsden put it, at the core of their movement's character. Was fundamentalism essentially sectarian, in the spirit of John Nelson Darby's Plymouth Brethren, fragmenting into proliferating cadres of the doctrinally and behaviorally pure? Or was it revivalist, in the spirit of Dwight L. Moody, building coalitions around a common-denominator faith in order to prompt another Great Awakening? In truth it was both, with competing impulses at work within it, and the NAE is a prime example. Although it was formed as a quasi-separatist alternative to the Federal Council, the NAE was also an ecumenical coalition in service of revival.

Why did the moderate fundamentalist organizers of the NAE find so many other evangelical and conservative Protestants willing to give them at least a sympathetic hearing? Part of the answer is that throughout the second quarter of the twentieth century fundamentalism was the most visible and vocal of these movements and traditions. At any given time in the history of American evangelicalism, one particular perspective or movement has had a "leavening" influence on the others. Like the Methodists in the early nineteenth century and the holiness evangelists and Bible teachers in the late nineteenth century, the fundamentalists were the salient evangelical movement in the 1920s, 1930s, and 1940s. Fundamentalist ideas, methods, and products were permeating the American evangelical and conservative Protestant mosaic, and fundamentalist leaders had the visibility, sweeping vision and convening power to attract a broad new evangelical coalition.

As we have seen, fundamentalists seemed to have a knack for drawing a crowd and communicating the gospel to it in modern accents. This fact had not been lost on Elwin Wright, and his pilgrimage from pentecostal sectarianism to evangelical ecumenicity was accomplished largely by his moving into fundamentalist circles. Fundamentalists may have seemed like backwoodsmen to mainline Protestants, but to a number of younger holiness and pentecostal leaders in the 1940s they looked positively upscale and progressive. Fundamentalism also became a vehicle of assimilation for many immigrants of Protestant heritage. It was a new way for them to sing Zion's songs in a strange land, to give their faith dynamic expression in a New World context. This should not be surprising, since fundamentalism was in a sense a sojourner's faith already, a reconstituted community for rural and small-town Americans who had come to live in the city. It combined a lively and up-to-date revival style with a message that said "this world is not my home." This blend seemed to appeal to many people of immigrant stock who wanted both to make good in America and yet to honor their parents' faith.[50]

Jacob Stam, a delegate at the St. Louis conference in 1942, provides a close-up study of this phenomenon. Stam was an immigrant from the Netherlands who first professed faith after being handed a Dutch New Testament by a roving evangelist. Not long after, he founded the Star of Hope Mission, an urban outreach among the immigrants in Paterson, New Jersey. At first the mission was officially sponsored by the Christian Reformed Church. The Stam family had been influenced by fundamentalist evangelists and Bible teachers, however, and when Christian Reformed officials started trying to control the Stams' revival work, the family shifted its allegiance to fundamentalism, which was tailor-made for supporting independent ventures such as theirs. Many fundamentalist congregations had counterparts to the Stam family in their midst, people of immigrant Protestant heritages who had found an attractive new religious home.[51]

Fundamentalist beliefs and emphases also penetrated ethnic Protestant denominations themselves. Some communions with roots in transatlantic revivalism, such as the Swedish and Norwegian branches of the Evangelical Free Church, became fully identified with the fundamentalist movement. Others with a stronger location in a historic tradition, such as the two major Mennonite denominations and the two Dutch Reformed bodies, were attracted to some aspects of fundamentalism and repelled by others.

The Christian Reformed Church provides a good example of this ambivalent reception. As a denomination of immigrants that sprang from a revival of Calvinism in the Netherlands, the Christian Reformed Church resisted trends that threatened either its Reformed or its Dutch distinctiveness. American revivalism certainly was one of those trends, but the liberalization of mainline Protestantism seemed even more menacing. So while Christian Reformed leaders criticized the shallowness and flippancy of gospel tabernacle religion, the denomination contributed some of its best scholars to the antimodernist cause, first at Princeton Theological Seminary and then at Princeton-in-exile, Westminster Theological Seminary in Philadelphia. On the popular level, many in the Christian Reformed churches were attracted to fundamentalist revival services and radio programs, and not a few from the Dutch enclaves of the Midwest attended summer Bible conferences or received some training at the Moody Bible Institute. During the 1920s there was a bitter controversy and two minor secession movements in Michigan and Illinois, each resulting in the loss of a half-dozen Reformed and Christian Reformed congregations to the fundamentalist movement. Denominational leaders had good reason, then, to feel anxious about fundamentalism.[52] On the popular level, however, the attraction remained strong. A letter written by two children from Holland, Michigan, to the hosts of a program for youngsters on Moody's radio station shows the competing loyalties many felt: "We listen to your Bible Class every Saturday morning," they reported. "Sometimes we have to hurry home from catechism."[53]

The Christian Reformed Church, like so many other denominations created by immigrants, rapidly shifted to English-language worship and instruction in the 1930s, and it became vitally important to many of its younger leaders to develop a contemporary, truly American expression of their faith. One of the leaders in this endeavor was Clarence Bouma, a professor at Calvin Theological Seminary. Bouma spent a semester in Boston teaching at Gordon College in 1940, and the following year, when he convened a conference on the Calvinist mission to the modern world, Bouma's new friend, Harold Ockenga, was a featured speaker. So it is not surprising to find that Bouma was a delegate at the St. Louis meeting in 1942 and an officer of the new NAE in 1943, or that the Christian Reformed Church was a charter NAE member. This was an uneasy alliance, however. The NAE's firm stand for fundamental doctrines was attractive to Christian Reformed leaders, but its "Arminian" revivalism, which delighted many of the Dutch rank and file, most assuredly was not.[54] The story of the "fundamentalist leaven" throughout evangelical or conservative Protestantism during these years follows strikingly parallel lines, whether one focuses on the history of Mennonites and Brethren, holiness Wesleyans, or Southern Baptists. Rarely imbibed without a critical response from thoughtful guardians in each tradition, fundamentalism still had its attractions and left its mark. Sometimes it had a definite following within the group. More commonly it was manifested in new doctrinal emphases, notably antimodernism, dispensationalism, and biblical inerrancy; distinctive institutional forms, such as Bible institutes and Bible conferences; or in the proliferation of popular religious consumer products, including gospel songs, Scofield Reference Bibles, or the *Old Fashioned Revival Hour* radio program.[55]

There was more than style, however, to fundamentalism's appeal. For ambitious younger clergy and lay leaders, embracing the fundamentalists' revival vision moved them a step closer to the main corridors of American life and involved them in a larger purpose, a "greater field of service," than did the tight little denominational circles in which they were reared. Fundamentalists' driving vision for revival stemmed in part from the fact that unlike many pietist, revivalist, and conservative Protestants in America, fundamentalists were not content to sequester themselves in a cultural corner, nurturing their distinctive beliefs while the world passed them by. Fundamentalists deeply resented their exclusion from the nation's cultural centers and they were striving to find a way back. They were, as Grant Wacker puts it, "by far the most culturally aggressive members of the evangelical family." Far more than the others, they held to the Puritan-Reformed idea of cultural responsibility or "custodianship," and thus felt driven, despite their alienation, to restore a "Christian America."[56] Such beliefs resonated well with aspirations to middle-class status and respectability. For second-generation holiness, pentecostal, or ethnic Protestants who were ambitious for a higher rung on life's ladder than their parents had achieved and a higher purpose for their ministry than the internal affairs of their own denomination, this agenda was absolutely beguiling. No one else articulated it quite so well as the moderate fundamentalist reformers who first organized the NAE.[57]

Fundamentalists' campaign to organize a new evangelical coalition was blessed by good timing as well. There was a war on, and American leaders at all levels were straining to find a larger purpose for their various efforts. Fighting a world war seemed to spur many to think expansively, and fundamentalists too were ringing out themes of global challenge. In the context of calls for a united nation to face the enemy and for a United Nations to keep the peace, America's second-class Protestants were daring to dream of "United Action." They were led, as we have seen, by the unlikeliest of ecumenists, a group of fundamentalists.

Nevertheless, far fewer evangelicals joined the NAE than its organizers had hoped. Preaching with all their might that evangelical unity was the salient issue of the hour, the organizers of the NAE could not convince the larger conservative denominations and many of the smaller evangelical ones that the NAE was the most compelling vehicle for such unity. The fundamentalist-colored vision and rhetoric of the NAE, its distracting fight with the separatists, and the sectarian spirit of many evangelical groups made it impossible for the NAE to achieve the grand national alliance its founders envisioned.

One illustration of the limits of fundamentalism as an ecumenical agent was the NAE's failure to recruit the Southern Baptist Convention. Here was a conservative and aggressively evangelistic denomination that seemed like an obvious fit, and whose five million members in 1940 would have added considerable heft and credibility to the NAE. Elwin Wright carefully courted Southern Baptist leaders, and a number of them became NAE officers. Nevertheless, the Southern Baptist Convention preferred to take its stand alone. Southern cultural nationalism, denominational solidarity and self-sufficiency, and some internal tensions caused by fundamentalist agitators combined to keep the Convention aloof from entangling alliances. O. W. Taylor, editor of the *Tennessee Baptist and Reflector*, had visited the first NAE convention in St. Louis, and afterward he voiced what would be the party line. He did not question the "motives or sincerity of the sponsors," but he concluded that Southern Baptist people "already have the evangelical values" the NAE was trying to promote and "need no further organizational set-up to possess them."[58] "We have our own" was becoming the virtual motto of the Southern Baptists, for out of a scattered and fractious movement of independent congregations they had created a self-sufficient religious empire. Southern Baptist leaders thought the last thing they needed was some entangling alliance with Yankee fundamental-ists, holiness come-outers, immigrants, and tongues-speakers.[59]

The Southern Baptists' response offers an important clue for understanding the NAE's limited success in representing the whole breadth of twentieth-century evangelicalism. Southern Baptists did not sense that the NAE offered them something they needed. Likewise, other evangelical denominations chose whether or not to affiliate with the NAE according to their perceived needs. The NAE, then, was treated more as an ordinary parachurch group rather than as a normative call to Christian unity. Southern Baptists, with their great num-bers and well-established agencies, did not need either the NAE's services or its collective voice. Unlike smaller groups, such as the Free Methodists, Mennon-ite Brethren, and Assemblies of God, which had much to gain from the legit-imacy and advocacy offered by the NAE, the Southern Baptists were a force to be reckoned with in and of themselves.

Thus while the NAE was becoming the symbol and catalyst of a new evan-gelical coalition, it was not to become the all-inclusive clearing house, coordi-nator, and holding company for things evangelical. In a free religious economy, such monopolies were impossible. The NAE's birth pointed out that uncom-fortable fact to the Federal Council of Churches, but the NAE's own natural constituency was in turn illustrating the same truth to the NAE's frustrated organizers. The most powerful and effective kind of American ecumenism was neither formal and ecclesial, corporate and bureaucratic, nor even more vol-untary and coalitional. It was ad hoc, local, and task-oriented.

Organizing for Revival

Perhaps the most pointed illustration of this reality came when Elwin Wright tried to use the NAE to provide a national clearing house and coordinating center for urban revivalism. Based on his success in mobilizing the scattered evangelical churches of New England to sponsor such events as Charles Fuller's radio rallies at the Boston Garden, Wright believed that the NAE provided the basis for organizing "campaigns of community-wide character and strength" all across America. A Department of Evangelism was founded shortly after the 1943 Chicago convention, with a mandate to hold regional conferences, develop models for all-city crusades, and provide training and technical advice to local revival committees.[60]

Almost immediately, however, the NAE found out that it was not going to be able to coordinate revivalism nationwide from a central office. By the time the first regional conferences were held in late 1944, evangelicals (mostly fun-damentalists) in several major cities had already initiated campaigns under the sponsorship of "Christ for America," an initiative launched by Horace F. Dean, vice president of the Philadelphia School of Bible. Its inspiration came from a revival campaign held in Philadelphia during 1942, sponsored by the Philadelphia Fundamentalist Association and featuring Hyman Appelman, an evangelist from Texas. This three-week crusade involved over two hundred churches and live radio broadcasts. Some eighty-five thousand attended, and two thousand made "decisions for Christ." Encouraged to hope for similar responses across the land, Dean organized a national committee to sponsor crusades in other large cities, featuring old-style Southern evangelists such as Appelman, John R. Rice, and Joe Henry Hankins.[61]

Although the NAE leaders gave these campaigns positive coverage, they were perturbed by Dean's actions. Elwin Wright voiced his objections in a letter to an NAE officer who was backing the effort. Dean had launched these meetings without consulting the NAE, perhaps, Wright suspected, because Christ for America wanted to attract supporters who favored the American Council. What was worse, Dean and Appelman did not invite the holiness and pentecostal churches to participate. This exclusion threatened to undo the NAE's careful coalition-building and divide its local chapters. Wright also complained that the campaign's evangelists were not equal to the challenge. He believed that the NAE provided a broader, more inclusive basis for urban evangelism, and an approach that would be fresher and more compelling.[62]

Wright was fighting a lost cause, however, for the sort of consolidation he sought went against the basic nature and structure of the groups that made up the NAE. The spirit of religious enterprise, which led visionaries to form ministries without consulting anyone but the Almighty, would not be channeled. Indeed, the sense of fresh possibilities that the NAE did so much to evoke was prompting dozens of new initiatives to spring up from the grassroots. It was fruitless for the NAE to try to coordinate it all. Nevertheless, the NAE's attempt to form an evangelical united front had unleashed an idea, a new collective identity, and a dynamic force for religious initiatives. "Evangelicalism" had been born.

9

YOUTH FOR CHRIST

In October of 1941, just when Elwin Wright was traveling to Chicago to negotiate with Carl McIntire, another kind of evangelical movement was making its premiere in New York. People who were listening to station WHN on Saturday night, October 25, heard these words: "From Times Square, New York, we bring you the Word of Life . . . on the air!" With that the Word of Life Fellowship, a fundamentalist young people's organization, started a bold new venture. On the one night of the week long thought to be deadly for organized religious activities, World of Life was hosting a youth rally at the Alliance Tabernacle, in the heart of Manhattan's entertainment district.[1]

Word of Life, headed by a young evangelist named Jack Wyrtzen, became an important model for the Youth for Christ movement which rapidly captured a national following in the mid-1940s. By the last days of World War II, weekly youth rallies were thriving in hundreds of cities and towns with hundreds of thousands of people attending. At the same time, soldiers and sailors were holding rallies in Europe, the Pacific, and East Asia. Young people's ministries sponsored some spectacular events in those years, such as Word of Life's Victory Rally on April 1, 1944, when twenty thousand people filled Madison Square Garden; and the Memorial Day 1945 rally of Chicagoland Youth for Christ at Soldier Field, with seventy thousand present. Prompted by the movement's exciting style and spectacular growth, a writer for the *Chicago Daily News* exclaimed that Chicagoland Youth for Christ was the "biggest sensation in the world of religious revivals since the days of Billy Sunday."[2]

The Youth for Christ sensation is scarcely remembered, even in evangelical circles, yet it deserves to be recalled and understood because it marks the dawning of an era. The Youth for Christ phenomenon was the first sign that the revival of revivalism, which had been percolating deep within the fundamentalist movement, was finally breaking out into public view. The people who designed and promoted these rallies were not the recognized godfathers of fundamentalism—the Ironsides, Houghtons, and Rileys—but a coalition of youthful, relatively unknown evangelists. Their kind of revivalism was much more daring and innovative than their predecessors'. Unlike the *Old Fashioned Revival Hour,* for example, which used new means to convey its message but opted for a rather well-worn style, Youth for Christ wed born-again religion to the style as well as the media of the entertainment industry. From a fundamentalist perspective, the rally leaders were borrowing from the very dens of the devil—Hollywood and Radio City—to accomplish the Lord's purposes. Dressing revivalism in more fashionable attire and merging it with Americans' growing concern for their fate in a troubled world, Youth for Christ pioneered a new evangelical outreach. The rallies blended fundamentalists and other evangelicals into a broad coalition and showed how the movement might win a valued place once more in the public life of the nation. Youth for Christ had a long period of gestation before it emerged, however, and that is where this story must begin.

A Fundamentalist Youth Movement

Since fundamentalism advertised itself as "old-time religion," a youth movement in its ranks might sound like a contradiction in terms. Yet the antimodernist impulse was by no means confined to the older generation. In fact, the members of fundamentalist factions seemed to have been younger, on the average, than their opponents. Fundamentalists were conscious of their appeal to the young and proud of it. The movement's Bible institutes catered to young adults, and so did the summer Bible conferences. Indeed, the fundamentalist protest against mainline Protestantism often focused on the loss of evangelical fervor among youth-oriented ministries. The problem, said a young Baptist pastor from Philadelphia in 1925, was that "you can take the 'C' out of the YMCA and nobody would ever notice the difference."[3] To compensate, fundamentalists founded their own youth groups such as the East Bay (Oakland) Young People's Christian Fellowship and the New England Fellowship's Surrendered Life League. Large congregations, such as Calvary Baptist Church in New York, had their own youth ministries, and in a number of cities younger pastors and business people formed weekly gatherings for teenagers and younger adults.[4]

A few of these youth ministry leaders set the pace, and they became widely imitated. Their careers show similar patterns and the development of a distinctive style. Each came to faith during adolescence or early adulthood. They were unusually restless, constantly pursuing new ventures, and so intense that others would say they were "on fire" for the Lord.[5] Immersed in the idiom of popular culture, these young evangelists instinctively tuned their old-time faith to the new sounds and images of the popular entertainment world.

One of these pioneers was Lloyd Bryant, who had grown up in a tough neighborhood in Boston and was converted as a teenager. After a sojourn in the advertising business, Bryant enrolled in the National Bible Institute in

New York, where he caught the attention of Will Houghton, who hired him in 1932 to revive the youth ministry at Calvary Baptist Church. Bryant renamed the program the "New York Christian Youth Center," and during the next eight years he conducted over five hundred rallies at the Alliance Tabernacle near Times Square and on 57th Street at Calvary Baptist itself. These events had an average attendance of over six hundred. Other youth workers contacted Bryant for advice, and he helped them organize the Association of Christian Youth in America, most of whose forty chapters were in the New York metropolitan area. The movement grew when Bryant embarked on a nationwide tour in 1937 and 1938. Although Bryant's organization faded fairly rapidly, he showed dozens of local leaders the formula for a successful young people's ministry, featuring rallies, banquets, conferences, retreats, and radio programs—events that teenagers would get excited about and share with their friends.[6]

Groups like Bryant's were springing up elsewhere. In Washington D.C., Glenn Wagner, a former collegiate football star, organized a "Christian Youth Fellowship" in the early 1930s that drew participants from fifty-six congregations. In 1934 a young evangelist named Walter Smyth opened a youth center in Philadelphia. And in Detroit, a rally and broadcast called *The Voice of Christian Youth* began in 1937, led by evangelist Oscar Gillian, who had started a similar program in southern California three years earlier.[7]

The youth ministry which had the most widespread influence, however, was Percy Crawford's *Young People's Church of the Air,* based in Philadelphia. A hard-driving preacher and entrepreneur of Canadian birth, Crawford left home when he was a teenager. After drifting about the West Coast for a few years, he landed in Los Angeles in 1923. There Crawford, who was then twenty-one, took a room at the hotel operated by the Bible Institute of Los Angeles (BIOLA). Two days later he attended services at the Church of the Open Door and, responding to the gospel invitation, became a born-again Christian. Almost immediately he began preaching on street corners. Crawford enrolled at BIOLA, graduated two years later, and then studied for two years apiece at the University of Southern California and Wheaton College, where he received his degree in 1929. Crawford enrolled in Westminster Theological Seminary in Philadelphia later that year and took a student pastorate at a struggling Presbyterian mission in Philadelphia's inner city.[8]

Crawford's ministry was unconventional from the start. He preached on summer evenings in 1930 from the porch of the Old First (Pine Street) Presbyterian Church near Independence Hall. Soon he was drawing crowds of up to three hundred, mostly young people. At the close of the summer, Crawford began a radio broadcast that soon became known as the *Young People's Church of the Air*. Crawford expanded his station coverage rapidly while holding evangelistic youth rallies all along the Atlantic seaboard. By 1934 he was driving an unheard-of forty thousand miles each year; directing Pinebrook, a teen conference center in the Pocono Mountains; and operating a Christian bookstore. Somehow he also found time to get married and pursue graduate studies at the University of Pennsylvania. By 1940, Crawford's program was on scores of stations nationwide, and The King's College, which he had founded, was in its second year of operation in Belmar, New Jersey.[9]

Crawford's distinctive style became the norm for youth evangelists. He loved sporty clothes, practical jokes, and fast cars, and his programs moved at breakneck speed as well. They featured trumpet trios playing jazzed-up gospel tunes, talented vocal soloists such as George Beverly Shea of New York, and Crawford's high-voltage messages. Crawford's sermons were dramatic, bristling with Scripture quotations, and delivered in the rapid-fire, animated manner of radio news reporters. Since he was heard across the nation, Crawford was teaching scores of youth leaders their trade.[10]

One of Crawford's protégés was Jack Wyrtzen. A Brooklyn-bred insurance agent who went to church on Sunday mornings, Wyrtzen also enjoyed the night life with his twelve-piece dance band. After Wyrtzen's girlfriend and future wife, Marge Smith, was converted at Percy Crawford's Pinebrook Conference in 1933, Wyrtzen and his friends soon were transformed into another sort of band—a travelling evangelistic team. They continued to work at their secular jobs but spent their evenings and days off preaching and performing anywhere they could get a hearing: in churches, under revival tents, on the street, in prisons and youth reformatories, over the radio, on or near military bases and in the work camps of the Civilian Conservation Corps. In 1939, Wyrtzen and his troupe formally organized as the Word of Life Fellowship.[11]

Two years later Wyrtzen quit his job in order to expand this ministry. Soon Word of Life was sponsoring radio rallies at the Alliance Tabernacle in Manhattan, weekly Bible clubs throughout greater New York, an evening Bible school, a bookstore, banquets, Hudson River cruises, and a missionary recruiting agency. By 1943 the rallies had moved to Carnegie Hall, and in April 1944 Wyrtzen scheduled a "Victory Rally" for Madison Square Garden, which twenty thousand people attended. Encouraged by this response, Word of Life repeated the feat the following September.[12]

By this time "Youth for Christ" rallies based on Wyrtzen's and Crawford's format had spread to other cities. Roger Malsbary, the pastor of the Christian and Missionary Alliance Church in Danville, Indiana, began a Saturday night rally in early 1943 that soon moved to nearby Indianapolis. In Minneapolis, a young publisher named George Wilson planned a youth rally for the Northwestern Schools' homecoming in April 1944. Three thousand came, and Minneapolis Youth for Christ was born.[13] Chicagoland Youth for Christ, which was situated at the institutional hub of fundamentalism, soon became the rally movement's center. This rally was led by Torrey Johnson, pastor of Chicago's Midwest Bible Church. As president of the Wheaton College Alumni Association and treasurer of the Chicago-area chapter of the National Association of Evangelicals, Johnson had the contacts to organize a citywide project but showed no inclination to start a Saturday night rally. Others in Chicago who had seen the impact of Youth for Christ, notably George Beverly Shea, who was now working for WMBI, pleaded with Johnson to take up the task. Finally he relented and in early 1944 quickly assembled a team of musicians, evangelists, and supportive businessmen. They acquired the Chicago Symphony's Orchestra Hall for the summer and secured broadcast time on WCFL of Chicago. Twenty-five area youth organizations backed the effort, which was supported by one hundred business men and women.[14]

On opening night, May 27, two thousand showed up to hear Billy Graham, a twenty-five-year-old pastor from the suburbs. The rallies thrived throughout the summer and encouraged the directors to plan a massive "Victory Rally" like Wyrtzen's to highlight their fall and winter season. They rented the cavernous Chicago Stadium and, to their delight, a capacity crowd of twenty-eight thousand showed up. A broadcast of the rally and coverage by the major Chicago newspapers and the wire services helped spread the rally idea rapidly, and requests for advice swamped the Chicagoland Youth for Christ offices. Johnson and his brother-in-law, evangelist Robert Cook, responded with a small book, *Reaching Youth for Christ,* which sold fifteen thousand copies within a year.[15]

Geared to the Times: Entertaining Evangelism

Johnson and Cook were painfully aware of how hackneyed evangelism had become, and their book stressed the need to update the idiom. They reminded directors that a rally had to compete with what the "world" had to offer. Young people were used to flawlessly produced entertainment, the authors insisted: "Dare to offer something shoddy and they'll shun your meeting." A successful rally needed split-second timing, zippy gospel music, "punchy" announcements, brief and rehearsed testimonies, and messages with current-events "lead-ins." Johnson had preached at the June 10, 1944 rally on "D-Day—Day of Destiny," moving rapidly from the beaches at Normandy to other, greater "D-Days"—at Bethlehem and Calvary.[16]

The rally directors often copied popular entertainers' personal styles as well as their program formats. One reporter thought that Torrey Johnson was the "religious counterpart of Frank Sinatra." Johnson too had curly hair, wore bow ties, and spoke "the language of bobby soxers." Other preachers emulated personalities whose seriousness and urgency were adaptable to the pulpit—the radio news commentators. Jack Wyrtzen modeled his rapid delivery after Floyd Gibbons, while Billy Graham imitated the clipped speech of Walter Winchell.[17]

Central to the new style was Youth for Christ's updated gospel music. Many of the rally directors and musicians had experience in dance bands or as disc jockeys, and they liked music with a contemporary flair. Tight-harmony girls' trios abounded, as did swing-style instrumentals. One of the Chicagoland rally's trumpeters was nicknamed the "Harry James of the Sawdust Trail." Norman Clayton, an organist for both Percy Crawford and Jack Wyrtzen, echoed the dreamy "sweet" musical style in his compositions, "He Holds My Hand" and "Now I Belong to Jesus." Wyrtzen's song leader, Carlton Booth, evoked yet another popular style. A little girl once told him, "You sing just like a cowboy!"[18]

Another key to successful revivalism, the Youth for Christ leaders believed, was good publicity. They created mountains of slickly produced advertisements and press releases, hand cards, mailing cards, posters and tracts. A number of them—Ted Engstrom of Grand Rapids, for example—had worked in printing, publishing or advertising. Of equal importance were the movement's many contacts with the press. Toronto's rally director, Charles Templeton, had been a sports cartoonist for the *Daily Globe*. Youth for Christ's chief publicist, Mel Larson, was a sportswriter in Minneapolis. Don Hoke, a frequent rally speaker, had been a stringer for the *Chicago Tribune*. Vaughan Shoemaker, the chief cartoonist for the *Chicago Daily News* and founder of the businessmen's Gospel Fellowship Club in downtown Chicago, gave the movement valuable support. So did the religion editor of the *Chicago Daily News*, William F. McDermott, and Wesley Hartzell, the reporter whom the Hearst chain's *Chicago Herald-American* assigned to the rallies. Eventually Hartzell joined Youth for Christ's publicity committee. Clearly, these connections explain much of the movement's success at capturing public attention.[19]

The high tide of Youth for Christ's public notoriety came in the summer of 1945, in the wake of an event that caught national attention, even in these war-preoccupied days. On the evening of Memorial Day, seventy thousand people gathered at Soldier Field in Chicago to witness an open-air pageant. Like other ceremonies on that day, this one remembered fallen servicemen and rededicated a nation still at war to a global mission. The rally had an additional purpose, however. It celebrated the first anniversary of Chicagoland Youth for Christ, which had become the center of the rapidly growing movement. Youth for Christ's leaders could only guess its scope at that time, but their estimates ran to 300–400 rallies with a weekly attendance of 300,000–400,000. Youth for Christ had gone international as well, establishing new rallies, or "beachheads," among American military men and women in Paris, London, Glasgow, Frankfurt, Honolulu, Havana, Manila, and Peking.[20]

Giving full vent, then, to both an exuberant evangelicalism and a war-inspired revival of the American civic faith, the Soldier Field pageant praised God and country with a three-hundred-piece band, a choir of five thousand, and several well-known vocalists, including George Beverly Shea. On the field, high school cadets performed a flag ceremony along with four hundred marching nurses. Next came missionary volunteers in national costumes dramatizing the duty to evangelize the world. Standing for America was the young evangelist, Billy Graham, who sounded the call for another great revival. On the platform war heroes attested to their faith, as did intercollegiate boxing champion Bob Finley. Track star Gil Dodds, the record-holder for the indoor mile, ran an exhibition lap before giving his testimony. The evening's main speaker was Percy Crawford, and at the close of his sermon, hundreds signed cards to witness that they had accepted Christ as their savior. As the meeting drew to a close, a spotlight circled the darkened stadium while a huge neon sign blazed "JESUS SAVES" and the choir sang "We Shall Shine as Stars in the Morning."[21]

Indeed they did, for the rally attracted major news coverage from the Chicago papers, the wire services, and *Newsweek* magazine. A few weeks later,

William Randolph Hearst editorially blessed the movement and ordered his twenty-two papers to feature local rallies. Not since the Scopes trial had evangelical Christianity received such coverage, and this time most of it was friendly. The movement continued to grow, reaching a peak in 1946 of some nine hundred rallies with an estimated attendance of one million.[22]

Victory in Jesus: Civic Faith and Evangelical Revivalism

How can one explain this rapid growth? Surely the expansive outlook of a rising generation of evangelicals was part of the formula, and so was the youth rally movement's restyling of revivalism and skillful promotion. But external factors played a significant part as well, creating a demand for Youth for Christ. The rallies were greatly helped, to begin with, by what has been called the "Spirit of Pearl Harbor." World War II was in many respects a tonic for Americans' faith in their nation's commonly stated ideals that lasted long into the postwar years.[23] While the Depression had discouraged many people about ever realizing the American dream, war mobilization brought unprecedented opportunity even to the poorest. In spite of the disruptions, pain and grief, or frustration at injustice that many experienced, the war years' prosperity, mobility, and common cause regenerated Americans' civic faith.

Popular entertainment unabashedly celebrated the American dream in these years, with *Oklahoma!* and *Our Town* evoking a nostalgic reaffirmation of traditional values. The same spirit inspired one of Norman Rockwell's most famous works: an illustration of the "Four Freedoms" articulated in President Roosevelt's famous speech in January of 1941. Meanwhile, Kate Smith had made a hit of Irving Berlin's "God Bless America." Even on the left the mood was affirmative. Paul Robeson, the radical black vocal artist who had been ostracized from the concert circuit, performed Edwin A. Robinson's "Ballad for Americans" with great gusto.[24]

Religious faith appeared to be one of the values most worth reaffirming. The critical, condescending tone of much public discussion of religion since the 1920s was now muted by the renewed respect for faith that emerged at all levels. Many thought the war effort required all the spiritual reserves the country could muster. Religious trends among liberal intellectuals included heightened respect for Reinhold Niebuhr's neo-orthodoxy and the neo-Thomist Catholic philosophy of Jacques Maritain, while many Jewish intellectuals recognized that Jewish identity needed a religious focus.[25]

Among ordinary Americans, religious attendance and membership swung sharply upward in all faiths, and wartime stories of heroic chaplains, fox-hole epiphanies, and interfaith fellowship abounded. For three years in a row, a religious novel was the nation's best-selling work of fiction. Two of these, A. J. Cronin's *The Keys of the Kingdom* (1941) and Franz Werfel's *The Song of Bernadette* (1942), were quickly converted into popular movie versions. *Going My Way,* a gently inspiring film that portrayed Bing Crosby and Barry Fitzgerald as Roman Catholic priests, won several Academy Awards in 1944.[26]

Alongside the increased religiosity, however, came a surge of hard-living hedonism. As historian Geoffrey Perrett noted, the war was spurring "both religious sentiment and permissiveness." Church attendance increased but so did alcohol and tobacco consumption. Meanwhile, women's fashions were skimpier, Hollywood grew more brazen, and live entertainment became more vulgar. In the boomtowns created by military camps and war industries, divorce, prostitution, and violent crime abounded.[27] People were singing "God Bless America," Donald Barnhouse observed, but he wondered just which America God was supposed to bless. The America that spent more on alcohol than on religion? The America of the divorce courts? The nation where gambling, prostitution, and patronage rackets were a way of life? God would surely judge this America if she did not repent. President Roosevelt's calls for national days of prayer on Thanksgiving 1942 and New Year's Day 1943 did not impress evangelist Hyman Appelman. How could God answer these prayers? Appelman warned the nation to heed the words of the Psalmist: "If I regard iniquity in my heart, the Lord will not hear me (Ps. 66:18)." Revival, not a rebirth of religiosity, was what America needed.[28]

To many, no doubt, the fundamentalists' old-fashioned moral thunderings sounded tedious, if they were heard at all. There was a new problem, however, called "juvenile delinquency," that concerned almost everyone, from J. Edgar Hoover of the FBI to the progressive sociologist Robert S. Lynd. Street gangs were emerging in most large cities, and bus and train stations were full of teenage "Victory Girls," who offered sexual favors to servicemen in exchange for a night on the town. The war's demands on families meant that children were often left unsupervised, with free time, spending money, and little sense that they had any meaningful tasks to perform. Communities tried to overcome the delinquency problem by giving the teenagers something to do and somewhere to go. Many high schools launched a "Victory Corps" for stamp, bond, and scrap drives, and sponsored parades and physical fitness programs. Others started social and recreation centers modeled after those for servicemen. By 1946 as many as three thousand communities had "Teen Canteens" or "Rec' Centers."[29]

The Youth for Christ movement, then, was a part of this rising concern about young people set in the context of an increase in public religiosity, a revival of American civic faith, and worries about the nation's moral fitness to cope with its challenges. The youth rallies enjoyed their greatest expansion during 1943–1946, the years when juvenile delinquency emerged as a national problem. Rally evangelists hammered at the sins of youthful desire while featuring carefully orchestrated visions of innocence, heroism, and loyalty to a global cause, all wrapped in a format and idiom borrowed from radio variety shows and patriotic musical revues. Young people were restless, Torrey Johnson, explained; they were looking for a challenge. "They want something that demands sacrifice, . . . that appeals to the highest and holiest . . . that is worth living for and dying for."[30] Personal faith in Christ, tied to devotion to the Allied cause and to world evangelization, was Youth for Christ's answer.

The rally evangelists often singled out young people's morals in order to convict them of their need to make a fresh commitment to Christ. These preachers had often sown a few wild oats themselves before conversion, so they spoke knowingly about teenage temptations and perhaps sounded more like older brothers than worried parents. In one sermon, Jack Wyrtzen translated the parable of the Prodigal Son into contemporary terms. The young runaway had started "hanging about beer joints," where he began "playing fast and loose with women" and was soon "eating out of the garbage pails of sin." A reporter remarked that the youngsters were listening to Wyrtzen with rapt attention, and that "some had grown a shade pale."[31]

By contrast, the music, the personal testimonies, and the evangelists' invitation to receive Christ as savior stressed the joy and satisfaction of Christian commitment. At the Word of Life meeting referred to above, the all-girl choir and soloist George Beverly Shea sang "Jesus Can Satisfy the Heart," "Now I Belong to Jesus," and "What A Friend We Have in Jesus." When Wyrtzen told the audience that by confessing their sins and committing themselves to Christ they would start "the joy bells ringing in their hearts," one reporter noted an "almost pathetic eagerness" on many faces.[32] At the larger rallies, the penitents who came forward for prayer and counselling sometimes numbered in the hundreds. What were they experiencing? Some hints come from testimonies at the rallies. One sailor testified: "I was a sinner, but now, praise the Lord, I am clean, through Christ." Said another young seaman attending the Chicago rally, "Ever since I left the protection of my home, I have felt almost adrift, with no sense of security. I don't want to get caught in the current of vice. I needed something to stabilize me and in my new faith in Christ, I have found it."[33] For young people who were eager for challenges but also homesick, morally confused, and guilt-laden, Youth for Christ's message seems to have been compelling.

The Youth for Christ rallies evoked considerable public comment, and most of it was favorable. Civic leaders praised the rallies for their community service. When William Randolph Hearst commended the movement in an editorial, he called it a "powerful antidote" to juvenile delinquency and urged communities to support it. Walter Anderson, chief of police in Charlotte, North Carolina, became a rally director, claiming that "Youth for Christ is doing more than anything else I know to stop juvenile delinquency." Governor Arthur B. Lainglie of Washington said that youth ministries' combination of wholesome fun and religious challenge was the best cure for juvenile crime. After viewing a Youth for Christ rally in the Washington State Capitol, President Truman was said to have remarked that these meetings were just what America needed. Such praise was eagerly accepted by the young evangelists. They were anxious to have a role that transcended the sectarian church life in which they were raised, and they were gratified to be doing something that was valued by the wider public.[34]

The movement encountered criticism as well. The fact that Youth for Christ was being run by conservative preachers and business leaders did not escape notice. William Randolph Hearst's endorsement, moreover, deepened the suspicions. What was Youth for Christ really up to? Rumors circulated that Youth for Christ was the creation of "fascist-minded" business interests. These allegations gained some credence because of what historian Leo Ribuffo has called the "Brown Scare." In a wartime climate tinged with fear of subversion, the Department of Justice arrested a group of right-wing radicals who sympathized with the Nazis and prosecuted them on conspiracy charges. At least one of this group, the Kansas preacher Gerald Winrod, was a fundamentalist with a considerable following. Although Winrod had been shunned by most mainstream fundamentalists, his indictment on federal conspiracy charges prompted many liberals to suspect that fundamentalists threatened American security. Given Youth for Christ's mass-rally pageantry, it was easy to caricature the movement as Nazi-inspired.[35]

When these charges appeared, Youth for Christ received a reluctant word of support from an unlikely source. In an editorial and a lead article, the *Christian Century* gave the youth rally phenomenon a careful examination. After chiding Youth for Christ for its shallowness and warning that its pervasive support from conservative businessmen might play into the wrong hands, the *Century* stated that the rumors of fascism had no basis. Indeed, the editors praised the Chicagoland Youth for Christ chapter for building cordial relationships with the city's black churches.[36]

Torrey Johnson was asked by a *Time* magazine reporter to respond to the charge that his movement had fascist tendencies. Johnson quickly dissociated his movement from the far right. He insisted that he did not know Gerald Winrod and that he disapproved of the demagogue's views. Johnson said that rally leaders had no "political axes to grind." Youth for Christ's only ambitions were religious ones, Johnson said. The movement was dedicated to "the spiritual revitalization of America" and "the complete evangelization of the world in our generation."[37] These were the longstanding goals of evangelical Protestantism, hailing back to the prior century. In the religious and civic climate of the mid-1940s, however, these aims took on fresh currency. Youth for Christ leaders had been invited, so to speak, to express their moral and spiritual custodianship for the present age. The last thing they wanted to do was to tarnish their image by any association with politicized fundamentalism, so the young evangelists assured the public that they would be civil. Like their fundamentalist forbears they yearned to restore "Christian America," but their means would be revival, not contentious cultural politics.

After the war came to a close, Youth for Christ's leaders found yet another convergence between their concerns and those of the nation's leaders. The United States' interests were clashing increasingly with those of the Soviet Union, and the concern expressed during the war for the nation's moral integrity took on renewed urgency. Global conquest had reawakened American civic and religious leaders' ideas of Manifest Destiny and prompted them to see their nation as the guardian of the "Free World" in the struggle against totalitarianism. If America was to fulfil this role, her people must be rededicated to freedom and reformed in morals—or so went the postwar jeremiads. The spread of juvenile delinquency and rising divorce rates, many thought, were part of a larger spiritual malady that might make it easier for subversive forces to capture the hearts and minds of the people.[38]

Youth for Christ leaders quickly latched onto this motif. "America cannot survive another twenty-five years like the last," Torrey Johnson warned. "If we have another lost generation, . . . America is sunk." Did the nation have the moral backbone to keep the world safe and free? That was the question of the hour. Johnson told rally leaders that "we are headed either for a definite turning to God or the greatest calamity ever to strike the human race."[39] Conservative evangelicals had been saying things like this for at least thirty years, but in the early postwar period, they were astonished to hear their prophetic warnings being echoed by the nation's political leaders. Only one day after he had witnessed Winston Churchill's grim "Iron Curtain" speech in Fulton, Missouri, President Truman told the delegates of the Federal Council of Churches convened in Columbus, Ohio, in March 1946 that without "a moral and spiritual awakening" America would be lost. The following month, General Dwight D. Eisenhower told a meeting of Army chaplains that there was no hope for mankind "except through moral regeneration." Eagerly responding to these jeremiads, Youth for Christ leaders offered to do their part.[40]

A remarkable convergence was taking place, then, between the national public mood during World War II and the early postwar years and the aspirations of a new generation of fundamentalist and evangelical leaders. The American nation had been offered another chance, many thought, to fulfill its manifest destiny at home and abroad, and the children of sectarian Protestantism felt welcome to make a fresh start as valued contributors to the national cause. Perhaps there really would be a "revival in our time." Perhaps the "Christian America" of evangelical mythic memory could be restored if enough people came to Christ in a new wave of evangelistic crusades.[41]

A New Coalition for Revival

When youth rally leaders from across the country met at the Winona Lake (Indiana) Bible Conference in July of 1945 to organize as Youth for Christ, International, they were elated and expectant. They had received national attention, and even President Truman had said good things about their work. What did this success mean for the larger cause of bringing a revival to America? Torrey Johnson told them that citywide revival campaigns looked possible once again, thanks to Youth for Christ. "We have within our hands the thing that every evangelist in the United States would like to have," Johnson told the assembled rally directors, "some kind of a set-up by which we can hold city-wide revival meetings." The youth rallies had brought together a "city-wide representation of businessmen, youth leaders and pastors" who would "iron out all the details and differences" in order to bring back urban revival campaigns.[42]

Johnson's crowing rhetoric aside, the youth rallies were bringing together a new coalition for evangelism. Its most direct purpose was to pursue urban revivalism on a massive, all-city scale. In its breadth and scope, however, this coalition was exactly what Elwin Wright and the other pioneers of the National Association of Evangelicals had envisioned. Youth for Christ succeeded where the NAE had failed because it offered a definite, timely, and locally realizable goal that was achievable by ad hoc, task-oriented cooperation and was not susceptible to the complications of formal interchurch alignments. Three ingredients came together to form these new coalitions. They included, first, the cadre of entrepreneurial pastors and laymen who became rally directors. These evangelists "spoke the language" of their pop culture context and they had the drive and talent to "sell the program."[43] Second, the rally leaders found a supportive network of "Christian businessmen" who were just then mobilizing. With similar yearnings for revival, instincts for mass marketing, and a pragmatic disregard for denominational differences, the Christian Business Men's Committees and similar organizations were natural partners for the youth evangelists. The third and most striking ingredient was the sponsoring churches themselves. Youth for Christ was mobilizing churches from both the NAE and the Federal Council—and beyond—to support revival meetings.

Youth for Christ's success and its promise for organizing citywide campaigns depended heavily on the encouragement, advice, and sponsorship of the rapidly growing Christian businessmen's movement. By 1945 at least thirty of the newly organized Christian Business Men's Committees were sponsoring or cosponsoring local Youth for Christ organizations.[44] Evangelical businessmen were held up as "outstanding Christians" and called on to speak at rallies alongside sports stars and military heroes. At the October 1944 Chicago Stadium Victory Rally, Robert F. Nelson, vice president of the Arma Corporation, brought greetings from the Word of Life rally in New York; Freelin A. Carlton, manager of Sears and Roebuck's flagship department store in Chicago, led in prayer; and Herbert J. Taylor, president of Club Aluminum, gave his testimony. R. G. LeTourneau, an earth-moving equipment inventor and manufacturer from Peoria and perhaps the most celebrated fundamentalist businessman at the time, was a frequent speaker on the national rally circuit.[45]

Evangelical businessmen played a vital role in forging the new network supporting Youth for Christ. What they provided was not merely money, though they did invest generously in the new ventures. While they were conservative in their political and social views, they were not seeking to shape the movement's ideology. They were not the "fascist-minded businessmen" that the Left imagined. Rather, like John D. Rockefeller, Jr., and other philanthropists who supported liberal mainline Protestantism, these evangelicals had found that the new ministries reflected their own convictions and provided an attractive outlet for their sense of religious calling. The most important thing businessmen provided was not money or ideological direction, but a fresh injection of the pragmatic, optimistic, enterprising, and nonsectarian spirit that had characterized evangelical revivalism in the past.

By New Deal standards many of these businessmen would be considered reactionaries, but within fundamentalist circles they were progressives. They were impatient with old-fashioned religious methods and with any leaders who were obsessed with secondary doctrinal matters. Business had taught them to be accommodating and to "follow and capitalize on public trends and opinions," as one spokesman put it. Now that the American public showed new interest in religion, the church should take advantage of the trend. Religious leaders needed to be flexible and to design ministries that were aimed at solving particular religious problems, such as reaching young people, or taking advantage of a particular opportunity, such as evangelizing East Asia. These values were ones that the evangelists in Youth for Christ were ready to hear, so they invited businessmen to strengthen their organizations with managerial advice as well as with funds.[46]

The support of prominent business leaders helped the Youth for Christ movement in another regard as well. It provided a measure of legitimacy that the movement could not earn in churchly circles. The youth evangelists tended to be from fundamentalist and other sectarian Protestant backgrounds, so their rallies operated outside of the mainline Protestant establishment. Many of the businessmen who supported the rallies, however, were part of the civic establishment. Some were leaders in service organizations, such as the Rotary or the Lions Club, that operated with broad, generally Protestant commitments to public service and civic uplift. If Youth for Christ could help with the juvenile delinquency problem, many civic leaders reasoned, then it was a good thing; so they helped to boost the movement. Herbert J. Taylor of Chicago, who was a national officer in the Rotary, introduced Youth for Christ leaders to the Rotary's nationwide network. Youth for Christ field representative Billy Graham reported in 1946 that he had been "promoting and selling Youth for Christ" extensively that year, visiting nineteen Rotary, Kiwanis, and other civic clubs, plus the conventions of the Gideons and the Christian Business Men's Committees. All of these groups, Graham said, gave him "wonderful cooperation."[47]

So here was yet another way to gain legitimacy without working through established churchly channels. Evangelical revivalists' first discovery of this kind had been radio broadcasting. Next came the NAE, which gave evangelicals their own, rival public voice. Now they were developing partnerships with business and civic leaders. These strategies soon proved to be a formula for successful religious enterprise, and they fueled the startup of dozens of independent ministries in the postwar years.[48]

The Youth for Christ movement did not avoid working with churches, however, if what one means by "church" is a local congregation, not the larger religious organization. Indeed, the networks of local churches that supported the movement were breathtakingly broad in many instances, bringing together congregations from denominations that had no formal relations with each other. Torrey Johnson noticed the unusual breadth of this ad hoc collaboration almost immediately and was excited about its potential. "I believe that God has raised up 'Youth for Christ' . . . to bring together churches and people who otherwise couldn't get together," he declared. In the Greater Oklahoma City Rally, for example, congregations from the Assemblies of God, Church of God, Fundamental Baptist, Free Methodist, Free-Will Baptist, Salvation Army, Pentecostal Holiness, Nazarene, and Wesleyan Methodist sects cooperated with congregations from the more respectable Southern Baptist, Disciples-Christian, Methodist, Presbyterian, and United Brethren denominations.[49]

Enlisting a measure of good will from a local congregation was one thing, but how about Youth for Christ's leadership? In some cities, the leaders were a tightly knit cadre of the like-minded. In the Little Rock, Arkansas, Youth for Christ chapter, however, the three codirectors were evangelist Jimmy Bell of the Methodist Church, Captain W. T. Young of the Salvation Army, and Robert C. Sellers, pastor of the First Assembly of God. In most churchly settings these three men would not be able to walk together, but apparently they were agreed when it came to Youth for Christ. What is even more striking, the first meeting place for the Little Rock rallies was Christ Episcopal Church.[50] Youth for Christ was showing that Elwin Wright's dream of evangelical cooperation of the most inclusive sort could become a reality.

The movement's breadth was made possible by the nondenominational nature of the whole enterprise. Because local churches and religious leaders were not asked to unite formally, questions of interdenominational relations seemed irrelevant. The premise was collaboration to pursue a common task. Not all congregations and religious leaders were interested, and not all Christians were invited. This was a Protestant affair, and in most cases a white Protestant one at that. But across the broad landscape of white Protestantism—sectarian evangelical, ethnic confessional, mainline ecumenical, and Southern conservative—a network was being linked together for the sake of reviving America and evangelizing the world. And Youth for Christ was the catalyst.

Conclusion

The Youth for Christ movement and the larger revival impulse that lay behind it were driven by two intense desires: for public respect and for spiritual awakening. They were hastened along by fundamentalists' instinctive ability to adapt their message to popular tastes and trends. Vance Havner's defiant claim in the early 1930s that fundamentalists were not "bound for extinction" simply because "the great broadcasting chains do not carry our message and because popular periodicals give us no space" seems to have shown, in a contrary, backhanded way, how aware fundamentalists were of what it would take to legitimize their movement. By the mid-1940s they had done exactly what Havner had boasted they never would: they had crowded "the show windows of modern publicity"; they were tuning the gospel to play on modern mass media and appeal to contemporary tastes. Were they also, in fact, "cheapening the goods," as Havner put it, to draw the crowds?[51]

Some said that they were. An anonymous contributor to *The King's Business* expressed shock that youth rallies would "play up to the world" in order to attract interest, and that gospel programs would be called "streamlined" or "'packed with thrills." It seemed unlikely that the rallies' sensationalism could produce deep spiritual change. Donald Grey Barnhouse also complained of the "sickening shallowness" of some of the rallies. He admonished his readers to separate themselves from "that which is frothy." Barnhouse's readers chided him for being so negative, however, and he retreated, admitting that he had preached at a few rallies himself. His criticism, he explained, was not that of a gossip tearing down someone's morals, but merely "that of a husband who tells his wife that her slip is showing."[52]

Indeed, it was very hard for fundamentalists to quarrel with Youth for Christ, even if some were offended by its mimicking of popular entertainment. Like many other American Protestants, fundamentalists instinctively bowed to their audience's tastes and values, and constantly adjusted their presentations in order to sustain a hearing. Fundamentalists had not given Billy Sunday much of an argument over his antics, so Youth for Christ imitations of Kate Smith's patriotic revues were not going to provoke much criticism, either.

Fundamentalists' mainline Protestant counterparts also went rather easy on Youth for Christ. A correspondent for the *Christian Century* in Pittsburgh found the youth rally there a bit garish for his tastes, but in the final analysis he could only say, "More power to 'em. They got the crowd; they won 70 of them. They are coming soon, whether Jesus is or not. I wish them well." Likewise, the prominent religious journalist Frank S. Mead acknowledged the criticisms of Youth for Christ's sensationalism and shallowness, but compared to mainline Protestants' failure to attract young people, Mead thought the youth rallies were wonderful. "You just don't laugh off success," he said.[53]

Indeed, Youth for Christ, like the *Old Fashioned Revival Hour,* was a smashing success—at least in ways that evangelical Protestants were accustomed to measure it. Both the movement's numerical growth and its organizational vitality were astonishing. The nation's civic leaders had praised it. And the rallies had been featured in the popular media. Since radio, magazines, and newspapers told the public, in effect, what was worthy of its attention, these media had the power to confer social status and public respect. Getting media attention certified that one mattered, virtually that one existed. Amid the roaring headlines produced by global war and the myriad stories about sports and popular entertainment, the Youth for Christ sensation of 1944–1946 was quickly forgotten. But for fundamentalists and other evangelicals, it was of enormous importance. Small triumphs in popular communications loomed large to them, for they were assurance that what their movement was doing really mattered.

If there was one thing that fundamentalists and other sectarian evangelicals had lacked—and yearned for—it was respect in the public eye.[54] The *Old Fashioned Revival Hour* and the Youth for Christ movement provided them with at least a taste of it, and this experience seemed to make their thirst for visibility and legitimacy virtually insatiable. Like every other interest group in postwar America's public arena, the evangelicals learned to work incessantly to get their share of media attention. This drive to be known and respected has been one of the most powerful propellants of the postwar evangelical resurgence. The Youth for Christ phenomenon, with its skillful use of the mass media and its "God Bless America" civic devotion, showed evangelicals how to get the public's attention and win a sympathetic hearing.[55]

This small measure of fame was the stuff of dreams for a group of young preachers from sectarian backgrounds. But building their own fame did not seem to be foremost on their minds. Their astonishing breakthrough in national exposure, they believed, gave them both the means and the opportunity to put "eternity's values" back into public view and to touch off what so many in the fundamentalist realm had been yearning for, another Great Awakening. Too restless and visionary to settle down to the task of ministering to teenagers, many of the movement's early leaders, notably Billy Graham and Bob Pierce (the Seattle rally director who founded World Vision), infused the postwar evangelical coalition with their energy. They created a variety of missionary and evangelistic ministries that became the organizational core of the "new evangelicalism."[56]

10

WORLD VISION

One of the most far-reaching religious developments of the 1940s received no headlines, even in the religious press. A major shift was beginning, virtually without notice, in the North American missionary enterprise. Just when American political leaders and the secular press were becoming more attentive to the nation's new role as a world power, fundamentalists and other evangelicals were developing a corresponding outlook, which the emerging younger leaders were calling a "world vision." What they meant by this, in Torrey Johnson's words, was that they were determined to accomplish, in their own lifetime, "the complete evangelization of the world."[1]

This motto was of course the famous missionary "watchword" of the Student Volunteer Movement for Foreign Missions which had arisen in the late nineteenth century. By the 1930s that organization had ceased to be influential, but fundamentalists and other evangelicals had kept the watchword of world evangelization alive through their support of conservative denominational mission boards and nondenominational "faith" missionary societies. In the wake of the Second World War, these missions were growing rapidly and new ones were being formed. This expansion would continue unabated for a generation, representing the greatest spurt of growth in the two-century career of modern missions. Yet this story has been neglected. There is much to discover and examine in the postwar missions surge, but perhaps the way to begin is to see it as an expression of the new, war-inspired global outlook and the growing momentum of evangelical revivalism. "Revival in America" and "the evangelization of the world" were nearly inseparable slogans among the leaders of the NAE and Youth for Christ leaders in the mid-1940s. Although the first catchphrase was of more immediate interest to them than the second, each could be understood only in reference to the other. It was America's destiny to evangelize the world, Harold Ockenga had told the founding convention of the NAE, but if that goal was to be addressed effectively, there must be a revival. As both the expectancy of revival and wartime visions of America's global destiny grew, so did fundamentalists' and other evangelicals' interest in foreign missions.[2]

Onward Christian Soldiers

The Second World War had an enormous impact on the North American missionary impulse. Unfortunately, the part of this story that is best known is how the war devastated missions work in East Asia and led to the "closing of the door" for China missions when the communists won the postwar struggle for power. Just as the story of modern missions is much broader than its career in the Far East, so must be our understanding of the Second World War's impact. Especially for North American evangelicals, the triumph of the Allied forces arrayed around the world excited the missionary imagination, and so did the technological mastery that made these operations possible. Furthermore, the experience of thousands of born-again soldiers and sailors, trained and transported at government expense to serve in faraway lands, led them quite naturally to a greater missions awareness. And thanks to veterans' educational benefits and the abundance of surplus war goods, government spending provided additional support for a postwar missions surge.[3]

It is hard to overstate the war's role in reviving the idea of "global conquest" among evangelical missions promoters. The very scale of the conflict was suggestive to those who dreamed of world evangelization. Rowland V. Bingham, the venerable Canadian founder of the Sudan Interior Mission, expressed astonishment at the scope of the war and the commitment being mobilized by the Allies. If Christians would "show one tithe of the interest that we have taken in winning the present conflict . . . and one tenth of the money we have been pouring out," he declared, "we will soon have an evangelized world." Another Canadian, Robert Hall Glover, who was the North American representative of the China Inland Mission, drew a lesson from the sweeping strategy of the war effort. Missions represented "another conflict on a world-wide scale," he asserted, and missionary forces, no less than armies, must have plans and definite goals. Now is the time, Glover urged, for missions to reassess their strategies and get ready to launch the last great push "into 'the regions beyond.'" This broad impulse for "postwar planning" prompted the pioneering missionary broadcaster, Clarence Jones, to apply the concept to the global advance of missions: "If industry, diplomacy, military, finance and every other branch of our modern civilization is changing its attitude, approach, and attack on the new global problems of tomorrow," Jones observed, "the Church dare not lag behind."[4]

Military imagery was no stranger to the modern missions movement and to American evangelicals in particular. World War II, however, brought a fresh new store of terms to give it new currency. Youth for Christ evangelists, whose rallies were springing up wherever the Allied forces were stationed, easily translated the missionary mandate into GI terms. After he was invited to hold Youth for Christ meetings in London, Torrey Johnson spoke brashly of the need to "invade England with the Gospel." Indeed, Youth for Christ leaders hoped that the "beachheads" opened up by their rallies in foreign lands would lead to more full-scale missionary "invasions" everywhere. In the new youth rally lexicon, churches became the "home bases" and the "arsenals" for world-wide victory; and missionaries were "Christian commandos." The imperial language of conquest had pervaded the British missionary rhetoric during the prior century and reached its apex, perhaps, at the great Edinburgh World Missionary Conference of 1910. But just when mainline Protestants were beginning to repent of the attitudes these words reflected, conservative evangelicals were investing the triumphal outlook with fresh relevance and imagery.[5]

Probably the most profound factor for prompting a new commitment for missions was the actual experience of American men and women in the military. The war put thousands of fundamentalist and evangelical young adults into risk-filled situations far from home, and thus focused and intensified their thoughts about life's meaning and direction. For young people brought up to believe that other nations were "mission fields" and that life's noblest calling was to take the gospel to foreign lands, military service in Europe or the Pacific could be powerfully suggestive. Evangelist Merv Rosell observed that "Iowans and Texans and New Yorkers and Californians have come back to America with a new understanding of a world need. . . . Boys who might have dozed through life in some quiet little town . . . now have spunk enough to undertake world conquest—for God."[6]

Donald Cook, a young airman who had been raised in the small town of Lisle, Illinois, was one who came back from the war with missions on his mind. Cook, who served in the Pacific as a navigator in the Army Air Force, was from a fundamentalist family, but he recalled that it was during his time in the military that he grew close to God. His term of duty helped him sort out his priorities, and he decided that making money was not the most important thing in his life. Cook had not yet determined to become "a full-time Christian worker" when he came home from the war, but serving in East Asia had put him "face-to-face with a mission field." The poverty he saw in the Philippines, Japan, and China just after the war impressed him deeply; he was moved by the great material need he saw and he suspected that there was an "inward need as well."[7] Untold thousands of evangelical women and men had experiences like Donald Cook's during the war, and even those who did not become career missionaries gained an appreciation for the missionary's task that fueled increasing interest and support.[8]

Some soldiers and sailors took up mission work while still in the armed forces. Of the many Youth for Christ–type evangelistic rallies that sprang up among the American troops, perhaps the one with the most lasting missionary impact was the *G.I. Gospel Hour,* begun in Manila among the American troops in May of 1945. By September of that year, the service men and women who led the rally were laying plans to develop a Bible institute and seminary to educate Filipinos and other Asians for ministry. The following year similar meetings were organized in Japan, and the chaplains involved founded a seminary for Japanese pastors. The two groups merged in 1947 to form a non-denominational mission society, the Far Eastern Gospel Crusade. By the mid-1950s, the agency had 135 missionaries working in the Orient.[9]

One feature of the war that intrigued missions leaders was its use of technology. Observed R. H. Glover, "We have seen Anglo-American military forces press their way with amazing speed to the farthest interior of every continent and the remotest parts of the island world." Because of the logistical prowess thus displayed, Glover thought that "favoring factors" for the "speediest possible completion of the missionary task" were "greater than ever before." Likewise, R. V. Bingham speculated that with airplanes and radio broadcasting at their disposal, postwar missionaries would be able to "finish the task" of world evangelization in five years and "bring in the great consummation of the age."[10]

Faith in technological signs and wonders to evangelize the world and usher in the end of the age has been a character trait of modern missions over the past two centuries, and American evangelicals in particular have been charmed by such visions.[11] During the 1940s, however, military logistics were in fact beginning to serve actual postwar missions expansion and not simply its expansive rhetoric. In 1942 two American fundamentalist missionaries, Paul Fleming and Bob Williams, were uprooted by the war from their work with tribes living in remote parts of southeast Asia. Back in the States they laid plans with a small group of pastors and businessmen to form a mission that would focus on ethnic groups as yet virtually untouched by modern living. The war in Asia and the Pacific, with its mechanized incursions into formidable jungles, impressed on them that an outreach to remote tribes could be mobilized with greater speed than ever before. They formed the New Tribes Mission on this basis and it quickly caught the imagination of scores of returning soldiers. The Christian GI, one New Tribes promoter asserted, was better prepared than almost anyone else to be a modern missionary. Soldiers who were familiar with "the equipment now used to penetrate dark, steaming jungles" would use "planes, radios, food processing . . . and modern equipment of all kinds . . . to wage this warfare." Only two years after its founding, New Tribes had commissioned fifty missionaries.[12]

Military personnel also founded the Missionary Aviation Fellowship. Among its lead organizers were Elizabeth "Betty" Greene, a flight instructor commissioned in the Women's Air Force, another Air Force flight instructor named Grady Parrott, Navy pilot James Truxton, and Charles Mellis, a B-17 bomber pilot stationed in England. Each saw the possibilities of using light aircraft to serve missionaries in remote regions. Encouraged by mission leaders, they recruited other evangelical pilots and were ready to begin when the war ended.[13]

Thanks to the huge stockpiles of war materials that were left when the conflict ceased, mission agencies were able to buy into the logistical prowess of the American war machine at bargain basement prices. One of the key roles of the newly formed Evangelical Foreign Missions Association, begun under the sponsorship of the National Association of Evangelicals, was to act as a bargain hunter and purchasing broker for missionary agencies. Jeeps, radios, medical supplies, processed food, even airplanes were "converted" to serve the religious offensive. Among the most striking illustrations of both the windfall in Army-surplus goods and the postwar crusading spirit were the B-17 bombers that the mission board of the Assemblies of God bought and refurbished to transport its new recruits to Latin America.[14]

The influx of war veterans with government educational grants did much to swell the enrollments of fundamentalist and evangelical colleges, seminaries, and Bible schools in the postwar years, and they brought a heightened missions interest with them.[15] Donald Cook, the young airman from Illinois mentioned above, returned home in 1947 and enrolled in Wheaton College, where he had been studying before the war. There was a large group of veterans on campus, he recalled, and he felt especially drawn to some "guys who'd been involved in the Far Eastern Gospel Crusade." They taught him to feel a spiritual "burden" for the salvation of the people of the Philippines and Japan, he said, and they showed him "how to do something" about his concern. After finishing college and then earning a seminary degree, Cook volunteered with the Overseas Missionary Fellowship and was sent to work in Japan.[16]

Due to the presence of dozens like Donald Cook on campus in the late 1940s, Wheaton College was energized for missions. More than one hundred students attended the weekly Foreign Missions Fellowship meetings, and many of these participated in missions prayer circles that were devoted to the needs of a particular continent or region. President Edman, a veteran of the mission field himself, worked hard to encourage missionary devotion. Younger students were sobered by the veterans' presence and often picked up their spiritual seriousness. One younger student who eventually went to serve in Belgium remembered the spiritual direction he received in a "Navigators" Bible study led by a Navy veteran.[17] The spiritually charged atmosphere at Wheaton during those years produced a campus-wide revival in February of 1950, and perhaps the largest crop of missionary recruits in the college's history. Some one hundred members of the class of 1950—more than a quarter of all the graduates—became foreign missionaries.[18]

Wheaton College's experience seems to have been typical of a number of missions-minded evangelical schools. For example, Columbia Bible College, a fundamentalist institution in Columbia, South Carolina, experienced a major postwar surge of missions commitment. It had placed one hundred of its alumni in missionary work over its nineteen-year history by 1942, but only eight years later the school reported that another 150 graduates had entered missionary service.[19]

A New Wave of Student Volunteers

As powerful a catalyst of missionary commitment as military service seemed to have been, there were also some energetic new missions promoters on the home front. As in the heyday of the Student Volunteer Movement fifty years earlier, the evangelical youth organizations of the 1940s were channeling many hundreds of young people toward missionary careers. The Youth for Christ movement, which rode on a wartime wave of emotion, was saturated with the missionary spirit. Torrey Johnson, the founding president of Youth for Christ

International, had a huge world map in his office emblazoned with the old Student Volunteer motto: "Evangelize the world in the present generation." Youth rally leaders across the nation were fervent promoters of missions. New Tribes founder Paul Fleming became a great publicist for his mission and others while he was directing the Los Angeles Youth for Christ rally. Inspired, apparently, by the military's example, Jack Wyrtzen set up a Word of Life missions recruiting office. Representatives of mission agencies were understandably eager for invitations to address the youth rallies. Clarence Jones, for example, who was the founder of the missionary radio station HCJB in Quito, Ecuador, became a fixture on the rally circuit. His romantic stories of pioneering in the Andes added spice to rally directors' programs, and the earnest young people at the meetings added to his supply of recruits and funds.[20]

Rally directors who had never gone on foreign missions themselves were catching the vision along with their youthful audiences. Several organized "invasion teams" and made a flurry of preaching tours to postwar Europe, Asia and the Pacific, and Latin America. By 1948 these evangelistic squads had visited forty-six countries. That year Youth for Christ International organized the first postwar evangelical missions conference, in Beatenburg, Switzerland. After some debate at that meeting Youth for Christ's leaders decided that its role in missions would be primarily promotion, not missionary sending.[21] A number of them, however, decided that foreign missions was their calling.

Dick Hillis, a former missionary to China who helped start the Los Angeles rally, led an evangelistic team in 1950 to minister to Chinese exiles in Taiwan. There he was challenged to begin a training program in Bible and evangelism for converts. That was the beginning of a mission that became known as Overseas Crusades. Paul Freed, director of the Greensboro, North Carolina, Youth for Christ rally, would establish Trans World Radio in 1954 as a result of his postwar overseas preaching tours. Robert Evans, a former Navy chaplain who had been wounded in the Normandy campaign, became Youth for Christ International's first executive director upon his discharge from the military. Europe beckoned, however, and Evans led an evangelistic team there soon after the war. His attention was drawn to the educational needs of young European converts, so Evans founded a Bible institute near Paris in 1949 and eventually developed a new missionary society, the Greater Europe Mission.[22]

This renewed vision for missionary service had no more able promoter than Bob Pierce, who had directed the Youth for Christ rally in Seattle. Pierce led Youth for Christ preaching teams on tours through India and China in the late 1940s. Astonished by the thousands who responded to the gospel during these campaigns, Pierce felt compelled to return to the Far East in 1950, where he encountered the ravages of war in Korea. Moved by the suffering of the people, Pierce came home and organized scores of "World Vision" rallies to enlist support. This was the beginning of World Vision, Incorporated, today one of the world's largest relief and development agencies.[23]

Another young people's movement was springing up during roughly the same years as the youth rallies, and it played an equally powerful role in raising missions consciousness and recruiting volunteers. Serving primarily the students of secular colleges and universities, Inter-Varsity Christian Fellowship was able to reach a talented cohort of young adults, hundreds of whom would join the conservative evangelical missionary forces whose ranks previously had been dominated by Bible school and church college graduates.

Inter-Varsity was a British import, with origins in the evangelical student societies at Cambridge and London in the late nineteenth century. The organization functioned in Great Britain as a conservative evangelical alternative to the Student Christian Movement, and it began work in Canada in 1928 under similar auspices. Howard Guinness, a medical student from London, was commissioned that year by British student leaders to organize chapters at Canadian universities. This work began to expand rapidly after C. Stacey Woods, an Australian graduate of Wheaton College, became its director in 1934.[24]

Over the next five years Woods received numerous requests for assistance from students in the United States. In 1939, with the permission of his board, Woods crossed the border. One of his first missions was to help students at the University of Michigan form the first Inter-Varsity chapter in the United States. With the financial support and organizational coaching of a prominent fundamentalist businessman, Herbert J. Taylor of Chicago, the Inter-Varsity Christian Fellowship of the United States of America was formally established in 1941. During the following decade this organization grew rapidly, to nearly 200 campus chapters in 1945 and over 550 by 1950.[25]

Inter-Varsity USA was missions-minded, for that was an important part of its British and Canadian evangelical legacy. The missions impulse grew much more prominent, however, after a merger in 1945 with an indigenous American group, the Student Foreign Missions Fellowship (SFMF). SFMF had been formed by students in the wake of campus revivals at Wheaton College and Columbia Bible College in 1936, with the support and encouragement of Robert C. McQuilkin, the president of Columbia Bible College. Its purpose was parallel to that of Inter-Varsity in that it was a response to the decline of evangelical commitment in a mainstream Protestant youth organization, in this case the Student Volunteer Movement for Foreign Missions. During the decade before the merger, SFMF organized chapters on thirty-six fundamentalist and other evangelical college and seminary campuses.[26]

The year after the merger, SFMF leaders J. Christy Wilson and H. Wilbert Norton organized the first Inter-Varsity student missions conference, which was held at the University of Toronto on December 27, 1946 to January 1, 1947. Five hundred seventy-six students attended that meeting to hear addresses and engage in Bible studies presented by Samuel Zwemer, who had been an early leader in the Student Volunteer Movement; Harold Ockenga, former president of the National Association of Evangelicals and pastor of the missionary-minded Park Street Church in Boston; Bakht Singh, a gifted Indian evangelist; and representatives of three of the leading training centers for faith missions: Wilbur M. Smith of the Moody Bible Institute, Robert C. McQuilkin of Columbia Bible College, and L. E. Maxwell of the Prairie Bible Institute. By the end of the conference, three hundred students had pledged to serve in foreign missions. This convention was the first of what became a regular biennial or triennial event for Inter-Varsity, held since 1947 on the campus of the University of Illinois at Urbana and eventually attracting some 15,000–19,000 students per conference.[27]

It is hard to overestimate the influence of Inter-Varsity in promoting foreign missions during the postwar era. This student ministry was itself organized as a faith missionary society, permeated with an ethos of prayer, personal consecration, and a pressing evangelistic concern known as a "burden for souls." Well-placed to ride the rising waves of postwar college enrollments and popular religious interest, Inter-Varsity organized cells of students on hundreds of campuses across the nation. These groups studied the Bible, held prayer meetings, and considered their life's calling as Christians. Given the insistent, nearly overriding demand that ran deep in American evangelical piety for every young person seriously to consider a call to "full-time Christian service," Inter-Varsity became a powerful contributor to the postwar missions surge, adding university-educated volunteers to a cause hitherto dominated by Bible school graduates.

The Evangelical Surge Begins

Just how dramatic was the postwar growth of evangelical foreign missions? From a total of about 12,000 career foreign missionaries in 1935, the North American Protestant missionary force increased to some 35,000 by 1980. While the mainline Protestant missionary force decreased from 7,000 to 3,000 over these forty-five years, the number of more "sectarian" evangelical missionaries grew from about 5,000 to 32,000. The evangelicals had posted some numerical gains in the late 1930s and early 1940s, but the most dramatic growth was a postwar phenomenon.[28]

New fundamentalist organizations founded in the 1930s and 1940s were among the fastest growing. Wycliffe Bible Translators, for example, was founded in 1933 by two missionaries to the Indian tribes of southern Mexico, L. L. Legters and W. Cameron Townsend. The mission was designed to evangelize remote ethnic groups by putting their languages into written form, teaching the people to read, and translating the Scriptures into their languages. Wycliffe had 107 workers in the field by the end of its first decade and three times that many by 1952. The Conservative Baptist Foreign Mission Society, founded in 1943 by the fundamentalist network within the Northern Baptist Convention as an alternative to the denominational board, had 114 missionaries under appointment after only three years and nearly double that number by 1952. As we have seen, the New Tribes Mission grew rapidly after its founding in 1942; a decade later New Tribes had 246 missionaries.[29]

The older faith missions were expanding as well. The Scandinavian Alliance Mission, founded by Swedish-American evangelist Fredrik Franson in 1890, had 183 active missionaries in 1940 and increasing support from non-Scandinavian fundamentalists. Renamed The Evangelical Alliance Mission (TEAM) in 1949, the agency reported 636 missionaries three years later. The

Africa Inland Mission (AIM), an American-based faith mission of 1895 vintage, had 283 missionaries by the end of World War II. Seven years later AIM had 465 missionaries.[30]

Denominational boards representing conservative evangelicals also experienced steady growth during this period, and some grew dramatically. The Church of the Nazarene more than doubled its missionary force between 1935 and 1952, from 88 to 200 missionaries; the same trend was true for the Southern Baptist Convention over these years, as its overseas complement increased from 405 to 855. Add to this the flourishing Foreign Missions Department of the Assemblies of God, which reported 230 missionaries in 1935 and 626 seventeen years later.[31]

Most of the mainline Protestant boards experienced decreases in staff between 1935 and 1952. One obvious cause of this decline was these agencies' heavy involvement in the Pacific and East Asia. Missions in those regions encountered great hardship and disruption during years of upheaval and war. Over this time span the Congregationalists' American Board of Commissioners for Foreign Missions decreased its deployment of missionaries from 587 to 488; the Northern Baptists' foreign missionary contingent declined from 495 to 354; and the northern Presbyterian force decreased from 1,356 to 1,116. Some boards—notably those of the Methodists, the Evangelical United Brethren and several Lutheran groups—posted gains over these years, and others would rally numerically in the late 1950s and early 1960s. Still, in retrospect, the trend is clear: in 1935 roughly 40 percent of the 12,000 Protestant missionaries were sent from North America by conservative evangelical boards and societies. By 1952 fully half of the 18,500 North American Protestant missionaries were sent by evangelical agencies. Among the largest gainers in these years were the identifiably fundamentalist mission societies, which accounted for one in seven of the total in 1935 and nearly one in three by 1952. These shifts took place in the midst of a growing North American presence in Protestant missions worldwide. Americans and Canadians constituted 41 percent of all the world's Protestant missionaries in 1936 and 52 percent in 1952. By 1969 they would amount to more than 72 percent of the total.[32]

By the early 1950s, therefore, a quarter of the world's Protestant missionary force consisted of fundamentalist, pentecostal, holiness, and other conservative evangelical missionaries from the United States and Canada. As the statistics for the subsequent thirty years now show us, that was only the beginning. The impact of this shift has scarcely begun to be studied. What has it meant for the character of world missions? What has been its effect on Third World Christianity's numerical growth, theology, ecclesiastical alignments, and social and political witness? These questions require more analysis. Suffice it to say that after the Second World War, American religious, cultural, and technological products were being exported in ever-increasing volume in the triumphal context of America's rise to world power. At a time when mainline Protestants were entertaining questions about the traditional missionary mandate's relevance and righteousness, fundamentalists and other evangelicals were asserting, more by their actions than by any sustained defense, the right of all the world's people to hear the gospel. That message was dominated, however, by the narrowly evangelistic theology of the nineteenth-century faith missions and by twentieth-century sectarian evangelicalism, and it was freighted with what Andrew Walls has identified as some typically American cultural baggage: "vigorous expansionism, readiness of invention, [and] a willingness to make the fullest use of contemporary technology, finance, organization, and business methods."[33] These traits had persisted over time, but they were certainly given a major boost by American conservative evangelical missions' ebullient postwar expansion.

The impact of this foreign missions avalanche on the domestic career of fundamentalism and other forms of evangelicalism in these years is also hard to assess. Certainly these movements and traditions were already heavily committed to foreign missions, and they resonated with heightened missions awareness and interest. The missionary enterprise was in fact reaping the benefits of these movements' successful institutional development and their growing boldness about communicating their message to the outside world. But did the lines of influence run the other way as well? Was the new evangelical coalition drawing great bursts of affirmation and momentum from its missionary accomplishments?

Missionary feats did not dominate the American fundamentalist and evangelical magazines nor the agendas of the preachers in the late 1940s and early 1950s, even though the call to missions was prominent. The missions surge was still in the making and too scattered institutionally for the postwar coalition's leaders to easily assess its collective impact and draw encouragement from it. For the moment, the prime ingredient of conservative evangelical missions was its urgency to complete the task before the doors of opportunity to foreign missionaries closed, before the Lord's imminent return.[34] The extraordinary postwar expansion of evangelical missions was, after all, the second part of a dual purpose, as Torrey Johnson put it, to bring about "the spiritual revitalization of America" and "the complete evangelization of the world in our generation."[35] This second, more ultimate, goal, many of Johnson's colleagues thought, was contingent upon achieving the first one, for America needed to be preserved as a gospel lighthouse in these tempestuous last days. So while the missionary force was multiplying, pleas for "revival in our time" and efforts to bring it about dominated the movement's agenda.

This call for revival, however, lacked one important ingredient for effecting a lasting recovery of evangelical religion in the mainstream of American public life. Evangelicals, and fundamentalists in particular, sensed that their marginal status reflected not just lack of popular interest or support, but their reputation for intellectual backwardness.[36] Unless the new coalition for revival improved its standing in the nation's houses of intellect, it would continue to experience problems getting others to take it seriously. So for a small group of younger fundamentalists, the call for revival had some broader cultural and theological resonances to it. A new Awakening would need its intellectual apologists if it was to effect a lasting reformation.

11

CAN FUNDAMENTALISM
WIN AMERICA?

In June of 1947, Harold John Ockenga, the pastor of Park Street Church in Boston and the former president of the National Association of Evangelicals, published a short article titled "Can Fundamentalism Win America?" Posing Protestant modernism, Roman Catholicism, and secularism as the three major contenders in a "struggle for power" for the dominant role in shaping "America's cultural pattern," Ockenga bluntly told his readers that in its current state, fundamentalism could never win America. It was divisive and utterly incapable of "cooperative action"; and it stood aloof with a negative social ethic "in an hour of crying social problems." Ockenga's purpose in mounting these criticisms emerged only at the end of the article, where he pointed to a "ray of hope" for the winning of America: the "spirit of cooperation, of mutual faith, of progressive action, and of ethical responsibility" that he saw in the National Association of Evangelicals.[1]

On its surface, this article appeared to be nothing more than a brief commercial for the NAE, and perhaps one more occasion for Ockenga, who had been harassed by the leaders of fundamentalism's separatist wing, to contrast their foibles to the NAE's virtues. Yet this article also signalled that a new dispensation was beginning within the career of fundamentalism. A progressive party was arising, and Ockenga was deeply involved in the events that marked its birth.

Winning America

"Winning America" was by no means a new phrase in the fundamentalist lexicon, but ever since the movement's defeats in the antimodernist campaigns of the 1920s and its subsequent sojourn out on the cultural margins, it had fallen into disuse. Winning Americans to faith in Christ was the one sense of the term that persisted. Ockenga, however, was going beyond that meaning; he clearly meant a victory in the contest for cultural power. This idea was at most implicit in the new revivalists' rhetoric, but it had become a lost cause for fundamentalists after the 1920s. By the late 1940s, however, a small group of reformers with cultural ambitions was emerging. They were drawn, for the most part, from a second generation of fundamentalists who were driven by the old desire to shape American culture according to evangelical norms. Two major developments in the 1940s that had encouraged such thoughts were the founding of the NAE and the Youth for Christ movement. Still, these developments had not brought fundamentalists and other evangelicals anywhere near a position of cultural salience. That was, in part, Ockenga's point, but his larger message was that there were new reasons to hope that "winning America" was an achievable goal.

Had the leaders of mainline Protestantism noticed Ockenga's article, they would have been either amused or annoyed by its presumption. They would not have questioned its basic premise, however, for "winning America" was very much on their own agenda. They saw their special mission in the postwar era to be the preservation of the Christian, democratic values Americans needed if they were to keep the peace at home and abroad and prosper once more. Church leaders had even put back into play the old vision of a national awakening. Not only were presidents and generals sounding like revivalists, but so were liberal Protestant clerics. If freedom was to prevail, warned G. Bromley Oxnam, the Methodist bishop and ecumenical pioneer, the postwar world needed a "revival of religion" that would let loose "the regenerating power of God's love and forgiveness, righteousness and justice."[2]

The prevailing religious opinion in postwar America has often been portrayed as favorable to interfaith cooperation, but in fact, the various parties had not given up on winning America. Mainline Protestantism's ecumenical impulse was motivated to a large extent by the belief that a united Protestant front was needed to withstand some very powerful threats to the American way of life. Winning America was a banner theme for the *Christian Century* in the mid-to-late 1940s. Editor Charles Clayton Morrison saw three powerful forces vying for sovereignty in American life: Protestantism, Catholicism, and secularism. Each was "possessed of the missionary spirit," and each "was out to win America."[3]

Of the two competitors the *Century* seemed more worried about the Roman Catholic Church. Catholicism was enjoying unprecedented vitality and respectability in America, and American Catholic leaders felt more confident than ever that they could promote their dream of applying the "culture of Catholicism" to every sphere of life. Mainline Protestant leaders were alarmed by this challenge to their influence, and the *Century* was filled with dire warnings about the alleged Catholic threat to American democratic values, most notably an eight-part series in 1944 and 1945 by the *Century's* associate editor, Harold Fey, titled "Can Catholicism Win America?"[4]

A second series in 1946, "Can Protestantism Win America?" argued that mainline Protestantism had lost a major contest with secularism. The "glittering achievements and messianic hopes" of secular thought had beguiled the church into surrendering vast areas of cultural influence, Morrison wrote. Protestant Christianity still enjoyed considerable power and it was still the foundation for the nation's democratic culture. But this was no time for Protestants to be complacent. Protestantism's greatest problem, Morrison insisted, was its lack of unity. "Anarchic sectarianism" still thrived on its fringes, and it was weakened by the economic waste and ecclesiastical scandal of denominationalism. Protestantism needed to unite so it could command the "religious resources" needed to build "an enduring order of mankind."[5]

Ockenga's vision for "winning America" was unusual only in its audacity, therefore. In mimicking the mainline Protestants' call to win America, he was imploring a ragtag evangelical team to mount a serious challenge on an already contested field. Nevertheless, for the first time in a generation, evangelicals were able to muster a team. They played very hard and, as a result, the field itself was changed. But that is getting ahead of the story. What is important to focus on here is the formation of an impulse to reform fundamentalism, unite like-minded evangelicals, and lead a two-pronged offensive for winning America—by means of a renaissance of orthodox Protestant thought and another Great Awakening.

Harold Ockenga was a likely leader for this initiative. He was the pastor, not of some tin-roofed tabernacle, but of an old and distinguished Congregational church that overlooked the Boston Common. Although he was the son of a Chicago transit worker and the graduate of a holiness Methodist college in rural Indiana, Ockenga had attended Princeton Theological Seminary, apprenticed with the Presbyterian conservative leader, Clarence Macartney, married above his social background, and earned a doctorate in philosophy at the University of Pittsburgh. The lay leaders of his congregation in Boston had sponsored his entry into the Rotary Club and a trusteeship at Suffolk University. Ockenga was still a long way from the city's most patrician circles, but his position now was unarguably respectable and worthy of some distinction.[6]

It would have been relatively easy for Ockenga to distance himself from his holiness and fundamentalist background and settle into a comfortable career within the Protestant mainline. But beneath Ockenga's cool, cerebral demeanor was an ardently evangelical heart and an ambition to achieve great things for the evangelical cause. His dream was to participate in some significant way in the "rescue of western civilization by a . . . revival of evangelical Christianity." By identifying himself with the NAE, Ockenga stood with the sectarians who were a scandal to respectable Protestantism. But he was convinced that with "the proper type of leadership" and a renewed outlook, this new movement could make a difference.[7]

Ockenga yearned for the evangelical faith to reshape his adopted city and region, and he was doing what he could to promote that cause. Ockenga and his influential parishioners became valuable supporters of the New England Fellowship's efforts, notably by helping to organize Charles Fuller's radio rallies in 1939 and 1941 in the city's largest arenas. Ockenga also joined the board of Gordon College and Divinity School, the region's leading evangelical educational center.[8]

Carrying the evangelical torch had its costs, especially in Boston, the early capital of religious liberalism and now a major center for secular intellectual life, where political affairs were dominated by the Catholic Irish. Ockenga encountered opposition, in fact, to his effort to be heard in the public square— quite literally, in this case, for he proposed to preach on the Boston Common. The Common, where the Sons of Liberty had spoken out against British oppression, had become a public shrine to free speech and an open forum where anyone might air his or her views. However, the city of Boston had an ordinance that forbade outdoor preaching without special permission. This law was an outrage to the city's evangelical ministers. Back in 1885 A. J. Gordon had sparked a citywide protest by getting himself arrested for defying the law, but the ordinance stood.[9]

Ockenga decided to bring evangelicalism back onto the square. He applied for a permit to preach on the Common and was denied. Like Gordon, he too went out and preached anyway. The city officials relented, and for two summers Ockenga sermonized from the Common's Parkman Band Stand on Sunday evenings. The attendance at these meetings grew, but so did "clerical pressure," according to Ockenga's biographer. In 1945 the permit was cancelled and the evangelicals were shooed off the square. Ockenga was not to be so easily excluded, however. He announced one Sunday that he wanted to build an outdoor pulpit onto his church, which stood right next to the Common. A businessman who had been converted under Ockenga's preaching donated funds for what became known as the "Mayflower Pulpit." So by the summer of 1946, Ockenga was able to give out the gospel to a public audience. Like other creative fundamentalist revivalists of his day, he found a way to bypass closed cultural channels and be heard.[10]

Getting heard afforded some legitimacy, but it was not enough. Ockenga was anxious to regain a full measure of public respect for the gospel, and he believed that it would take nothing less than another Great Awakening sweeping over the region, like that under Jonathan Edwards and George Whitefield two hundred years before. So profound was his spiritual and emotional struggle over this matter that at one point, it is reported, he actually lost his preaching voice. Ockenga became convinced that an evangelical revival, with cultural victories following, would not come without reformation. Old-school fundamentalism could not win America. What was needed, Ockenga insisted, was "a progressive fundamentalism with an ethical message."[11]

The New School

Another of Ockenga's concerns was being echoed by the scholarly Wilbur M. Smith of the Moody Bible Institute. Smith had just published a hefty treatise, *Therefore Stand: A Plea for a Vigorous Apologetic in the Present Crisis of Evangelical Christianity* (1945), in which he argued that it was the church's business to influence the nation's intellectual life. For fundamentalists this was a rare thought, however, and Smith sensed that it would take a "whole new group of conservative Christian scholars" to mount the "vigorous apologetic" he envisioned.[12] Smith could not have known that very soon he would find himself in a such company, for the idea of mounting a more positive intellectual and cultural witness was growing among some younger fundamentalists.

Indeed, Harold Ockenga recently had discovered that a group of younger theologians were living virtually in his backyard. They had come to Harvard Divinity School or, in the case of two of them, Boston University's School of Theology, to learn their trade and earn their credentials as theologians. During the mid-to-late 1940s there were more than a dozen evangelical Protestants earning Harvard doctorates: three from the Wesleyan holiness movement's Asbury College and Seminary, two from the Churches of Christ, one who was a pentecostal, and eleven from a fundamentalist background.[13] Among the fundamentalists were Samuel Schultz and Kenneth Kantzer, both of whom would go on to teach at Wheaton College, where Merrill Tenney (Ph.D., Harvard 1944) had preceded them; John Gerstner, who would become the church historian at Pittsburgh Theological Seminary; Burton Goddard and Roger Nicole, who had begun what would turn into long careers at Gordon Divinity School; Terelle Crum, of the Providence Bible Institute; and five who would join the faculty of Fuller Theological Seminary: Edward John Carnell, Gleason Archer, George Eldon Ladd, Paul King Jewett, and Glenn Barker. Carnell also enrolled in the doctoral program in theology at Boston University, where he was joined for several summers by Carl F. H. Henry, a fellow Wheaton graduate who was on the faculty of Northern Baptist Theological Seminary in Chicago.[14]

Why had these conservative evangelicals converged on Harvard? Edward Carnell's biographer, Rudolph Nelson, observed that the Divinity School was eager to find new sources of students after a period of declining enrollment. The Depression and the war had contributed to this problem, but so had the changing intellectual tide in Protestant theology. Harvard's classically liberal historicism and humanism were less attractive to mainline Protestants in the 1940s than was neo-orthodox theology. Nevertheless, if the Divinity School could locate some new source of good students who were less influenced by current theological fashions, Harvard's reputation and mystique would attract many. If one were gunning for a Ph.D., as the young Edward Carnell put it, the potential benefits from going to Harvard made it worth at least a shot.[15]

At the same time that Harvard Divinity School was looking for a few good students, fundamentalist colleges and seminaries had produced some graduates who felt called to be scholars, especially in the fields of philosophy, theology, and biblical studies. Leading producers of aspiring intellectuals were Wheaton College, where a dynamic philosophy professor, Gordon H. Clark, had developed a number of bright young disciples; and Westminster Theological Seminary, where the conservative scholarly commitments of the old Princeton prevailed. In both cases what stirred the imagination of the fundamentalist students was the idea of a "historic Christianity" that had more breadth and depth than the sectarian piety they had inherited. Orthodox Christianity did not have to insult the intellect, Clark and the Westminster professors insisted. It had provided some of the most important intellectual foundations for Western culture. In the present crisis, these Calvinist philosophers argued, only a revival of biblical faith and a recovery of the Reformed Christian "world-and-life-view" could save and rebuild the West.[16] For a bright young fundamentalist who felt stifled by the movement's legalism, intellectual thinness, and alienation from mainstream society, the idea of a culturally responsible and intellectually profound faith was positively intoxicating. A twentieth-century reformation would need its reformers, however, and those who heeded the call would have to equip themselves for the task. And what better place to do that than Harvard?[17]

The fundamentalist graduate students knew full well that the theological reputation of Harvard Divinity School was "ultraliberal," and that its perspective on the study of the Scriptures was said to be "naturalistic." For a fundamentalist, pentecostal, or sectarian evangelical of another sort, enrolling in Harvard was like walking into the belly of the beast. Yet the danger may have been more imagined than real. Kenneth Kantzer recalled that he and his friends at graduate school "went through many soul-searching and mind-stretching experiences," yet he did not know of one who left the evangelical fold. Their persistence is not surprising. Most were already married, employed, and seminary-educated, so their basic convictions and commitments had been settled. The soul-destroying modernism that their elders had portrayed held no terror for them, they discovered, as they engaged it in its own lair.[18]

Indeed, one of the important discoveries these graduate students made was that their liberal mentors were admirable people. Among the professors at the Harvard Divinity School and Boston University's School of Theology were some who liked to bait conservative students, but most were gracious and scrupulously fair, insisting on intellectual rigor and honesty. For conservative graduate students reared on stories about believers being ridiculed and browbeaten in university classrooms, this was something of a revelation. Some suspected that they were being treated more kindly in the liberals' home institutions than the liberals would be in theirs. Personal graciousness and a willingness to engage in a civil debate, the graduate students were learning, should be the marks of the conservative no less than the liberal.[19]

Another critical lesson to be learned along the banks of the Charles was one that is common for doctoral students. As Kantzer put it, he and his colleagues discovered what it meant to lead "the disciplined life of a scholar." There were scarcely any scholarly role models for them within fundamentalism, so only now could they appreciate how many hours of study, how many years of work it took to master one's field and to make a contribution to it. This lesson had a sobering effect on their vision for mounting a renaissance of orthodox Christian thought. On the one hand, as they digested mountains of books and engaged in exhaustive research, their studies confirmed what they had been told about the richness of the Christian intellectual heritage; they also saw the deep problems encountered by the liberal humanist approach to the modern world's predicament. On the other hand, they came to realize that the cost of scholarly achievement, like the cost of spiritual discipleship, was dear indeed. If it was their mission to create a fresh and intellectually powerful evangelical literature, it would be a monumental task.[20]

A related and perhaps more painful truth was revealed in graduate seminars: fundamentalism needed a major intellectual overhaul. The doctoral students had assumed that Harvard professors would not be enamored of conservative or evangelical theology, but they were dismayed to find out how marginal these traditions were to contemporary theological discourse. Other than Machen's work, there was scarcely a book written by an evangelical or conservative Protestant in the past half-century that compelled contemporary scholars' attention. Convinced that "the Gospel deserved better," as Carl Henry later recalled, the students determined that they would "make a contribution." If fundamentalism was to make a difference in America, it would have to win a hearing in the cultural centers. Its advocates would never get the chance, however, unless they minded their manners and did their homework.[21]

One more very important lesson seemed to have been driven home to these young theologians. Much as they might criticize liberal theology for tending to reduce religion to ethics, they could not help but notice the deep concern of their professors "to serve the present age," as Charles Wesley had put it, for the sake of social righteousness. Carl Henry, for example, was studying under Edgar Brightman and the other "personalist" theologians at Boston University who were deeply devoted to the Social Gospel movement. Two years after they approved Henry's dissertation, they would be imparting some of their vision to another extraordinary student, Martin Luther King, Jr. Henry has claimed that his encounter with Brightman and the others had little to do with his developing a critique of fundamentalism's lack of social concern. But it is hard to believe that it was only a coincidence that Henry was putting the finishing touches on *The Uneasy Conscience of Modern Fundamentalism* (1947) in the summer of 1946 while he was studying in Boston.[22]

Henry and the others formed more of a cohort than a cohesive group during their graduate studies. They had few enough occasions to reflect together on what they were learning at Harvard and Boston, much less to form any collective vision for reforming fundamentalism. With courses to teach, churches to pastor, and families to tend, the fundamentalist graduate students had to catch up with each other on the way to and from classes, in the library, and now and then over a meal in each others' homes.[23] Several had more contact, however, through Gordon College and Divinity School. T. Leonard Lewis, a colleague of Carl Henry's at Northern Baptist Theological Seminary in the early 1940s, had become Gordon's president, and he recruited several of the graduate students to teach. Henry lectured there during his summer sojourns at Boston University, while Carnell, Ladd, Jewett, Goddard, and Nicole held more regular faculty appointments.[24]

Another point of reference was Harold Ockenga. The Park Street pastor remained somewhat aloof from the doctoral students, but they shared his vision for a renewal of western culture and agreed with his call for a more progressive fundamentalism. Some received invitations to preach at Park Street, and one of them, Gleason Archer, assisted Ockenga for a time. Carl Henry also won the favor of an Ockenga-penned Foreword to *The Uneasy Conscience*.[25] Ockenga also organized a few seaside seminars for evangelical theologians during the mid-1940s, such as the "Plymouth Conference for the Advancement of Evangelical Scholarship" held in August 1945. Henry, Tenney, and Crum were invited, along with Lewis and Goddard. There they met with other important fundamentalist and Reformed intellectuals, notably Everett Harrison of Dallas Theological Seminary, Stacey Woods of the Inter-Varsity Christian Fellowship, Allan MacRae of Faith Theological Seminary, Clarence Bouma of Calvin Theological Seminary, and Cornelius Van Til of Westminster. Other meetings were less formal, and the occasions were few. Still, Ockenga used these affairs to encourage the younger theologians and to solicit their thoughts about how to strengthen evangelical scholarship. These contacts would serve Ockenga well in his next venture.[26]

In the fall of 1946 the radio evangelist Charles E. Fuller separately contacted both Ockenga and Wilbur M. Smith of the Moody Bible Institute to enlist their participation in his plan to build a training college for missions and evangelism. Fuller's wife, Grace, was also influential in shaping this idea and so was their son, Dan, who had just entered Princeton Theological Seminary. Charles Fuller wanted the school to be practical in orientation, but on a higher level than the average Bible institute. It was important to the Fullers to do nothing in a shoddy way, and their commitment to quality struck a responsive note with both Ockenga and Smith. Yet neither felt free to participate.[27]

Fuller was persistent, however, and he invited the Ockengas to visit at the Fullers' Palm Springs resort home in February of 1947. As they talked over the college idea once again, Ockenga stressed the need for something more ambitious: a scholarly institution, offering graduate-level education in theology and convening the nation's best evangelical scholars to pursue their work. The Fullers accepted this idea and persuaded Ockenga to help them develop it. Not long after, they enlisted Smith as well, and he eagerly agreed to the plan because he had been dreaming for some time of an evangelical institution of this sort. In *Therefore Stand*, Smith had challenged evangelicals to develop "a seminary for advanced studies" that would help raise up "a new generation of apologists." Now, with the backing of perhaps the most famous and well-financed fundamentalist preacher of their day, Smith and Ockenga were being handed the opportunity to build an institution where an evangelical scholarly renaissance could begin.[28]

It was agreed that Ockenga was to take the lead in organizing the new school. Thanks to his earlier efforts at convening theologians, the Park Street pastor was well prepared for the task. Within three years' time he recruited a very talented faculty of younger, reform-minded scholars, notably Everett Harrison, who was on leave from Dallas to finish his doctorate at the University of Pennsylvania; Carl Henry; and Harold Lindsell, Henry's colleague at

Northern who had earned a doctorate in history from New York University. These three joined Smith as the founding faculty for the first year. Among the additional faculty members joining them by 1950 were three of the Harvard fundamentalists: Gleason Archer, Edward Carnell, and George Ladd.[29]

The new school seemed admirably situated for supporting new directions. It was amply financed, located in the Far West, where people felt free from the constraints of established patterns and institutions, and founded at a time when both the fundamentalist movement and the American people more generally were surveying a postwar world that seemed to demand a different outlook. As George Marsden has noted in his history of Fuller Seminary, its organizers presented the school's opening in the fall of 1947 as "a truly epochal event, the beginning of a new age for evangelicalism." To a full house at the Pasadena Civic Auditorium, Ockenga, who had agreed to serve as president in absentia, traced out what was by then a recurring theme among fundamentalist reformers, the need "to rethink and to restate the principles of western culture." The only hope for meeting the challenge of this age, Ockenga insisted, was for a resurgence of evangelical theology, the only theology adequate to the task. Fuller Seminary, then, would not only educate ministers and missionaries but would be a place where scholars would spark the "revival of Christian thought and life" needed to "rebuild the foundations of society."[30]

That was a tall order for a new school, which in its first year had just four professors and fifty students, and met in the educational wing of a church in Pasadena. Still, the talented faculty whom Ockenga was assembling shared his vision, and Fuller Theological Seminary was a great tonic for their scholarly aspirations. Carl Henry recalled that the professors thrived there. With the conviction that they were engaged in a great and noble enterprise, and in an atmosphere that encouraged them to write, everyone "seemed perpetually at their typewriters or deep in drafts of manuscripts." Each scholar was endeavoring to make a contribution that the theological world would have to take seriously, that would signal the emergence of a new evangelicalism, that would contribute to Christian cultural renewal in the West.[31]

The Task at Hand:
To Strengthen Fundamentalism or Revise It?

For each professor, the shape and thrust of the contribution would be somewhat different. For Carnell, the task was to write intellectual arguments for the truth and power of traditional Christian belief. For Harrison, it was to use the critical methods of biblical study to conservative ends. For Ladd it was much the same, with the added quest of replacing dispensationalism with an evangelical view of the kingdom of God and the end-times that was more conversant with classic Christian beliefs and more able to sustain evangelical social engagement. For every one, however, there seemed to be a basic issue to resolve about their goals: Were they content to strengthen fundamentalism's intellectual contribution and moderate its excesses, or was their task a more substantial revision of some of its distinctive beliefs? This question is basic to the history of Fuller Theological Seminary and the "new evangelicalism." It has been addressed, thanks to Marsden, and much of the ensuing drama it provoked was played out in the 1950s and 1960s. What is important to see in the very early years, however, are the sources of these conflicting impulses. The experiences of two of Fuller's original faculty, Wilbur M. Smith and Carl F. H. Henry, illustrate the formation—and tensions—of "progressive fundamentalism."

At the time he accepted the Fullers' invitation to anchor the faculty of their new seminary, Wilbur Moorehead Smith was one of fundamentalism's most widely admired Bible teachers. He was, as George Marsden put it, a "purebred fundamentalist." His father, a Chicago businessman, had served on the board of the Moody Bible Institute and his mother's father had worked with evangelist Reuben A. Torrey. Smith had been named after William G. Moorehead, an editor of the Scofield Reference Bible, who had presided at his parents' wedding. After nearly two decades of pastoral service within Presbyterian churches in Delaware, Maryland, Virginia, and Pennsylvania, Smith had accepted a call to the Moody Bible Institute in 1937. By all appearances this was the apex of his career. Even though he held a full-time teaching position, Smith was constantly preaching and lecturing, especially at weekend and summer Bible conferences. His pen was no less productive. Since the early 1930s he had been a frequent contributor, and sometimes an editorial associate, of several leading magazines: the *Sunday School Times*, the *Moody Monthly*, *Our Hope*, and *Revelation*. His specialty was book reviews and interpretations of world events in the light of prophecy. In 1934 Smith also became the editor of the annual Sunday school teacher's guide, *Peloubet's Select Notes on the International Sunday School Lesson*.[32]

By the mid-1940s, however, Smith was growing restless. He sensed that fundamentalism had grown intellectually dull, bitter, and ungracious, and had lost its hearing in the circles of thoughtful discourse. He was growing impatient with its penchant for offering "ephemeral pamphlets" when serious scholarly works were needed and perfunctory practical training for its leaders rather than the intellectual rigors of graduate study.[33] On the surface it might seem odd for Smith to harbor such feelings. After all, he had never had the patience to finish a degree of any sort. He had enrolled at Moody before finishing high school, but left after a year to study at the College of Wooster in Ohio. A year before graduation Smith accepted an assistantship at a Presbyterian church in Wilmington, Delaware, and was ordained without a degree while serving the Presbyterian congregation in Ocean City, Maryland. Smith become an authority within fundamentalism because of his native intellectual ability and his teaching skills, not because of his formal credentials.[34]

Nevertheless, Smith was a genuine intellectual. He read insatiably and had collected a personal library of some fourteen thousand volumes. He appreciated high-order thinking and he loved the company of scholars. Smith thrived on the fellowship and debates of the theological societies. He had participated in one during his pastorate in Baltimore in the 1920s, and while at Moody he had joined the Chicago Society for Biblical Research, where he met faculty members from McCormick Theological Seminary and the University of Chicago Divinity School. Associating with liberal scholars was certainly a questionable activity by fundamentalist standards, yet Smith was permitted to participate. He found the discussions to be very stimulating. By contrast, the level of discourse at the Moody Bible Institute was increasingly frustrating for Smith, and he complained to friends that the school lacked intellectual commitment and vision.[35]

Another formative experience for Smith was the conflict in the Presbyterian Church. From 1930 until 1937, Smith pastored a congregation in Coatesville, Pennsylvania, a town not far from Philadelphia. That region was the epicenter of the denomination's fundamentalist–modernist conflict. Smith left no doubts as to his theological loyalties. J. Gresham Machen preached his installation sermon, and three years later Smith joined the executive committee of Machen's Independent Board of Presbyterian Foreign Missions.

For the next four years Smith found himself in the eye of a raging ecclesiastical storm. The Presbyterian General Assembly proscribed the Independent Board in 1934 and several of its leaders, including Machen, were tried and suspended from the ministry. Smith's presbytery initiated no actions against him, and for a time he and his congregation were able to escape controversy. All around them, however, debates raged over whether or not fundamentalist congregations should separate from the "apostate" Presbyterian Church. In 1936 the General Assembly finally ordered Smith's presbytery to take action against him. Machen also tried to persuade Smith that his memberships with both the Presbyterian Church and the Independent Board were incompatible. Smith finally agreed with that logic, but instead of joining the separatists, he resigned from the Independent Board. The following year Will Houghton invited Smith to join Moody's faculty, and to his great relief Smith was able to walk away from the turmoil.[36]

Smith's experience as a nonseparating fundamentalist was fairly typical of a whole wing of the movement. These conservatives had grown exceedingly weary of the incivility, doctrinal hair-splitting, and church-rending tactics they had witnessed among fellow fundamentalists. Yet they recognized that their orientation was not in favor among their denominations' leaders. So they felt most at home with the independent ministries of the fundamentalist network. Independency, not overt separatism, was their instinctive choice, and in America's relatively undisciplined religious economy, they were free to pursue it.

Wilbur Smith was not one to preach against the sins of the fundamentalists, but he was clearly longing for something better. He wanted to see the faith defended in a more winsome, intellectually compelling, and respectable manner. By the mid-1940s he was forming a vision of what a new agenda might look like, and he shared it in the last chapter of his book, *Therefore Stand* (1945). Smith had no desire to revise any of the basic tenets of fundamentalism. Indeed, his vision for the movement focuses on classic fundamentalist themes: standing fast in the faith at a time when there were many inducements toward "indifference or denial," vigorously defending the gospel in the face of a "vast conspiracy" to intimidate Christians into not intruding their faith into public conversation, and insisting that the mainline churches teach the Bible and put Christ back into the center of their message. Smith's outlook, then, was largely defensive. The problem with fundamentalism, Smith was saying, was that it was not doing its defending with sufficient determination, graciousness, and intellectual power.[37]

To counter this problem, Smith called for a "vigorous offensive in the defense of the Christian faith," and suggested some measures that would restore some vigor. First on his list was "the training of a new generation of apologists," or intellectual missionaries. What was needed was a new seminary for advanced studies. The mission of these apologists would be to create "a new body of apologetical literature, . . . powerful works, attractively written, which will present the great truths of the Christian faith" in a manner that would demand attention. Smith felt acutely the disrespect that orthodox Christianity suffered in intellectual circles and yearned for fundamentalists to make a compelling answer. He was especially worried about the paganizing effects of contemporary campus life, and saw it as the field where "a new evangelical literature could have its greatest ministry. Smith added a related item to his wish list: "a truly great journal established for the defense of the faith," something more like the *Princeton Theological Review* than the *Moody Monthly*.[38]

There was little in Smith's outlook or agenda that could not be found somewhere within the older fundamentalist movement. Smith was an avid dispensationalist, and his view of evangelicals' role in society seemed largely formed by those views. Smith seemed bound to the beliefs of his predecessors, D. L. Moody and James M. Gray, whose sense of social, cultural, and ecclesiastical mission was limited to "holding the fort" until Jesus came to the rescue. *Therefore Stand* called for fundamentalists to mount a more vigorous and compelling apologetic, but largely for the purposes of better defending the ramparts they still held.

Wilbur Smith's colleague at Fuller, Carl F. H. Henry, shared the elder teacher's intellectual hunger and his yearning for a respectable expression of Christian orthodoxy. He too had encountered a bitter struggle between denominational loyalists and separatists.[39] Henry and Smith could agree, then, on the need to mount a more powerful scholarly witness to the faith, and for a more engaging and less sectarian approach than old-school fundamentalism seemed able to muster. Yet they had important differences, which would make Henry more than just a more scholarly and civil fundamentalist. He was a genuine revisionist, and he was to become the chief theological advocate for a "new evangelicalism."

Henry's and Smith's differing outlooks on fundamentalism and the church's role in the world came in part from their very different personal vantage points. Smith was born into the very core of the nascent movement's leadership and institutional life, and he entered the pastorate at the very moment when the fundamentalist–modernist controversies were beginning. He instinctively turned, again and again, to the classic fundamentalist posture of shock, outrage, and resentment at the demise of evangelical influence in American culture and the erosion of evangelical emphases within the older denominations.

Carl Henry, on the other hand, was an adopted son of the movement, who came to personal faith in Christ in 1933, at the age of twenty. By the time he graduated from Wheaton College in 1938, the fundamentalist–modernist controversies were over. Converts often are the most zealous of adherents, and Henry was eager to serve the faith in any way he could. Still, he had been a newspaper reporter and editor before entering the fundamentalist subculture, and his hunger for engaging the larger world of public affairs persisted. Over the years he maintained a mental vantage point from which he could see the movement's shortcomings and prod its leaders to make their message relevant to the needs of the day.[40] Unlike Smith, Henry took the decline of evangelicalism within the American Protestant mainline and its social and cultural marginalization to be settled facts. Rather than focusing his intellectual energy on a defensive holding action against these trends, Henry seemed much more interested in taking advantage of fresh opportunities to advance the evangelical cause in a cultural moment when chastened religious liberals and secularists were looking for new answers.

Henry was only thirty-four years old when he accepted the appointment to Fuller, but he had accomplished a great deal by that time, both in practical ministry and in scholarship. While serving on the faculty of Northern Baptist Theological Seminary, Henry found that his proficiency as a publicist was in high demand. He wrote a popular history of the Pacific Garden Mission, volunteered as a press agent for the early meetings of the National Association of Evangelicals, and helped organize an Easter sunrise service at Soldier Field for the Christian Business Men's Committee. In 1943 he published a second book, based on his doctoral dissertation at Northern, which offered advice on creating *Successful Church Publicity*.[41] Henry also continued to feed his immense intellectual appetite. This required some talent at mental gear-shifting, for while he was churning out articles and speaking at Youth for Christ rallies in the mid-1940s, he was also learning about Thomist philosophy at Loyola University and Calvinist philosophy with William Harry Jellema at Indiana University. In the spring of 1946 Henry was the publicist of the "Life Begins" evangelistic campaign in Chicago, which featured the old-time revivalists Paul Rood, John R. Rice, and Bob Jones, Sr. That summer, however, he was studying for his doctorate at Boston University and teaching at Gordon College. Meanwhile, *Remaking the Modern Mind* was being readied for publication, and Henry was editing the manuscript of *The Uneasy Conscience of Modern Fundamentalism*.[42] By the time Henry moved to Fuller Seminary, he had earned his credentials both as a working theologian and as an activist.

Henry's first two theological books laid out a two-pronged agenda that drew on both his studies and his ministry. They called for the rescue of western civilization through a powerful reassertion of an evangelical Christian "world-and-life view," and for the reformation of fundamentalism in order to equip it for that task. *Remaking the Modern Mind* (1946) was a sweeping examination of modern thought fashioned somewhat after the grand surveys of contemporary sages Jacques Barzun, Arnold Toynbee, and Reinhold Niebuhr. In it Henry argued that western culture was in a state of collapse and that its foundational humanistic faiths could no longer sustain it. In the midst of this crisis, Henry asserted, orthodox Christians faced a historic opportunity to show that the "controlling ideas of the Hebrew-Christian world-life view" could meet the cultural challenge.[43] In *The Uneasy Conscience*, however, Henry argued that fundamentalism could not take up this challenge. It was more interested in curbing individual sin than combatting social evil, more interested in divining all the details surrounding the Second Coming than working to advance Christ's kingdom now. Fundamentalism's ethical and social irrelevance was a scandal, for it trivialized the gospel and abandoned the field of social reform to secularists and religious liberals.[44] Yet fundamentalism could be redeemed, Henry insisted. If it recovered an evangelical social ethic and followed through on it, the world would witness another Reformation.[45]

Having arrived at Fuller, where the launching of such an effort had become the school's mission, Henry felt encouraged to sketch out for a broader audience what this new impulse might look like. He did this in a three-part series, "The Vigor of the New Evangelicalism," which was published in *Christian Life* magazine in 1948. Henry picked six issues upon which to concentrate. The first, which was presented as a prologue to the rest, was a reprise of *The Uneasy Conscience*. Was evangelicalism's "only message for today the proclamation of individual rescue," he asked, or did the gospel "have implications also for the most pressing social problems of our day?" Henry argued that there must be two parts to evangelicals' message: the prophetic, which declares God's impending judgment and the need for repentance; and the social, which declares that "there is not a problem of human existence but that Christianity . . . somehow has implications for its solution." As evangelicals learned to balance these two messages more properly, Henry claimed, their movement would "find a new vitality."[46]

Henry then set out to distinguish the new evangelicalism from the older fundamentalism by seeking to correct some of its faults. The first deficiency, Henry wrote, was fundamentalism's inattention to the encounter between biblical revelation and modern philosophy. Put this way, the issue would seem to be of little interest to the typical fundamentalist reader of *Christian Life*. Henry plunged in anyway, and the topic's relevance gradually appeared. Henry charged that fundamentalists' lack of engagement with modern intellectual trends had done incalculable damage to the faith. Collegians who had been confronted with intellectual arguments against Christian belief were being counselled simply to cast aside their questions and rely on pure faith. Many had lost their faith as a result. Henry stressed that the "younger evangelicals" of his circle were trying to confront antireligious ideas head on. Rather than bowing to the argument that the Bible had to be examined on terms set by modern secular philosophy, they were trying to turn the tables by bringing "the philosopher to terms with prophets and apostles."[47]

Henry turned next to something more controversial, fundamentalists' prophecy-charged world view. Fundamentalist savants were so certain that the present age was the final one, Henry charged, that they seemed to "fall all over each other in the rush to make it clear that they have no message which is relevant" to the modern predicament. Their outlook on the world was counsel for temporal despair; all of their hope was pinned on an imminent divine rescue. Henry insisted that "the new evangelicalism" would balance the apocalyptic outlook of fundamentalism with the message that "while the Lord tarries, the gospel is still relevant to every problem."[48]

Henry also complained that fundamentalism's preoccupation with the Second Coming and the minutiae of prophecy led people to lose perspective on what was truly important. Henry sadly recalled one of his former professors, who had poured himself into a treatise on whether the church would go through the Great Tribulation on earth in the last days or be raptured up to heaven before it began. Meanwhile, Henry noted, the professor seemed oblivious to the tribulation that churches were enduring at that moment in many places around the world. The new evangelicalism, he insisted, would remedy this travesty by seeking a more "properly balanced" approach to prophecy, stressing not the details but the grand themes of prophecy: the triumph of righteousness, the defeat of evil, and Christ's sure return.[49]

Henry turned next to fundamentalists' "spiritual isolationism." Their sectarian posture was having devastating consequences, he feared. Around the world, the church was growing and flourishing as never before, but fundamentalists focused on "the oppression of Satan" rather than "the lordship of Christ." Henry contrasted this negative outlook to the new evangelicalism, which, he said, applauded the formation of the NAE and other signs of a rising "ecumenical spirit in the evangelical camp."[50]

The final distinctive idea Henry wanted to highlight was pretty much for theologians only. He criticized conservative Protestants' characteristic way of studying theology, claiming that their seminaries usually required courses in systematic theology but made biblical theology optional. The problem with this was that evangelicals' various theological systems generally led them away from each other. The new evangelicalism, Henry insisted, would rediscover the apostolic core of doctrine in the Scriptures and produce a new theological consensus that would bring orthodox Protestants together instead of driving them apart.[51]

Henry's new evangelicalism, therefore, was a faith that would affirm the great fundamentals but avoid the "deficiencies" of fundamentalism. It would be intellectually engaged, socially aware, balanced and realistic about prophecy, positive about Christian unity, and based on a fresh and relevant rendering of biblical teaching. Henry believed that these new evangelical emphases were emerging at a propitious time. Western civilization was experiencing a crisis of confidence and was on the brink of the abyss. Liberalism had suffered a "severe set-back," but if conservative evangelicals did not rise to the challenge, the demise of liberalism could mean the emergence of "a secularism even worse than that of recent decades." The fate of an entire generation, Henry insisted, "will depend under God upon the vigor of the evangelicals."[52]

Henry's breathless rhetoric about evangelicals' historic task reveals perhaps the most important difference between the new evangelicalism, as he sought to articulate it, and the refined and reinvigorated fundamentalism that his colleague, Wilbur Smith, envisioned. Smith's instincts were defensive, and his rhetoric bristled with allusions to fortresses and ramparts. He mainly wanted fundamentalists and other conservative Protestants to contend for the faith without being so contentious. Smith did argue for some changes; he insisted that conservatives build the infrastructure to sustain a more vigorous intellectual defense of the faith, and, like almost every other leader in the camp, he was eager for a revival. Yet he did not envision a more positive agenda for theological thought or cultural engagement.

Henry, by contrast, had a nearly boundless vision of what evangelical revival and cultural reformation could accomplish. His manifesto, *The Uneasy Conscience of Modern Fundamentalism,* brimmed with hope for a new reformation. Henry did not expect that evangelicalism would create a fully Christian civilization, but certainly it could "engender reformation here, and overthrow paganism there; it can win outlets for . . . redemption." He envisioned, for example, Christian statesmen echoing "the great evangelical affirmations throughout world politics," and an evangelical intellectual revival that would "develop a competent literature in every field of study" and create a complete academic system, from grade schools to universities. Evangelicals' primary task was to preach the gospel "of individual regeneration," but do so in a way that it "can be recognized as the best solution of our problems." Christianity is a "world-and-life view," Henry insisted, not just an individual rescue. A Christian community living out that conviction would have a profound influence as "salt and light" throughout society, and the world might well see, as a result, "a new reformation."[53]

What made for the difference between this bolder vision of the movement's future and Wilbur Smith's more constrained outlook? One very obvious factor is a theological one. Henry and Smith had diverging views of biblical prophecy and its implications for the church's mission. Wilbur Smith was a classic dispensationalist. He believed that human civilization was caught in an unstoppable progression of evil, moving relentlessly toward the great and final judgment of God. The church's social and cultural mission was to give a clear and compelling witness to the truth in these dark times, to save as many as possible from the wrath to come. At best one could defend some final strongholds in society, and hope for a revival that would empower the defenders on the ramparts and reap a last great harvest of the redeemed before the Redeemer's return. Smith was not among the most alienated of dispensationalists, but this persuasion's prophetic determinism left only a minor place for any Christian witness other than personal evangelism.

Henry explicitly rejected this view of the church's mission. By placing the kingdom of God beyond the second coming of Christ, dispensationalists had cut the nerve of evangelical social and cultural witness, he believed. Evangelicals had to recover a theology of the kingdom that would enable them to be its advance agents and effect significant social transformation before Christ's return to establish the kingdom in its fullness. One of the central themes of the new evangelicalism, then, would be a movement from dispensationalism and the sectarian, culturally alienated position that it suggested.[54]

Such revisions had to be handled with great care, however, because dispensationalism had an honored position, virtually that of a "fundamental." Those who did not agree with its tenets had learned to keep quiet. Yet as fundamentalists encountered other Bible-believing Christians via the NAE or the Youth for Christ movement, they saw that one could be orthodox in doctrine and ardently evangelical in mission without being schooled in the Scofield Reference Bible. Headlong attacks on dispensationalism were not prudent, but some soft-peddling was occurring even within the dispensationalist camp. Thus the "new evangelicalism" had room for the "soft" dispensationalism of Everett Harrison and Charles Fuller himself, even while Henry, Ladd, and others suggested that the system had serious inadequacies.[55]

Henry's outlook differed from Smith's for another important reason. Unlike Smith, Henry had not directly encountered the process of marginalization from religious and social respectability. Without a doubt he shared Smith's yearning for respect and standing, but perhaps it seemed more readily attainable to him than it did to the older man. Smith was among the leaders who had both experienced and helped produce the movement's alienation; he had counted the cost and identified with the dissenters. Henry, on the other hand, had fundamentalism's status presented to him as a given. It would be very difficult for him to feel the same identification with the movement's original mission that Smith did. This differing vantage point was obviously generational. Henry's graduate school colleagues were second-generation fundamentalists who had grown up under a social stigma they had not chosen. They and he were eager to recapture some respectability for the movement and for themselves. Both Henry and the rest had known, and had grown to dislike, the penury of "full-time Christian service" within fundamentalism, and they could not help but notice its contrast to the lives of the gentlemen theologians with whom they studied in Boston. It is revealing that some of the most prominent details of Henry's memoirs concerning the late 1940s were his purchases. The young family that struggled along in faculty housing and with second-hand cars in Chicago came to Pasadena in a new Buick, and they were able to purchase a home. This too was an important dimension of the neo-evangelical impulse. Bound up with doctrinal revisions and the recovery of social concern was the determination to stake a fresh claim on middle-class respectability.[56]

The "younger evangelicals," as Henry called his cohort, would eventually make their viewpoint the dominant one for the new evangelicalism, but they did not want to alienate fundamentalist moderates like Smith and Charles

Fuller. Such leaders provided high visibility and instant respect within fundamentalist circles, and important continuity with the past. They also represented a very large contingent of fundamentalist pastors and lay leaders who were wary of revising their beliefs and orientation so dramatically as Henry was suggesting, but who were looking for an evangelical faith that was more irenic and inclusive, and more "geared to the times," as the Youth for Christ evangelists put it, than was the older fundamentalism. Keeping them on board would require some delicacy, especially when it came to issues like dispensationalism and the relationship between evangelism and social reform.

Perhaps Henry and his colleagues were too delicate, however, for it took nearly a decade for their reformist message to prompt much discussion in the major networks of fundamentalist discourse. It was odd that an experienced publicist such as Henry had difficulty provoking sustained interest or debate. His impassioned manifesto, *The Uneasy Conscience*, sold relatively few copies. His articles in *Christian Life* prompted a few letters but did not seem to have much impact. Even when the NAE's magazine, *United Evangelical Action*, tried to stir up a debate with opposing articles on the question "Is Dr. Henry Right?," little came of it. Part of the problem was the need for proper rumination. New ideas, attitudes, and visions take some digesting, some repeating, and a good forum for discussion and debate. Not until *Christianity Today* was founded in 1956 with Henry as editor did the new evangelical reformers have the means to promote and sustain their new perspective.

Spoiling for a Fight: Resurgent Separatism

One item on the new evangelicalism's agenda provoked an immediate reaction, however: its criticism of fundamentalism's sectarian spirit. The militant, separatist wing of fundamentalism was vigorous and growing in the late 1940s, and was more than willing to play the adversary. Harold Ockenga rang the opening bell for a new round with Carl McIntire, for example, in his address for the opening of Fuller Seminary, when he proclaimed that the new school would be "positive" in its ecclesiastical emphasis, and that it repudiated "the 'come-out-ist' movement." This was a direct jab at McIntire and his forces, made the more pointed by Ockenga's adding that Fuller graduates would have no time for the "kind of negativism" that existed "to attack others, and to derogate others, and to drag them down, and to besmirch them." McIntire of course gave as good as he got, for the evils of compromise at Fuller Seminary became a recurring theme in the *Christian Beacon*, and the separatist wing of fundamentalism became suspicious of the new school from the very start.[57]

Using separatism as a negative reference point for the new evangelicalism was attractive to many moderate fundamentalists and other reform-minded evangelicals, but the costs may have been greater than they anticipated. Separatist fundamentalists, like all the others, were thriving in the postwar years, and Carl McIntire was emerging as a key spokesman for them. McIntire's little denomination, the Bible Presbyterian Church, would never amount to much, but the militant pastor from southern New Jersey was a gifted publicist. For a time his organizations, the American Council of Christian Churches and the International Council of Christian Churches, enjoyed growing support from other separatist groups, and McIntire garnered public recognition for these agencies far beyond what their numbers might suggest was appropriate. The *Christian Beacon*, McIntire's weekly religious newspaper, was a widely read organ of separatist opinion in which McIntire practiced his talent for sensational and aggressive religious journalism.[58]

Carl McIntire's influence was in many respects a function of the dynamism of the separatist wing of fundamentalism. While the Presbyterian separatist sects remained tiny, other groups were burgeoning and new ones were being formed. The General Association of Regular Baptist Churches, for example, had grown to include 468 congregations by the late 1940s, and it had some outspoken and well-placed leaders, such as David Otis Fuller of Grand Rapids, who was on the board of Wheaton College. Likewise, the Independent Fundamentalist Churches of America, a loosely affiliated fellowship of pastors serving independent Bible churches, had a membership of 1,129 clergy by 1948 and included some of the leaders of Dallas Theological Seminary and the Moody Bible Institute. Both of these groups joined McIntire's American Council, so schools and ministries at the fundamentalist center, such as Dallas, Wheaton, Moody, and most of the faith missions, still could not afford to choose sides in a debate over separatism.[59]

Indeed, the separatist impulse was on the move once again in the late 1940s. The Northern Baptist Convention, which had been plagued by fundamentalist defections, was once again hemorrhaging dissident churches. Scores of conservative congregations within the Convention supported the formation in 1943 of an alternative mission board, the Conservative Baptist Foreign Mission Society (CBFMS). At issue was the denominational board's commitment to evangelical criteria for selecting missionaries and for setting priorities for mission activity. When it became clear at the denomination's annual convention in 1946 that a rival mission agency would not be tolerated, CBFMS supporters organized the Conservative Baptist Association and hundreds of congregations joined it. Northern, Western, and Eastern Baptist seminaries, which had been formed to train conservative evangelical pastors for the denomination, were caught up in the fray. While many of the Conservative Baptist leaders were not radical sectarians of the McIntire type, they felt compelled to uphold separation as a sometimes necessary option in the life of the church, and they could not accept wholesale denunciations of "come-out-ism."[60]

The most fertile seedbed for separatism in the postwar era would be the South, where populist and sectarian movements had flourished since the 1890s. Just when the Southern Baptist Convention thought it had contained the separatist movement that J. Frank Norris had stirred up, a fresh crop of dispensational and antidenominational sentiment began to sprout in Southern Baptist territory. Independent evangelists, such as Vance Havner of North

Carolina, John R. Rice, the former protégé of Norris, and Bob Jones, who was then building a sparkling new campus in Greenville, South Carolina, were popularizing dispensational beliefs and fomenting populist criticism of the Southern Baptist "machine"; and in their wake a number of relatively small, localized Baptist separatist movements were erupting, such as the one precipitated by Lee Roberson of Highland Park Baptist Church in Chattanooga. Independent fundamentalist schools in the South, notably Bob Jones College, Dallas Theological Seminary and Columbia Bible College, now had networks of loyal alumni who were steeped in fundamentalist beliefs and outlook. They were starting up independent but Baptist-like congregations, often called "Bible churches." These churches and the networks they formed were explicitly fundamentalist in doctrine and implicitly separatist in outlook. They gave new vigor and an expanding constituency to the separatist persuasion in fundamentalist circles.[61]

Harold Ockenga was not picking a safe sparring partner, therefore, when he excoriated "come-out-ism." Perhaps more than he knew, he was beginning to alienate a vigorous, growing, and very considerable wing of the fundamentalist movement with connections to some of the movement's most important centers. Bold talk of a new evangelicalism, then, was bound to make conservative leaders at fundamentalism's institutional core—Moody, Wheaton and Dallas—very nervous, and reluctant to highlight such themes for discussion and debate.[62] In part because of this reluctance, there were no great divides opening up yet in the fundamentalist movement.

Bob Jones, Sr., for example, who would eventually become a bitter opponent of any trend towards moderation, was still very much in fellowship with the progressives, even to the point of being an officer in the National Association of Evangelicals. Henry invited him to speak in chapel during Fuller Seminary's inaugural year. The veteran evangelist was working on a grand institutional plan of his own, the relocation and expansion of Bob Jones College into "the world's most unusual university." No doubt Jones felt a bit of institutional rivalry as he came to Pasadena, and perhaps some resentment at the high-handed treatment Fuller's faculty was giving old-fashioned fundamentalism. His chapel address was a tongue-lashing on the sin of intellectual pride.[63] Still, Jones had come when he was invited. Some fault lines were appearing, but the new evangelicals still had no identity distinct from the older fundamentalism. Because each faction was still in vital contact with the other and since each was seeking a base within the Dallas-Moody-Wheaton middle ground of the movement, the new evangelicals would have to take the separatists far more seriously than they may have wanted.

The Outlines of a New Movement

Even though moderate fundamentalists and other evangelical leaders were slow to take up the new evangelicalism promoted by Henry and Ockenga, the early stages of a new movement were beginning to form by the late 1940s.

Nowhere was this nascent network more evident than in the activities of the leaders at Fuller Seminary, Carl Henry, Wilbur Smith, and Harold Ockenga. Each continued to divide his time between the life of the mind and the call to evangelical action, and they found their way to groups and ministries that shared their more progressive perspectives. The networks they helped to form in the early postwar years would become the backbone of the new evangelicalism a decade later.

One of the most important of these organizations was of course the National Association of Evangelicals. The NAE was a natural haven for the progressives, but it could not promote their more pointed agenda. Critical to the NAE's success was the support of as many fundamentalist leaders and institutions as possible. With McIntire and others trying to undermine the NAE's credibility, the last thing the organization wanted was to stir up more opposition by, for example, debating the validity of dispensationalism. Still, the NAE had taken a stand favoring two of the new evangelicalism's issues: it stood against divisiveness among evangelicals and it stood for a more positive ministry to society.

Although the promotion of scholarship was never high on the NAE's agenda, the fellowship did yield the platform on occasion to the reformers and it did provide a base from which they could build networks and launch new pursuits. Ockenga was of course a major spokesman for the organization, and Wilbur Smith had been invited to give the closing address at the 1946 annual meeting in Minneapolis. His topic, not surprisingly, was "The Urgent Need for a New Evangelical Literature." Carl Henry, for his part, served as book review editor of *United Evangelical Action* and on two NAE committees. He chaired a group that selected an annual list of recommended books, and he served on a task force mandated to prepare an evangelical philosophy of education in response to the much-discussed Harvard report, *General Education in a Free Society* (1945). On both of these panels Henry met theologians and liberal arts educators who shared his vision for an evangelical intellectual revival.[64]

Before long, this emerging network of evangelical theologians developed its own organization. Faculty members of the Gordon Divinity School issued a call, replete with the signatures of two dozen leading evangelical scholars, for a two-day meeting in Cincinnati December 27–28, 1949. Sixty professors attended, and Carl Henry delivered the keynote address, a critical overview of the last "Fifty Years of Protestant Theology." Thereafter the assembly founded the Evangelical Theological Society, an independent association with an "affiliated" status in the NAE.[65]

Perhaps the most compelling arena of ministry for the emerging new evangelical movement was among college and university students. The most important campus ministry at the time was the Inter-Varsity Christian Fellowship. Inter-Varsity, as we have seen, was a newcomer to the United States, having arrived from Great Britain by way of Canada only in 1939, but it was growing rapidly by the late 1940s. Inter-Varsity brought into the American evangelical domain a number of traits that had developed within the British evangelical student movement. The most important of these, perhaps after the missionary impulse, was a high regard for the life of the mind. The British movement had produced a cadre of evangelical graduate students and younger lecturers in theology and biblical studies, and through the Inter-Varsity connection, some of their books, notably F. F. Bruce's *The New Testament Documents: Are They Reliable?* (1943), were making the rounds of the American campus movement by the late 1940s. Travelling Inter-Varsity agents, who often sold or gave away books, also introduced American students to the works of C. S. Lewis, the Oxford don who had become a popular fiction writer and an influential apologist for Christianity in wartime Britain. For evangelical students who yearned for Christian thought that could compete with the secular ideas they were encountering, these brilliant representations of Christianity were exciting indeed.[66]

Inter-Varsity's intellectual mission reflected the passions of C. Stacey Woods, the American-educated Australian who was leading the North American movement. Woods wanted the students to be challenged intellectually and to encounter scholarly Christianity, but he also wanted them to find some American role models. He quickly found the cadre of American fundamentalist and Reformed theologians Harold Ockenga had been convening, and he encouraged them to participate in his movement. Ockenga spoke at Inter-Varsity's first foreign missions conference in Toronto over the Christmas–New Year's holiday, 1946–1947, and he also addressed an international student meeting organized by Inter-Varsity in Lausanne, Switzerland, in the summer of 1948. Wilbur Smith was an early and eager contributor to the evangelical student cause. He spoke regularly to campus groups, contributed articles to *HIS,* Inter-Varsity's magazine, and eventually joined its editorial staff. One of Smith's compositions, *The Man Who Lived Again* (1944), an apologetic for the resurrection of Christ, was one of the American Inter-Varsity's first publications. Smith spoke at the first two student missionary conferences during the Christmas–New Year's holiday, in 1946–1947 and 1947–1948; and in 1949 he held a series of noon meetings at UCLA, where 400–500 students attended each time. Carl Henry was on the Inter-Varsity campus circuit in the mid-1940s, speaking at the universities of Chicago, Illinois and Michigan as well as teaching at Inter-Varsity's Campus in the Woods in Ontario in 1947. Henry wrote a small book for Inter-Varsity, *Giving a Reason for Our Hope* (1949), which was drawn from his Friday-night discussions with college students at the First Baptist Church of Hollywood.[67]

These contributions to campus discourse were not the high-powered scholarship that Smith and Henry envisaged, but the Fuller professors were happy to serve a movement with which they shared so many ideals and commitments. The works of biblical scholarship coming out under British Inter-Varsity's own imprint did display the high caliber of scholarship to which they aspired. Inter-Varsity in the United States shared the reform-minded fundamentalists' concern for intellectual engagement, practical ecumenism among evangelicals of every kind, and an emphasis on the "great verities" of historic

Christianity, as Carl Henry put it, rather than on sectarian minutiae. Thousands of alumni from Inter-Varsity campus chapters formed a natural constituency for the new evangelicalism when it finally emerged as a visible entity in the following decade.

Another vital ingredient in the developing new evangelical network was the innovators in evangelism. Among the fundamentalists, everyone—moderates and militants alike—were mounting citywide initiatives and forming new parachurch ministries to press forward in evangelism. At the innovative edge of this movement, however, were the organizers of Youth for Christ rallies and the burgeoning Christian Business Men's Committees. The leaders of these efforts were not intellectuals by any stretch of the imagination, but they were coming to some of the same conclusions that the younger theologians at Fuller had reached. In their efforts to mount city-wide evangelistic campaigns, these groups, which usually were led by a core of fundamentalist organizers, reached out beyond their usual institutional and sectarian redoubts and welcomed evangelicals from other traditions. Their prevailing outlook was much like that of the NAE: evangelicals should stress their common commitments, not the things which divided them; they should join for cooperative action in these days of unprecedented challenge and opportunity; and they should work harder at bringing their faith out into the marketplace rather than hiding it within sectarian fortresses. There were revival showers on the horizon, many thought. They were not yet pouring down upon the nation, but "mercy drops" were falling. Now was the time to work together to make it happen.[68]

The revival of revivalism taking place in the late 1940s was a major source of confirmation for Ockenga, Henry, and the others. It meant that the new evangelicalism they were articulating had something like a popular expression and a grassroots constituency. Their ties went much deeper as well, for as Carl Henry had repeatedly emphasized, the keystone to a new evangelical theology and social ethic was personal regeneration. The renaissance of evangelical thought that they were working for and the reformation of western culture they were hoping for could only begin with a revival of born-again Christianity. These scholars were not merely distant cheerleaders for the work of evangelism. They believed that everyone, whether professor or factory worker, was called to be a "soul winner." So Henry, Smith, and Ockenga yearned for revival, supported the new evangelistic measures, and participated in them as well, according to their talents. Wilbur Smith, whose finely honed sense of personal dignity made him more at home at the Bible conference lectern than the youth rally, still did his part by speaking repeatedly at Percy Crawford's young people's camp and at the "Forest Home" conferences for college students in the nearby San Bernardino Mountains. Carl Henry, as we have seen, had served several of the citywide campaigns in Chicago and with Youth for Christ around the Midwest. In Pasadena he became the organizer of the annual Easter sunrise service at the Rose Bowl. For him, this work was part and parcel of the "vigor of the new evangelicalism."[69]

Harold Ockenga was perhaps the most intensely committed to advancing the cause of revival. He longed for it and prayed constantly for another Great Awakening in New England. At times his yearning was so great that he prostrated himself under the rug in his study, weeping and pleading with the Lord in prayer. He had done his part in New England. Souls were being saved and evangelical Christians were growing more bold in their witness, but there was no general outbreak of religious interest. Even the creation of that "ray of hope," the NAE, had not ushered in a new Awakening, despite expectations that with the NAE's formation, America's revival was breaking forth. Seven years later, despite many positive signs, nothing truly extraordinary had happened. Without a revival, not even the vigor of a new evangelicalism could win America. Would revival ever come?[70]

12

REVIVAL IN OUR TIME

On a quiet day in 1944, somewhere in the South Pacific, a young chaplain in the U.S. Army Air Force sat forlornly on a beach, looking out to sea. He wondered if he would ever see his family again. He was Edwin Orr, an evangelist and native of Northern Ireland. Homesickness was unusual for Orr, for his earnest face, horn-rimmed glasses, and slender frame concealed a restless spirit. Orr had traveled much of the globe in the decade before the war on a mission to prepare the churches for a great revival. Now Orr was doing his part for the war effort, ministering to an American fighter squadron. He counselled his men through the loneliness, danger, and uncertainty they faced, but on this particular day Orr seemed to have come down with the same sort of emotional virus that afflicted them, and he needed some answers. The guidance Orr was seeking came soon, and straight from the Lord, he believed. Orr felt suddenly convinced that his life would be spared, and that the Lord had two tasks for him to accomplish. He was to "become a historian of the great religious awakenings of the Nineteenth Century, and an eye-witness of the beginnings of the awakenings of the Twentieth Century."[1]

By the time the war was over Orr had decided that he would pursue a doctorate at Oxford University on the history of the nineteenth-century awakenings. Orr got his discharge from the Army in Manila, where he had been helping the local Youth for Christ rally, and then set off for South Africa, where his family had settled for the war's duration. Once there, Orr saw them off on a ship to England and then hitch-hiked his way up through Africa and finally to England. Orr enrolled in Oxford, and in two years completed his dissertation on the Second Great Awakening in Great Britain and America. Now he was free to take on the second part of his calling: to report on and participate in the great twentieth-century Awakening.[2]

In the fall of 1948 Orr received an invitation from his friend and fellow revival promoter, Armin Gesswein, to come over to California and help him.

211

Deciding that this was the Spirit's call to the second part of his mission, Orr went to Los Angeles to help Gesswein and other revivalists prepare for the "Christ for Greater Los Angeles" campaign, scheduled for September of 1949. The evangelist leading the campaign was a young crusader from the Youth for Christ rally circuit. His name was Billy Graham. Orr the revivalist and chronicler of revivals found himself in exactly the right place at exactly the right time. The Los Angeles campaign would catapult Billy Graham into national fame and become one important sign that a remarkable revival of religious interest was taking place in America. Orr played a minor role in these events and, more importantly, he wrote a number of accounts of them. In these he blended first-hand knowledge, a researcher's eye for important details and relationships, and a revivalist's reading of the spiritual temper of the times.[3]

Orr was only one of many who have tried to make sense of the postwar religious quickening that included the rise of Billy Graham. Some have seen it as an anxious nation's response to the fearsome global challenge of the Cold War. Others have argued that the boom in church membership and ecclesiastical construction was stimulated by postwar demographics: the large cohort of young couples who all began families after the war and the migration of the middle class to new suburban communities. Sociologist Will Herberg had another explanation: the growing "other-directedness" of middle-class America. Herberg postulated that joining a congregation was becoming a major way of adjusting and belonging in postwar society. Meanwhile, evangelical interpreters such as Orr have portrayed the revival as God's chosen moment, for which Billy Graham was the divinely anointed prophet.[4]

It is not necessary to deny the importance of any of these factors. One critical component has not been sufficiently addressed, however: the impact of a fundamentalist-led revival of revivalism, of which Billy Graham was a product. It may be extreme to claim that if the dynamic preacher from North Carolina had not been available, this revival movement might well have created him. Yet his emergence in Los Angeles in 1949 and his successes thereafter in one citywide campaign after another were made possible by a revivalist movement that had been mobilizing for some time. By the late 1940s, as we have seen, fundamentalists and other evangelicals were putting their new revival techniques to work with ever-increasing vigor and expectation.

The postwar religious revival was much more widespread and general in its scope than could be attributed to the fundamentalist-led evangelical coalition, but its efforts added new active ingredients to the postwar social and religious cauldron. Discussion of the postwar revival has concentrated mostly on possible changes in the public climate that might have been reflected in an increase in religious demand. The infusion of a fresh supply of religious products is an important part of the equation as well. Whether or not Americans' demand for religious identification and expression was growing, the aggressive marketing of evangelical Protestantism attracted many and seemed to raise the general level of interest in religion. The new revivalism and its charismatic young champion made a major contribution to the supply side of the equation of public religiosity in America.[5]

The Sound of a Going

Evangelical revivalism, spearheaded by enterprising fundamentalists and sparked by young peoples' rallies, had accomplished a major mobilization during the years of World War II. Even though the youth rally movement began to settle down during the late 1940s, the larger enterprise that had been set in motion continued to flourish and gain momentum. The resumption of peacetime life did nothing to hinder it, and in fact the new conditions seemed to encourage revivalism. There was, on the one hand, a pervasive sense of peril. After nearly two decades of economic depression and world war, most Americans worried that peace and prosperity would not last. The expansion of communism overseas was a major cause for concern, but so was moral decline at home. Yet promise was in the wind as well, for the end of the war seemed like the end of an era. The Depression was definitely over, the United States had emerged as the world's premier economic and military power, and many of the debates and polarities of earlier decades now seemed less relevant. For many, even those who had suffered oppression, this new, more promising age seemed to offer another chance to gain their portion of the American dream.[6]

The many signs of growing religious interest during the war continued and even gained momentum in the late 1940s. New churches were being erected at a phenomenal rate, with over a billion dollars of Protestant ecclesiastical construction underway by 1949. The Roman Catholic Church was baptizing one million babies every year in the late 1940s and building a total of 125 new hospitals, 1,000 new elementary schools, and 3,000 new parishes. National religious membership statistics swelled, surpassing the 50 percent mark of the total population for the first time. Bible sales doubled between 1947 and 1952. According to the Roper opinion polls, the clergy were gaining more esteem as well. In 1942 they placed third, behind government and business leaders, summoning a 17.5 percent response to the question, "Which one of these groups do you feel is doing the most good for the country at the present time?" In 1947 clergy placed first, with a 32.6 percent response.[7]

The new revivalists had mobilized quickly during the war, and now they had an impressive infrastructure. Citywide networks of churches along with local chapters of the NAE, the Gideons, and the Christian Business Men's Committees that had supported the Youth for Christ rallies were still in place, made confident by their successes and looking for more evangelistic work to do. If these groups could gather a crowd to fill a civic auditorium or an indoor arena for a Saturday night rally, why not do it for two or three weeks for an extended revival meeting?

One of the earliest attempts to gear up extended citywide campaigns was sponsored by the "Christ for America" committee. This organization, which was inspired by a successful three-week crusade in Philadelphia in 1942, was seeking to promote revival crusades in other cities. The evangelists most often drafted to preach the Christ for America campaigns were of the more traditional sort, notably Hyman Appelman, Bob Jones, and John R. Rice. Theirs was hardly a revivalism that was geared to the times. Even so, between 1943 and 1948 the organization was very busy, sponsoring more than fifty metropolitan evangelistic campaigns. The old-time campaigners had full appointment books, and prominent fundamentalist pastors, such as Oswald J. Smith of Toronto, Harold Ockenga of Boston, and William Ward Ayer of New York, were enticed to come out from behind their downtown pulpits to mount the revival hustings.[8]

The renewed interest in revivalism was in fact a pan-evangelical phenomenon. Among the Southern Baptists, the Youth for Christ sensation had prompted a Southern Baptist look-alike organization and then a denomination-wide revival campaign. By the late 1940s Southern Baptists were baptizing hundreds of thousands each year. In the networks of pentecostalism, a movement called the "healing revival" was growing, led by a younger generation of evangelists whose expansive visions and extraordinary gifts were drawing crowds for weeks on end in city after city. The most charismatic of the lot was Oral Roberts, a handsome young pastor from Oklahoma. Even among nonrevivalist conservative Protestants, something like a revival spirit was breaking out. Dr. Walter Maier, the nationally renowned radio pastor of the *Lutheran Hour*, was holding rallies in the massive indoor arenas of midwestern cities and at the Hollywood Bowl as well.[9]

The evangelists on the Youth for Christ circuit whose programs had sparked this new movement were not to be outdone. They too wanted to lead extended citywide meetings, and they had no trouble in finding opportunities. Those who received the most calls included Merv Rosell, who had trained under William Bell Riley but restyled his work for the youth rally circuit; Jack Shuler, who was the son of Robert (Fighting Bob) Shuler, the Methodist radio preacher from Los Angeles; Charles Templeton, the charming and eloquent youth rally leader from Toronto; and Billy Graham, the Wheaton College graduate from North Carolina who had been groomed for leadership by Torrey Johnson. In 1948, Johnson himself felt the call to "wider fields of service," so he left the presidency of Youth for Christ in order to try some citywide campaigning.[10]

A revival was in its strictest sense a season of spiritual renewal within the churches that might then grow into a greater awakening of religious commitment in society. So in many cases the urban revival campaigns were built upon a base of pastors, lay leaders, and local congregations organized and dedicated to the task. During the 1930s, Edwin Orr and a number of others had been traversing the nation, stressing the need for repentance, a fresh enduement of spiritual power, and earnest prayer for a national revival. Small groups of pastors, businessmen, women's societies, and young people were gathering here and there to pray and work for revival. The Christian Business Men's Committees alone had 197 chapters functioning by 1949.[11]

In several major metropolitan areas there were large and denominationally diverse meetings of pastors praying for revival. The organizer of a number of them was Armin R. Gesswein, a former minister in the Lutheran Church–Missouri Synod. Gesswein had experienced conversion under the preaching of the radio evangelist Paul Rader, felt called to the ministry, and went to study at Concordia Theological Seminary in St. Louis, where Walter Maier was a professor. During his first pastorate, Gesswein began to have fellowship with evangelicals who were outside the Lutheran fold. This practice got him in trouble with the strictly separatist Missouri Synod, however. Dismayed by his denomination's sectarian spirit, Gesswein resigned his pastorate and became the minister of an independent church nearby. When Gesswein was invited to conduct a preaching tour in Norway during 1937 and 1938, he encountered a revival that was sweeping through both the state-sponsored Lutheran Church and the free churches. He came home inspired by what he had witnessed in Norway and determined to see a revival of that kind happen in the United States. He began to travel from city to city on a teaching mission, holding retreats and establishing prayer meetings for revival among pastors of many denominations. Gesswein helped to start a meeting in Los Angeles in 1941 and 1942 but then went on his way, settling for a time in Boston, where he taught at Gordon College.[12]

When the war was over Gesswein returned to Southern California, settled in Pasadena, and began to plant ministers' revival prayer meetings throughout the region. He also continued to organize groups elsewhere, notably in the San Francisco Bay area, Seattle, and Minneapolis–St. Paul. Meanwhile, in the fall of 1948, Gesswein's friend, confidant, and advisor, Edwin Orr, had come to help him. One of their first joint efforts began that October when they went to Minneapolis and St. Paul to lead a series of meetings on revival with a minister's group called the United Spiritual Advance. Orr returned the next spring to lecture at Bethel College and Seminary. A revival broke out on the campus and spread quickly to the other two fundamentalist schools in town, St. Paul Bible Institute and the Northwestern Schools. Students moved out from there to organize revival prayer meetings at another half-dozen denominational colleges nearby and at the University of Minnesota. In a month's time the meetings had also spread to the more than fifty churches of the United Spiritual Advance. News of these meetings stimulated similar developments in Seattle, Portland, Chicago, San Francisco, and Los Angeles, with Orr and Gesswein giving guidance and keeping revival expectation percolating.[13]

Increasingly, however, this duo's attention turned to Southern California. In September 1948 Gesswein and Orr helped to organize a retreat at the Pacific Palisades conference grounds for their revival prayer network. About 120 ministers gathered from a variety of denominations, ranging from Lutheran to Methodist to pentecostal. Said Norman Grubb, a British missions promoter who was at the meeting: "It was a time in the heavenlies. The real break came the first night after impromptu testimonies to revival, from Mennonite and Presbyterian missionaries. Many were on their faces till 1 A.M. confessing need and failure. The next day and night took us to the heights, again ending about 1 A.M., after very many had come forward to have united hands laid on them for a new experience of the Holy Spirit in themselves and their churches."[14] Gesswein and Orr held another conference the following spring with Harold

Ockenga as guest speaker. Some four hundred ministers and their spouses attended, and according to one account, half of the participants each night "continued in penitence and prayer until the early hours of the mornings." In response to this stirring, the "Christ for Greater Los Angeles" evangelistic committee sponsored Orr and Gesswein to conduct a month of meetings throughout the Los Angeles area to speak on "revival and how it may be attained."[15] Orr and Gesswein held one more prayer conference in September 1949, just before the Christ for Greater Los Angeles committee's citywide "Big Tent Campaign." The committee had organized several citywide campaigns since its start in 1944, featuring first Hyman Appelman, then Jack Shuler, and most recently, Charles Templeton. This year their featured evangelist would be Billy Graham, so Orr invited Graham to help lead this third and final Pacific Palisades prayer conference.[16]

While Orr and Gesswein worked to mobilize pastors for revival, Henrietta Mears, who was the director of religious education at Hollywood Presbyterian Church, was inspiring and challenging hundreds of the region's young adults. Mears was a wealthy, talented, and vibrant woman who had worked for several years at William Bell Riley's church and school in Minneapolis, but she moved out from under Riley's constraining leadership in 1928 to settle in southern California. Mears's dynamism made an immediate impact at Hollywood Presbyterian, where in less than three years she built Sunday School enrollment from 450 pupils to more than 4,000. Faced with a lack of evangelical curricular materials, Mears created her own and then founded Gospel Light Publications in 1933 to market them. By the late 1940s Gospel Light had become one of the largest evangelical publishing firms.[17]

Ministry to young adults was another passion for Mears, and she took special delight in challenging them to engage in ministry. By the late 1940s a number of her protégés were building an evangelical student movement on nearby campuses. Most notable was the work at UCLA led by a young Oklahoman named Bill Bright. Bright urged Mears to provide a place for college-age young adults to hold retreats, so she developed Forest Home, a conference center in the San Bernardino Mountains. Six hundred students attended her initial "College Briefing" conference in 1947.[18] At one of the Forest Home gatherings in the summer of 1949, a vocalist from Hollywood was converted. She approached Mears about starting a prayer meeting for people in show business. Mears opened her lovely home in Westwood to the celebrities, including, for example, Roy Rogers and Dale Evans; and with the help of Edwin Orr, her weekly gathering was soon attracting up to forty entertainers. In September of 1949, Mears's annual College Briefing Conference at Forest Home attracted some five hundred students to hear Billy Graham and Edwin Orr, and a revival broke out. According to the veteran campus evangelist, "Dad" Elliott, it was the most unusual meeting "since the glorious days of the Student Volunteers."[19]

Among the evangelically inclined of southern California, then, revival was in the air. Conferences and weekly prayer meetings provoked revival expectancy to new heights. By the eve of the evangelistic campaign in September 1949, there were some eight hundred prayer groups throughout the region. The evangelical forces of the city were mobilized as never before.[20]

The Prophet

By the eve of the Los Angeles crusade, Billy Graham had been engaged in citywide evangelistic campaigns for some time. During most of 1945 and 1946 he had been a headliner for Youth for Christ, visiting forty-seven states in the first year and in the process being named United Airlines' top civilian passenger. Although Graham was but one of a cohort of talented young preachers and certainly not the most eloquent among them, the other revivalists noticed Graham's remarkable way with an audience. Billy may have talked too loud and too fast and his gestures might have been a bit wild, but people sat up and listened to the tall and slender young man with wavy blond hair, piercing, deep-set blue eyes, and a resonant, trumpet-like voice. Graham had developed his preaching style from listening to radio announcers, merging their timing and timeliness with his own passion to save lost souls. Graham's intensity and earnestness were contagious. Others on the circuit were more talented, but Graham had a stronger effect on the crowds. Charles Templeton, who had toured with Graham, observed that Billy consistently convinced more people to respond at the invitation than he did.[21]

Graham got his first taste of citywide crusades while touring England in the winter of 1946–1947. The mission of his entourage was to hold Youth for Christ rallies in many cities and help local groups organize Youth for Christ chapters. Over six months, Graham spoke at 360 meetings. In addition to one-night rally engagements he held more extensive campaigns in Belfast, Birmingham, London, and Manchester. The cultural clash at these meetings was nearly palpable as the young, upbeat Americans with their pastel suits and hand-painted ties interacted with their British hosts. British reactions to the American preachers were mixed, ranging from disapproval and resentment to delight at the Americans' freshness and energy. Regardless of their hosts' disposition, the Youth for Christ preachers enjoyed strong public interest as they spoke to packed auditoriums in city after city.[22]

These engagements called for a great deal of exertion and the team experienced many obstacles along the way, but this tour was in some respects a can't-lose situation. The young evangelists were able to learn some things about citywide revivalism in another land, where they could walk away from their mistakes. If they were at least moderately successful, they would bring home the cachet of a victory for the Lord overseas. A transatlantic evangelistic tour had done wonders for the evangelistic careers of Moody and Sankey in the 1870s, and Graham was by no means the only hopeful American preacher to make the crossing in the late 1940s.[23]

Graham's British tour was the occasion for the young evangelist to look inward, at the state of his own soul, and outward, to the hope of revival just over the horizon. Two British preachers became his guides in these moments of reflection. The first was Stephen Olford, a young Welsh evangelist, who spent two intense days on retreat with Graham in rural Wales, where they studied the Bible together and prayed about the work of the Holy Spirit in their lives. As Olford recalled it, Graham questioned him about his own experience, and Olford told of totally surrendering his life to the Lord and then being filled with the Spirit and empowered as never before in his ministry. Graham said that he wanted this blessing too. According to Olford, Graham then pledged to God a total dedication of his life, and shortly thereafter, like so many other leaders before him in the fundamentalist lineage, he experienced a powerful presence of the Spirit. The result, claimed Olford and the others on the tour, was that Graham's preaching did indeed take on an added measure of authority and force.[24]

The other British mentor for Graham was Edwin Orr. He and Graham had met briefly in 1940 in Tampa where Graham was a student at the Florida Bible Institute and Orr was sequestered at a trailer park working on a book. They met again in early 1947 in the somewhat more auspicious setting of Oxford, where Orr was writing his doctoral dissertation on the Second Great Awakening. Orr led Graham over to Lincoln College, where John Wesley, George Whitefield, and some fellow students had founded the "Holy Club." Said Graham as he looked into the room where they had met, "This is holy ground." He and Orr talked about the marks of a true revival, and before they left, they prayed that God would favor his people with another Great Awakening.[25]

Their desire was a common one at the time, but was Graham thinking about some special role that he might be called to play? He very well might have been wondering about these things, because the dynamic young preachers on the rally circuit could not help but believe that they were on the cutting edge of God's advance in their day. In their private thoughts and prayers they may have wondered whether the Lord had a special role for them in bringing revival.

It would be presumptuous to speak of such things, but fundamentalist spirituality encouraged these imaginings. God had a special plan for every believer, a singular role for each to play in the great drama of redemption. And for the more devoted souls, there was something more, a definite call to full-time Christian service as pastor, missionary, or evangelist. Under such circumstances, young fundamentalist leaders were encouraged to lift their sights beyond their current duties and look for that wider field of service just over the horizon.

Fundamentalism encouraged heroic ambition by the way it remembered the past. Stories abounded of missionaries like Hudson Taylor who had risked all and accomplished wonders in faraway places, and humble "prayer warriors" like George Muller who had seen answers to their prayers beyond their imagining. Evangelists such as Charles G. Finney had become mighty instruments of the Spirit in bringing great revivals. Young people read about these heroic deeds and the more earnest among them yearned to be "used of the Lord" for something as wonderful.[26] The movement's remembrance of revivals highlighted the role of the singular spiritual hero, the prophet-evangelist who became the Lord's trumpet to sound the message of warning, repentance, and salvation. As the expectation of a revival spread in the 1940s, leaders began to voice the question: Where was the prophet to lead it? Vance Havner was one of the most insistent in claiming that God's way of bringing revival was first to send a prophet. In one of his published sermons, Havner launched into a litany of sorts, reciting "that noble line of prophets and preachers" that ranged from Samuel to Jeremiah to Amos "the country preacher" to John the Baptist to Paul, and then since Bible times, to "Savonarola and John Knox and Martin Luther and John Wesley and George Whitefield and Charles G. Finney and Dwight L. Moody and Billy Sunday. . . . Down through the ages it has ever been thus," Havner insisted. "The hearts of men have grown skeptical and dis-illusioned and doubtful until another Elijah came along who walked with God and could pray down fire from heaven, and then revival has come." To Havner the implication was clear: "May God raise up another such prophet today!"[27]

Part of the expectation that a new prophet would arise was that this person would be an Elisha, not an Elijah, a younger preacher who would inherit the prophet's mantle from his elders. Revival promoter Ernest Wadsworth of the Great Commission Prayer League reasoned that since "God is grieved with many of the older generation who are set in their ways, . . . we must look to the young. We need a Whitefield, a Wesley, a young Spurgeon more than ever." If revival was to come, "godly men of the old generation must lay hands on young Timothys."[28]

There was one leader of the older generation who desperately wanted to lay his mantle on one of the young sons of thunder. William Bell Riley was in his late eighties by the end of the war, and his health was failing. He had retired in 1942 from a forty-five-year pastorate at First Baptist Church of Minneapolis, and in other ways as well he was putting the finishing touches on his career. Riley's Northwestern Schools were flourishing, and by the mid-1940s North-western alumni pastored 70 percent of the Baptist churches in Minnesota. When Riley was elected president of the Minnesota Baptist Convention in 1944 and 1945, he organized its separation from the Northern Baptist Con-vention to join the new Conservative Baptist Association. Riley no longer dreamed of a national fundamentalist victory, but he had a formidable regional empire to hand on to a successor.[29]

Riley was a bitter old man who was not encouraged by many trends in the 1940s. One bright spot he saw, however, was the Youth for Christ movement. The Minneapolis rally had started in his former church under the leadership of a Northwestern alumnus, George Wilson. Riley was delighted by this new ini-tiative, and he wanted one of its dynamic young preachers to succeed him. Riley apparently approached both Billy Graham and Torrey Johnson in 1946 about becoming the next president of the Northwestern Schools. Johnson gave Riley a firm negative reply and Graham tried to do the same.[30]

Riley would not back away from Graham, however. Like Edwin Orr, he had first met Graham at the Florida Bible Institute, and Riley, who grew up on a farm in Kentucky, immediately took a liking to the lanky, earnest southerner.

Nevertheless, Graham had become settled in his call to be a traveling evangelist, and he was just as certain that administrative duties were not for him. He gave Riley a second polite refusal and insisted that he could not maintain a revival preaching schedule and also run the schools. Graham also expressed worries in private that Riley's legacy was not all that attractive. The old warrior had frequently lashed out at his foes, real and imagined, with anti-Semitic, conspiratorial tirades. So Graham told Riley, in the best evangelical terms of finality he could muster, that he had received no assurance that taking on the presidency of the Northwestern Schools would be God's will for him.[31]

Riley refused to take this for an answer. The bedridden and dying old preacher called Graham to his side in the summer of 1947 and, in the midst of a violent thunderstorm, gave Graham an unforgettable charge: "Beloved, as Samuel appointed David King of Israel, so I appoint you head of these schools. I'll meet you at the judgment-seat of Christ with them." Graham reluctantly agreed to serve as interim president if Riley expired before the end of the school year. Riley died in early December, and Graham kept his promise, thereby becoming the youngest college president in America at the tender age of twenty-nine. Here was a mantle for a young prophet, even if it was redolent of a bitter brand of fundamentalism. Graham received a second conferral of blessing the following summer when his erstwhile alma mater, Bob Jones College, awarded him an honorary doctorate. Thus doubly anointed, Graham was gaining a reputation in fundamentalist circles as a rising star.[32]

Meanwhile, in the fall of 1947, while still under the employ of Youth for Christ, Graham had begun to hold citywide campaigns in America. His first was in Grand Rapids, Michigan, where the Graham campaign tried the youth rally approach, promoting the evangelist as "A Young Athlete with a Twentieth-Century Gospel Message." Graham's next stop was his hometown, Charlotte, and once again the campaign was as much Saturday night gospel variety show as traditional revival meeting. A return visit to England ensued in early 1948. All the while the Graham entourage, which now featured soloist George Beverly Shea, associate evangelist Grady Wilson, and song leader Cliff Barrows, continued to appear on behalf of Youth for Christ.[33]

In the fall of 1948 Graham and Barrows left Youth for Christ to work full-time in citywide campaigns. They returned to England for meetings in Birmingham in August and September; then held meetings that fall in Augusta, Georgia, and Modesto, California. Graham then spoke at the Inter-Varsity missions conference at the University of Illinois just after Christmas. In the first half of 1949 the Graham team held meetings in Miami and Baltimore; in July they campaigned in Altoona, Pennsylvania. The Miami and Baltimore campaigns were not blessed with extraordinary results, and the Altoona meeting was downright discouraging. It was plagued by feuding local clergy, a deranged woman who disrupted the meetings, and a poor response to Billy's invitations.[34]

Crusading for the Lord seemed to have lost some of its luster during the summer of 1949. Compared to the acclaim Graham had previously received at youth rallies in major cities, his current trajectory of achievements now seemed to be flattening out, if not descending. Ahead was a campaign in Los Angeles, the largest American city to which the young evangelist had been invited for extended meetings, but Graham had reason to worry about making a difference there. Two of Graham's former colleagues, Jack Shuler and Charles Templeton, each had met with an indifferent response there. Could Graham do any better?

Not the least of his worries was friction among the clergy, especially the fundamentalists. Some of these pastors doubted that a revival was possible, given the lateness of the prophetic hour. The mainline church was in a terminal decline from which it would not recover before the Lord's return. Graham contacted the leading fundamentalist Bible teacher of the day, Harry Ironside of the Moody Memorial Church in Chicago, to refute this argument. Then some dissenters refused to associate with congregations that were still affiliated with the "apostate" mainline Protestant denominations. Graham complained to Orr in February of 1949 that he had "never felt such hindrance and obstruction in my own spirit about a campaign." Orr counselled that perhaps they should wait for the tide of revival expectation to rise some more. As late as August 1949, a month before the scheduled beginning, there was still a question about going forward.[35]

Graham seemed to be troubled with doubts of several kinds that summer including some intellectual questions about his faith and ministry. The major source of these troubling thoughts was his friend, Charles Templeton, who had resigned from full-time Youth for Christ work in 1948 to attend Princeton Theological Seminary. Templeton tried to persuade Graham to get some deeper theological grounding, arguing that their Youth for Christ enthusiasm would wear thin before long. Graham reluctantly decided against it. Thereafter, during the academic year of 1948–1949 and into the summer, Graham met several times with Templeton. Their conversations turned repeatedly to theology and the authority of the Scriptures, with Templeton arguing that modern scholarship made it impossible to hold to a fundamentalist theology and the unerring authority of the Bible. Graham stood by his views, but he continued to wrestle with these issues.[36]

Graham also seemed to be wondering where the Lord was leading him. Not long after the Altoona debacle, he had a speaking engagement at the Maranatha Bible Conference in western Michigan. Inspired by the northern lights one evening, Graham and several other preachers began to talk about the Second Coming. What signs might they see in the sky just before the Rapture? Would Christ come soon? Graham hesitated. Voicing a yearning from deep within himself, he said, "I sure would like to do something great for Him before he comes."[37] But what did the Lord have for Billy Graham to do? Were he and his team turning into just another group of journeymen evangelists? With God's grace the Altoona experiences would be few, but campaigns in cities the size of Grand Rapids, Modesto, and Augusta might become the norm. Perhaps Templeton was right about the need to acquire greater intellectual depth to sustain him. Perhaps Riley had been right about Northwestern Schools offering a fallback career when his evangelistic work burned out. But Graham longed to do something greater. After the men closed their fellowship under the stars that night with a prayer, they found Billy prostrate on the grass, groaning and begging the Lord for a chance to serve him in some greater way.[38]

Despite Graham's doubts about going forward, the preparatory work for the meetings in Los Angeles continued apace. A great deal of revival expectation had been stirred up in the region by Orr, Gesswein, and Mears, and the Christ for Greater Los Angeles Committee had done its work more thoroughly than ever before. Some 250 churches—perhaps a quarter of the Protestant congregations in the city—were endorsing the meetings. Many of the fundamentalist critics had signed on, and a vexing final problem, a suitable site for the meeting's tent in downtown Los Angeles, had been solved. Grady Wilson, who had become an "advance man" for the team, came out and organized even more prayer meetings for the campaign than the eight hundred enlisted by Orr and Gesswein. A Youth for Christ style promotional campaign ensued and Graham cultivated the support of business and civic leaders, including the mayor of Los Angeles. Graham also sought the help of Henrietta Mears's Hollywood Christian Group. One participant, Stuart Hamblen, a former cowboy who was a popular radio show host in town, agreed to endorse the meetings.[39]

Still, Graham was uneasy, and Templeton's accusation that Billy was "committing intellectual suicide" by refusing to question the Bible's authority kept nagging at him. Was Templeton right? Was he too poorly prepared intellectually to take on a big city crusade like this one? Only a few weeks before the meetings, as Graham and Grady Wilson were crossing the desert on the way to Henrietta Mears's Forest Home student conference, Wilson noticed that Graham was weeping as he drove the car. These doubts were pressing him down as never before and he felt wholly inadequate to the task ahead. Grady counselled Billy to pull off the road for a time of prayer. Two hours later, feeling relieved and recharged, they hopped back into the car and drove on.[40]

Graham's doubts were waiting for him up at Forest Home, however, for Charles Templeton was speaking there also. Apparently, all of Templeton's questions about the Bible's authority came out once more. Edwin Orr was at the meeting as well, speaking to the students about the need to surrender their lives to the Lord, and this topic also fed Graham's feelings of inadequacy. In the middle of one night he came to Orr's cabin and expressed a hunger for the "deeper blessing" in his own life and ministry. Orr expressed surprise, for he had thought of Graham as "surrendered," as the Keswick holiness parlance would have it. Billy poured out his frustrations, saying that he felt as though he were continually falling short of God's best in his ministry. So Orr counseled him concerning "God's provision for . . . victory over sin in true sanctification and surrender to His Will." Graham told Orr that he had thought himself to be surrendered. Orr probed a bit. Was he emotionally surrendered? Yes. Volitionally surrendered? Yes. Intellectually? Graham asked what that meant. Orr queried whether the evangelist preached "the Way of Surrender" with full assurance of its truth. This was not quite what was bothering Graham, but Orr had come uncomfortably close to the evangelist's painful doubts. Graham went off to pray.[41]

As the story has been told, Graham walked alone through the mountain forest that night, struggling with his doubts and his feelings of inadequacy. As he sat on a rock, with his Bible open, he finally decided to give up his questioning, admitting to God that he could not resolve all of his intellectual difficulties but surrendering, nonetheless, to the authority of the Bible, which he would simply accept by faith as God's Word. Having settled this matter, Graham felt greatly relieved and energized. Now he was ready to preach the Word to Los Angeles.[42] According to Orr, Graham came back to him later that night saying that "he had been filled afresh with the Spirit of God," and adding that "God had given him a vision that something unusual was going to happen down the mountain in Los Angeles."[43]

The power and authority of Graham's preaching in Los Angeles came as a surprise, even to his team. Those who came to the big tent in downtown Los Angeles saw a man of incredible intensity. Graham seemed to embody the message of God's passion: his judgment against human rebellion and his sacrificial love. Graham's transparent sincerity and earnestness, his ringing voice, the electric flash of his deep-set eyes, his relentless physical energy as he paced the platform and slashed the air with his gestures, and his confident use of the book he brandished, compelled the attention of the crowd. This was a modern-day prophet with a word from the Lord.[44]

In his lead-off sermon, "We Need Revival," Graham read a long passage from the first chapter of Isaiah (verses 1–20), which told of the desolation to come, likening the people's impending fate to that of Sodom and Gomorrah: "your cities are burned with fire" and "your land, strangers devour it in your presence, and it is desolate." Graham wanted the Angelenos to know, right off, that there was a choice before them, "of either revival or judgment." Theirs was a "city of wickedness and sin" that was world famous for its "crime and immorality. God Almighty is going to bring judgment upon this city unless people repent and believe—unless God sends an old-fashioned, heaven sent, Holy Ghost revival."[45] There was a fresh urgency to Graham's warning of a coming firestorm. Graham reminded people of the shocking recent news, that "Russia has now exploded an atomic bomb." People's fears of a world war returning were being stoked again, and this time the destruction would be more terrible than ever, just like the Bible's account of the end of Sodom and Gomorrah. Said Graham, "I sincerely believe that it is the providence of God that He has chosen this hour for a campaign—giving this city one more chance to repent of sin and turn to a believing knowledge of the Lord Jesus Christ."[46]

Graham then launched into a litany of the shocking trends that were afoot in the contemporary world: the widespread denial of God and God's moral law, the demise of marriage and the home, an "unchecked crime wave" in Los Angeles that the mayor had said was out of hand. Graham relentlessly reported the bad news of the day: media saturated with sex, a drinking problem that had become epidemic, and teenage delinquency. Finally, on the global scene, there was a great conflict looming, with western culture ranged against communism, "a religion that is inspired, directed and motivated by the Devil himself." And now there was the specter of atomic war. Every "paragraph" the preacher spoke carried a vivid illustration from current events. And after each came the trumpet call: "We need revival!" Graham had developed this sort of journalistic preaching on the Youth for Christ circuit, and he worked to keep it fresh with recent and close-to-home examples. The result was powerful indeed: The warnings of the ancient prophets were made as immediate as the network news.[47]

Indeed, Graham seemed to be taking on the mantle of the prophet. Repeatedly he referred to Isaiah and to Amos, but he was not simply quoting from these passages; he was reenacting their messages in a contemporary context and idiom. Could it be that he now believed that this was the moment, that America's next Great Awakening was breaking, and that he was its prophet? Again, to say so would have been presumptuous. But the thought seemed to be crossing his mind. In one sermon there was a revealing reference to Amos as the "hillbilly preacher." Was the young man from the hills of North Carolina inserting himself into the prophet's role? Hear his own words:

> Let me tell you something: when God gets ready to shake America, He may not take the Ph.D. and the D.D. [did Graham have his encounters with Templeton in mind?]. God may choose a country boy [from Charlotte?]. God may choose a shoe salesman like He did D. L. Moody [or a Fuller Brush salesman—one of Graham's summer jobs?]. He may choose a baseball player like he did Billy Sunday [Graham's early press releases stressed his ball-playing ability]. . . . God may choose the man that no one knows, a little nobody [fresh from a campaign in Altoona?], to shake America for Jesus Christ in this day. . . . We need a voice that sounds forth, "Thus saith the Lord."[48]

For three weeks Graham sounded forth from the big tent. Attendance was fairly good but it was beginning to flag. The response during the altar calls was acceptable but not extraordinary. Three weeks was the planned time frame for the meetings. Should they be brought to an end? The weather was colder than usual, and the committee decided to determine whether to extend or close the campaign by asking for a specific sign from God. They prayed for the arrival of a warm front before the services ended that evening if the campaign were to continue. During that service the weather did change, and the meetings were extended.[49] Still, as Edwin Orr might have observed, evangelistic meetings were not to be equated with a revival. Los Angeles seemed to be encountering the Billy Graham meetings without breaking stride, much as it had scarcely noticed the earlier efforts of Rice, Shuler, and Templeton.

Shortly into the fourth week of the meetings, however, something extraordinary began to happen: some celebrities got religion. The heart and soul of Los Angeles was the entertainment business, and the Hollywood stars were the staple of the local news media. Graham understood the value of celebrities for drawing interest to revival meetings; it was a lesson he had learned well on the Youth for Christ circuit. Hollywood's luminaries, to say the least, were far less likely to project a clean-cut image than the collegiate sports stars and war heroes had at the Saturday-night rallies. Nevertheless, Graham continued to cultivate the interest of Henrietta Mears's Hollywood Christian Group. Little seemed to come of it, however, other than some promotions on the radio show of Stuart Hamblen.

Hamblen's endorsements were a mixed blessing, for he was no saint. The son of a Methodist preacher and an early recruit for the Hollywood Christian Group, he still loved the honky-tonk lifestyle. Hamblen was troubled by the contradiction in his life, however, and his wife, Susie, who had recently become a Christian, was pleading with him to "get saved." Hamblen's godly parents were praying for him, and Edwin Orr had been working on him also. Orr had to report, however, that although Hamblen had been "on the brink of decision," he had "drowned his conviction in alcohol."[50] Hamblen attended several of Graham's meetings and had joined Graham for a couple of late dinners afterward. But he rejected Billy's invitations to repent and be saved. Late one sleepless night during the fourth week of the campaign, Hamblen was both drunk and remorseful. He drove into Los Angeles, showed up at Graham's apartment, and asked Billy to help him. Billy counseled him from the Scriptures and they prayed, and Hamblen was converted. Soon after, he announced this change of heart to his radio audience, declared that he was finished with wild living, and urged his listeners to go hear Billy Graham.[51]

Now here was something for Los Angeles to notice. Word of Hamblen's conversion hit the newspapers and airwaves, and a small crowd of reporters and photographers showed up at the revival tent. Graham asked what brought them out, and one reporter said he was on orders from William Randolph Hearst to "puff Graham." Graham's meetings were blessed with the conversions of some other notables. Louis Zamperini, an American track star at the 1936 Berlin Olympics who later survived a Japanese POW camp, was saved, he declared, at the Graham meetings. So did Jim Vaus, the son of a Bible teacher at BIOLA, who had become a wiretapper for a notorious West Coast gangster, Mickey Cohen. With an eager press gallery ready to record such novelties, the Graham campaign stayed on the front pages.[52]

Graham worried about the publicity. Would the glare of the flashbulbs kill off the spirit of revival? He met Edwin Orr in a parked car near the tent to get some advice. Orr brought along his Oxford dissertation on the Second Great Awakening, and he showed Billy what one observer had said: "The press . . . is taken possession by the Spirit, willing or unwilling, to proclaim His wonders." Orr counseled that "the Lord may make the American Press act as His publicity agent for nothing. So don't be afraid of it." Media interest multiplied, and the big tent became the place to see and be seen in Los Angeles. Graham became a celebrity and was even offered a screen test. By the end of its eight-week run, the campaign had a total attendance of a third of a million. Nearly three thousand inquirers had prayed for salvation and many more had come forward to be restored in their faith.[53]

Becoming a sensation in the nation's entertainment capital brought national and international media exposure as well. *Time, Life,* and *Quick* ran stories, as did the Associated Press, United Press, International News Service, and two London daily newspapers. The story in *Time* reflected that journal's usual amused contempt toward popular religion, stressing the "big circus tent" and the large collections, and emphasizing Graham's "trumpet-lunged" vocalizations and kinetic preaching style. *Life* let the pictures tell the story. Two dramatic images depicted a handsome, intense, dynamic Graham at the pulpit, and a wide-angle shot portrayed the crowd, six thousand strong, packed inside the tent. A closeup caught a tearful inquirer, and two photos featured Graham's celebrity converts, Stuart Hamblen and Louis Zamperini. *Life*'s coverage, then, suggested that something fresh and dramatic was happening. For Graham's evangelical supporters, the content of the articles did not seem to matter too much. Media coverage in itself was what counted. It meant that Billy Graham's ministry was part of the public record. Now he mattered, and by implication, so did they. Their efforts to bring revival to America had become legitimate news."[54]

Another Great Awakening?

The next engagement for the Graham team was scheduled to be a ten-day campaign in Boston, from December 30, 1949 to January 8, 1950, which had been organized principally by the Park Street Church. Graham had been invited by Harold Ockenga and a small committee, led by the young businessman Allan C. Emery, Jr., whose father had organized the Billy Sunday meetings in Boston a generation earlier. Graham's Boston visit, however, had not received anything like the months of preparation and publicity that had been invested in the Los Angeles campaign.

Apparently Ockenga once had been rather cool toward sponsoring Graham in Boston. He had turned down a request in 1947 to host a Youth for Christ rally at Park Street Church with Graham as the featured preacher. As the fundamentalist graduate students at Harvard Divinity School had learned, Ockenga did not offer his pulpit to just anyone, much less a slangy youth evangelist. Moreover, Ockenga's yearning for revival had a deeply personal dimension. Park Street Church was virtually the regional cathedral of evangelicalism, and Ockenga had been preaching, praying, and organizing for a revival for years. A New England revival would need some latter-day Jonathan Edwards or Charles Finney to bring down fire from God, and Ockenga seemed to be the most likely candidate. So why should he deign to invite Graham, a relatively unknown young evangelist?[55]

Over the next two years, Ockenga grew more willing to try Graham out. Older, more conventional revival preachers, such as Bob Jones and Oswald Smith, had come and gone in recent years without anything extraordinary happening, so perhaps Park Street Church should to ask someone new to come. In late 1948 Emery and another Park Street businessman promised they would guarantee the expense if Ockenga would rent the six-thousand-seat Mechanics Hall in Boston for a New Year's Eve rally with Graham in 1949. Ockenga agreed, and the date was set. After Graham became a national sensation out in Los Angeles that fall, the decision to invite the young evangelist looked much better. At the same time it was becoming clear that Ockenga was not going to be the nation's next great revival prophet. He had been the evangelist that November for a twenty-day campaign in Syracuse, New York, deep in the "burned-over district" of revival enthusiasm back in Finney's day, but only three hundred people made decisions at the meetings. Ockenga seemed to have determined that if he was not to be the next Finney, then perhaps he could be the revival's sponsor. So Billy Graham would come to Boston and preach in the historic Park Street Church where Finney had preached in 1831. By the eve of the campaign, he had convinced some one hundred churches to endorse the campaign.[56]

Graham arrived in Boston only six weeks after his Los Angeles meetings. Thanks to the stories in *Time, Life,* and the wire services, public interest was high. Even though the Mechanics Hall rally was not heavily publicized, a capacity crowd of more than six thousand showed up, and the Boston newspapers gave the event front-page treatment. Ockenga and his committee were astonished. Sensing a major opportunity, they rented Mechanics Hall for the following afternoon, New Year's Day, which was also a Sunday. With little more publicity than announcements in churches that morning, the arena was almost completely filled again. Preaching that evening at Park Street Church, Graham drew a capacity crowd of 2,500, and another 2,000 were turned away. The Park Street sanctuary was packed again for the January 2 service, and the campaign leaders looked for a larger meeting place. Mechanics Hall was available for the next four nights, and the committee secured it. Every night there the crowd was equal to or surpassing the building's seating capacity.[57]

On Tuesday of that week the editor of the *Boston Post,* Edward Dunn, called Ockenga and asked whether the campaign would be meeting in the Boston Garden. Ockenga replied that he had been told the place was booked solid for three months. Dunn asked whether the group would rent the Garden if they could get it for a night, and Ockenga agreed. Thanks to Dunn, the committee secured the arena for Monday, January 16, and patched together a series of venues to effectively extend the campaign to that date. The revival meetings moved from Mechanics Hall to the Opera House to Symphony Hall and back to Mechanics Hall, but at each site the people outnumbered the seats.[58]

On the day of the Boston Garden meeting, a crowd began to form outside the arena at 4:30 P.M. One hour before the 8:00 service the Garden was packed, with 16,000 people in the arena and another 2,500 in the lobbies. Eventually a crowd of some ten thousand gathered in the streets outside. Graham preached that night on Noah and the judgment of God, drawing on Christ's words, "As it was in the days of Noah, so shall it be also in the days of the Son of man" (Luke 17:26). Graham rang out the warning loud and clear that the days of God's judgment were at hand. Given the current generation's sinful abandon and the new nuclear threat from the Soviet Union, Graham thundered, the present day was very much like the days of Noah. People should heed Christ's warning and repent of their sins.[59]

The audience readily responded. At least 1,500 people left their seats and moved toward the rostrum when Graham invited them to accept Christ. People of all ages and races came forward, a *Boston Globe* reporter observed. He noted that "there was, among those hundreds, no seeming hysteria. Those who cried looked as though they shed tears of relief or happiness. Others walked forward quietly, serenely, as if they knew a long time ahead that they were ready to look for the better life that Graham told them Christ offered."[60] Something like one person for every twelve who gathered inside the building went forward. This was a much larger response than Graham was accustomed to seeing, and it persuaded the sponsoring committee that they had a revival on their hands.[61]

The Boston press was extraordinarily interested in this campaign. For each of its eighteen days, the campaign appeared on page one of at least one of the Boston daily newspapers. On the day after the meeting at the Boston Garden, the three morning papers each carried reports on the front page, featured several photos, and devoted well over one hundred column inches each to the story. As in Los Angeles, the wire news services carried stories on the meetings. This was astonishing to the meetings' organizers, for only a decade ago, Charles Fuller's massively attended radio rallies in Boston Garden and in other major venues on the East Coast stirred scarcely any journalistic interest.[62]

What accounted for the difference? Popular religious interest was on the rise, and the press was certainly responding to it. But there was something new on the "supply" side of the equation as well. The new revivalists had become more sophisticated about publicity. In Boston as in Los Angeles, the Graham meeting's organizers employed a tactic that they had learned during the Youth for Christ rallies. They encouraged the support of a sympathetic journalist—in this case the assistant city editor of the *Boston Herald*—to promote news coverage for the campaign.[63] Still, this coverage seemed remarkable in Boston, where evangelicals were more marginal than perhaps in any other major city in America. Here, in the graveyard of many earlier revival campaigns, people seemed mightily interested in this one. The meetings attracted a total attendance of 105,000 people, and more than 3,000 came forward to seek salvation. Even the Roman Catholic diocesan newspaper published a positive editorial titled "Bravo Billy!" These were signs and wonders indeed, and the committee was loath to let this season of revival pass by quickly.[64]

It was impossible to secure enough dates at local arenas to keep the campaign going, so Graham and his team left for Columbia, South Carolina, where they were scheduled to hold five weeks of meetings in February and March. They promised to return later that spring, and Ockenga helped organize a tour through New England that would bring Graham to each of its major cities, from Portland to Bridgeport. The Graham team returned on March 28, and at each site the leaders of the Evangelistic Association of New England, the New England Fellowship and cadres of Christian businessmen organized the meetings. Everywhere capacity audiences greeted Graham, whose South Carolina campaign had prompted a fresh wave of national publicity. Hundreds came forward at the close of each meeting, even at a few where Jack Wyrtzen and Ockenga filled in when Graham became sick and had to rest. These meetings, Ockenga enthused, were New England's greatest since the days of George Whitefield.[65]

The New England campaign reached a climax with a four-night engagement at the Boston Garden on April 19–22, followed by a final open-air rally on Boston Common on Sunday, April 23. The rally was Ockenga's idea; Graham would preach where George Whitefield had preached in 1740, and where Ockenga had tried to establish a beachhead in 1944. Now, thanks to Graham, he was back; they had won their hearing in the public square, and a crowd of some fifty thousand showed up. Graham preached one of his favorite sermons, "Prepare to Meet Thy God." This was a heady moment, one of the first of many occasions in the months and years to come when Billy Graham would speak an evangelical word in the public square.[66]

It was a time of deep vindication for Harold Ockenga. The "ray of hope" he had seen three years earlier for the prospects of evangelicals' winning back lost influence in America seemed to have broken through on that cold and rainy day in April. Ockenga was nearly beside himself with enthusiasm that spring. He was utterly convinced that the "America's revival" was breaking at last. On April 18 Ockenga had reported to the annual convention of the National Association of Evangelicals meeting in Indianapolis that he had just come "'hot' from revival" in New England, where Billy Graham was about to begin a four-night engagement at the Boston Garden after an astonishingly successful revival tour through the region. Ockenga told the crowd: "You do not have to wait till next year. You don't have to wait ten years. You don't have to pray any more, 'Lord, send a revival.' The revival is here!" No other movement in his memory, Ockenga insisted, could compare with what he had witnessed in New England. He was utterly convinced that the evangelist he had been working alongside was the one who had been anointed to bring revival to America.[67]

So the time had come at last. Now, more than ever, Ockenga pleaded, America needed revival showers of blessing. Prophecies in the books of Hosea 6, Joel 2, and Peter's sermon on the day of Pentecost in Acts 3, pointed to one last revival before "the great holocaust of judgment falls upon the earth." The revival now breaking, Ockenga speculated, "may be the revival of the last time. It may be that God is now taking out his elect . . . before the awful wrath of God will be loosed in the atomic warfare of this day."[68]

Extraordinary Times

This was the kind of biblical interpretation that would make most of the scholars at Fuller Seminary cringe in embarrassment for their president, yet it spoke to a pervasive feeling rippling through the evangelical networks nationwide that these were extraordinary times. Not only was Billy Graham's evangelistic team marching from victory unto victory with one major urban campaign after another—in Portland, Oregon, Minneapolis, and Atlanta following Boston— but many others who had taken to the field were witnessing unusual interest and success. Merv Rosell, for example, was holding successful citywide campaigns in Long Beach, Kansas City, Des Moines, Phoenix, Denver, and Chicago. Torrey Johnson, the former president of Youth for Christ, held meetings in Oakland, California, while Bob Cook, the new president of Youth for Christ, held a citywide campaign in San Diego; Jack Shuler brought the new revivalism to Fort Wayne, Sioux Falls, and Louisville; and Jimmy Johnson, a Youth for Christ evangelist from North Carolina, delivered the gospel to Memphis.[69]

America's small towns were getting involved as well. Youth for Christ and the Christian Business Men's Committees paved the way for many of these meetings and supplied them with new approaches. A few examples from 1950: a "Lancaster for Christ" campaign in southeastern Pennsylvania, sponsored by Youth for Christ and the Christian Business Men's Committee; revival meetings featuring YFC accordionist Arnie Hartman, organized by the Christian Business Men in Grass Valley, northern California; and a YFC-style campaign in Coon Rapids, Iowa, featuring the novel ministry of Dr. Wendell Hansen and his "Bible Birds."[70]

Meanwhile, the itinerant teaching of Orr and Gesswein had helped touch off a chain reaction among evangelical colleges and seminaries. In October 1949, the Northern Baptist Theological Seminary in Chicago was experiencing revival, and this outbreak was followed a month later by an awakening at North Park College across town. In December revival came to California Baptist Seminary, a sister school to Northern. This series of events attracted national notice when on February 5, 1950, during Wheaton College's customary evangelistic service at the beginning of the semester, a spontaneous eruption of confessions of sin, one after another, swept through the meeting and continued for about forty hours.[71] Vaughan Shoemaker, an evangelical leader who was a cartoonist at the *Chicago Daily News*, wrote a story on the Wheaton revival, and soon it was picked up by the wire services, radio, television, *Time*, and *Life*. Two-and-a-half weeks later a similar outpouring of confession and testimonies occurred at Asbury College in Wilmore, Kentucky, and continued for nearly five days. Once again the press and the electronic media turned out in full force. Throughout the early months of 1950 the campus revivals spread, to Simpson College in Portland, Oregon, Seattle Pacific College, Greenville College in downstate Illinois, and Los Angeles Pacific College.

Media coverage varied in tone once again, ranging from *Time*'s snickering account of this new oddity from the Bible Belt to some expressions of genuine appreciation. Wrote syndicated columnist Walter Kiernan, "Looking back at it, that outburst of sin-confessing at Wheaton College may be one of the top stories of the year. . . . Some say it was hysteria, some say it was pure emotion, but it may be that even today the spiritual can meet the material and top it if given half a chance."[72] The *Long Beach Press-Telegram*'s editors observed that the college revivals showed that "there never was a time when mankind needed the redemptive and sustaining power of conversion to God more than it needs it to-day."[73]

Such thoughts were not unusual in 1949 and 1950. In times like those, when the contest with communist regimes for global influence carried the added threat of a nuclear holocaust, American people searched for sources of courage, integrity, and hope. One powerful wellspring, lying not too far from the surface, was the nation's evangelical heritage. Conservative evangelical Protestants were discovering that if they made the right sort of approach, with the right sort of prophet speaking for them, they could get a hearing—on network radio, in the national news media, in businessmen's club dining rooms, on Boston Common, and even at the White House.[74] After years of alienation, the fundamentalists, at least the more moderate and mannerly ones, were back. And this time they were leading a broad—one might even say ecumenical—coalition from many Protestant movements and traditions for the sake of revival.

Had a national revival come? In the busyness and cultural diversity of mid-century America, it was doubtful that anything like a Great Awakening could command national or even local interest for very long. Even so, the new revivalism had won a share of the public's attention. It had been reported on television and noticed by the *New York Times,* even if not yet by the *Christian Century.* Evangelical religion was carving out some new cultural space for itself. Charles and Grace Fuller's *Old Fashioned Revival Hour* continued to compete head-on in prime time with the best of secular radio. Christian Business Men's Committees now enjoyed interlocking national leadership with other service organizations, notably the Rotary. An offshoot of the CBMC, the "leadership prayer breakfast" movement, was making inroads on Capitol Hill. Stuart Hamblen's conversion during the Graham meetings in Los Angeles was part of a larger awakening among Hollywood stars. When actress Colleen Townsend announced in 1950 that she was giving up her film contract with Twentieth Century Fox to engage in ministry full-time, *Life* gave her a three-page spread. Other notable converts were Roy Rogers, Dale Evans, and Tim Spencer of Rogers's Sons of the Pioneers musical group. Hamblen's post-conversion song "It Is No Secret What God Can Do" sold over a million records, rose up the Hit Parade charts, and sparked a strong gospel trend in the recording industry.[75]

All of these occurrences were part of the trend that many observers of the postwar scene, then and since, have called a religious revival. The revivalists, however, often seemed more reluctant than the secular press to call this new interest in religion a full-blown revival. Edwin Orr thought that the nation was on the verge of a third Great Awakening, but he insisted that it had not yet "reached the pitch of effectiveness of either of its predecessors." Real revival would amount to more than what was going on just then, insisted evangelist Fred B. Hoffman. It would "regenerate the whole life of America" and would be manifest "in every church, in every city and town and village and rural community" of the nation. Here was a mythic understanding of revival that could never be fulfilled across a vast and variegated modern nation like the mid-century United States.[76]

Still, the leaders of the new evangelical coalition were feeling mightily encouraged. They had learned how to get the public's attention and how to make a contribution to public life. They had also learned how to sustain a nearly continuous "sound of a going" that would repeatedly convince the hopeful to mobilize for the next Awakening. And not least, they lived in a nation whose public discourse had a decidedly revivalistic structure and cadence. Over the next generation America's secular pundits would discern one national crisis after another and call repeatedly for national renewal. The postwar evangelical coalition that the moderate fundamentalists had organized would be ever ready to take such jeremiads as their cue. A place had opened up for these religious outsiders in the main halls of American public life. It was a place that in many respects they had created for themselves. Perhaps the dream of a great and sweeping revival would continue to elude them. But they had been revived and, to a certain extent, rehabilitated as well.

CONCLUSION

Fundamentalists and their allies in the postwar evangelical coalition were beginning to occupy a different place in American life by 1950 than they had only a decade earlier. Mainline Protestant leaders were not quite aware as yet that there was another Protestant force out there that they had to take seriously; the *Christian Century* published no stories or commentary on Billy Graham's phenomenal urban campaigns in 1949 and 1950. Still, it was increasingly more difficult for the Protestant establishment to assume that all of those "other" Protestant people and their activities occupied only the margins of American religion and culture. The postwar evangelical movement reached into the older denominations, the offices of Capitol Hill, the studios of Hollywood, and up the Hit Parade charts as well. The *New York Times* had decided that the resurgence of revivalism was news fit to print, so the *Century* would soon follow suit. In a national climate that foresaw both fresh promise and new perils for the postwar era, the older lines of religious conflict and the boundaries between respectability and marginality appeared to be less relevant than before the war. Mainline Protestantism was much more evangelical in its rhetoric and actions than it had been in years, and the more sectarian wing of Protestantism seemed increasingly interested in taking on some public responsibility. What has not often been recognized, however, is that one of the most important driving forces behind the postwar resurgence of religion was a cadre of "progressive fundamentalists."

The fundamentalist movement had made a major comeback, and its leaders made this recovery possible through some amazing feats of religious creativity and imagination. They turned failure into vindication, marginality into chosenness, survival into an opportunity for expansion, and a religious depression into a prelude for revival. The contemporary fruit of their dynamism is all around us today, to be seen in burgeoning independent megachurches, thriving and ever-diversifying parachurch ministries, an astonishing popular appetite for spine-chilling interpretations of biblical prophecy, and a major upsurge of religiously inspired conservative cultural politics—all of which have been driven by a finely honed instinct for popular appeal and well-practiced skills in communications and marketing. Certainly fundamentalism is not the only popular religious impulse informing these contemporary trends. Two other critically important parts of this story, which are just now beginning to be told, are the expansive postwar careers of both the pentecostals and the Southern Baptists. Yet it was the fundamentalists, by and large, who pioneered, organized, and led the center-stage events of the postwar religious resurgence.

The recovery of American fundamentalism has some insights to offer, I believe, for our understanding of the broader evangelical tradition of which fundamentalism was a variant, of religion's place in modern America, and of course about the character of fundamentalism itself.

Modern Evangelicalism

A Symbiotic Relationship with Modernity

Historians and social scientists have been misled repeatedly about the character, thrust, and long-term prospects of evangelical Christianity because of one overriding assumption: Modernization always produces secularization. They have expected to see religion decline to the point of irrelevance as a way of understanding how the world works and as a force in public affairs. It has been easy for scholars to assume, as an eminent sociologist of religion confessed, that "the point of view variously called evangelical, fundamentalist, holiness, Pentecostal, or millenarian was moribund in America. . . . The whole conservative religious scene . . . was out of step with the America I knew. Therefore it could be dismissed."[1]

Such assumptions have a certain logic to them, for secularization surely has happened in the modern world. In the West, where Christianity once constituted the official intellectual, spiritual, and ethical rubric for all of life, and where the church played a dominant role in public affairs, that faith has become fragmented and has also been forced to compete with other powerful worldviews, both religious and nonreligious. But what is becoming clearer in recent years is that religions are competing rather well in this pluralistic setting. The prevailing intellectual assumption that religion is moribund is being dismantled before our eyes, if not yet in theory then at least in the daily headlines.

The story of American fundamentalism's recovery adds a confirming note to an alternative understanding of religion's role in the modern world and, more specifically, the fate of evangelical Christianity. Rather than viewing evangelicalism as a throwback, as a religion of consolation for those who cannot accept the dominant humanist, modernist, liberal, and secular thrust of mainstream society, perhaps it is more accurate to see evangelicalism as a religious persuasion that has repeatedly adapted to the changing tone and rhythms of modernity. As Martin Marty once put it, "there has been a symbiosis between unfolding modernity and developing Evangelicalism." Indeed, Marty asserted, "Evangelicalism is the characteristic Protestant way of relating to modernity."[2]

This may seem like a strained interpretation, but it is altogether true. Setting his discussion in the context of the past two-and-a-half centuries of the "modern era" in the West, Marty explains that evangelicals have adapted well to the characteristic features of the modern world. Evangelicals have responded readily to modernity's compartmentalization of life because theirs is an intensely personal religious experience. Modern society is often structured to favor voluntarism and choice-making, Marty argues further; and evangelicals have responded with aggressive recruiting and creative institution-making while more established faiths have tended to take the church's place in life for granted. Because the modern temper is intense, impatient, and egalitarian, Marty continues, modern people commonly expect to have quick and personal access to knowledge and experience. By offering authoritative religious knowledge and intense religious experiences to "whosoever will" rather than reserving them for scholars and mystics, evangelicals have provided an accessible faith for millions of modern people, including at least a quarter of today's American adult population.[3]

A cursory look at the history of evangelical movements confirms this point. At every turn these movements benefited from or even advanced the forces of social and technological change. One may take this interpretive line back even farther than Marty does to the original evangelical movement, the Protestant Reformation. It was both aided by and helped to fortify the dynamic trends in early modern Europe, such as the rise of literacy, vernacular literature, and national consolidation. The Puritan and Pietist awakenings of the seventeenth century emphasized a personal experience of God's grace at a time when new understandings of the self and experimental norms for science were growing. The evangelical revivals of the eighteenth century, spurred on by George Whitefield and the Wesleys, experimented with new forms of religious association and communication in the marketplace at a time when the idea of untrammeled markets—for both commodities and ideas—was being tested in theory and in practice. In the wake of the American Revolution, a generation of populist revival preachers challenged the religious and social authority of the older denominations and encouraged ordinary people to read the Bible and organize churches for themselves. When during the late nineteenth century urban Protestantism became increasingly genteel and less hospitable to the common people, Dwight L. Moody and a generation of innovative evangelists developed a style of religious life that welcomed one and all. And while religious progressives made common cause with the managerial and professional revolution at the turn of the century, holiness, fundamentalist, pentecostal and other sectarian rebels fought to take back control of their religious lives, using all the tools of modern culture to create alternative communities.

The fundamentalist-led revival of revivalism in the 1940s marks the beginning of the latest chapter of this story. Post–World War II American culture has been dominated, Marty reminds us, by yet another wave of modernization, which features "electronic communication, rapid transportation, mobile and kinetic styles of living, affluence, and a sense of entitlement in large publics."[4] What an irony, then, that fundamentalism, which advertised itself as "old-time religion," should lead the way in engaging this new social context. And yet it did. By the 1940s a rising generation of fundamentalist leaders had gravitated toward radio broadcasting and the new, electronically inspired entertainment style and promotional techniques, which they adapted to their own uses. While World War II was escalating personal mobility and the breakdown of regional and cultural insularity in America, fundamentalists led other evangelicals in emerging from their ethnic, sectarian, and regional redoubts to form a united front for revival and world evangelization. Taking on the "radio style" that the Youth for Christ movement introduced, franchised, and marketed across the entire nation, this new coalition made evangelical Christianity more portable and more conversant with the kinetic popular culture and mobile lifestyles of the postwar era. As evangelicals experienced new affluence and sent more of their children to college, the need to reform their movement's alienation from the more sophisticated levels of discourse became more pressing. University-educated evangelicals provided a natural constituency for the "neo-evangelical" pioneers and reformers who first coalesced in and around the NAE and then Fuller Theological Seminary in the 1940s. Since the revival-charged years of 1949–1950, leaders of the new evangelical coalition have used their gifts of organization and communication to press for a hearing in American public life. In all of these ways, the heirs of fundamentalism led other evangelical movements and traditions out to ride postwar America's new cultural wave.

The Fundamentalist Era

Fundamentalists' role in shaping American evangelicalism has been the subject of some debate in recent years. In the first scholarly attempts in the 1970s to account for the continuing vitality of evangelicalism, interpreters tended to assume that there was a direct and simple progression from the fundamentalism of the first half of the twentieth century to the evangelicalism of the second half.[5] Others, notably the leading historians of the Wesleyan holiness and pentecostal strains of American Christianity, took issue. They insisted that evangelical Christianity in America is a vast and varied mosaic, as historian Timothy L. Smith once put it, and that even the evangelical coalition that formed in the postwar years largely consisted of pietist or revivalist Protestants who were not of direct fundamentalist lineage.[6]

One of these critics, Donald W. Dayton, argues further that a "presbyterianizing" distortion of American evangelical history has occurred, by which historians who are themselves of the post-fundamentalist, neo-evangelical lineage have recast American religious reality to conform to their own image of what evangelicalism should be. The key culprit, Dayton alleges, has been George M. Marsden, whose magisterial *Fundamentalism and American Culture* has done more than any other treatment to confirm American intellectuals' equation of "fundamentalist" and "evangelical." A better way of understanding what evangelicalism is all about, Dayton insists, is to see it not as essentially rationalist, conservative, doctrinally orthodox, and antimodernist, like fundamentalism, but as an essentially experiential, populist, sectarian, millenarian, anticreedal, doctrinally innovative, and often socially radical religious impulse. Historians should use this "pentecostal paradigm" for interpreting evangelicalism and its role in modern religious history, Dayton argues, and set fundamentalism off as an anomaly, a sidebar to the main story.[7]

Dayton, Marsden, and others, including myself, have argued at length about such matters.[8] While not wanting to return to that discussion, I do wish to state fundamentalism's role in the larger history of modern evangelicalism. Briefly put, fundamentalism was by far the most influential evangelical movement in the United States during the second quarter of the twentieth century. Fundamentalists' religious ideas and emphases dominated popular evangelicalism and actually permeated other traditions. Dispensationalist movements, to cite one example, arose and grew within the Southern Baptist Convention. Many holiness Wesleyans came to accept the doctrine of biblical inerrancy even though that belief is not a Wesleyan way of understanding the Bible's inspiration and authority. Enough Dutch Calvinists, German-speaking Mennonites and Scandinavian Lutherans were attracted to the fundamentalists' Bible institutes, radio programs, and gospel tabernacles to raise sharp concern among these traditions' leaders. And finally, the more moderate wing of fundamentalism formed the organizing center for the National Association of Evangelicals. For all of their sectarian and antiworldly posturing, fundamentalists were more engaged with mainstream America than any of the other evangelical movements or traditions at the time. It was principally their example and their leadership that propelled a new evangelical coalition and resurgence in postwar America.

To assert these facts is neither to endorse the fundamentalists' leavening of other traditions nor to trivialize the unique identity and contributions of the other groups. Nevertheless, from the controversies of the 1920s at least until the rise of the charismatic movement in the 1960s, fundamentalism was the most dynamic and widely influential American evangelical impulse. During the long reign of Billy Graham as the world's most prominent and influential evangelical, the postfundamentalist party of evangelical leaders and their institutions has enjoyed more influence than the number of its self-identified adherents might seem to warrant. The role of fundamentalism and its moderating heirs during our century has been similar, then, to the influence of Methodism during the first half of the nineteenth century and the pervasive reach of the holiness movement throughout the second half of that century. Understanding that fundamentalists and their moderate heirs had a period of ascendancy also helps us perceive, by implication, that we are now entering a new chapter of evangelical history, in which the pentecostal-charismatic movement is quickly supplanting the fundamentalist-conservative one as the most influential evangelical impulse at work today.

A better understanding of this pattern—the rise and fall of the relative influence of one popular movement after another—adds another kind of thematic unity to the history of modern evangelicalism. The story adheres not only because there have been some central or "classic" touchstones of belief and outlook, or because of the continuing dynamic interplay with the evolution of modern society, but also because of this recurring motif. Evangelicalism, as Timothy Smith has taught us, is actually more like a kaleidoscope than a mosaic. Over time the pieces overlap, change position, and form new patterns, and new colors can emerge to cast their hues across the rest. To insist that one paradigmatic viewpoint can make sense of the whole career of modern evangelicalism is to neglect the repeated twists and turns of that kaleidoscope. There has been a "fundamentalist era" in the patterns and tones of American evangelicalism just as surely as there was once a "Methodist era." However that fact might strike the interpreter, it happened, and the consequences are readily apparent. Historians of evangelicalism may not always be enamored of these trends, but as historians they should take heed to R. Laurence Moore's warning that regret is no substitute for historical analysis.[9]

Religion and American Culture

The Blessings of Secularity

The story of fundamentalism's recovery suggests some important things about religion's role in American culture as well. First, it offers some clues to the puzzle of why the nation is so pervasively religious yet simultaneously so thoroughly secular in structure. Unlike the situation in Europe or in many nations of Africa, religious institutions and traditions in the United States are afforded very little by way of a formally instituted place in public life, such as in government, industry, law, communications, education, or health care. In part because of the formally instituted roles for religion in these other nations, the difference between an officially favored religion and a "dissenting" one is built into the national structure. In the United States, even though there have been very real differences in prestige and influence between longstanding respectable traditions and upstart movements, there is no firm legal or institutional difference.

As the story of fundamentalism's recovery shows, the structural secularity of the United States has not inhibited religiosity nearly so much as it has opened up multiple opportunities for religious movements and persuasions to win popular interest and support. Conversely, attempts by mainstream religious groups to protect institutional prestige and privilege have given them only temporary advantages. Fundamentalists were denied radio broadcast time on major networks because of arrangements made by the Federal Council of Churches to ban paid religious programming and allow free time only to respectable religious bodies. But this exclusive arrangement was not embedded in national law. New networks and individual stations eager for revenue welcomed paying religious broadcasters. Fundamentalists and other religious interlopers found ways to get a hearing whether or not NBC and the Federal Council of Churches thought they were fit for prime time.

Likewise, the secularization of American universities made it possible for evangelical upstarts like Inter-Varsity and Campus Crusade to compete with the more respectable campus ministries of the mainline denominations, which found themselves increasingly on the sidelines of university life. In similar fashion, the absence or relative weakness of institutionalized chaplaincies in business, the military, and government made it possible for independently organized groups like the Christian Business Men's Committees, the Navigators' ministry to the military and the leadership prayer breakfast movement to freely recruit adherents and provide unofficial chaplaincy services. In sum, the very secularity of American society—as well as its fluidity and pluriform nature—has made it possible for creative and entrepreneurial religious movements to win a hearing, a following, and, eventually, a measure of respectability.

The Decline of Denominationalism

Given these conditions, the recovery of fundamentalism—and with it, the reputation of evangelicalism more broadly—was fairly rapid. It was only twenty-five years from the Scopes trial to the rise of Billy Graham, and only twenty-seven more to the point where a born-again Southern Baptist was elected president of the United States and a *Newsweek* cover story proclaimed the "Year of the Evangelical." Factors that speeded the recovery, as we have seen, included both the supply and demand sides of American religion, both the creation of attractive new religious "products" and a major change in the national religious mood during World War II and the beginning of the Cold War. Yet there was another change afoot that the fundamentalist movement helped to stimulate and from which it benefited. Although the nascent change was nearly invisible at the time, the foundations were being laid for a major shift among the basic institutional carriers of American religious life. Large Protestant denominations have been losing members, income, and influence while special-purpose, nondenominational religious agencies have grown, multiplied, and taken on increasing importance in shaping and carrying people's religious identity.

The much-discussed weakening of mainline Protestantism, then, is not simply a function of secularization or of religious and cultural pluralism. There is a profound "restructuring of American religion" going on as well, as Robert Wuthnow pointed out in his book by that title. The growing irrelevance of denominations is a major feature of that structural change. The trends of postwar American life—especially the increase in personal mobility and the growth of a shopping mall consumerist ethic—have seriously weakened denominational loyalties. Special-purpose, nondenominational religious agencies have proved to be a better fit with these trends, and increasingly they are becoming the focus of American Christians' religious identity and the channels of their

religious activity. Denominations, which were in effect the full-service department stores of American religious life, increasingly find that their members
"shop around" to meet their religious needs. They order books and other
educational materials from a variety of religious publishing houses. They support foreign missions and domestic ministries organized independently by
parachurch agencies, and they join nondenominational fellowships for prayer,
Bible study, marriage enrichment, and even recreation. Thus while grassroots
religious activity is thriving, the older Protestant denominations are in serious
decline, and even some of the younger and more conservative ones have
begun to stagnate numerically and financially. Meanwhile, wholly independent
congregations have become one of the nation's largest categories of Protestant
affiliation. These churches rely solely on parachurch ministries for identity,
outreach, and services.[10]

It is important to remember who pioneered this new way of organizing religious life. Because fundamentalists still needed channels for fellowship and
outreach after they became alienated from the mainline denominations, they
brought the parachurch model of religious endeavor to new levels of use and
identity-carrying importance. By relying so heavily on independent ministries,
fundamentalists largely avoided the sectarian pattern of forming new and
exclusive denominations followed by earlier evangelical movements such as
the holiness Wesleyans and the pentecostals. The handful of small denominations they did form never tried to create a full range of services; they simply
did not need to. Beginning with the Christian Business Men's Committees
and the Youth for Christ movement in the 1940s, these parachurch agencies
began to reach beyond fundamentalism and other varieties of sectarian evangelicalism to involve evangelically minded mainline Protestants. Mainline congregations began to pick and choose among the agencies that might serve
them rather than automatically selecting their own denominations' products.
So the mobilization for revival in the 1940s, spearheaded by progressive fundamentalists and carried by parachurch agencies, set in motion what has
become a major decentralization of American religion. This structural readjustment has been no less profound than the similar trends among the nation's
institutions of government, business and education.

There is an irony here. Fundamentalists turned to independent ministries in
part to compensate for the services they lost when they became disenchanted
with the agencies of mainline Protestantism. But by pursuing these survival
tactics out on the margins, fundamentalists started a trend that has led to
the weakening of the most central and powerful corporate expressions of
American religion.

The Taming Power of Popularity

The recovery of American fundamentalism illustrates yet another important
feature of religion's role in America: the assimilative power of American popular culture. In the relatively open, market-like setting for religion that Ameri-

can law and society provides, religious innovation flourishes, just as the European and early American spokesmen for officially sanctioned religion feared it would. But the social anarchy that they believed would result has not come to pass. American society is much less bounded and distinct in its roles and institutions than European society but it still possesses a number of unifying forces. One of the most powerful of these has been the sovereignty of popular appeal. Religious movements in America have possessed both the right and the opportunity to be as innovative, demanding, and strange as their leaders might envision them to be, but they also have had the opportunity to win widespread support. The chance to grow and to win a massive following immediately puts some tension into a new religious movement. On the one hand, the classic posture of new movements is to be prophetic, to challenge the established order and offer an alternative vision. Grassroots religious movements are sectarian virtually by definition; they tend to establish clear boundaries of belief and behavior that will mark their followers as distinct and special, as a chosen and set-apart people. But in a situation where such movements can hope to grow and flourish if they are broadly attractive, their leaders find it tempting to smooth out some of their rough edges.

The recovery of fundamentalism provides a powerful case in point. Even during the years when fundamentalists seemed most deeply alienated from mainstream America, the movement's leaders retained what historian Grant Wacker has called a "custodial ideal," a proprietary sense of responsibility for American national morality and spirituality, and alongside it a vision for leading another Great Awakening that would restore their lost moral and spiritual influence.[11] They pursued these aims with a revivalist's instinct for popular appeal. Beginning in earnest with the Youth for Christ movement, a cadre of younger fundamentalist leaders worked to address the wartime generation's hopes and fears, market their message with polish and civility, and affirm the "American Way of Life." To be sure, these new revivalists tried to challenge the nation. Billy Graham pointedly insisted that Americans had to be spiritually transformed if the nation was to survive. But as Martin Marty once observed, no matter how earnestly Graham called the nation to repent, his audiences seemed more charmed than convicted. This clean-cut young man seemed to many to embody American virtue, and his utterances comported well with the conventions of American folk piety.[12] The new engagement with American mainstream culture that Graham's generation of revivalists, parachurch entrepreneurs, and neo-evangelical theologians sought brought them closer to the absorbing and domesticating vortex of American national culture.

Because fundamentalism had built its identity upon a finely tuned sense of alienation, the "new evangelicalism" raised many worries and considerable opposition. For a number of the movement's more militant leaders, this new approach of intellectual engagement looked suspiciously like a compromise of religious principle. Bob Jones was moved to protest repeatedly that an evangelical was "someone who says to a liberal, 'I'll call you a Christian if you'll call me a scholar.'"[13] An even more pressing concern for most fundamentalists was their ability to maintain a distinctive way of life in a culture that continually invited their participation. Were the consumer habits of the white suburban middle class compatible with the separated life? Questions about fundamentalist norms of personal and family behavior began to grow more frequent in the fundamentalist press after World War II. The question raised by an author in the *Moody Monthly* in the mid-1950s was in many respects the central one: "How different shall we be?"[14] Fundamentalists' and other evangelicals' yearning for acceptance and respect drove them toward an embrace with middle-class white America, while their opposition to the secularizing trends of public life kept them at arm's length.

The result has been a rather strange dance, so to speak, in which conservative evangelicals emulate many trends of popular culture while continuing to denounce America's transgressions. The emergence of fundamentalist separatist leaders such as Jerry Falwell as major players in the new Religious Right in American politics makes this trend seem even more dramatic. Catching the public's attention with some Bible thumping rhetoric about God's judgment on the nation's sins, these leaders, like Billy Graham before them, have been quick to beg pardon for any offenses they might have given and turn on the charm. Fundamentalists like to be liked, yearn to be accepted, and dream of regaining a sweeping influence for their faith across the nation. American public life, on the other hand, offers the opportunity for the marginalized to develop market appeal and come closer to the center. It often displays a facile tolerance, a tendency to absorb, approve, and domesticate traditions and movements on previously established, safe cultural terms. Sometimes Americans kill their rebels and prophets, but a more likely fate for them is to be assimilated, tamed, and even converted, somehow, into a commercial profit. Things could be worse. One alternative, which haunts this nation and troubles so many others these days, is the specter of a religiously fueled civil war.

American Fundamentalists: "A Very Special People"

The central task of this book has been to trace fundamentalism's passage through a critical but largely hidden period of its development, and along the way to provide a better understanding of the movement's character as well. Much of this narrative has had a corrective motive behind it. Because fundamentalism developed strong elements of social and religious reaction and protest, it has been tempting to reduce the movement to a mere expression of these dynamics. Too often scholars and journalists alike have been fooled into underestimating fundamentalists' strength and staying power because of their reductionistic approach to the movement's character. They have not fully understood that fundamentalism has been a popular religious movement with some positive purposes and a distinctive set of beliefs. Fundamentalists would not be fundamentalists without deep-seated feelings of dispossession, resentment, and alienation, and it is important to understand the sources of these emotions.

Just as critical to the movement, however, has been its creation of a way of life, enveloped by distinctive beliefs, behavioral norms, and aspirations that have made fundamentalism into a genuine religious tradition. Nevertheless, for all its separatist rhetoric and behavior, this tradition has not been totally counter-cultural. Rather, it has produced subcultures, much like ethnic communities, that function as "halfway houses" in which people find respite from the pressures of the world, where they experience support, accountability, and a sense of mission for their daily existence. Fundamentalists' ideal has been to live as exemplary people out in the world, daring like Daniel to be different and to stand alone when faithfulness to God demanded it, but also like Daniel to be useful, well-regarded servants of the common good, even in a pagan society.

Nevertheless, fundamentalists were tempted to envelop themselves in a protective shadow culture. Pastors instilled in their congregations a fear of moral and religious pollution. They worked with their parishioners to create alternatives to the world's allurements in order to keep them within the safe havens of the movement's institutions. In many respects, fundamentalism became a defensive and inward-looking mutation of nineteenth-century American evangelicalism. Too often, however, these traits have been highlighted without any attention being given to others of equal importance. Fundamentalism could be energizing and encouraging as well as small-minded and restrictive. It gave ordinary people the opportunity to create their own institutions and to make things happen, to experience God's presence and seek to do God's will through channels they designed and controlled themselves. They created new ministries with all the entrepreneurial and innovative energy of their secular counterparts in business, education, and entertainment. It is simply wrongheaded, then, to continue to paint fundamentalism as dysfunctional or as the refuge of the psychologically wounded. Millions of otherwise ordinary Americans found it to be an attractive and empowering way of investing their lives in a larger purpose.

One needs to ask, of course, what that purpose was. After all, one might say these same things about the Communist Party, the Kiwanis Club, or the Ku Klux Klan. How about the fundamentalists? What did they stand for? What kinds of behavior did their beliefs prompt in them? These kinds of questions have received a great deal of scholarly attention in recent years, so this book offers few stark surprises concerning them. Fundamentalist preachers sounded off, for example, on the role of women in home, church and society in terms that were often archtraditional, even at times misogynous. But the story of women's experiences within fundamentalism is not so simple. Oppressive though some of the movement's explicit teaching on women's roles, marriage, and the family undoubtedly was, its entrepreneurial spirit and informal structure offered more opportunities for women to take initiative and leadership in religious work than did mainline Protestantism.

Fundamentalism's intellectual legacy is at least two-sided as well. On the one hand, the movement was heir to a campaign in the late nineteenth century to repopularize the gospel, which led many evangelical leaders of Moody's day to neglect their intellectual responsibilities. The result was a near-abdication of any voice in academe at a time when the intellectual foundations of Judeo-Christian theism were being questioned as never before. Fundamentalist leaders were caught unprepared to respond to the critiques of scientific naturalism, whether applied to natural history or the study of the Bible. They fought with rusty intellectual weapons and very often resorted to anti-intellectual ridicule or the use of disreputable ideas and theories, such as those of the young-earth creationists. They left an enduring legacy of populist intolerance of ideas that cannot be explained in layman's terms and impatience with disciplined thinking in general. Yet a few intellectual sparks and yearnings survived in the movement, and by the late 1940s these produced a cadre of young theologians and biblical scholars. Making no small plans, they envisioned an intellectual rebirth for orthodox Protestantism and they allied themselves with the postwar revivalists in an effort to build a new and improved evangelical movement.

Fundamentalists' views of the prophetic trends in history, current affairs and the future bore a mixed set of results as well. Bizarre predictions of the end of world civilization dominated fundamentalist prophetic literature. Yet their readings of the prophecies of Ezekiel, Daniel, and Revelation assured fundamentalists that there was divine purpose at work in the great upheavals of the twentieth century. As eager interpreters of the "signs of the times," they were among the first Americans to see—and denounce—the Nazis' persecution of the Jews. But these beliefs also led them to take a rather passive, spectator's view of current events and to be susceptible to some of the most vicious conspiracy theories that were afoot in those days. Many found themselves embracing aspects of Zionism and anti-Semitism at the same time.

Fundamentalists' prophecy beliefs also confirmed and intensified their sense that they were God's faithful remnant, the keepers of the truth in the last days. It assured them that they and not the liberals were right about the state and direction of world civilization, but it also prompted them to remain passive and detached about the world's problems. The world was in a terminal downward spiral; social and political reforms were largely useless. But the one thing still in their power to control was their own religious community; the one positive task that was still placed in human hands was the gathering in of all those whom God would rescue from the coming disaster. So while dispensational prophecy pushed fundamentalists toward social and political alienation and passivity, it energized them religiously. They felt vindicated, chosen, and anointed to do God's work before the night came, when no more work could be done.

Even though fundamentalists often derided the prevailing optimism of America's cultural leaders, they had their own equivalent: revivals. Millenarian logic might point inescapably to the decline of all nations and the coming of the Antichrist, but fundamentalists could not give up on the idea that perhaps one last wave of spiritual revival and cultural rechristianization could sweep over America. This mythic ideal of the great revival was every bit as potent among fundamentalists as their views of the Apocalypse. The very bleakness of their situation—and America's—in the 1930s became a source of hope, for in a revivalist view of church history, bad times meant that revival was probably on its way. So the hope for revival energized fundamentalists and gave them a positive mission at a time when many of them were tempted to isolate themselves and wait for the Apocalypse.

Fundamentalists' yearning for a revival, moreover, revealed their latent interest in cultural politics. They were highly sensitive to the balance of cultural influence and power in the nation and haunted by the memory of a time when America had seemed much more evangelical. Frontal attacks on the secularizers had failed in the 1920s, but by the late 1930s fundamentalists were beginning to mobilize again, this time for another Great Awakening in America. Implicit in that vision was a social and cultural subplot: revival was a way to "heal their land." So while leaders of the new revivalism such as Torrey Johnson could honestly say that they had no political agendas to pursue, their message had a subtext that was deeply cultural and implicitly political. In time the subtext would surface once again, when the disparity between the liveliness of American popular religiosity and the continuing decline of Christian influence in national institutions and public morality became too striking to ignore. The result, as we have seen in recent years, has been the rise of a new "Religious Right," driven by the mythic vision of a "Christian America" over which fundamentalists, more than any other Protestant movement or tradition, held custody.

In sum, the ideas and character of the fundamentalists are easy to caricature but they were anything but two-dimensional. George Marsden's characterization of the movement as being filled with "paradoxical tensions" is probably the best we have. Fundamentalists at turns could be deeply alienated from the mainstream of American culture while still yearning to engage that culture for the sake of the gospel. They could be profoundly sectarian in their desire to "come out and be separate" from secular society and liberal Protestantism, while on the other hand they spearheaded a powerful ecumenical impulse, based on a common commitment to spiritual renewal and evangelism. They could be petty and legalistic in their demands on each other's beliefs and behavior, an oppressive trait to some free spirits among them. At the same time, however, the close communities that fundamentalists created gave millions of ordinary Americans the fellowship, moral accountability, and sense of direction they craved.

Fundamentalists propagated a frightful vision of the world's last days that struck many as bizarre, if not dangerous; but at the same time the prophetic texts bore an uncanny resemblance to the fantastic and horrific events of an age of economic depression, dictatorships, and global war. Fundamentalists frustrated optimistic liberals with their predictions of "wars and rumors of wars" and their disparagement of hope for moral progress in what liberals envisioned as the "Christian century." But in the end, fundamentalists had the more realistic outlook.

Fundamentalism could be profoundly anti-intellectual, but it also sustained a deep reverence for and desire to defend God's truth and a longing to learn from the Scriptures. These traits led at least some of the movement's sons and daughters to become scholars. The fundamentalist movement portrayed itself as standing for the eternal verities in the face of destructive modern innovation, billing itself as the "old-time religion" of America's better days gone by. But no other religious persuasion, including self-consciously modern and progressive liberal Protestantism, better understood or more effectively used the power of mass marketing and mass media. Fundamentalists could be bitter, contentious, and spoiling for a fight, but they could also be sweet-spirited in yielding to their Lord, to each other, and to the call to serve in the world's hard places. Self-righteous militancy and self-mortifying piety could coexist, and it often did, to a perplexing degree, in the same individuals.

In sum, American fundamentalists showed the same propensity for contradiction and conflicting interest that British novelist Somerset Maugham saw in the American people more generally. They were, all at once, "so cocksure on the outside, so diffident within, so kind, so hard, so trustful and so cagey, so mean and so generous."[15] Fundamentalists have been "a very special people," said Garrison Keillor, who was raised in the tradition. Their mission, he believed, has been "to shake us up . . . with a very strong and very clear message."[16] But after having done some shaking, repeatedly they have been eager to find some way to be liked and to be useful. Like the Puritans, the fundamentalists have been easy to vilify. But also like the Puritans, their staying power and influence demand serious attention.

APPENDIX

Fundamentalists' Views of Prophecy
and the End of Time

Fundamentalists' views about the end-times, about how to interpret the Bible, and about God's role in the course of history were not simple; in fact, they can be very confusing to the uninitiated. Simply to call them millenarian and leave it at that is to do them a great disservice, for *millenarian* has become a generic category for religious and social movements that are driven by visions of imminent doom, a golden age to come, or some combination of the two. Although there were a few exceptions, fundamentalists were, as a rule, millenarians of a particular sort—*premillennialists*. Premillennialists believe that Jesus Christ will personally and bodily return to earth to defeat the forces of evil and establish the millennium, the age during which, many Christians have affirmed, God's kingdom of holiness, justice, peace, and prosperity will prevail on earth for a thousand years. Modern Christian premillennialism is an internally varied and complex theological persuasion, so it is important to briefly trace its origins, precepts, and convergence with fundamentalism.

One of the first things to understand about premillennialism is that it is not a new doctrine; indeed, it is in many respects a modern successor to the apocalyptic millenarianism that was prevalent in the early church (as opposed to more gradualist, progressive views of the spread of God's kingdom that developed later). Christian millenarianism was revived by radical religious movements during the late Middle Ages and spread through left-wing Protestant ranks during the Reformation. It continued to have wide circulation during the seventeenth and eighteenth centuries, especially among the English Puritans and the Pietists in Europe. In the wake of the French Revolution and the rise of Napoleon, millenarian views issued forth again, both in populist folk versions and in more sophisticated scholarly forms.

Agreed that there will be a literal thousand-year reign of peace and righteousness on earth, and that Christ will return beforehand to personally usher it in by his power, modern premillennialists have differed on many other details. The varieties, terminology, and particulars of premillennialism can be bewildering, so it is important to pause here and offer some definitions and distinctions.

First, there have been two basic schools of premillennial thought: the historicists, who believe that the prophecies in the Bible about the end of time are being progressively fulfilled in history; and the futurists, who assert that most of these prophecies await fulfillment. To give one example, historicists traditionally interpreted the Beast or Antichrist figure described in the books of Daniel and Revelation to mean the papacy, while the futurists insisted that this "Man of Sin" will be a single person, who will appear mysteriously on the world scene sometime in the future.

Another major interpretive difference has to do with the sequence of events in history's last days that premillennialists call the rapture of the Church, or the departure from this earth and entry into glory with Christ of all true Christians, living and dead. Historicists have generally believed that this would occur simultaneously with Christ's second coming and that until then the church could expect to be persecuted, with its tribulations intensifying toward the end. Most futurists, however, believed that the church would be suddenly drawn up in a secret rapture, after which the rest of the world would experience a period of extreme turmoil, usually called the Great Tribulation. During this time the Antichrist would arise, and he would persecute any who refused to worship and obey him. His hateful violence would be focused most intently on those Jews who still hoped for the Messiah. These two very different scenarios and those who believed in them were often referred to, respectively, as the posttribulational and the pretribulational views of the rapture of the church.

Finally, one must understand the term *dispensationalism,* or dispensational theology. In Protestant parlance, dispensations are ages in divine history in which God's plan of salvation for humanity is marked by special characteristics. Traditional Christian teaching designates the periods of the Old and New Testaments—or of Israel and the church—as the two major dispensations. Several leading premillennialists in the late nineteenth century, however, began to teach a more elaborate view, which they called dispensational theology. First propagated in North America in the 1860s and 1870s by the British Plymouth Brethren Bible teacher John Nelson Darby and his popularizer, C. H. Mackintosh, dispensationalism became even more widespread after it was accepted by a number of distinguished American pastors and evangelists, such as James H. Brookes, Dwight L. Moody, and two of Moody's protégés, Reuben A. Torrey and Cyrus I. Scofield, and inscribed in the notes of the popular Scofield Reference Bible (1909).

Dispensationalists divided the history of God's dealing with humanity into several dispensations, or periods of time, during which humanity would be tested according to the revelation they had of God's will and the covenants or promises that God made with them. In each of these ages, God dealt with people according to a different method. Each dispensation was meant to provide a way of salvation for humanity, and each ended in judgement, as humans failed the test. Thus, for example, the Flood of Noah's time ended the dispensation of Conscience, while the dispensation of Promise, under Abraham, Isaac, Jacob, and Joseph, ended with captivity in Egypt. These various ages were pointing toward a final golden age, when a messianic kingdom would come to earth.

When Jesus came and announced the messianic kingdom, Israel, God's chosen people, rejected him, so the kingdom was postponed. The current era, then, is not really a distinct dispensation at all. Rather, several dispensationalists called it the "Great Parenthesis," during which God was gathering a new people from among the Gentiles, the church. Prophecies concerning the time of the Second Coming and the millennial kingdom were being postponed. Therefore God has two distinct peoples: Israel, the heirs to the prophetic promises of an earthly kingdom; and the church, whose chief inheritance is heaven.

Because dispensationalists differentiated between teaching and prophecies aimed at Israel and those directed to the church, their interpretation of prophetic themes in current affairs was preoccupied with worldwide Jewry and Zionism. Indeed, dispensationalists believed that very few of the biblical prophecies applied to the church, which would leave the world scene in the secret rapture before many of the apocalyptic portents appeared.

This premillennialist, futurist, dispensational theology had a profound effect on the fundamentalist worldview and temperament. Distinctive dispensational beliefs—that all of the fearsome events of the Apocalypse portrayed in the Bible would be literally fulfilled in the near future, that an unholy conspiracy involving an apostate church and a satanically inspired Antichrist was in the offing, that the Jews would face terrible persecution before their redemption, and that the church's main mission was not working for the kingdom of God on earth but rescuing souls from the wrath to come—all contributed to fundamentalism's alarmist, conspiratorial, and alienated outlook.

NOTES

Preface

1. "Vanishing Fundamentalism," *Christian Century,* 24 June 1926, 799.
2. Ernest R. Sandeen, *The Roots of Fundamentalism: British and American Mille-narianism, 1800–1930* (Chicago: University of Chicago Press, 1970); and George M. Marsden, *Fundamentalism and American Culture: The Shaping of Twentieth-Century Evangelicalism, 1870–1925* (New York: Oxford University Press, 1980) have become the definitive works on the movement's early years. Marsden, *Reforming Fundamentalism: Fuller Seminary and the New Evangelicalism* (Grand Rapids, Mich.: Eerdmans, 1987); and Rudolph L. Nelson, *The Making and Unmaking of an Evangelical Mind: the Case of Edward Carnell* (New York: Cambridge University Press, 1987) contain suggestive looks at fundamentalism's career in the 1930s and 1940s, although each focuses on the post-1945 era.
3. Sandeen, *Roots of Fundamentalism,* xvii.
4. These two of Marsden's many insights about the movement are found in *Fundamentalism and American Culture,* 6–7.
5. On the issue of insider status and religious history, see Leonard I. Sweet, "Wise as Serpents, Innocent as Doves: The New Evangelical Historiography," *Journal of the American Academy of Religion,* 56 (1988), 397–415.

Introduction

1. The one book that purports to survey this period is Louis Gasper, *The Fundamentalist Movement* (The Hague: Mouton, 1963). This work actually focuses on the rise of two rival fundamentalist-led cooperative ventures, the American Council of Christian Churches in 1941 and the National Association of Evangelicals in 1942; and the proliferation of fundamentalist-inspired parachurch agencies around the mid-to-late 1940s. Gasper makes some fairly accurate assertions about fundamentalism's character and career during the 1930s, but these are not sustained by narrative detail or extensive documentation. Douglas E. Herman, "Flooding The Kingdom: The Intellectual Development of Fundamentalism, 1930–1941" (Ph.D. diss., Ohio University, 1980) limits

its discussion to fundamentalists' use of their five or six cardinal doctrines. Two topical studies that reveal a great deal about fundamentalism in the 1930s and 1940s are William Vance Trollinger, *God's Empire: William Bell Riley and Midwestern Fundamentalism* (Madison: University of Wisconsin Press, 1990); and Virginia Lieson Brereton, *Protestant Fundamentalist Bible Schools, 1880–1940* (Bloomington: Indiana University Press, 1990). George M. Marsden, *Reforming Fundamentalism: Fuller Seminary and the New Evangelicalism* (Grand Rapids, Mich.: Eerdmans, 1987); Rudolph L. Nelson, *The Making and Unmaking of an Evangelical Mind: The Case of Edward Carnell* (New York: Cambridge University Press, 1987); and Mark A. Noll, *Between Faith and Criticism: Evangelicals, Scholarship, and the Bible in America* (San Francisco: Harper & Row, 1986) also contain suggestive glimpses of fundamentalism's career in the 1930s and 1940s, although each focuses on the post-1945 era.

2. Edward John Carnell, *The Case for Orthodox Theology* (Philadelphia: Westminster, 1959), 113–126.

3. Nelson, *The Making and Unmaking of an Evangelical Mind;* Marsden, *Reforming Fundamentalism,* 172–96, 257–59.

4. One of the best comparative overviews of the recent usage of "fundamentalism" as a category of militant traditionalism among many of the world religions is Bruce B. Lawrence's *Defenders of God: The Fundamentalist Revolt against the Modern Age* (San Francisco: Harper & Row, 1989). The Fundamentalism Project, sponsored by the American Academy of Arts and Sciences and directed by Martin E. Marty and R. Scott Appleby at the University of Chicago, produced a massive compendium of scholarship that now serves as a benchmark for the comparative religions approach to fundamentalism. See Marty and Appleby, eds., *Fundamentalism Observed,* The Fundamentalism Project vol. 1 (Chicago: University of Chicago Press), (1991); *Fundamentalisms and Society: Reclaiming the Sciences, The Family, and Education,* The Fundamentalism Project, vol. 2 (1993); *Fundamentalisms and the State: Remaking Polities, Economics and Militance,* The Fundamentalism Project, vol. 3 (1993); and *Accounting for Fundamentalism: The Dynamic Character of Movements,* The Fundamentalism Project, vol. 4 (1994).

5. One example of such confused and confusing usage is R. Laurence Moore, *Religious Outsiders and the Making of Americans* (New York: Oxford University Press, 1986), ch. 6, "The Protestant Majority as a Lost Generation—A Look at Fundamentalism," which makes most evangelical and/or conservative Protestants out to be "fundamentalists." Moore offers some very important insights about fundamentalism strictly defined, but many of these points are misapplied when extended to the other movements and traditions. For a better solution, see George Marsden, "Introduction: The Evangelical Denomination," in *Evangelicalism and Modern America,* ed. George Marsden (Grand Rapids, Mich.: Eerdmans, 1984), vii–xvi; and Timothy L. Smith, "The Evangelical Kaleidoscope and the Call to Christian Unity," *Christian Scholar's Review* 15 (1986): 125–40.

6. George M. Marsden, *Fundamentalism and American Culture: The Shaping of Twentieth-Century Evangelicalism, 1870–1925* (New York: Oxford University Press, 1980), 4.

7. Sandeen, *The Roots of Fundamentalism: British and American Millenarianism, 1800–1930* (Chicago: University of Chicago Press, 1970), xiii–xxiii. See also Sandeen, "Toward a Historical Interpretation of the Roots of Fundamentalism," *Church History* 36 (March 1967): 66–83.

8. Marsden, *Fundamentalism and American Culture,* 3–6, 199–205. See also Marsden, "Defining Fundamentalism," *Christian Scholar's Review* 1 (Winter 1971):

141–51; and Ernest R. Sandeen, "Defining Fundamentalism: A Reply to Professor Marsden," *Christian Scholar's Review* 1 (Spring 1971): 227–32.

9. Marsden, "Fundamentalism," *Encyclopedia of the American Religious Experience: Studies of Traditions and Movements,* 3 vols., ed. Charles H. Lippy and Peter W. Williams (New York: Scribner's, 1988), II:947, 947–62.

10. Grant Wacker, "Uneasy in Zion: Evangelicals in Postmodern Society," in Marsden, ed., *Evangelicalism and Modern America,* 22–24, labels this proprietary feeling a "custodial" ideal.

11. Moore, *Religious Outsiders,* ch. 6.

12. Grant Wacker, The Holy Spirit and the Spirit of the Age in American Protestantism, 1880–1910," *Journal of American History* 72 (June 1985): 45–62.

13. Milton L. Rudnick, *Fundamentalism and the Missouri Synod: A Historical Study of Their Interaction and Mutual Influence* (St. Louis, Mo.: Concordia, 1966), 84–90; Theodore Graebner, *The Problem of Lutheran Union and Other Essays* (St. Louis, Mo.: Concordia, 1935), 50–52, 62–66, 70–72; F. E. Mayer, *The Religious Bodies of America* (St. Louis, Mo.: Concordia, 1954), 419–26, 480–81.

14. James J. Thompson, Jr., *Tried as by Fire: Southern Baptists and the Religious Controversies of the 1920s* (Macon, Ga.: Mercer University Press, 1982), 137–65; Kenneth C. Hubbard, "Anti-Conventionism in the Southern Baptist Convention, 1940–1962" (Th.D. diss., Southwestern Baptist Theological Seminary, 1968), 83–94.

15. Robert Mapes Anderson, *Vision of the Disinherited: The Making of American Pentecostalism* (New York: Oxford University Press, 1979), 5–6, 147–52; William W. Menzies, *Anointed to Serve: The Story of the Assemblies of God* (Springfield, Mo.: Gospel Publishing, 1971), 24–28, 180–81.

16. Timothy L. Smith, *Called unto Holiness: The Story of the Nazarenes: The Formative Years* (Kansas City, Mo.: Nazarene Publishing, 1962), 315–21; Harry A. Ironside, *Holiness: The False and the True* (New York: Loizeaux Brothers, 1939).

17. Both of the two most significant earlier (pre-Sandeen) studies of fundamentalism used this thesis: Stewart G. Cole's *The History of Fundamentalism* (New York: Richard Smith, 1931); and Norman F. Furniss's *The Fundamentalist Controversy, 1918–1931* (New Haven, Conn.: Yale University Press, 1954). So did Richard Hofstadter's influential studies, *Anti-Intellectualism in American Life* (New York: Knopf, 1962); and *The Paranoid Style of American Politics and Other Essays* (New York: Random House, 1963). A more recent version of this perspective is William G. McLoughlin's *Revivals, Awakenings, and Reform: An Essay on Religion and Social Change in America, 1607–1977* (Chicago: University of Chicago Press, 1978); and his "The Illusions and Dangers of the New Christian Right," *Foundations* 25 (1982): 128–43.

18. Martin E. Marty insists that evangelicals (in general, and presumably, fundamentalists in particular) have had a symbiotic relationship with modernity. See his "The Revival of Evangelicalism and Southern Religion," in *Varieties of Southern Evangelicalism,* ed. David Edwin Harrell, Jr. (Macon, Ga.: Mercer University Press, 1981), 7–22. Arguments against reductionistic interpretations of fundamentalism are in Marsden, *Fundamentalism and American Culture,* 199–205; and in Leo P. Ribuffo, *The Old Christian Right: The Protestant Far Right from the Depression to the Cold War* (Philadelphia: Temple University Press, 1983), xi–xix, 258–74. Moore, *Religious Outsiders* (143–49, 164–72) states a case for the movement's functional success. Ernest R. Sandeen's "Fundamentalism and American Identity," *Annals of the American Academy of Social and Political Sciences* 387 (January 1970): 56–65, is provocative and suggestive on all of these points.

19. Walter Edmund Warren Ellis, "Social and Religious Factors in the Fundamentalist-

Modernist Schisms among Baptists in North America, 1895–1934" (Ph.D. diss., University of Pittsburgh, 1974), 29–30, 75–82, 116–23, 159–76.

20. *Ibid.,* 119, 175; Nathan O. Hatch, *The Democratization of American Christianity* (New Haven, Conn.: Yale University Press, 1984) 210–19; Hatch, "Evangelicalism as a Democratic Movement," in Marsden, ed., *Evangelicalism and Modern America,* 71–82.

21. Everett L. Perry, *The Presbyterian Church in Metropolitan Erie, Pennsylvania* (New York: Board of National Missions of the Presbyterian Church of the U.S.A., 1948); see also Ellis, "Social and Religious Factors," 119–25.

22. This idea is the operative assumption behind Douglas W. Frank's *Less than Conquerors: How Evangelicals Entered The Twentieth Century* (Grand Rapids, Mich.: Eerdmans, 1986), a provocative historical and theological evaluation of fundamentalist evangelicalism.

23. Anthony F. C. Wallace, *Rockdale: The Growth of an American Village in the Early Industrial Revolution* (New York: Knopf, 1978), 394–97, 422–24. See also Eric Foner, *Free Soil, Free Labor, Free Men: The Ideology of the Republican Party before the Civil War* (New York: Oxford University Press, 1970), 11–39.

24. Sandra Sizer, "Politics and Apolitical Religion: the Great Urban Revivals of the Late Nineteenth Century," *Church History* 48 (March 1979): 81–98.

25. This "status revolution" which eroded the influence of more traditional evangelicals was first hypothesized by Richard Hofstadter in his *The Age of Reform: From Bryan to F.D.R.* (New York: Knopf, 1955), and has been reinterpreted by Burton L. Bledstein, *The Culture of Professionalism: The Middle Class and the Development of Higher Education in America* (New York: W.W. Norton, 1976). Riley's alarm at these trends and his determination to combat them appear in his *The Menace of Modernism* (New York: Christian Alliance, 1917), 79–100.

26. Marsden, *Fundamentalism and American Culture,* 194–95, 204–5. Fundamentalism's appeal to ethnic Protestants will be discussed more fully in chapter 8.

Chapter 1

1. Ernest R. Sandeen, *The Roots of Fundamentalism: British and American Millenarianism, 1800–1930* (Chicago: University of Chicago Press, 1970), 269.

2. "Vanishing Fundamentalism," *Christian Century,* 24 June 1926, 799; H. Richard Niebuhr, "Fundamentalism," *Encyclopedia of the Social Sciences* (New York: Social Science Research Council, 1931), 525–27; see also Stewart G. Cole, *The History of Fundamentalism* (New York: Richard Smith, 1931), 324–28.

3. Mencken, *Prejudices: Fifth Series* (New York: George H. Doran, 1926), reprinted selection in *The Discontent of the Intellectuals: A Problem of the Twenties,* ed. Henry May (Chicago: Rand McNally, 1963), 25–30; Lippmann, *A Preface to Morals* (New York: Macmillan, 1929), 31–32.

4. O. W. Van Osdel, "Good Soldiers of Jesus Christ," *Baptist Bulletin* 1 (April 1933): 1.

5. Louis Gasper, *The Fundamentalist Movement* (The Hague: Mouton, 1963), 21; R. Laurence Moore, *Religious Outsiders and the Making of Americans* (New York: Oxford University Press, 1986), 165–70.

6. The clearest statements of these views appear in Richard Hofstadter, *Anti-Intellectualism in American Life* (New York: Knopf, 1963), 117–36; and more recently in William G. McLoughlin, *Revivals, Awakenings, and Reforms* (Chicago: University of

Chicago Press, 1978), 4–6, 18, 143–48, 185–93, 212–14. For some fairly standard treatments, see William Leuchtenburg, *The Perils of Prosperity:1914–1932* (Chicago: University of Chicago Press, 1958), 223; and George E. Mowry, *The Urban Nation: 1920–1960* (New York: Hill & Wang, 1965), 28.

7. R. Laurence Moore, "Insiders and Outsiders in American Historical Narrative and American History," *American Historical Review* 87 (April 1982): 406. See also Leo P. Ribuffo's criticism of consensus historians' treatment of fundamentalism in his *The Old Christian Right: The Protestant Far Right from the Depression to the Cold War* (Philadelphia: Temple University Press, 1983), xi–xix, 258–74.

8. Ernest R. Sandeen, "Fundamentalism and American Identity," *Annals of the American Academy of Social and Political Sciences* 387 (January 1970): 64–66; George M. Marsden, *Fundamentalism and American Culture: The Shaping of Twentieth-Century Evangelicalism, 1870–1925* (New York: Oxford University Press, 1980), 204–5, 221–28.

9. Sandeen, *Roots of Fundamentalism*, 268.

10. Marsden, *Fundamentalism and American Culture*, 3–8, and Part Four, "Interpretations."

11. Mark A. Noll, *The Scandal of the Evangelical Mind* (Grand Rapids, Mich.: Eerdmans, 1994), 109–45.

12. Luther P. Gerlach and Virginia H. Hine, *People, Power, Change: Movements of Social Transformation* (Indianapolis: Bobbs-Merrill, 1970), 183–86; Moore, *Religious Outsiders*, 25–47.

13. Harry Emerson Fosdick, quoted in Robert Moats Miller, *Harry Emerson Fosdick: Preacher, Pastor, Prophet* (New York: Oxford University Press, 1985), 214; Robert T. Handy, "The American Religious Depression, 1925–1935," *Church History* 29 (March 1960): 1–29.

14. The impression of fundamentalism being hopelessly split by the lack of cooperation among its leaders is portrayed most convincingly in C. Allyn Russell, *Voices of American Fundamentalism: Seven Biographical Studies* (Philadelphia: Westminster Press, 1976); and Russell's subsequent articles, "Mark Allison Matthews: Seattle Fundamentalist and Civic Reformer," *Journal of Presbyterian History* 57 (Winter 1979): 447–66; "Donald Grey Barnhouse: Fundamentalist Who Changed," *Journal of Presbyterian History* 59 (Spring 1981): 33–57; and "Thomas Todhunter Shields: Canadian Fundamentalist," *Foundations* 24 (January–March 1981): 15–31.

15. Marsden, *Fundamentalism and American Culture*, 184–93, is an able summary of these aspects of the movement's record. See also Hofstadter, *Anti-Intellectualism in American Life*, 117–36, for the argument that fundamentalism was essentially a pathological reaction to modern thought, characteristically expressed in "pseudo-conservative" political crusades.

16. Vance Havner, "Come and See—The Road to Certainty," *Moody Bible Institute Monthly* [hereinafter *MM*] 34 (January 1934): 211.

17. "Bible Schools that are True to the Faith," *Sunday School Times* [hereinafter, *SST*] 1 February 1930, 63. The Bible institute movement was not limited to fundamentalism. The Wesleyan holiness movement also created such agencies, most notably God's Bible School in Cincinnati. So did pentecostal groups such as the Assemblies of God, who sponsored Central Bible Institute in Springfield, Missouri. An excellent history of the Bible school movement's rise and development is Virginia Lieson Brereton, *Training God's Army: The American Bible School, 1880–1940* (Bloomington: Indiana University Press, 1990).

18. Ernest R. Sandeen first suggested this feature of the Bible schools, pointing out that the scope of Bible institute activity was such that the schools functioned as denominational surrogates for their constituents (Sandeen, *Roots of Fundamentalism,* 241–43). William Vance Trollinger, *God's Empire: William Bell Riley and Midwestern Fundamentalism* (Madison: University of Wisconsin Press, 1990), tests Sandeen's suggestion in a thorough case study, with positive results.

19. Renald E. Showers, "A History of Philadelphia College of Bible," (M.Th. thesis, Dallas Theological Seminary, 1962), 69, 81, 86; *Brief Facts about the Moody Bible Institute of Chicago* (Chicago, 1928); *Moody Bible Institute Bulletin* [hereinafter *MBI Bull*] 12 (November 1932): 14; *MBI Bull* vol. 16 (November 1936): 15.

20. "Institute Items," *The King's Business* 3 (November 1912): 295–96; Showers, "Philadelphia College of Bible," 69, 89; *A Brief Story of the Bible Institute Colportage Association of Chicago: Forty-five Years of Printed Page Ministry* (Chicago: Bible Institute Colportage Association, 1939).

21. "Interdenominational Christian Magazines," *SST,* 7 February 1931, 72.

22. Daniel P. Fuller, *Give the Winds a Mighty Voice: The Story of Charles E. Fuller* (Waco, Tex.: Word Books, 1972), 75–77; "WMBI," *MM* 30 (January 1930): 270; "Radio Station WMBI," *MM* 31 (May 1931): 480; "The *Sunday School Times* Radio Directory," *SST,* 30 May 1931, 313.

23. *MBI Bull* 12 (November 1932): 14; ibid. 16 (November 1936): 15; "Miracles and Melodies," *MM* 42 (April 1942): 487; figure on radio staff itinerary compiled from the annual reports of the Radio Department of the Moody Bible Institute of Chicago for the years 1929–1941; "President's Report," *MBI Bull* 17 (October 1937): 3; "Enrollment," typescript table found in File Drawer G, the Moodyana Collection, Moody Bible Insitute; "And Now for 50,000," *MM* 41 (September 1940): 4; *N. W. Ayer and Son's Dictionary of Newspapers and Periodicals* (Philadelphia: N. W. Ayer & Son, 1933).

24. Nathan R. Wood, *A School of Christ* (Boston: Gordon College, 1953), 165–66.

25. "The Sweep of Northwestern Schools," *The Pilot* 17 (January 1937): 108; William Vance Trollinger, Jr., "Riley's Empire: Northwestern Bible School and Fundamentalism in the Upper Midwest," *Church History* 57 (June 1988): 197–212.

26. "A Magazine for All," *MM* 40 (February 1942): 249.

27. "1937 Commencement," *The King's Business* 28 (June 1937): 205, mentions such a program, which was instituted in 1935; Gene A. Getz, *MBI: The Story of Moody Bible Institute* (Chicago: Moody Press, 1969), reports that Moody had a pastor's course from 1922 on.

28. Donald G. Tinder, "Fundamentalist Baptists in the Northern and Western United States, 1920–1950" (Ph.D. diss., Yale University, 1969), 245–53, relates the story of Central Baptist. For the histories of Northern, Eastern, and Western, see respectively Warren Cameron Young, *Commit What You Have Heard: A History of Northern Baptist Theological Seminary, 1913–1988* (Wheaton, Ill.: Harold Shaw, 1988); Gilbert L. Guffin, ed., *What God Hath Wrought* (Philadelphia: Judson Press, 1960); and Albert Wardin, Jr., *Baptists in Oregon* (Portland: Judson College, 1969), 423–34.

29. Leland D. Hine, "A Denomination Assists a Seminary," *Foundations* 7 (January 1964): 63–76.

30. Tinder, "Fundamentalist Baptists," 242–99, provides an informative summary of Northern Baptist fundamentalists' seminary-building. The above two paragraphs owe much to his observations. On Gordon and Northwestern, see Wood, *A School of Christ,* 100–6, 110, 141–43, 162–66; and short notices on Northwestern's new seminary program in *The Pilot* 15 (July 1935): 274, and vol. 16 (December 1935): 72.

31. Tinder, "Fundamentalist Baptists," 299–305.

32. See for example, James D. Mosteller, "Something Old—Something New: The First Fifty Years of Northern Baptist Theological Seminary," *Foundations* 8 (January 1965): 31–34.

33. Rudolf A. Renfer, "A History of Dallas Theological Seminary" (Ph.D. diss., University of Texas, 1959).

34. George M. Marsden, *Reforming Fundamentalism: Fuller Seminary and the New Evangelicalism* (Grand Rapids, Mich.: Eerdmans, 1987), 31–44, gives a background of the Presbyterian fundamentalism that created Westminster.

35. Edward Heerema, *R.B.: A Prophet in the Land: Rienk Bouke Kuiper, Preacher–Theologian–Churchman* (Jordan Station, Ont.: Paideia Press, 1986), 126; see also George M. Marsden, "Perspective on the Division of 1937," in *Pressing Toward the Mark: Essays Commemorating Fifty Years of the Orthodox Presbyterian Church,* ed. Charles G. Dennison and Richard C. Gamble (Philadelphia: Orthodox Presbyterian Church, 1986), 295–328.

36. Heerema, *R.B.,* 146–49; "Dr. Buswell Joins Faith Theological Seminary," *SST,* 17 February 1940, 137; Edward A. Steele III, "Buswell, The Man," *Presbyterion: Covenant Seminary Review* 2 (Spring–Fall 1976): 10–11; Edwin H. Rian, *The Presbyterian Conflict* (Grand Rapids, Mich.: Eerdmans, 1940), 102–3.

37. The origins of the "neo-evangelical" theological renaissance among the heirs of the fundamentalist movement and the role of fundamentalist seminaries in the 1930s and 1940s are discussed in chapter 11 of this book and more at length in Rudolph Nelson, *The Making and Unmaking of an Evangelical Mind: The Case of Edward Carnell* (New York: Cambridge University Press, 1987); Mark A. Noll, *Between Faith and Criticism: Evangelicals, Scholarship, and the Bible in America* (San Francisco: Harper & Row, 1986); Marsden, *Reforming Fundamentalism;* and Carl F. H. Henry, *Confessions of a Theologian: An Autobiography* (Waco, Tex.: Word Books, 1986).

38. Bruce Leslie, "Between Piety and Expertise: Professionalization of College Faculty in the 'Age of the University,'" *Pennsylvania History* (July 1979): 245–65; John Barnard, *From Evangelicalism to Progressivism at Oberlin College, 1866–1917* (Columbus: Ohio State University Press, 1969); George M. Marsden, *The Soul of the American University: From Protestant Establishment to Established Nonbelief* (New York: Oxford University Press, 1994).

39. See, for example, G. D. Franklin, "Rationalism in Kalamazoo College," *Baptist Temple News,* 25 October 1924, 1–2; and "Support Only Christian Colleges," *MM* 29 (June 1929): 471.

40. "What About Your Son or Daughter?" *MM* 38 (July 1938): 560.

41. Virginia Lieson Brereton, "The Bible Schools and Conservative Evangelical Higher Education, 1880–1940," in *Making Higher Education Christian: The History and Mission of Evangelical Colleges in America,* ed. Joel A. Carpenter and Kenneth W. Shipps (Grand Rapids, Mich.: Eerdmans, 1987), 125–26.

42. William C. Ringenberg, *The Christian College: A History of Protestant Higher Education in America* (Grand Rapids, Mich.: Christian University Press and Eerdmans, 1984), 166–87, is an informative overview of these efforts.

43. These and several other similar colleges were advertised in *MM* 31 (September 1930–August 1931), passim.

44. Harry J. Albus, "Christian Education Today," *Christian Life* 10 (September 1948): 26, 46.

45. William J. Jones, "A Study in Contrasts," *Bulletin of Wheaton College* 8 (October 1931): 7; Thomas A. Askew, Jr., "The Liberal Arts College Encounters Intellectual

Change: A Comparative Study of Education at Knox and Wheaton Colleges, 1837–1925" (Ph.D. diss., Northwestern University, 1969); Michael S. Hamilton, "The Fundamentalist Harvard: Wheaton College and the Enduring Vitality of American Evangelicalism, 1919–1965" (Ph.D. diss., University of Notre Dame, 1994).

46. "Wheaton College, 'For Christ and His Kingdom,'" *Baptist Bulletin* 1 (November 1935): 5, 11–12; "The World Is Wondering about Wheaton," *Baptist Bulletin* 3 (March 1938): 14; the *New York Times* annual survey of higher education in the 11 October 1936 issue confirms the claims of Wheaton's leading the nation in growth for that year (II, 5:1).

47. "Wheaton College, Harvard of the Bible Belt," *Change* 6 (March 1974): 17–20; William G. McLoughlin, *Billy Graham: Revivalist in a Secular Age* (New York: Ronald Press, 1960), 34; Henry, *Confessions of a Theologian*, 60–76; Nelson, *The Case of Edward Carnell*, 28–41.

48. "Shall I Go to a Summer Bible Conference?" *SST,* 18 May 1935, 337, is a valuable introduction.

49. "Forthcoming Conferences," *MM* 34 (July 1934): 528; "Forthcoming Conferences," *MM* 35 (August 1935): 589.

50. "Forthcoming Conferences," *MM* 30 (June 1930): 517; "Forthcoming Conferences," *MM* 41 (June 1941): 614.

51. C. H. Heaton, "The Winona Lake Bible Conference," *Watchman-Examiner,* 4 September 1941, 826.

52. Ibid.

53. "Why Attend A Summer Conference?" *SST,* 15 May 1937, 348.

54. Edwin L. Frizen, Jr., "An Historical Study of the Interdenominational Foreign Mission Association in Relation to Evangelical Unity and Cooperation" (D.Miss. project, Trinity Evangelical Divinity School, 1981), 2–3, 74–75, 78, 80–81.

55. "Why Attend A Summer Conference?"

56. Herman S. Hettinger, "Broadcasting in the United States," *Annals of the American Academy of Political and Social Sciences* 177 (January 1935): 6.

57. "A Directory of Evangelical Radio Broadcasts," *SST,* 23 January 1932, 44–45.

58. Exclusion of "sectarian" and controviersial religious broadcasting was in fact one of the aims of such programming policy. Spencer J. Miller, "Radio and Religion," *Annals of the American Academy of Political and Social Sciences* (January 1935) 177: 136–40; Fuller, *Give the Winds A Mighty Voice,* 101–3.

59. Quentin Schultze, "Evangelical Radio and the Rise of the Electronic Church, 1921–1948," *Journal of Broadcasting on Electronic Media* 32 (Summer 1988) 296–97.

60. Fuller, *Give the Winds A Mighty Voice,* 151–57.

61. "Another Year of Miracle Gospel Broadcast," *SST,* 21 October 1939, 720–22; Fuller, *Give the Winds A Mighty Voice,* 113–22, 140.

62. Wilbur M. Smith, *Before I Forget* (Chicago: Moody Press, 1971), 98–105.

63. Wesley R. Willis, *200 Years—And Still Counting!* (Wheaton, Ill.: Victor Books, 1979), 77–81; Ethel May Baldwin and David V. Benson, *Henrietta Mears and How She Did It* (Glendale, Calif.: Regal Books, 1966), 60–72; Clarence H. Benson, *A Popular History of Christian Education* (Chicago: Moody Press, 1943), 229–30. In the mid-1940s, Benson's All-Bible Graded Series formed the core of a new Sunday school publishing firm, Scripture Press.

64. By contrast, mainline Protestant Sunday school enrollments were declining; over the same period those of the northern Presbyterian Church decreased by 18 percent. These trends are discussed in Robert W. Lynn and Elliott Wright, *The Big Little School: 200 Years of the Sunday School,* rev. and enl. ed. (Nashville, Tenn.: Abingdon, 1980), 133.

65. *Fundamentalism in American Religion, 1880–1950: A 45–Volume Facsimile Series Reproducing Often Extremely Rare Material Documenting the Development of One of the Major Religious Movements of Our Time* (New York: Garland Publishing [1987]), a publisher's catalogue, reflects the options for book publishing available to fundamentalists in the publishing information listed for the books in the series. See also Marie D. Loizeaux, *A Century of Christian Publishing* (Neptune, N.J.: Loizeaux Brothers, 1976); Eugene Schuyler English, *H.A. Ironside, Ordained of the Lord* (Grand Rapids, Mich.: Zondervan, 1946), 133–36; Getz, *MBI: The Story of Moody Bible Institute,* 229–37; and Joseph H. Hall, "The Controversy over Fundamentalism in the Christian Reformed Church, 1915–1966" (Th.D. thesis, Concordia Theological Seminary, 1974), 140–55 (on Eerdmans and Zondervan).

66. Marsden, *Fundamentalism and American Culture,* 96–99; Smith, *Before I Forget,* 75–82; Marsden, *Reforming Fundamentalism,* 35, 40, 87; Introduction, *Modernism and Foreign Missions: Two Fundamentalist Protests,* ed. Joel A. Carpenter (New York: Garland Publishing, 1988).

67. David A. Rausch, "Our Hope: An American Fundamentalist Journal and the Holocaust, 1937–1945," *Fides et Historia* 12 (Spring 1980): 89; Arno C. Gaebelein, *Half a Century: The Autobiography of a Servant* (New York: Our Hope, 1930), 85–87. See also David A. Rausch, *Arno C. Gaebelein, 1861–1945: Irenic Fundamentalist and Scholar* (Lewiston, N.Y.: Edwin Mellen Press, 1983).

68. C. Allyn Russell, "Donald Grey Barnhouse: Fundamentalist Who Changed," *Journal of Presbyterian History* 59 (Spring 1981): 33–57.

69. John W. Bradbury, "Curtis Lee Laws and the Fundamentalist Movement," *Foundations* 5 (January 1962): 52–58.

70. C. Allyn Russell, "Thomas Todhunter Shields: Canadian Fundamentalist," *Foundations* 24 (January–March 1981): 15–31.

71. C. Allyn Russell, *Voices of American Fundamentalism: Seven Biographical Studies* (Philadelphia: Westminster Press, 1976), 79–106.

72. Leo P. Ribuffo, *The Old Christian Right: The Protestant Far Right from the Depression to the Cold War* (Philadelphia: Temple University Press, 1983), 81–88.

73. Russell, "J. Frank Norris, Violent Fundamentalist," in *Voices of American Fundamentalism,* 20–46.

74. Robert L. Sumner, *Man Sent from God: A Biography of Dr. John R. Rice* (Grand Rapids, Mich.: Eerdmans, 1959), 91–96. Before Rice died in 1980, *The Sword of the Lord* reached a circulation of three hundred thousand (Robert Sumner, "John R. Rice, A Man Sent from God," *Fundamentalist Journal* 1 [December 1982]: 25).

75. Handy, "American Religious Depression;" Clifton J. Philips, "Changing Attitudes in the Student Volunteer Movement of Great Britain and North America, 1886–1928," in *Missionary Ideologies in the Imperialist Era, 1880–1920,* ed. Torben Christiansen and William R. Hutchison (Aarhus, Denmark: Aros Publishers, 1982), 131–45; Paul A. Varg, *Missionaries, Chinese, and Diplomats: The American Protestant Missionary Movement in China, 1890–1952* (Princeton, N.J.: Princeton University Press, 1958), 147–66; and especially William R. Hutchison, *Errand to the World: American Protestant Thought and Foreign Missions* (Chicago: University of Chicago Press, 1987), 146–75.

76. Curtis Lee Laws, "Shall Baptists Go Out of Business?" *Watchman-Examiner,* 2 January 1936, 13; "The Tragedy of the Northern Baptist Convention" *Watchman-Examiner,* 11 June 1936, 699; "The Tragedy of It All," *Baptist Bulletin* 6 (July 1940): 1; *Annual of the Northern Baptist Convention, 1937* (Philadelphia: American Baptist Publication Society, 1937), 28.

77. James Alan Patterson, "The Loss of a Protestant Missionary Consensus: Foreign

Missions and the Fundamentalist–Modernist Conflict," in *Earthen Vessels: American Evangelicals and Foreign Missions, 1880–1980,* ed. Joel A. Carpenter and Wilbert R. Shenk (Grand Rapids, Mich.: Eerdmans, 1990), 73–91.

78. James A. Patterson, "Robert E. Speer, J. Gresham Machen, and the Presbyterian Board of Foreign Missions," *American Presbyterians: Journal of Presbyterian History* 64 (Spring 1986): 58–68, shows that this is exactly how Robert Speer felt about his opponents.

79. These figures are drawn from Joseph I. Parker, ed., *Interpretative Statistical Survey of the World Mission of the Christian Church* (New York: International Missionary Council, 1938), 40–45; and R. Pierce Beaver, "The Protestant Misssionary Enterprise of the United States," *Occasional Bulletin of the Missionary Research Library* 4, 7, 8 May 1953, 1–15. For an explanation of how these statistics were derived from the sources, see Joel A. Carpenter, "Appendix: The Evangelical Missionary Force in the 1930s," in *Earthen Vessels,* 335–42.

80. D. E. Hoste, "For the Evangelization of Unreached Areas," *China's Millions* 37 (May 1929): 67–68; background information on the recruits was collected from their testimonies published in *China's Millions* 37–40 (1929–1932), passim. For a list of the North American recruits, see "North America's Contribution to the Two Hundred," *China's Millions* 40 (February 1932): 30.

81. Robert Hall Glover, "What Is A Faith Mission?" *Missionary Review of the World* 58 (September 1935): 409–11; Ernest Gordon, "A Survey of Religious Life and Thought," *SST,* 24 June 1939, 430; Robert Hall Glover, "Decrease in Mission Giving—Its Real Cause and Cure," *Revelation* 7 (June 1937): 241.

82. Gary Corwin, "Evangelical Separatism and the Growth of Independent Mission Boards, 1920–1945: Some Preliminary Observations from the History of the Sudan Interior Mission," paper presented at the conference "A Century of World Evangelization," Wheaton College, Wheaton, Illinois, June 17, 1986; Rowland V. Bingham, *Seven Sevens of Years and a Jubilee! The Story of the Sudan Interior Mission* (Toronto: Evangelical Publishing, 1943), 62.

83. "Suggestions for Your Christmas Giving," *SST,* 26 December 1931, 737.

84. John B. Cole, "What Hath God Wrought," *Alumni News* 8 (June 1934): n.p. (Bible Inst. of Pa.); J. Davis Adams, "Facing Our Twentieth School Year," *Serving and Waiting* 23 (November 1933): 150 (Phila. School of Bible); R. Arthur Mathews, *Towers Pointing Upward* (Columbia, S.C.: Columbia Bible College, 1973), 143; Marguerite C. McQuilkin, *Always in Triumph: The Life of Robert C. McQuilkin* (Columbia, S.C.: Columbia Bible College Bookstore, 1956), 88–91, 102–15; *Northwestern Pilot* 7 (December 1926): 2; *The Pilot* 17 (October 1936): 16; "Twentieth Anniversary," *The King's Business* 18 (March 1927): inside back cover; "Giving to BIOLA Means Giving to Missions," *The King's Business* 29 (February 1938): 62; "The World-Wide Ministry of Moody Students," *MBI Bull* 15 (March 1936): 18; "Fields of Service," *MBI Bull* 16 (September 1936): 9; Parker, *Interpretative Statistics,* 43.

85. Dr. and Mrs. Howard Taylor, *"By Faith . . ." Henry W. Frost and the China Inland Mission* (Philadelphia, China Inland Mission, 1938), 308–12; Frizen, "An Historical Study of the IFMA," passim; Renald E. Showers, "A History of Philadelphia College of Bible" (M.Th. thesis, Dallas Theological Seminary, 1962); passim.

86. *Winona Echoes,* the annual volumes of addresses published by the Winona Lake Bible Conference demonstrate the ubiquity of missions speakers; on annual missions conferences, see Harold Lindsell, *Park Street Prophet: A Life of Harold John Ockenga* (Wheaton, Ill.: Van Kampen Press, 1951), 97–107; and Carol Talbot, *For This I Was Born: The Captivating Story of Louis T. Talbot* (Chicago: Moody Press, 1977), 145–46.

87. See chapter 4 for a more sustained look at missions-minded piety, and see chapter 10 for an account of accelerated mission expansion after World War II. For glimpses of the role played by church and home in encouraging young people to volunteer for missions, see the following oral history records: Jeannette Louise Martig Thiessen (Collection 260), Paul Kenneth Gieser (Collection 88), Susan Schultz Bartel (Collection 57), Elizabeth Stair Small (Collection 164), Zoe Anne Alford (Collection 177), Jennie Eliza Kingston Fitzwilliam (Collection 272), all in the Archives of the Billy Graham Center, Wheaton College, Wheaton, Illinois.

88. The best available treatment of the career of mainline Protestantism in the twentieth century is William R. Hutchison, ed., *Between the Times: The Travail of the Protestant Establishment in America, 1900–1960* (New York: Cambridge University Press, 1989).

89. Richard G. Hutcheson, *Mainline Churches and the Evangelicals: A Challenging Crisis?* (Atlanta, Ga.: John Knox Press, 1981), 67–79, is a helpful survey of the contemporary evangelical parachurch phenomenon.

90. This major shift is examined in Robert Wuthnow, *The Restructuring of American Religion: Society and Faith since World War II* (Princeton, N.J.: Princeton University Press, 1988), pp. 71–240.

91. James M. Gray, *The Static and the Dynamic: An Examination of Dr. Harry Emerson Fosdick's "Now Famous Sermon" on Progressive Christianity; Address before the Graduating Class of the Moody Bible Institute of Chicago, April 20, 1922* (Chicago: Bible Institute Colportage Association, 1922), 15.

Chapter 2

1. "The Sin of Timidity," *Revelation* 2 (December 1932): 489. For an outline and interpretation of Barnhouse's career, see C. Allyn Russell, "Donald Grey Barnhouse: Fundamentalist Who Changed," *Journal of Presbyterian History* 59 (Spring 1981): 33–57.

2. Editorial, *Bibliotheca Sacra* 88 (October 1931): 385.

3. Virginia Hine, "Bridge Burners: Commitment and Participation in a Religious Movement," *Sociological Analysis* 31 (1970): 61–66.

4. Nathan O. Hatch, "Evangelicalism as a Democratic Movement," in *Evangelicalism and Modern America,* ed. George Marsden (Grand Rapids, Mich.: Eerdmans, 1984), 71–82; Nathan O. Hatch, "Epilogue: The Recurring Populist Impulse in American Christianity," 210–19 in *The Democratization of American Christianity* (New Haven, Conn.: Yale University Press, 1984).

5. Dana L. Robert, "Arthur Tappan Pierson and Forward Movements of Late-Nineteenth-Century Evangelicalism" (Ph.D. diss., Yale University, 1984); A. E. Thompson, *The Life of A. B. Simpson* (Brooklyn, N.Y.: Christian Alliance Publishing, 1920); C. Allyn Russell, "Adoniram Judson Gordon: Nineteenth-Century Fundamentalist," *American Baptist Quarterly* 4 (March 1985): 61–89; Helen C. A. Dixon, *A. C. Dixon: A Romance of Preaching* (New York: G. P. Putnam's Sons, 1931).

6. Reuben A. Torrey, for example, who became the first dean of Moody's Bible institute in Chicago, earned undergraduate and master's degrees from Yale, and pursued postgraduate studies for a year in Germany. For a brief but perceptive analysis of his career, see William G. McLoughlin, *Modern Revivalism: Charles Grandison Finney to Billy Graham* (New York: Ronald Press, 1959), 366–77.

7. Laurence R. Veysey, *The Emergence of the American University* (Chicago: University of Chicago Press, 1965); Burton Bledstein, *The Culture of Professionalism: The Middle Class and the Development of Higher Education in America* (New York: W. W.

Norton, 1976); George M. Marsden, *The Soul of the American University: From Protestant Establishment to Established Unbelief* (New York: Oxford University Press, 1994).

8. An important exception was the scholarly work being done at Princeton Theological Seminary. But even there, as Mark A. Noll notes, thought was taking a reactive more than a creative direction. See Noll, *Between Faith and Criticism: Evangelicals, Scholarship, and the Bible in America* (San Francisco: Harper & Row, 1986), 11–56; and his introduction to *The Princeton Defense of Plenary Verbal Inspiration,* ed. Mark A. Noll (New York: Garland, 1988).

9. C. Allyn Russell, *Voices of American Fundamentalism: Seven Biographical Studies* (Philadelphia: Westminster, 1976), ch. 4, "William Bell Riley, Organizational Fundamentalist," and William Vance Trollinger, *God's Empire: William Bell Riley and Midwestern Fundamentalism* (Madison, University of Wisconsin Press, 1990), ch. 1, "The Leader," are excellent background studies of Riley's rise to fame.

10. Riley, *The Finality of the Higher Criticism, or, The Theory of Evolution and False Theology* (Minneapolis: By the author, 1909), 38–39, 42–43, 56–60.

11. Riley, *The Menace of Modernism* (New York: Christian Alliance Publishing, 1917), 71–75, 151–56, 172–80.

12. Ibid., 76–104.

13. Ibid., 156, 84, 177–78.

14. Ferenc M. Szasz, "William B. Riley and the Fight Against the Teaching of Evolution in Minnesota," *Minnesota History* 41 (Spring 1969): 201–16.

15. Ibid., 213–15; Russell, *Voices,* 96–99.

16. See, for example, Riley's *Wanted—A World Leader!* (Minneapolis: By the author, 1939), which mixes premillennial expectations of the rise of the Antichrist with theories of a Jewish conspiracy for world domination.

17. William Vance Trollinger, Jr., "Riley's Empire: Northwestern Bible School and Fundamentalism in the Upper Midwest," *Church History* 57 (June 1988): 197–212.

18. Eric Sevaraid, *Not So Wild A Dream,* 2d ed. (New York: Atheneum, 1976), 71.

19. William Bell Riley, *The Conflict of Christianity with Its Counterfeits* (Minneapolis: Irene Woods, 1940), 6.

20. See Joel A. Carpenter, ed., *Fighting Fundamentalism: Polemical Thrusts of the 1930s and 1940s* (New York: Garland, 1988) for more discussion of this subject and some illustrative documents.

21. See the Appendix for a brief description of this doctrinal viewpoint. For helpful introductory discussions of premillennialism and dispensationalism, see Timothy P. Weber, *Living in the Shadow of the Second Coming: American Premillennialism, 1875–1982,* enl. ed. (Chicago: University of Chicago Press, 1987), 9–24; and George M. Marsden, *Fundamentalism and American Culture: The Shaping of Twentieth-Century Evangelicalism, 1870–1925* (New York: Oxford University Press, 1980), 48–71.

22. "Fear not, little flock; for it is your Father's good pleasure to give you the kingdom" (Luke 12:32).

23. Ernest R. Sandeen, *The Roots of Fundamentalism: British and American Millenarianism, 1800–1930* (Chicago: University of Chicago Press, 1970), 71–80, 101–2; Marsden, *Fundamentalism and American Culture,* 70–71; William E. Blackstone, *Jesus Is Coming,* presentation ed. (New York: Fleming H. Revell, 1908), 151–58; 231–33.

24. Marsden, *Fundamentalism and American Culture,* 146–48, is an able summary and interpretation of this attack. See also Shailer Mathews, *Will Christ Come Again?* (Chicago: American Institute of Sacred Literature, 1917), reprinted in *The Fundamentalist–Modernist Conflict: Opposing Views on Three Major Issues,* ed. Joel A. Carpenter (New York: Garland, 1988).

25. "Unprincipled Methods of Post-Millennialists," *The King's Business* 9 (April 1918): 277.

26. Reuben A. Torrey, *What the War Teaches, or, The Greatest Lessons of 1917* (Los Angeles: BIOLA Book Room, 1918), 9–11, reprinted in *Conservative Call to Arms*, ed. Joel A. Carpenter (New York: Garland, 1988).

27. Reuben A. Torrey, *"Will Christ Come Again?" An Exposure of the Foolishness, Fallacies and Falsehoods of Shailer Mathews* (Los Angeles: BIOLA Book Room, 1918), 32, reprinted in Carpenter, ed., *The Fundamentalist–Modernist Conflict*. Torrey quotes II Peter 3:3. Mathews, *Will Christ Come Again?*, 21.

28. William Adams Brown, quoted in Sydney E. Ahlstrom, *A Religious History of the American People* (New Haven, Conn.: Yale University Press, 1972), 896–97. The definitive study of the Interchurch campaign is Eldon G. Ernst, *Moment of Truth for Protestant America: Interchurch Campaigns Following World War One* (Missoula, Mont.: American Academy of Religion/Scholars Press, 1974).

29. "The Federation of the World," *Christian Worker's Magazine* 11 (November 1910): 178; "A New Type of Christianity," *Christian Worker's Magazine* 11 (September 1910): 11–13; "Bishop Hoss and Church Union," *Christian Worker's Magazine* 12 (January 1912): 331; "The Palace of Peace," *Christian Worker's Magazine* 14 (October 1913): 74.

30. James M. Gray, *The Proposed World Church Union: Is It of God or Man?* (Chicago: Bible Institute Colportage Association, 1919), 12, reprinted in Carpenter, ed., *The Fundamentalist–Modernist Conflict*.

31. Harry Emerson Fosdick, *Shall The Fundamentalists Win? A Sermon Preached at the First Presbyterian Church, New York, May 21, 1922* (New York, 1922), 13–14, reprinted in Carpenter, ed., *The Fundamentalist–Modernist Conflict*.

32. William M. Runyan, *Dr. Gray at Moody Bible Institute* (New York: Oxford University Press, 1935), 30–79.

33. James M. Gray, "Scholarship and Evangelical Christianity," *MM* 29 (October 1928): 54.

34. "Hopeful Signs for 1908," *The Institute Tie* 8 (July 1908): 856; "Church and Labor," *Christian Worker's Magazine* 11 (May 1911): 758–59; "Social Problems," *Christian Worker's Magazine* 12 (May 1912): 588.

35. "The President and the Classes," *The Institute Tie* 10 (August 1910): 944; "Power to Trust," *The Institute Tie* 9 (January 1909): 378; "Wild Utterances," *Christian Worker's Magazine* 15 (July 1915): 666; "Are the Young Men's Christian Associations of This Country Doing Harm or Good?" *The Institute Tie* 7 (July 1907): 488–89; "The Christian Endeavor Convention," *Christian Worker's Magazine* 15 (July 1915): 667; "Labor's Appeal," *The Institute Tie* 10 (March 1910): 536–37.

36. Charles R. Erdman, "Premillennialism Defended Against Assailants," *Christian Worker's Magazine* 16 (August 1916): 914–15; W. H. Griffith Thomas, "Premillennialism and the Bible," ibid., 918–19.

37. James M. Gray, "Current Criticism of Premillennial Truth," *Christian Worker's Magazine* 18 (March 1918): 548–51; "Postmillennialism and Pacifism," *Christian Worker's Magazine* 19 (October 1918): 83; and "Religious Heterodoxy and the World War," *Christian Worker's Magazine* 19 (December 1918): 226.

38. "R. A. Torrey Replies to Dr. O. E. Brown," *MM* 26 (December 1925): 161–62; Charles T. Page, "D. L. Moody and George Adam Smith—R. A. Torrey Corroborated," *MM* 26 (February 1926): 263; W. E. Biederwolf, "Fosdickism in the *Ladies Home Journal*," *MM* 26 (December 1925): 158–59; "Mr. Bryan Replies to the *Chicago Tribune*," *MM* 23 (August 1923): 701–4. Paul Waggoner, "The Treatment of

Fundamentalism in Major American Periodicals, 1918–1941" (M.A. thesis, Trinity Evangelical Divinity School, 1982), documents the pervasive antifundamentalist slant in the major secular magazines.

39. "The Fight Against Evolution," *MM* 26 (April 1926): 364.

40. R. J. Alderman, "Evolution Leads to Sodom," *MM* 23 (September 1922): 12; John G. Reid, "Dr. Harry Emerson Fosdick, A Demonic Disguise?" ibid. (February 1923): 247.

41. "The Ku Klux Klan," *MM* 23 (February 1923): 240; "The Sacco-Vanzetti Case," *MM* 28 (October 1927): 47–48; "Selective Immigration," *MM* 26 (November 1925): 100; "Governor Smith's Religion," *MM* 27 (March 1927): 324; James M. Gray, "The Jewish Protocols," *MM* 22 (October 1921): 598.

42. "The 'Social Gospel' or the 'Gospel for the Individual,'" *MM* 23 (October 1922): 43; T. J. Bach, "Convention of the Student Volunteer Movement," *MM* 28 (March 1928): 314; "'Al' Smith among the Prophets," *MM* 34 (September 1933): 3. Smith's alienation by the early 1930s is discussed in Oscar Handlin, Al Smith and His America (Boston: Little, Brown, 1958), 167–89.

43. "Fighting Days," *MM* 34 (February 1934): 252.

44. Marsden, *Fundamentalism and American Culture,* 182.

45. J. C. Massee, "The Thirty Years' War," *The Chronicle* 17 (April 1954): 106–16.

46. Trollinger, "Riley's Empire," 209–11; Albert W. Wardin, Jr., *Baptists in Oregon* (Portland: Judson Baptist College, 1969), 418–21; Bruce Shelley, *Conservative Baptists: A Story of Twentieth-Century Dissent* (Denver, Colo.: Conservative Baptist Theological Seminary, 1960), 37, 72; Robert G. Torbet, *A History of the Baptists,* rev. ed. (Valley Forge, Pa.: Judson Press, 1963), 433–34.

47. The *Christianity Today* magazine referred to here was published from 1930 to 1936, and was aimed specifically at a Presbyterian readership. It had no connection to the contemporary magazine of the same title that was founded in 1956.

48. George M. Marsden, *Reforming Fundamentalism: Fuller Seminary and the New Evangelicalism* (Grand Rapids, Mich.: Eerdmans, 1987), 36–37.

49. Joseph M. Stowell, *Background and History of the General Association of Regular Baptist Churches* (Hayward, Calif.: J. F. May Press, 1949), 1–37; Robert Delnay, "A History of the Baptist Bible Union" (Th.D. diss., Dallas Theological Seminary, 1963).

50. Stowell, *Background and History,* 28–37; C. Allyn Russell, "Thomas Todhunter Shields: Canadian Fundamentalist," *Foundations* 24 (January–March 1981): 15–31; Russell, *Voices of American Fundamentalism,* 40.

51. Lefferts E. Loetscher, *The Broadening Church: A Study of the Theological Issues in the Presbyterian Church since 1869* (Philadelphia: Westminster, 1954), 136–48; Edwin H. Rian, *The Presbyterian Conflict* (Grand Rapids, Mich.: Eerdmans, 1940), 60–150; Ned B. Stonehouse, *J. Gresham Machen: A Biographical Memoir* (Grand Rapids, Mich.: Eerdmans, 1954), 493–505; Wilbur M. Smith, *Before I Forget* (Chicago: Moody Press, 1971), 106–23; and George M. Marsden, "Perspectives on the Division of 1937," in *Pressing Toward the Mark: Essays Commemorating Fifty Years of the Orthodox Presbyterian Church,* ed. Charles G. Dennison and Richard C. Gamble (Philadelphia: Orthodox Presbyterian Church, 1986), 295–328.

52. William A. Bevier, "A History of the I.F.C.A." (Th.D. diss., Dallas Theological Seminary, 1958), 27–41, 65–69, 77–78, 85–87, 95–98, 111–19, 271, 274.

53. See, for example, *Enterprising Fundamentalism: Two Second-Generation Leaders,* ed. Joel A. Carpenter (New York: Garland, 1988), which contains short biographies of Houghton and Ayer and details their work at Calvary Baptist Church.

54. H. G. Hamilton, "Secretary Lerrigo Struggles Hard to Explain," *Baptist Bulletin*

1 (August 1933): 2; O. W. Van Osdel, "How About It?" *Baptist Bulletin* 1 (November 1933): 2; "An Open Letter to Dr. W. B. Riley from Dr. R. T. Ketcham," *Baptist Bulletin* 2 (November 1936): 3–4; R. T. Ketcham to Virgil Bopp, undated taped correspondence (ca. 1974) on file at the Ketcham Library, Grand Rapids Baptist College, Grand Rapids, Michigan.

55. Robert T. Ketcham, "The Three-Fold Purpose of the Association," *Baptist Bulletin* 1 (June–July 1935): 7.

56. Robert T. Ketcham, *Facts for Baptists to Face* (Gary, Ind.: By the author, 1936), 2, 39. See J. Murray Murdoch, *Portrait of Obedience: The Biography of Robert T. Ketcham* (Schaumberg, Ill.: Regular Baptist Press, 1979), for a detailed chronicle of Ketcham's career; a helpful shorter account is Ruth Ryburn, "The Outworking of Obedience," *Baptist Bulletin* 31 (March 1966): 9–12.

57. R. T. Ketcham to Virgil Bopp; Ketcham, "The Princeton [Illinois] Case," *Baptist Bulletin* 5 (May 1940): 10.

58. U.S. Department of Commerce, Bureau of the Census, Religious Bodies, 1936, vol. II, *Denominations, A to J: Statistics, History, Doctrine, Organization, and Work* (Washington: U.S. Government Printing Office, 1941), 86; "Fellowshipping Churches of the G.A.R.B.C.," *Baptist Bulletin* 14 (August 1948): 5–18.

59. John W. Bradbury, "The N.B.C. Fundamentalists," *Watchman-Examiner* 12 (August 1937): 916–18.

60. W. B. Riley, "The Denominational Division among Baptists," *The Pilot* 20 (January 1940): 104–5.

61. "Notes on Open Letters: Dr. Riley and the Northern Baptist Convention," *SST,* 24 July 1937, 522.

62. Russell, *Voices of American Fundamentalism,* 101–2.

63. Chester E. Tulga, *The Foreign Missions Controversy in the Northern Baptist Convention, 1919–1949* (Chicago: Conservative Baptist Fellowship, 1950).

64. "Three Years' Advance for CBFMS," *Conservative Baptist Foreign Mission Society News and Views* 3 (January 1947): 1.

65. Torbet, *History,* 400–401, 435–36.

66. "N.A.E., Fuller Seminary, Championed by Ockenga," *Christian Beacon,* 10 May 1951, 1, 4–5, 8.

67. Joel Carpenter, "The Fundamentalist Leaven and the Rise of an Evangelical United Front," in *The Evangelical Tradition in America,* ed. Leonard I. Sweet (Macon, Ga.: Mercer University Press, 1984), 257–88; Ockenga, "Can Fundamentalism Win America?" *Christian Life and Times* 2 (June 1947): 13–15; "Ockenga Attacks 'Come-Outers' at Seminary Opening," *Christian Beacon,* 9 October 1947, 8; "N.A.E., Fuller Seminary, Championed by Ockenga"; Marsden, *Reforming Fundamentalism,* 60–67.

68. See Paul M. Harrison, *Authority and Power in the Free Church Tradition: A Social Case Study of the American Baptist Convention* (Princeton, N.J.: Princeton University Press, 1959), which examines the deep tension within one denomination between the populist, local-democratic values upon which it was founded and the managerial ethos that pervaded its twentieth-century reorganization. No wonder the Northern Baptists' ranks were so decimated by dissent and schism over the first half of the current century.

69. Murdoch, *Portrait of Obedience,* 65–82; Wilbur M. Smith, *A Watchman on the Wall: The Life Story of Will H. Houghton* (Grand Rapids, Mich.: Eerdmans, 1951), 46–49; Norman H. Maring, *Baptists in New Jersey: A Study in Transition* (Valley Forge, Pa.: Judson Press, 1964), 323–27, 334; Isaac M. Haldeman, *Why I Am Opposed*

to the Interchurch World Movement (New York: n.p., n.d.), 22–23, 43–47, reprinted in Carpenter, ed., *The Fundamentalist–Modernist Conflict.*

70. Russell, *Voices of American Fundamentalism,* 37–38.

71. Marsden, *Fundamentalism and American Culture,* 110; on issues of Presbyterian ecclesiology and separatism more generally, see Marsden, *The Evangelical Mind and the New School Presbyterian Experience* (New Haven, Conn.: Yale University Press, 1970), 67–87, 212, 229.

72. J. Gresham Machen, "A True Presbyterian Church at Last," *Presbyterian Guardian,* 22 June 1936, 110.

73. See, e.g., Sandeen, *Roots of Fundamentalism,* 260–64.

74. Marsden, "Perspective on the Division of 1937"; Marsden, "The New School Heritage and Presbyterian Fundamentalism," *Westminster Theological Journal* 32 (May 1970): 129–47.

75. "Churches in the General Association of Regular Baptist Churches," *Baptist Bulletin* 3 (February 1938): 11–13; Robert L. Sumner, *Man Sent from God: A Biography of Dr. John R. Rice* (Grand Rapids, Mich.: Eerdmans, 1959), 70–96; Walter E. Ellis, "Social and Religious Factors in the Fundamentalist–Modernist Schisms among Baptists in North America, 1895–1934" (Ph.D. diss., University of Pittsburgh, 1974), 30–32, 96–121; Everett L. Perry, "The Role of Socio-Economic Factors in the Rise and Development of American Fundamentalism" (Ph.D. diss., University of Chicago, 1959), 287–319, 349–69; Donald G. Tinder, "Fundamentalist Baptists in the Northern and Western United States, 1920–1950" (Ph.D. diss., Yale University, 1969), 141–62.

76. Hugh Hartshorne and Milton C. Froyd, *Theological Education in the Northern Baptist Convention: A Survey* (Philadelphia: Judson Press, 1945), for example, makes some interesting comparisons between fundamentalist and nonfundamentalist pastors in the Northern Baptist Convention, but comparisons of separatist and nonseparatist Baptist fundamentalists are not available.

77. Smith, *Watchman,* 16–24; Murdoch, *Portrait of Obedience,* 19–25; Lindsell, *Park Street Prophet,* 26–34; Carl McIntire, "Not I, But Christ," *Servants of Apostasy* (Collingswood, N.J.: Christian Beacon Press, 1955), 362; Smith, *Before I Forget,* 11–15; Stonehouse, *J. Gresham Machen,* 23–46.

78. The differences in clientele and outlook between separatists and the emerging postwar party of nonseparatist "new evangelicals" receive illuminating treatment in James Davison Hunter, *American Evangelicalism: Conservative Religion and the Quandary of Modernity* (New Brunswick, N.J.: Rutgers University Press, 1983), 73–170; George W. Dollar, *A History of Fundamentalism in America* (Greenville, S.C.: Bob Jones University Press, 1973), 187–289; and Martin E. Marty, "Tensions within Contemporary Evangelicalism," in *The Evangelicals: What They Believe, Who They Are, Where They Are Headed,* ed. David F. Wells and John D. Woodbridge (Nashville, Tenn.: Abingdon, 1975), 170–88.

79. The most balanced brief account of Norris's turbulent career is in Russell, *Voices,* 37–43. Norris's reputation for violence was sealed after he shot and killed a man in 1926 during an argument in the pastor's study. Norris was tried for murder but was acquitted.

80. Ibid., 44–46; "W. B. Riley Quits Frank Norris," *The Pilot* 18 (April 1938): 205–6; Sumner, *Man Sent from God,* 101–12; Murdoch, *Portrait of Obedience,* 147–53, 177–87, 202–7.

81. Ketcham, *Facts for Baptists to Face,* 18–19.

82. Smith, *Watchman on the Wall,* 40–50, 168.

83. Riley, "The Denominational Division among Baptists," 104–5; "Churches in

the General Association of Regular Baptist Churches," 11–13; Trollinger, "Riley's Empire," 209–11.

84. Lindsell, *Park Street Prophet,* 31–35; McIntire, "Not I, But Christ," 361–66.

85. Ketcham, "An Open Letter to W. B. Riley," 4.

86. See David D. Allen, "Compromise, Confusion, and Cowardice," *The Voice* 22 (May 1944): 6–7; and William McCarrell, "Why I Left the Congregational Denomination," *The Voice* 23 (February 1945): 8–9, two installments in a series of reminiscences on the decision to separate that was published in the magazine of the IFCA. See also the editorial "Denominational Revolt," *Watchman-Examiner,* 22 April 1937, 467–68.

87. Wardin, *Baptists in Oregon,* 455–69; Sumner, *Man Sent from God,* 64–86.

88. "Apostasy," *Revelation* 3 (February 1933): 52. Philippians 3:13–14 (KJV) states: "Brethren, I count not myself to have apprehended: but this one thing I do, forgetting those things which are behind, and reaching forth unto those things which are before, I press toward the mark for the prize of the high calling of God in Christ Jesus." It was an oft-quoted maxim for disciplined Christian living.

89. "Should A Christian Ever Leave His Church?" *Revelation* 2 (December 1932): 489.

90. "Fighting Days," *MM* 34 (February 1934): 252.

91. "Notes on Open Letters: 'Ought I to Leave My Church?'" *SST,* 14 May 1932, 262. See also the editorial "Come Out From Among Them?" *Revelation* 2 (December 1932): 488; Grant Stroh, "Practical and Perplexing Questions," *MM* 32 (January 1932): 256; "Separation," *Revelation* 3 (February 1933): 51–52; "Practical and Perplexing Questions: Editorial," *MM* 32 (March 1932): 329.

92. "Ought I to Leave My Church?" 262.

93. Rowland V. Bingham, *Seven Sevens of Years and a Jubilee!* (Toronto: Evangelical Publishers, 1944), 105.

94. Andrew Porter, "Evangelical Enthusiasm, Missionary Motivation and West Africa in the Late Nineteenth Century: The Career of G. W. Brooke," *Journal of Imperial and Commonwealth History* 6 (October 1977): 25–28.

95. Virginia Lieson Brereton, "The Bible Schools and Conservative Evangelical Higher Education, 1880–1940," in *Making Higher Education Christian: The History and Mission of Evangelical Colleges in America,* ed. Joel A. Carpenter and Kenneth W. Shipps (Grand Rapids, Mich.: Eerdmans, 1987), 114–15.

96. "Another Milestone On Our Way," *Christian Worker's Magazine* 20 (July 1920): 851.

97. "Bible Schools that are True to the Faith," *SST,* 1 February 1930, 63; "The *Sunday School Times* Radio Directory," *SST,* 30 May 1931, 313; "Sound Interdenominational Missions," *SST,* 26 December 1931, 737; "Your Christmas Giving," *SST,* 6 December 1930, 731–34; "Interdenominational Evangelical Magazines," *SST,* 7 February 1931, 72.

98. Interview of Torrey Maynard Johnson (Collection 285), Archives of the Billy Graham Center, Wheaton College, Wheaton, Illinois.

Chapter 3

1. See, for example, Deut. 14:2, II Cor. 6:17, I Pet. 2:9.

2. Donald G. Mathews, *Religion in the Old South* (Chicago: University of Chicago Press, 1977), 18–38, 81–135, traces the change in white evangelicals' status from marginality to virtual establishment in the antebellum South. The transformation was

less dramatic in the North, but see Mary P. Ryan, *Cradle of the Middle Class: The Family in Oneida County, New York, 1790–1865* (New York: Cambridge University Press, 1981); and Randolph A. Roth, *The Democratic Dilemma: Religion, Reform, and the Social Order in the Connecticut River Valley of Vermont, 1791–1850* (New York: Cambridge University Press, 1987).

3. The best treatment of the holiness movement in its protean stages remains Timothy L. Smith, *Called Unto Holiness: The Story of the Nazarenes: The Formative Years* (Kansas City, Mo.: Nazarene Publishing House, 1962); but see also Melvin E. Dieter, *The Holiness Revival of the Nineteenth Century* (Metuchen, N.J.: Scarecrow Press, 1980); and Jean Miller Schmidt, "Holiness and Perfection," *Encyclopedia of the American Religious Experience,* 3 vols., ed. Charles H. Lippy and Peter W. Williams (New York: Scribner's, 1988), II:813–29. Shirley Nelson, *Fair, Clear and Terrible: The Story of Shiloh, Maine* (Latham, N.Y.: British American Publishing, 1989), is a haunting account of one of the perfectionist communities that the holiness movement spawned at the turn of the century.

4. A number of studies of the militant, separatist wing of contemporary fundamentalism take such an approach. The best are Nancy Tatom Ammerman, *Bible Believers: Fundamentalists in the Modern World* (New Brunswick, N.J.: Rutgers University Press, 1987); Alan Peshkin, *God's Choice: The Total World of a Fundamentalist Christian School* (Chicago: University of Chicago Press, 1986); and Frances FitzGerald, "Liberty Baptist—1981" and "Liberty Baptist—1986," in her *Cities on a Hill: A Journey through Contemporary American Cultures* (New York: Simon and Schuster, 1986), 120–201. See also "Born Again," a documentary film produced in 1988 by anthropologist James Ault that portrays a contemporary fundamentalist congregation. A superb study of a congregation influenced by the more moderate "new evangelical" heirs of fundamentalism is R. Stephen Warner, *New Wine in Old Wineskins: Evangelicals and Liberals in a Small Town* (Berkeley: University of California Press, 1988). Of the very few studies that use historical sources to take a close look at fundamentalist community life during the 1920s and 1930s, the two noteworthy ones are Virginia Lieson Brereton, *The Formation of the Bible Schools, 1880–1940* (Bloomington: Indiana University Press, 1990); and William Vance Trollinger, *God's Empire: William Bell Riley and Midwestern Fundamentalism* (Madison: University of Wisconsin Press, 1990).

5. Shirley Nelson, *The Last Year of the War* (New York: Harper & Row, 1978), 5.

6. "Oh, for the Bad Old Days," *MM* 37 (November 1936): 107.

7. J. Edwin Orr, *This Is The Victory* (London: Marshall, Morgan, & Scott, 1936), 91–92. Orr quotes his American friend, fundamentalist evangelist Clifford Lewis.

8. Virginia Lieson Brereton, "The Bible Schools and Conservative Evangelical Higher Education, 1880–1940," in *Making Higher Education Christian: The History and Mission of Evangelical Colleges in America,* ed. Joel A. Carpenter and Kenneth W. Shipps (Grand Rapids, Mich.: Eerdmans, 1987), 125–27.

9. Paul Bechtel, *Wheaton College: A Heritage Remembered, 1860–1984* (Wheaton, Ill.: Harold Shaw, 1984), 236. There were, of course, degrees of strictness. Billy Graham's odyssey from Bob Jones College to the Florida Bible Institute and then to Wheaton College was in part a reflection of his desire to train in places that were more encouraging and less intrusive. For Graham, Wheaton was liberating after the boot camp atmosphere at the evangelist Jones's school. See William Martin, *A Prophet with Honor: The Billy Graham Story* (New York: William Morrow, 1991), 70–84.

10. Buswell, *The Christian Life,* vol. 4 of *The Lamb of God* (Grand Rapids, Mich.: Zondervan, 1937), 87–88.

11. George M. Marsden, "Perspectives on the Division of 1937," in *Pressing toward*

the Mark: Essays Commemorating Fifty Years of the Orthodox Presbyterian Church, ed. Charles G. Dennison and Richard C. Gamble (Philadelphia: Orthodox Presbyterian Church, 1986), 295–328, is a thorough and astute treatment of this episode.

12. "The Sin of Timidity," *Revelation* 2 (December 1932): 489.

13. The most comprehensive statement of the fundamentalist ideals and expectations for the "Christian home" was compiled by evangelist John R. Rice. This work, *The Home: Courtship, Marriage and Children* (Wheaton, Ill.: Sword of the Lord, 1945) was a compendium of sermons and pamphlets on related topics, such as "Courtship and the Dangers of Petting," "Normal Sex Life in Marriage," "Wives Be Subject to Husbands," and "Winning Children to Christ in the Home," that Rice had produced over the years. For some richly detailed accounts of fundamentalist homes, see the oral history interviews of Vincent Leroy Crossett (Collection 288), Susan Schultz Bartel (Collection 57), Elisabeth Howard Elliot (Collection 278), Jeannette Louise Martig Thiessen (Collection 260), and Torrey Maynard Johnson (Collection 285) in the Archives of the Billy Graham Center, Wheaton College, Wheaton, Illinois.

14. See, for example, Walter E. Ellis, "Social and Religious Factors in the Fundamentalist–Modernist Schisms among Baptists in North America, 1895–1934" (Ph.D. diss., University of Pittsburgh, 1974), 161–75, which shows an unusually large number of young single men and women joining a fundamentalist congregation. See also the membership rolls of Calvary Undenominational Church and Wealthy Street (now Wealthy Park) Baptist Church, both in Grand Rapids, Michigan, for the fairly common occurance of membership entries showing one parent—usually a mother—plus children. Oral history interviews of Elizabeth Stair Small (Collection 164) and Ruth Sundquist (Collection 266), both in the Archives of the Billy Graham Center, document the experience of families that were incompletely converted to fundamentalist Christianity.

15. Everett L. Perry, "The Role of Socio-Economic Factors in the Rise and Development of American Fundamentalism" (Ph.D. diss., University of Chicago, 1959), 65–72, 412–25, 427–37, 440–46, 452–93, carefully describes several independent fundamentalist congregations in the Chicago area around 1944. See also Wilbur M. Smith, *A Voice for God: The Life of Charles E. Fuller, Originator of the Old Fashioned Revival Hour* (Boston: Fellowship Press, 1949), 88–94; Daniel P. Fuller, *Give the Winds a Mighty Voice: The Story of Charles E. Fuller* (Waco, Tex.: Word Books, 1972), 55–64; "Our Providence Service," *The Radio Caroller Announcer* 1 (May 1929): 11, 23; "The Providence Gospel Centre," *The Announcer* 1 (January 1930): 3; Angeline Dantuma, "Doors of Utterance," *The Announcer* 1 (February 1930): 10, 18–19; Mel Larson, *Young Man on Fire: The Story of Torrey Johnson and Youth for Christ* (Chicago: Youth Publications, 1945), 49–72; announcements of coming events at Calvary Baptist Church, New York, for the year 1939, which appear in *The Calvary Pulpit and Monthly Messenger,* ser. I, nos. 11–21 (1939); and the collected weekly bulletins for the years 1934–1941 on file at Wealthy Street (now Wealthy Park) Baptist Church, Grand Rapids, Michigan.

16. Perry, "Social and Economic Factors," 72–74, 91–94, 98–103.

17. Walter Lippmann, *A Preface to Morals* (New York: Macmillan, 1929), 31–32; H. L. Mencken, quoted from the *American Mercury* in Donald G. Barnhouse, "First Century Christianity," *Revelation* 3 (February 1933): 44.

18. "Annual Report of the Broadcasting Station of the Moody Bible Institute of Chicago for the Year Ending April 30, 1938," 28; "Annual Report of the Broadcasting Station . . . 1939," 311; both on file at station WMBI, Moody Bible Institute, Chicago.

19. Robert Wuthnow, *The Restructuring of American Religion: Society and Faith*

since World War II (Princeton, N.J.: Princeton University Press, 1988), 160–62, 168–72, confirms fundamentalists' fears, for it argues that colleges and universities have been among the most powerful religious and political liberalizing forces in twentieth-century America. George M. Marsden, *The Soul of the American University: From Protestant Establishment to Established Unbelief* (New York: Oxford University Press, 1994), traces the process of secularization in American higher education.

20. R. K. Johnson, *Builder of Bridges: The Biography of Dr. Bob Jones, Sr.* (Murfreesboro, Tenn.: Sword of the Lord, 1969), 195–98.

21. Gaebelein, "The Christian Graduate in the World Today," *Bulletin of Wheaton College* 8 (August 1931): 4.

22. James Oliver Buswell, Jr., "Reflecting on My 'Liberal' Education," *Serving and Waiting* 15 (February 1926): 548. See also Granville Hicks, "The Son of a Fundamentalist Prophet," *The Christian Register,* 10 March 1927, 197–98, reprinted in *The Uncertain World of Normalcy: The 1920s,* ed. Paul A. Carter (New York: Pitman, 1971), 143; "Satan in the Professor's Chair, by a Junior at College," *MM* 23 (January 1923): 200–201.

23. See, for example, Simon Littlefaith (pseud.), "How I Kept My Faith During College Years," *SST,* 7 March 1931, 134; O. Thompson, "A Sad Condition," *Evangelist* 1 (September 1931): 6; Joseph Stowell, "Death on the Campus," *Baptist Bulletin* 5 (July 1939): 1, 3–4; "Support Only Christian Colleges," *MM* 29 (June 1929): 471.

24. "What About Your Son or Daughter?" *MM* 38 (July 1938): 560.

25. Advertisement, *Watchman-Examiner,* 25 April 1933, 476; "Wheaton College," *Bulletin of Wheaton College* 13 (June 1936): 4.

26. "Wheaton College," 4–5; William J. Jones, "A Study in Contrasts," *Bulletin of Wheaton College* 8 (October 1931): 5–7.

27. Clarence E. Mason, "Where Shall I Go To College?" *Bulletin of Wheaton College* 8 (October 1930): 4.

28. "Social Security," *MM* 35 (January 1935): 215; "Bank Runs Invited," *SST,* 26 May 1934, 341; "Clouds without Water," Baptist Evangel, 1 August 1936, 3, 6.

29. Harry Emerson Fosdick, "The Peril of Worshiping Jesus," *The Church Monthly* 5 (January 1931): 43–48, reprinted in *The Fundamentalist–Modernist Conflict: Opposing Views on Three Major Issues,* ed. Joel A. Carpenter (New York: Garland, 1988).

30. See Marsden, *Fundamentalism and American Culture,* 4; Marsden, *Reforming Fundamentalism,* 4, 10; and Marsden, "Fundamentalism," in *Encyclopedia of the American Religious Experience: Studies of Traditions and Movements,* 3 vols., ed. Charles H. Lippy and Peter W. Williams (New York: Scribner's, 1988), II:947.

31. E. W. Crowell, "Why God Is Judging America," *Baptist Bulletin* 3 (May–June 1938): 5–6, 11–12.

32. One of the most famous and widely read of the fundamentalist behavioral guardians was the evangelist John R. Rice. See, for example, his *Lodges Examined by the Bible* (Findlay, Ohio: Fundamental Truth Publishers, n.d.), *What's Wrong with the Dance?* (Grand Rapids, Mich.: Zondervan, n.d. [ca. 1935]), and *What Is Wrong with the Movies?* (Grand Rapids, Mich.: Zondervan, 1938).

33. Riley, *The Confict of Christianity with Its Counterfeits* (Minneapolis: Irene Woods, 1940), 6.

34. Studies of contemporary separatist fundamentalism stress this continual struggle to maintain ideological closure. See Ammerman, *Bible Believers,* 40–71; and Peshkin, *God's Choice,* passim. According to Luther P. Gerlach and Virginia H. Hine, *People, Power, Change: Movements of Social Transformation* (Indianapolis: Bobbs-Merrill,

1970), 159–82, such behavior is common to grass-roots movements and functionally important for a variety of reasons.

35. Interview of Torrey Maynard Johnson (Collection 285), Archives of the Billy Graham Center.

36. Sandeen, *The Roots of Fundamentalism: British and American Millenarianism, 1800–1930* (Chicago: University of Chicago Press, 1970), 269.

37. Rice, *What's Wrong with the Dance?*, passim, 22 (long quote).

38. I am endebted to historians Margaret Bendroth and Edith Blumhofer for these insights. See Margaret L. Bendroth, *Fundamentalism and Gender, 1875 to the Present* (New Haven, Conn.: Yale University Press, 1993), 31–53; and Edith L. Blumhofer, "A Confused Legacy: Reflections on Evangelical Attitudes toward Ministering Women in the Past Century," *Fides et Historia* 22 (Winter/Spring 1990): 49–61. See also Betty DeBerg, *Ungodly Women: Gender and the First Wave of American Fundamentalism* (Minneapolis: Augsburg Fortress, 1990), which argues that a reaction to the increasing influence and freedom of women was one of the most important determinants in the rise of fundamentalism. This argument claims too much, I think, but antifeminism was definitely one of the several "antis" the movement developed in its formative stages.

39. Rice, *Bobbed Hair, Bossy Wives and Women Preachers* (Wheaton, Ill.: Sword of the Lord, 1941), 77, 65.

40. A. J. Gordon, "The Ministry of Women," *Missionary Review of the World* 17 (1894): 910–21. See also Janette Hassey, *No Time for Silence: Evangelical Women in Public Ministry around the Turn of the Century* (Grand Rapids, Mich.: Zondervan, 1986).

41. Blumhofer, "Reflections on Evangelical Attitudes," 55–58.

42. D. E. Hoste, "For the Evangelization of Unreached Areas," *China's Millions* 37 (May 1929): 67–68; "Editorial Notes: A Call for New Workers," *China's Millions* (July 1929): 111. For a list of North American candidates, see "North America's Contribution to the Two Hundred," *China's Millions* 40 (February 1932): 30.

43. For an example of someone who did nearly all of these things at one time or another during the 1930s and 1940s, listen to the oral history interview of Elizabeth Morell Evans (Collection 279), Archives of the Billy Graham Center. Ethel May Baldwin and David V. Benson, *Henrietta Mears and How She Did It* (Glendale, Calif.: Regal Books, 1966), tells the story of one of the most influential of a cadre of women fundamentalist Sunday school specialists. See also Bendroth, *Fundamentalism and Gender,* 73–89; and Michael S. Hamilton, "Women, Public Ministry, and American Fundamentalism, 1920–1950," *Journal of Religion and American Culture* 3 (Summer 1993): 174–80.

44. Bendroth, *Fundamentalism and Gender,* 63; William J. Hopewell, *The Missionary Emphasis of the General Association of Regular Baptist Churches* (Chicago: Regular Baptist Press, 1963), 55, documents the stepping down of Lucy Peabody. This incident is also treated in Ruth Tucker, "Women in Missions: Reaching Sisters in 'Heathen Darkness,'" in *Earthen Vessels: American Evangelicals and Foreign Missions, 1880–1980,* ed. Joel A. Carpenter and Wilbert R. Shenk (Grand Rapids, Mich.: Eerdmans, 1990), 270–71.

45. Margaret L. Bendroth, "Fundamentalism and Femininity: The Reorientation of Women's Roles in the 1920s," *Evangelical Studies Bulletin* 5 (March 1988): 1.

46. "The Place of the Bible," *Revelation* 8 (May 1938): 195.

47. Some important secular pundits agreed with the fundamentalists about the new theories' faith-destroying implications (if nothing else), so the liberals' revisionist views drew fire from both sides. For fundamentalists' arguments, see Donald Grey Barnhouse, "First Century Christianity," *Revelation* 3 (February 1933): 44; and Alexander

Fraser, "The Indiscipline of the Era," *MM* 40 (September 1939): 16. For a secular intellectual's similar reasoning, see Walter Lippmann, *A Preface to Morals* (New York: Macmillan, 1929), 25–35; and for an insightful commentary on these views and liberal Protestants' embattled mediating position, see William R. Hutchison, *The Modernist Impulse in American Protestantism* (Cambridge, Mass.: Harvard University Press, 1976), 257–87.

48. Mark A. Noll, Introduction to *The Princeton Defense of Plenary Verbal Inspiration,* ed. Mark A. Noll (New York: Garland, 1988); Randall H. Balmer, "The Princetonians and Scripture: A Reconsideration," *Westminster Theological Journal* 44 (Spring 1982): 352–65.

49. Lewis Spitz, "History: Sacred and Secular," *Church History* 47 (1978): 5–22; B. B. Warfield, "Calvin's Doctrine of Creation," *Princeton Theological Review* 13 (1915), reprinted in *The Princeton Theology, 1812–1921,* ed. Mark A. Noll (Grand Rapids, Mich.: Baker, 1983), 293–98. I am indebted to Mark Noll for this insight. See his response to an earlier version of my work on this subject, "Primitimism in Fundamentalism and American Biblical Scholarship: A Response," in *The American Quest for the Primitive Church,* ed. Richard T. Hughes (Urbana: University of Illinois Press, 1988), 120–28.

50. Mark A. Noll, *Between Faith and Criticism: Evangelicals, Scholarship, and the Bible in America* (San Francisco: Harper & Row,1986), 32–47, 56–61.

51. George M. Marsden, *Fundamentalism and American Culture: The Shaping of Twentieth-Century Evangelicalism, 1870–1925* (New York: Oxford University Press, 1980), 63–65.

52. Ernest R. Sandeen, *The Roots of Fundamentalism: British and American Millenarianism, 1800–1930* (Chicago: University of Chicago Press, 1970), xiii.

53. I am indebted here to Timothy Weber, *Living in the Shadow of the Second Coming: American Premillennialism, 1875–1982,* rev. ed. (Chicago: University of Chicago Press, 1987), 9–24, 36–42; but see also Sandeen, *Roots of Fundamentalism,* 59–70; and Marsden, *Fundamentalism and American Culture,* 48–66.

54. Noll, *Between Faith and Criticism,* 51–61.

55. Noll, Introduction, *The Princeton Defense.*

56. Marsden, *Fundamentalism,* 56, 122.

57. Noll, *Between Faith and Criticism,* 56–61; Marsden, *Fundamentalism and American Culture,* 191, 212–21. Both Noll, *Between Faith and Criticism,* 91–121, and Marsden, *Reforming Fundamentalism: Fuller Seminary and the New Evangelicalism* (Grand Rapids, Mich.: Eerdmans, 1987), 13–82, also tell of a small cohort of younger fundamentalist scholars who in the late 1930s and the 1940s were beginning to restore some intellectual integrity to fundamentalists' study of the Bible.

58. George M. Marsden, "Understanding Fundamentalist Views of Science," in *Science and Creationism,* ed. Ashley Montagu (New York: Oxford University Press, 1984), 95–116.

59. Ronald L. Numbers, *The Creationists: The Evolution of Scientific Creationism* (New York: Knopf, 1992), 60–71, 102–17. Numbers also recounts the rise of the American Scientific Affiliation in 1941, an organization of university-trained scientists from fundamentalist and other conservative Protestant communities. These scientists eventually developed several theories of theistic creation that could be reconciled with evolutionary theory, and thus parted ways with the more unrelenting anti-evolutionists (*The Creationists,* 158–83).

60. Wilbur M. Smith, *A Watchman on the Wall: The Life Story of Will H. Houghton* (Grand Rapids, Mich.: Eerdmans, 1951), 142–48; Gene A. Getz, *MBI: The Story of the Moody Bible Institute* (Chicago: Moody Press, 1969), 314–21.

61. This idea is borrowed from sociologist Michael A. Cavanaugh, the author of "A Sociological Account of Scientific Creationism: Science, True Science, Pseudoscience" (Ph.D. diss., University of Pittsburgh, 1983), as quoted in George M. Marsden, "Creation versus Evolution: No Middle Way," *Nature,* 13 October 1983, 572.

62. See the entire second half of Numbers, *The Creationists,* which documents the resurgence of the movement; see also Edward J. Larson, *Trial and Error: The American Controversy over Creation and Evolution* (New York: Oxford University Press, 1985), which focuses on the legal aspects of the ongoing conflict.

63. Albright summarized the implications of recent findings for biblical studies and theology in his "Archaeology Confronts Biblical Criticism," *American Scholar* 7 (April 1938): 176–88. See also his *From the Stone Age to Christianity: Monotheism and the Historical Process* (Baltimore: The Johns Hopkins University Press, 1940).

64. "An Inconsistent Archaeologist," *MM* 31 (May 1931): 437–38; "Behind the Times," *Revelation* 1 (September 1931): 304; "Archaeology and the Bible Agree Again!" *SST,* 28 November 1931, 669–70; and "Confirming Moses," *MM* 34 (April 1934): 348.

65. H. E. Irwin, "Testing the Higher Criticism in the Law Courts," *SST,* 21 January 1933, 43–44.

66. "Steps Down," *Revelation* 9 (September 1939): 350.

67. Phil Saint, "A Rare Species," *Presbyterian Guardian,* 7 October 1935, 28.

68. This paragraph borrows heavily from a passage in Timothy Weber, "The Two-Edged Sword: The Fundamentalist Use of the Bible," in *The Bible in America: Essays in Cultural History,* ed. Nathan O. Hatch and Mark A. Noll (New York: Oxford University Press, 1982), 102.

69. Virginia Lieson Brereton, *The Formation of American Bible Schools, 1880–1940* (Bloomington: Indiana University Press, 1990), 97–98.

70. See, for example, the dialogue throughout Shirley Nelson's novel about fundamentalists, *The Last Year of the War* (New York: Harper & Row, 1978).

71. Advertisement, *MM* 28 (September 1927): inside cover; John Hay, "A New Society: The S.T.T.L. [Spare Tire Testimony League]," *MM* 37 (June 1937): 520; "Gospel Advertising," *Alliance Weekly,* 10 October 1936, 646.

72. Martin E. Marty, "America's Iconic Book," in *Humanizing America's Iconic Book,* ed. Gene M. Tucker and Douglas A. Knight (Chico, Calif.: Scholar's Press, 1982), 18.

73. Everett L. Perry, "The Role of Socio-Economic Factors in the Rise and Development of American Fundamentalism" (Ph.D. diss., University of Chicago, 1959), 67, 74, 98–99.

74. Thomas Howard, *Christ The Tiger* (Wheaton, Ill.: Harold Shaw, 1967), 75–76.

Chapter 4

1. This expression comes from the third chapter of the Gospel of John, where Jesus tells the religious leader Nicodemus: "Except a man be born again, he cannot see the Kingdom of God" (John 3:3).

2. Henry C. Vedder, *The Fundamentals of Christianity: A Study of the Teachings of Jesus and Paul* (New York: Macmillan, 1922), 187–95; Harry Emerson Fosdick, "True Christianity is Progressive," in *Fundamentalism versus Modernism,* ed. Eldred C. Vanderlaan (New York: H. W. Wilson, 1925), 52; and Shailer Mathews, *The Faith of Modernism* (New York: Macmillan, 1925), 155–62 exemplify liberal Protestants' criticisms of substitutionary blood atonement.

3. Dyson Hague, "At-One-Ment by Propitiation," *The Fundamentals* 11 (Chicago: Testimony Publishing, n.d. [c. 1914]), 23–42; J. Gresham Machen, *Christianity*

and Liberalism (New York: Macmillan, 1923), 117–56; John Horsch, *Modern Religious Liberalism: The Destructivenenss and Irrationality of the New Theology* (Scottdale, Pa.: Fundamental Truth Depot, 1921), 94–104.

4. Fundamentalists used terms such as *conversion* and *born again,* which are common to most Christians, in ways that were shaped by the revivals of the eighteenth and nineteenth centuries and the rise of evangelical movements in transatlantic Protestantism. For fundamentalists as well as for most other evangelicals, an experience of conversion, of a dramatic turn from a life marked by sinfulness to a new life of godliness, was virtually the only way to be saved. Evangelicals usually disallowed or at least distrusted the more gradual and often less experientially intense paths to saving faith taught by Catholics, Lutherans, and many of the older Calvinist denominations. The idea of being born again, which the more sacramental churches attached to the rite of baptism, thus came to be equated with conversion. Many evangelicals, such as those in the Wesleyan holiness movement or the pentecostals, developed other significant spiritual and emotional waymarks beyond conversion, but for fundamentalists the conversion event had unrivalled experiential importance.

5. Daniel P. Stevick, *Beyond Fundamentalism* (Richmond, Va.: John Knox, 1964), 57–58, makes this observation and reconstructs a typical fundamentalist "liturgy" of invitation.

6. "Tell Me! Oh, Tell Me!" *The Pilot* 10 (May 1930): 253; "A Hebrew Christian Testimony," *Moody Church News* 21 (November 1936): 7; Will H. Houghton, "Is Life Worth Living?" *MM* 42 (March 1942): 398–99, 429, are typical of the frequent testimonies of conversion and accounts of "soul-winning" experiences.

7. See the accounts of "going forward" in the oral history interviews of Raymond Bates Buker, Jr. (Collection 262), Jennie Eliza Kingston Fitzwilliam (Collection 272), Elisabeth Howard Elliot (Collection 278), and George Murray Winston (Collection 306), in the Archives of the Billy Graham Center, Wheaton College, Wheaton, Illinois.

8. See, for example, Albert W. Lorimer, *God Runs My Business: The Story of R. G. LeTourneau* (New York: Fleming H. Revell, 1941), 108, 158; Elmer L. Wilder, "The Gospel in Cellophane," *The King's Business* 30 (September 1939): 338–39.

9. George M. Marsden, *Fundamentalism and American Culture: The Shaping of Twentieth-Century Evangelicalism, 1870–1925* (New York: Oxford University Press, 1980), 80–93.

10. Donald W. Dayton, Introduction to *The Prophecy Conference Movement,* 4 vols., ed. Donald W. Dayton (New York: Garland Publishing, 1988), I:[vii–xvi].

11. One can see this narrowing process very clearly in the career of Amzi Clarence Dixon, distinguished pulpiteer of the late nineteenth and early twentieth centuries. See A. C. Dixon, *Evangelism Old and New: God's Search for Man in all Ages* (New York: American Tract Society, 1905), esp. 32–57; Helen C. A. Dixon, *A. C. Dixon: A Romance of Preaching* (New York: G. P. Putnam's Sons, 1931), 145–56; and Brenda M. Meehan, "A. C. Dixon: An Early Fundamentalist," *Foundations* 10 (January 1967): 50–63.

12. Virginia Lieson Brereton, "The Bible Schools and Conservative Evangelical Higher Education, 1880–1940," in *Making Higher Education Christian: The History and Mission of Evangelical Colleges in America,* ed. Joel A. Carpenter and Kenneth W. Shipps (Grand Rapids, Mich.: Eerdmans, 1987), 110–36.

13. David R. Enlow, *Men Aflame: The Story of Christian Business Men's Committee International* (Grand Rapids, Mich.: Zondervan, 1962), 5–24; Mel Larson, *Youth for Christ: Twentieth-Century Wonder* (Grand Rapids, Mich.: Zondervan, 1947), 30–50.

See also Bruce Shelley, "The Rise of Evangelical Youth Movements," *Fides et Historia* 18 (January 1986): 45–63.

14. The best analysis of Rader and the widespread emulation of his tabernacle style is Larry K. Eskridge, "Only Believe: Paul Rader and the Chicago Gospel Tabernacle, 1922–1933" (M.A. thesis, University of Maryland, 1985). See also Everett L. Perry, "The Role of Socio-Economic Factors in the Rise and Development of American Fundamentalism" (Ph.D. diss., University of Chicago, 1959), which contains a wealth of detail about selected "gospel tabernacle" and Bible church" congregations in metropolitan Chicago. For an example of how the tabernacle style was disseminated, see the widely used and long-lived songbook, *Tabernacle Hymns No. 2,* comp. Paul Rader (New York: Alliance Publishing, 1921), which put revival-style gospel songs in the hymnal racks of thousands of fundamentalist churches.

15. "Debtor to the Jews," *MBI Bull* 10 (April 1931): 12.

16. Carl Bode, *Mencken* (Carbondale, Ill.: Southern Illinois University Press, 1969), 149–51.

17. Interview with Torrey Maynard Johnson, 23 October 1984 (Collection 285), Archives of the Billy Graham Center,.

18. Shirley Nelson, "Before Jo and Ed: Backgrounds," lecture presented at a colloquium, "Evangelicals in Modern America: Personal Perspectives," held at Wheaton College, Wheaton, Illinois, 31 October 1988.

19. Superb explications of the centrality of the new birth for earlier evangelical communities are Donald G. Mathews, *Religion in the Old South* (Chicago: University of Chicago Press, 1977), 10–38; and George Rawlyk, *Ravished by the Spirit: Religious Revivals, Baptists, and Henry Alline* (Montreal: McGill-Queen's University Press, 1984), 109–36. Marsden, *Fundamentalism and American Culture,* 44–46; and Sandra Sizer, *Gospel Hymns and Social Religion* (Philadelphia: Temple University Press, 1978), 50–82, 112–15, show the continuing importance of a common born-again experience for evangelical community in Moody's day; while Shirley Nelson, *Last Year of the War* (New York: Harper & Row, 1978), 20–26, portrays a powerful bonding among young women at a Bible school in the 1940s after they related their conversion testimonies.

20. Formerly the Heart of Africa Mission, founded by one of the famous "Cambridge Seven" missionary volunteers, C. T. Studd. For background, see Norman P. Grubb, *C. T. Studd, Athlete and Pioneer* (Atlantic City, N.J.: World-Wide Revival Prayer Movement, 1943); and N. P. Grubb, *Successor to C. T. Studd: The Story of Jack Harrison* (London: Lutterworth, 1949).

21. Interview of Helen Torrey Renich (Collection 124), Archives of the Billy Graham Center.

22. George M. Marsden, "Fundamentalism," in *Encyclopedia of the American Religious Experience,* 3 vols., ed. Charles H. Lippy and Peter W. Williams (New York: Scribner's, 1988), II:952. See also Marsden's extended treatment of the Victorious Life holiness teaching in *Fundamentalism and American Culture,* 72–101.

23. Steven Barabas, *So Great Salvation: The History and Message of the Keswick Convention* (London: Marshall, Morgan & Scott, 1957); and John Pollock, *The Keswick Story: The Authorized History of the Keswick Convention* (London: Hodder & Stoughton, 1964). For a treatment of the movement's development in North America, see C. Melvin Loucks, "The Theological Foundations of the Victorious Life: An Evaluation of the Theology of the Victorious Christian Life in the Light of the Present and Future Aspects of Biblical Sanctification" (Ph.D. diss., Fuller Theological Seminary, 1984).

24. Loucks, "Theological Foundations of the Victorious Life," 33–108.

25. Barabas, *So Great Salvation,* 148–55. For a fuller treatment of the faith missions ethos in American fundamentalism, see my chapter, "Propagating the Faith Once Delivered: The Fundamentalist Missionary Enterprise, 1920–1945," in *Earthen Vessels: American Evangelicals and Foreign Missions, 1880–1980,* ed. Joel A. Carpenter and Wilbert R. Shenk (Grand Rapids, Mich.: Eerdmans, 1990), 92–132.

26. Mrs. Howard Taylor, *The Triumph of John and Betty Stam* (Philadelphia: China Inland Mission, 1925), 39. See also Andrew Porter, "Late Nineteenth-Century Missionary Expansion: A Consideration of Some Non-Anglican Sources of Inspiration," in *Religious Motivation: Biographical and Sociological Problems for the Church Historian,* ed. Derek Baker (Oxford: Basil Blackwell, 1978), 358–59.

27. Interview of Ruth Sundquist (Collection 266), Archives of the Billy Graham Center. On the vintage character of the "being willing to be made willing" appeal, see William Borden's use of it some thirty years earlier on the Student Volunteers circuit in Mrs. Howard Taylor, *Borden of Yale, '09: The Life that Counts* (Philadelphia: China Inland Mission, 1926), 216–18; and see the interview of Eleanor Ruth Elliott for her encounter with this appeal at a Christian Endeavor conference circa 1920.

28. Mrs. Howard Taylor, *Borden of Yale,* 218; see also David M. Howard, "The Road to Urbana and Beyond," *Evangelical Missions Quarterly* 21 (January 1985): 17, for a contemporary example of this argument.

29. This is, of course, the title of one of the devotional favorites of the fundamentalist movement, reprinted many times: Oswald Chambers, *The Golden Book of Oswald Chambers: My Utmost for His Highest: Selections for the Year* (London: Simpkin, Marshall, 1927). Chambers was a young Bible teacher who worked for the YMCA during World War I, and in that capacity served the British troops in Egypt. He died there in 1917. His devotional works, published posthumously from his lectures and addresses, express a fairly radical (some might say morbid) version of the Keswick movement's stress on self-denial.

30. Lillie F. Oliver, *Richard Weber Oliver, A Challenge to American Youth* (Providence, R.I.: Challenge Publishing Company, 1932), 108–60, offers some valuable first-hand accounts of life within a small fundamentalist Bible school in Massachusetts.

31. W. Phillip Keller, quoted in John Kayser, "How A Bible Institute Imparts Missionary Vision," *Evangelical Missions Quarterly* 21 (October 1985): 406–7. Valuable descriptions of life at Bible schools can be found in Isobel Kuhn's memoirs, *By Searching* (London: China Inland Mission, 1957), 60–70; Interviews of Elizabeth Stair Small (Collection 164), Zoe Anne Alford (Collection 177), Helen Nowack Frame (Collection 255), Ruth Sundquist (Collection 266), Jennie Eliza Kingston Fitzwilliam (Collection 272), in the Archives of the Billy Graham Center. See also Brereton, "Bible Schools," 122–28. Bible school life receives sensitive, carefully detailed treatment in Shirley Nelson's *The Last Year of the War,* a novel situated at a school closely resembling the Moody Bible Institute in the mid-1940s.

32. Brereton, "Bible Schools," 121–22; Kuhn, *By Searching,* 65–70, 79–93; E. Schuyler English, *By Life or By Death: Excerpts and Lessons from the Diary of John C. Stam* (Grand Rapids, Mich.: Zondervan, 1930), 20, 27, 34; Taylor, *John and Betty Stam,* 17–23.

33. "The World-Wide Ministry of Moody Students," *MBI Bull* 15 (March 1936): 18; "Fields of Service," *MBI Bull* 16 (September 1936): 9; Joseph I. Parker, ed., *Interpretative Statistical Survey of the World Mission of the Christian Church* (New York: International Missionary Council, 1938), 43.

34. Rowland V. Bingham explained the nonsectarian principles for the Sudan Inte-

rior Mission in his history of the mission, *Seven Sevens of Years and a Jubilee!* (Toronto: Evangelical Publishers, 1943), 101–8. Both Ralph Davis of the Africa Inland Mission and T. J. Bach of the Scandinavian Alliance Mission were involved in the early planning for the National Association of Evangelicals. For fundamentalists' role in organizing the NAE see Joel A. Carpenter, "The Fundamentalist Leaven and the Rise of an Evangelical United Front," in *The Evangelical Tradition in America,* ed. Leonard I. Sweet (Macon, Ga.: Mercer University Press, 1984), 257–88. On the renewal of the WEF, which tended to follow evangelical missions networks, see David M. Howard, *The Dream that Would Not Die: The Birth and Growth of the World Evangelical Fellowship, 1846–1986* (Exeter, England: Paternoster Press, 1986).

35. Paul M. Bechtel, *Wheaton College: A Heritage Remembered, 1860–1984* (Wheaton, Ill.: Harold Shaw, 1984), 146–50; interviews of Helen Torrey Renich (Collection 124), and Torrey Maynard Johnson, Archives of the Billy Graham Center.

36. Interviews of Donald Cook (Collection 259), Jeannette Martig Thiessen, and Helen Torrey Renich, Archives of the Billy Graham Center.

37. Marsden, *Reforming Fundamentalism: Fuller Seminary and the New Evangelicalism* (Grand Rapids, Mich.: Eerdmans, 1987), 45–46; H. Wilbert Norton, *To Stir The Church: A Brief History of the Student Foreign Missions Fellowships, 1936–1986* (Madison, Wis.: Student Foreign Missions Fellowship, 1986); Bechtel, *Wheaton College,* 194; Richard V. Pierard, "*Pax Americana* and the Evangelical Missionary Advance," in Carpenter and Shenk, eds., *Earthen Vessels,* 155–79.

38. Quoted in Douglas W. Frank, *Less than Conquerors: How Evangelicals Entered the Twentieth Century* (Grand Rapids, Mich.: Eerdmans, 1986), 119–20. For an extended discussion and critique of Charles G. Trumbull's teaching on the Victorious Christian Life, see ibid., 109–23, 145–54.

39. James Alan Patterson, "The Loss of a Protestant Missionary Consensus: Foreign Missions and the Fundamentalist–Modernist Conflict," in Carpenter and Shenk, eds., *Earthen Vessels,* 84; "In the Interests of Fair Play: Is There More than One Side to the Stanley Jones Matter?" *The King's Business* 18 (November 1927): 708–12; Marsden, *Reforming Fundamentalism,* 39–40.

40. Andrew Porter, "Evangelical Enthusiasm, Missionary Motivation and West Africa in the Late Nineteenth Century: The Career of G. W. Brooke," *Journal of Imperial and Commonwealth History* 6 (October 1977): 25–29; and Porter, "Cambridge, Keswick, and Late-Nineteenth-Century Attitudes toward Africa," *Journal of Imperial and Commonwealth History* 5 (October 1976): 5–34, examine this perfectionist dynamic at work on the mission field a generation earlier.

41. Marsden, *Reforming Fundamentalism,* is replete with examples of such attitudes, but according to Leonard I. Sweet, it is culpable for exercising too much restraint in exposing them. See Sweet, "Wise as Serpents, Innocent as Doves: The New Evangelical Historiography," *Journal of the American Academy of Religion* 56 (December 1988): 404–7.

42. Virginia Lieson Brereton, *Training God's Army: The American Bible School, 1880–1940* (Bloomington: Indiana University Press, 1990, 112–25. Nelson, *The Last Year of the War,* 120–28, is a fictional, albeit authentic episode of such manipulative spiritual counselling.

43. See the reminiscence of Amy Carmichael's impact on novelist Elisabeth Elliot, "The Person Who Influenced Me Most," *Christianity Today,* 7 October 1983, 26–31. See also the interview of Elisabeth Howard Elliot (Collection 278), Archives of the Billy Graham Center.

44. Tozer, *The Pursuit of God* (Harrisburg, Pa.: Christian Publications, 1948), 8. This

book is a refinement of themes developed in over a decade of column-writing for the *Alliance Weekly*.

45. Marsden, "From Fundamentalism to Evangelicalism: A Historical Analysis," in *The Evangelicals: What They Believe, Who They Are, Where They Are Changing*, ed. David F. Wells and John D. Woodbridge (Nashville, Tenn.: Abingdon, 1975), 129–33.

46. Peter Berger, "A Sociological View of the Secularization of Theology," *Journal for the Scientific Study of Religion* 8 (Spring 1967): 11–12.

47. Editorial, *Evangelical Beacon*, 22 September 1936, 12.

48. John R. Riebe, "The Separated, Not Segregated Life," *MM* 38 (April 1938): 407.

49. Russell T. Hitt, "Capital of Evangelicalism," *Christian Life* 5 (April 1952): 17. See also Ernest R. Sandeen, "Fundamentalism and American Identity," *Annals of the American Academy of Social and Political Sciences* 387 (January 1970): 60–61, which discusses the importance of such "institutional parallelism" for fundamentalism's longevity.

50. Edward John Carnell, "Post-Fundamentalist Faith," *Christian Century*, 26 August 1959, 971.

51. Edward John Carnell, "Orthodoxy: Cultic vs. Classical," *Christian Century*, 30 March 1960, 377–78.

52. Carnell, *The Case for Orthodox Theology* (Philadelphia: Westminster, 1959), 113–26.

53. Carnell, "Orthodoxy: Cultic vs. Classical," 377.

54. Moore, *Religious Outsiders and the Making of Americans* (New York: Oxford University Press, 1986), 149.

Chapter 5

1. An excellent explanation of the dispensational premillennialist viewpoint and this scenario for the end-times is found in Timothy P. Weber, *Living in the Shadow of the Second Coming: American Premillennialism, 1875–1982*, enl. ed. (Chicago: University of Chicago Press, 1987), 9–24. See also C. Norman Kraus, *Dispensationalism in America: Its Rise and Development* (Richmond, Va. John Knox Press, 1958); and Robert G. Clouse, ed., *The Meaning of the Millennium: Four Views* (Downers Grove, Ill.: InterVarsity Press, 1977).

2. Robert S. and Helen M. Lynd, *Middletown in Transition: A Study in Cultural Conflicts* (New York: Harcourt Brace, 1937), 491.

3. The best overview of intellectual ferment in the 1930s is Richard S. Pells, *Radical Visions and American Dreams: Culture and Social Thought in the Depression Years* (New York: Harper & Row, 1973). See also Warren Susman, "The Thirties," in *The Development of an American Culture*, ed. Stanley Coben and Lorman Ratner (Englewood Cliffs, N.J.: Prentice-Hall, 1970), 170–218; and Susman, Introduction, *Culture and Commitment, 1929–1945*, ed. Susman (New York: George Braziler, 1973), 1–19, which argue that the search for security was the era's dominant theme.

4. Lynd and Lynd, *Middletown in Transition*, 318.

5. Donald Grey Barnhouse, "Russia Wins The War!" *Revelation* 9 (December 1939): 477.

6. Barnhouse, "Tomorrow: Current Events in the Light of the Bible: Maelstrom," *Revelation* 10 (August 1940): 354, 376–77.

7. James M. Gray's editorials in the *Christian Worker's Magazine* reflect this line of thought; see, e.g., "The Federation of the World," 11 (November 1910): 78; "The Palace of Peace," 14 (October 1913): 74; "Bishop Hoss and Church Union," 12 (January 1912): 331; and "A New Type of Christianity," 11 (September 1910): 11–13. William E.

Blackstone's *Jesus Is Coming*, enl. ed. (Chicago: Fleming H. Revell, 1908), 230–42 addresses all of these themes as well. See also David A. Rausch, *Zionism within Early American Fundamentalism, 1878–1918: A Convergence of Two Traditions* (New York: Edwin Mellen Press, 1979), 262–69; and Weber, *Living in the Shadow*, 137–43.

8. On Balfour and Bolshevism, see Dwight Wilson, *Armageddon Now! The Premillenarian Response to Russia and Israel since 1917* (Grand Rapids, Mich.: Baker Book House, 36–85; on modernism and evolution, see George Marsden, *Fundamentalism and American Culture: The Shaping of Twentieth-Century Evangelicalism, 1870–1925* (New York: Oxford University Press, 1980), 141–64.

9. Leonard Sale-Harrison, "Mussolini and the Resurrection of the Roman Empire," *MM* 29 (April 1929): 386–87. For discussions of the speculation about Mussolini as Antichrist, see Wilson, *Armageddon Now!*, 81–84; and Weber, *Living in the Shadow*, 178–82.

10. Ralph C. and Edith F. Norton, "A Personal Interview with Mussolini," *SST*, 13 August 1932, 423.

11. Announcement, *SST*, 30 November 1935, 806.

12. Bauman, "'I Believe in the Resurrection of the Empire,'" *SST*, 2 December 1939, 886–87. See also Bauman, *Light from Bible Prophecy as Related to the Present Crisis* (New York: Revell, 1940), 16–24.

13. "Pastor Niemoeller is in Solitary Confinement," *Revelation* 8 (August 1938): 333 (quote); editorial notes, *Revelation* 6 (June 1936): 17; "Seeing Straight in Germany," *Revelation* 7 (December 1937): 494–95, 516–20.

14. Bauman, *N.R.A.—The Sign and Its Spiritual Significance* (n.p., n.d. [c. 1933]); see also Bauman, "The Blue Eagle and Our Duty as Christians," *SST*, 16 September 1933, 583–84; Barnhouse, "The Mark for Commerce," *Revelation* 3 (August 1933): 311–12; Walter P. Knight, "The Mark of the Beast, or Is AntiChrist at Hand?" *MM* 34 (July 1934): 493; "The Blue Eagle," *Revelation* 3 (September 1933): 329.

15. "An Age of Dictators," *MM* 33 (July 1933): 480. See also "Is The Ship of State Drifting?" *MM* 34 (June 1934): 443; editorial, *Bibliotheca Sacra* 93 (April–June 1936): 130–31; and M. H. Duncan, "Trends Toward Liberalism in America," *MM* 38 (November 1937): 118.

16. Wilson, *Armageddon Now!*, 215–18; Weber, *Living in the Shadow*, 201–3.

17. Mencken, quoted from the *American Mercury* in an editorial, "Mencken," *Revelation* 2 (May 1932): 204.

18. "Rehearsals," *SST*, 8 April 1933, 241.

19. All quoted in Charles G. Trumbull, *Prophecy's Light on Today* (New York: Revell, 1937), 60–61.

20. Cowley, *The Dream of the Golden Mountains: Remembering the 1930s* (New York: Penguin Books, 1981), 31–45, 171–75; advertisement, *MM* 40 (November 1940): 135.

21. Havner, *It Is Time* (New York: Revell, 1943), 83–85.

22. "Who Now Are the Pessimists?" *MM* 32 (February 1932): 280; see also Enock C. Dyrness, "Becoming Pessimistic," The Evangelist 42 (April 1931): 8; "The Reign of Fear in Europe," *SST*, 31 May 1941, 437; "The Failure of Christians," *MM* 40 (November 1939): 115; Trumbull, *Prophecy's Light on Today*, 28–30.

23. Bauman, *Light from Bible Prophecy*, 67.

24. Cf. Norman Thomas, *America's Way Out: A Program for Democracy* (New York: Macmillan, 1931). Although Thomas was the leader of the Socialist Party and thus the advocate of a "way out" that most Americans thought was way out of bounds, he, like the fundamentalists, was picking up on an important popular concern of his day.

25. "Old Time Prophecy and New Time Events," *SST,* 14 November 1937, 637; Trumbull, Introduction to Bauman, *Light from Bible Prophecy,* 3 (quoting Luke 21:26); Trumbull, *Prophecy's Light on Today,* 34 (quoting Titus 2:13).

26. "Words of Comfort for Dark Days," *SST,* 8 June 1935, 385–86.

27. Ibid., 385, 391.

28. Ibid., 391; Trumbull quotes II Tim. 3:2–3 and Psalm 42:7.

29. Trumbull, "Words of Comfort" (quoting Luke 21:28), 341.

30. Louis Bauman, *The Time of Jacob's Trouble* (Long Beach, Calif.: By the author, 1939), 114.

31. Weber, *Living in the Shadow,* 137–41. See also Yaakov Ariel, *On Behalf of Israel: American Fundamentalist Attitudes toward Jews, Judaism, and Zionism, 1865–1945* (Brooklyn, N.Y.: Carlson Publishing, 1991).

32. Weber, *Living in the Shadow,* 144.

33. "Debtor to the Jews," *MBI Bull* 10 (April 1931): 12. See also J. A. Vaus, "Jewish Department of the Bible Institute of Los Angeles," *The King's Business* 21 (October 1930): 460.

34. "Debtor to the Jews," 12; Isobel Kuhn, *By Searching* (London: China Inland Mission, 1957), 65–70.

35. Jacob Gartenhaus, editorial in the *Hebrew Christian Alliance Quarterly,* quoted in *The Pilot* 10 (May 1930): 253.

36. O. W. Stambrough to D. O. Fuller, editor, published in *Baptist Bulletin* 3 (February 1938): 13.

37. "Fairness to the Jews," *Revelation* 4 (January 1934): 7; Louis Bauman, "The Great Red Dragon and the Woman's Child—in 1934," *The King's Business* 25 (March 1934): 94; "This Magazine Not Anti-Semitic," *The Pilot* 14 (April 1934): 195; Will H. Houghton, "The Jew—His Present and Future," *SST,* 11 August 1934, 511; Donald G. Barnhouse, "Anti-Semitism in America," *Revelation* 6 (May 1936): 229; "Dwelling in the Tents of Shem," *Bibliotheca Sacra* 96 (April–June 1939): 133–34. For discussions of stereotyping in an American context, see Jonathan D. Sarna, "American Anti-Semitism," in *History and Hate,* ed. David Berger (Philadelphia: Jewish Publication Society, 1986), 115–27; and John Higham, *Send These to Me: Jews and Other Immigrants in Urban America* (New York: Athenaeum, 1975), 116–37.

38. John Robertson Macartney, "The Spread of Communism in Our Land," *MM* 35 (May 1935): 413; Mark Matthews, "The Place of the Jews," *Revelation* 2 (July 1932): 284, 307–8.

39. See especially Bauman, *The Time of Jacob's Trouble.*

40. "Jews in Germany," *MM* 33 (May 1933): 322; "The Jews in Germany," *MM* 34 (July 1934): 506; Birnbaum, "Conrad Hoffman's World Report on the Jews," *MM* 35 (December 1934): 167. For examples of similarly diverging perspectives, see W. B. Riley, "Why Recognize Russia and Rag Germany?" *The Pilot* 14 (January 1934): 109–10; and Barnhouse, "Seeing Straight in Germany," 495, 516–17.

41. "Hitler's Cake," *Revelation* 3 (September 1933): 329; and "Fairness to the Jews," *Revelation* 4 (January 1934): 7; Barnhouse, "Anti-Semitism in America," *Revelation* 6 (May 1936): 229; Bauman, "The Great Red Dragon and the Woman's Child—in 1934," 94; Bauman, *Time of Jacob's Trouble;* "The Spirit of Persecution," *Bibliotheca Sacra* 94 (January 1937): 6–7; "Dwelling in the Tents of Shem," *Bibliotheca Sacra* 96 (April–June 1939): 133–34; and "Warnings from History," *Bibliotheca Sacra* 96 (July–September 1939): 263; LeBaron W. Kinney, "Why Are the Jews Hated?" *Revelation* 9 (February 1939): 59, 80.

42. "For Fear of the Jews," *The Pilot* 13 (July 1933): 298–99.

43. Weber, *Living in the Shadow*, 184–89. But see David A. Rausch, "Our Hope: An American Fundamentalist Journal and the Holocaust, 1937–1945," *Fides et Historia* 12 (Spring 1980): 89–103, for a much more favorable reading of Gaebelein's views. Weber and Rausch debated their differences in the *Journal of the Evangelical Theological Society:* Rausch, "Fundamentalism and the Jew: An Interpretive Essay," vol. 23 (June 1980): 105–12; Weber, "A Reply to David Rausch's 'Fundamentalism and the Jew,'" vol. 24 (March 1981): 67–71; Rausch, "A Rejoinder to Timothy Weber's Reply," vol. 24 (March 1981): 73–77; Weber, "A Surrejoinder to David Rausch's Rejoinder," vol. 24 (March 1981): 79–82.

44. Ross, *So It Was True: The American Protestant Press and the Nazi Persecution of the Jews* (Minneapolis: University of Minnesota Press, 1980), 30–36, 70, 103–3, 161–62, 195–96, 273–74.

45. Ibid., 70, 103–4, 161–62, 195–96, 273–74; notice, *Moody Church News* 21 (April 1936): 5; Advertisements of these relief groups can be found in *Revelation* 10 (October 1940): inside front cover; vol. 14 (July 1944): 307; vol. 14 (December 1944): inside front cover. These notices appeared in other major magazines as well, notably the *Moody Monthly,* the *Sunday School Times,* and *The King's Business.* For a discussion of rescue efforts, see interview of George Murray Winston (Collection 306), Archives of the Billy Graham Center, Wheaton College, Wheaton, Illinois.

46. A classic critique of millenarian cultural pessimism and passivity is Shailer Mathews, *Will Christ Come Again?* (Chicago: American Institute of Sacred Literature, 1917), reprinted in *The Fundamentalist–Modernist Conflict: Opposing Views on Three Major Issues,* ed. Joel A. Carpenter (New York: Garland, 1988).

47. Quoted in the editorial "The World's Redemption," *Alliance Weekly,* 5 September 1936, 566.

48. "The Church's Greatest Failure," *SST,* 28 October 1939, 749. He quotes Acts 15:14.

49. See, for example, James M. Gray's editorials "The Second Coming of Christ and Reform Movements," *The Institute Tie* 10 (July 1910): 856; "Social Problems," *Christian Worker's Magazine* 12 (May 1912): 588.

50. "A Crop Survey," *SST,* 28 July 1934, 485.

51. C. P. Perrie, letter to the editor, *New York Times,* 3 September 1933, E5.

52. "The Blue Eagle," *Revelation* 3 (September 1933): 329. Other commentary on the Blue Eagle includes Barnhouse, "The Mark for Commerce"; Louis S. Bauman, "The Blue Eagle and Our Duty as Christians," *SST,* 16 September 1933, 383; "NRA," *MM* 34 (November 1934): 96.

53. "Is the Ship of State Drifting?" *MM* 34 (June 1934): 443.

54. David Brion Davis, ed., *The Fear of Conspiracy: Images of Un-American Subversion form the Revolution to the Present* (Ithaca, N.Y.: Cornell University Press, 1971); Davis, *The Slave Power Conspiracy and the Paranoid Style* (Baton Rouge: Louisiana State University Press, 1969); and Higham, *Send These to Me: Jews and Other Immigrants in Urban America,* 116–37, which discusses the extent and limits of Populists' conspiratorial anti-Semitism. Fundamentalists' inheritance and refitting of older conspiracy themes is shown most clearly in Richard Taylor, "Beyond Immediate Emancipation: Jonathan Blanchard, Abolitionism and the Emergence of American Fundamentalism," *Civil War History* 27 (1981) 260–74, in which he shows Blanchard, an evangelical abolitionist reformer, transforming the antebellum conspiratorial view of the Masons and the "Slave Power Conspiracy" into a proto-fundamentalist outlook after the Civil War.

55. The best exposition of this theme is in Marsden, *Fundamentalism and American Culture,* 141–70, 184–92, 206–11.

56. "Defenders' Convention A Great Success," *Christian Fundamentals in School and Church* 9 (January–February–March 1927): 8–10.

57. Norman F. C. Cohn, *Warrant for Genocide: The Myth of the Jewish World Conspiracy and the "Protocols of the Elders of Zion"* (New York: Harper & Row, 1969), 25–76.

58. On Ford's attack, see ibid., 158–64; and Leo P. Ribuffo, "Henry Ford and *The International Jew,*" *American Jewish History* 69 (June 1980): 437–77.

59. Leo P. Ribuffo, *The Old Christian Right: The Protestant Far Right from the Great Depression to the Cold War* (Philadelphia: Temple University Press, 1983), 97; Weber, *Living in the Shadow,* 154–56.

60. The *Moody Monthly* series ran from August through October 1931. A fundamentalist "expert" on communism, Elizabeth Knauss, published a series of articles in Riley's monthly magazine, *The Pilot,* which ran from October of 1932 through June of 1933.

61. Arno C. Gaebelein, *Half A Century: The Autobiography of a Servant* (New York: "Our Hope" Publishing Office, 1930); David A. Rausch, *Arno C. Gaebelein, 1861–1945: Irenic Fundamentalist and Scholar* (New York: Edwin Mellen, 1983).

62. Arno C. Gaebelein, *The Conflict of the Ages: The Mystery of Lawlessness—Its Origin, Historic Development and Coming Defeat* (New York: "Our Hope" Publishing Office, 1933).

63. Weber, *Living in the Shadow,* 155–57.

64. Ibid., 189–91.

65. "The *Times* and the Jews," *SST,* 6 January 1934, 2; "Anti-Semitism and the Protocols," *MM* 34 (January 1934): 209; "Fairness to the Jews," *Revelation* 4 (January 1934): 6–7.

66. Weber, *Living in the Shadow,* 190; Timothy P. Weber, "Saved or Slaughtered: Ambivalence in Fundamentalist and Jewish Relations between the Wars," paper presented at the annual meeting of the American Historical Association, Cincinnati, Ohio, 29 December 1988, p. 9.

67. Barnhouse, "The Tanaka Secret Memorial," *Revelation* 5 (April 1935): 140; Bauman, "The Great Red Dragon and the Woman's Child," 94; Brooks, "Manifesto to the Jews," *Prophecy Monthly* 2 (October 1939): 1–19. See also J. A. Vaus, "In the Jewish World," *The King's Business* 25 (January 1934): 16. Vaus was the director of BIOLA's Jewish ministries program. He and others who led such missions, such as Solomon Birnbaum of the Moody Bible Institute, enjoyed close contact and often identification with the Jewish community. They provided a strong counterpoint to fundamentalists' other sources of information.

68. William Bell Riley, "For Fear of the Jews," *The Pilot* 13 (July 1933): 298–99; Riley, "American Jews and American Communism," *The Pilot* 15 (June 1935): 249–50; Riley, "Cohn vs. Riley," *The Pilot* 15 (May 1935): 218, 220; and Riley, "Character Slanders by Pseudo-Communists," *The Pilot* 20 (September 1940): 340, 346.

69. Ribuffo, *The Old Christian Right,* 109–18.

70. Ralph L. Roy, *Apostles of Discord: A Study of Organized Bigotry and Disruption on the Fringes of Protestantism* (Boston: Beacon Press, 1953), 354–55, notes Norris's stance; David Otis Fuller, "Hands Off the Jews!", sermon listed and abstracted in the November 25, 1937 bulletin of Wealthy Street Baptist Church, Grand Rapids, Michigan, now in the archives of Wealthy Park Baptist Church.

71. It is helpful to see fundamentalists' outlook and behavior within the context of American attitudes toward Jews more generally. Leonard Dinnerstein, "Christian-

Jewish Relations in the United States between World War I and World War II," a paper presented at the annual meeting of the American Historical Association, Cincinnati, Ohio, 29 December 1988, shows how pervasive anti-Semitism was in America at the time. A longer perspective is presented in Jonathan D. Sarna, "Jewish-Christian Hostility in the United States: Perceptions from a Jewish Point of View," in *Uncivil Religion,* ed. Robert N. Bellah and Frederick E. Greenspahn (New York: Crossroad, 1987), 5–22.

In his treatment of the issue in *The Old Christian Right,* Leo P. Ribuffo makes it clear that even Gerald Winrod's views, objectionable as they were for their anti-Semitism, were by no means the worst to be found. He argues that the Kansas preacher's dispensational views both contributed to his anti-Semitism and limited it. Winrod never exhibited the extreme hatred toward all Jews that characterized others on the Far Right in his day. Ribuffo's final assessment is that dispensationalism acted as an intensifier of Gentile Americans' typical mixed feelings of fascination, admiration, disapproval, and suspicion toward the Jews (97–115).

72. Ribuffo, *The Old Christian Right,* 249.

73. D. J. Fant, "This Machine Age," *Alliance Weekly,* 22 October 1932, 674–75.

74. "Civilization's Peril," *MM* 40 (July 1940): 591.

75. "It Must Not Happen Again," *MM* 41 (August 1941): 691–92.

76. "Evolution and This War," *SST,* 2 August 1941, 4.

77. Thomas M. Jacklin, "Mission to the Sharecroppers: Neo-Orthodox Radicalism and the Delta Farms Venture, 1936–1940," *South Atlantic Quarterly* 78 (Summer 1979): 302–16, provides an insightful look at neo-orthodox social action. See also Paul A. Carter, *The Decline and Revival of the Social Gospel: Social and Political Liberalism in American Protestant Churches, 1920–1940,* rev. ed. (Hamden, Conn.: Archon Books, 1971), 153–62, 213–19.

78. "The Church and Politics," *Revelation* 1 (June 1931): 200.

79. R. Laurence Moore, *Religious Outsiders and the Making of Americans* (New York: Oxford University Press, 1986), 149. Ribuffo's *The Old Christian Right* makes the case throughout that the views of the Far Right, not to mention those of more moderate fundamentalists, were very much in continuity with those of the American mainstream.

80. Houghton, *Let's Go Back to the Bible* (New York: Revell, 1939), 71.

81. Moore, *Religious Outsiders,* 159.

82. The classic study is Norman R. C. Cohn, *The Pursuit of the Millennium: Revolutionary Messianism in Medieval and Reformation Europe and Its Bearing on Modern Totalitarian Movements* (New York: Harper & Row, 1957). For examples of the more radical kinds of modern millenarianism, see J. F. C. Harrison, *The Second Coming: Popular Millenarianism, 1780–1850* (New Brunswick, N.J.: Rutgers University Press, 1979); W. H. Oliver, *Prophets and Millennialists: The Uses of Biblical Prophecy in England from the 1790s to the 1840s* (Auckland, N.Z.: Oxford University Press, 1978); and Grant Underwood, "Millenarianism and the Early Mormon Mind," *Journal of Mormon History* 8 (1981): 63–77. Underwood's superb historiographical essay should also be consulted; it is far more broad ranging than its title, "Early Mormon Millenarianism: Another Look," *Church History* 54 (June 1985): 215–29.

83. This kind of millennial thinking has a long history as well. Ernest R. Sandeen, *The Roots of Fundamentalism: British and American Millenarianism, 1800–1930* (Chicago: University of Chicago Press, 1970), gives a brief but helpful treatment and shows its influence on the rise of fundamentalism. There were some millenarian "fanatics" that had at least tangential relationships to early fundamentalism. The radical holiness movement that gave rise to pentecostalism was its main source. See, for example, the

following treatments of two holiness faith-healers who were self-proclaimed millenarian prophets: Shirley Nelson, *Fair, Clear and Terrible: The Story of Shiloh, Maine* (Latham, N.Y.: British American Publishing, 1989), is about the perfectionist commune established by Frank W. Sandeford; and Grant Wacker, "Marching to Zion: Religion in a Modern Theocracy," *Church History* 54 (December 1985): 496–511, looks at Zion, Illinois, the community founded by John Alexander Dowie.

84. Weber, *Living in the Shadow,* 43–81.

85. "How Should Christians Draw Up Their Wills in View of the Lord's Return?" *SST,* 25 March 1933, 210, 221. The editors advised him and their other readers to make orthodox Jewish friends the executors of their estates in the event of Rapture, and to direct them to distribute their estates for the evangelization of the Jews.

86. Barnhouse, "Maelstrom," 377.

87. See James West Davidson, *The Logic of Millennial Thought: Eighteenth-Century New England* (New Haven, Conn.: Yale University Press, 1977).

Chapter 6

1. "Revolution, Rapture, Revival," *Revelation* 2 (May 1932): 205.

2. "The Year Closes," *MM* 39 (December 1938): 171.

3. George M. Marsden, *Fundamentalism and American Culture: The Shaping of Twentieth-Century Evangelicalism, 1870–1925* (New York: Oxford University Press, 1980), 43.

4. Arno C. Gaebelein, *World Prospects: A Study in Sacred Prophecy and Present-Day World Conditions* (New York: Our Hope, 1934), 163.

5. Harold Lindsell, *Park Street Prophet: A Life of Harold John Ockenga* (Wheaton, Ill.: Van Kampen Press, 1951), 5.

6. "A Call to Prayer for Revival," *Revelation* 2 (May 1932): 205.

7. "Business Is Sick," *MM* 31 (October 1930): 52.

8. See, for examples, S. Paul Weaver, "Pray for Revival," *SST,* 31 March 1934, 209–10; J. D. Williams, "God's Cure for Depression," *Alliance Weekly,* 29 October 1932, 693; "A Call to Prayer for Revival"; "Business Is Sick."

9. "In the Tops of the Mulberry Trees," letter from William Allen Dean to Donald Grey Barnhouse published in *Revelation* 4 (October 1934): 381. Dean quotes from II Samuel 5:24, where King David was told by the Lord that the sign that the Lord was going "out before thee, to smite the host of the Philistines" would be "the sound of a going in the tops of the mulberry trees." Apparently, this obscure reference was used in evangelical circles to refer to a sign from the Lord to take the initiative.

10. J. Elwin Wright, "A New Year's Message," *The Sheaf of the First Fruits* 30 (January 1932): 2. For similar assessments, see "Fundamentalism's Light in a Dark World," *SST,* 9 July 1932, 361–62; and three editorials: "The Spirit of the Times," *The Evangelist* 4 (October 1934): 4; "Where Social Welfare Ended," *MM* 33 (November 1932): 96–97; and "Our Opportunity in a Business Depression," *SST,* 22 November 1930, 685.

11. J. Edwin Orr, *The Church Must First Repent* (London: Marshall, Morgan & Scott, 1937), 84–86. See a similar argument in Grace W. Woods, *By Way of Remembrance* (Atlantic City, N.J.: World Wide Revival Prayer Movement, 1933), 49–50.

12. Harry A. Ironside, *Notes on the Minor Prophets* (New York: Loizeaux Bros., 1909), 128–31; Arno C. Gaebelein, *The Annotated Bible: The Holy Scriptures Analyzed and Annotated,* 9 vols. (New York: Our Hope, 1913–1924), V:108; Edwin C. Diebler, "The Relation of the Church to the Kingdom," *Bibliotheca Sacra* 97 (1940): 359;

Harry Allan Ironside, *Lectures on the Book of the Acts* (New York: Loizeaux Bros., 1943), 46–49; Merrill F. Unger, "The Baptism with the Holy Spirit," p. II, *Bibliotheca Sacra* 101 (1944): 366, 373–74.

13. Ironside, *The Lamp of Prophecy* (Grand Rapids, Mich.: Zondervan, 1940), 148.

14. Timothy P. Weber, *Living in the Shadow of the Second Coming: American Premillennialism, 1875–1982,* enl. ed. (Chicago: University of Chicago Press, 1987), 19–20, 43–47, explains these unique features of dispensationalism.

15. Armin R. Gesswein, "Revival versus Apostasy," in *Preparing the Way* (Atlantic City, N.J.: World Wide Revival Prayer Movement, 1941), 28.

16. See Ernest M. Wadsworth, *Will Revival Come?* (Chicago: Great Commission Prayer League, 1937), 31–36; Paul W. Rood, *Let The Fire Fall* (Grand Rapids, Mich.: Zondervan, 1939), 32–33; Orr, *The Church Must First Repent,* 81–90; Vance Havner, *Road to Revival* (New York: Revell, 1940), 57–58.

17. Finney's work was so pervasively influential that revival promoters repeated his principles, and sometimes even his anecdotes, apparently without knowing the source. See, for example, Vance Havner, *It Is Time* (New York: Revell, 1943), 67.

18. Orr, *The Church Must First Repent,* 14–17.

19. Morphologies of revival like this one appear in Wadsworth, *Will Revival Come?,* 24–29; Havner, *It Is Time,* 63–69; George T. B. Davis, "How Prayer Brings Revival," in *Christ for America: A Nationwide Campaign for Union Evangelistic Meetings by Cities* (New York: Revell, 1943), 27–34; Paul W. Rood, *Can We Expect A World-Wide Revival?* (Grand Rapids, Mich.: Zondervan, 1940), 14; Armin Gesswein, "How Does A Revival Begin?" *MM* 44 (October 1943): 61–62, 86; Wilbur M. Smith, *The Glorious Revival under King Hezekiah* (Grand Rapids, Mich.: Zondervan, 1937).

20. These two quotes are in Orr, *This Is The Victory* (London: Marshall, Morgan & Scott, 1936), 92, 38. See also Havner, *Road to Revival,* 44–45; Oswald J. Smith, *The Revival We Need* (London: Marshall, Morgan & Scott, 1933), 47–49; Wadsworth, *Will Revival Come?,* 17–19; H. M. and G. W. Woods, "Letter No. 5," in Woods, *By Way of Remembrance,* 41–42.

21. Apparently, this rationalistic approach to conversion, like dispensationalism, came to the fundamentalists by way of the Plymouth Brethren. See Phyllis D. Airhart, "'What Must I Do To Be Saved?' Two Paths to Evangelical Conversion in Late Victorian Canada," *Church History* 59 (September 1990): 372–85.

22. Rudolph Nelson, *The Making and Unmaking of an Evangelical Mind: The Case of Edward Carnell* (New York: Cambridge University Press, 1987), esp. pp. 28–53, discusses the importance of apologetics to fundamentalists in the 1930s; see the whole book for a more extended discussion of the subject.

23. Grant Wacker, "The Functions of Faith in Primitive Pentecostalism," *Harvard Theological Review* 77 (1984): 353–75, gives an excellent account of the emotional and spiritual satisfactions pentecostals enjoyed.

24. Havner, *It Is Time,* 76.

25. Havner, *Road to Revival,* 57.

26. Wadsworth, *Will Revival Come?,* 20.

27. Grant Wacker, "The Holy Spirit and the Spirit of the Age in American Protestantism, 1880–1910," *Journal of American History* 72 (June 1985): 45–62.

28. The role of Keswick holiness teaching in fundamentalist faith missions and the influence of these missions and their piety on the larger fundamentalist movement are discussed and documented in detail in my essay, "Propagating the Faith Once Delivered: The Fundamentalist Missionary Enterprise, 1920–1945," in *Earthen Vessels: American*

Evangelicals and Foreign Missions, 1880–1980, ed. Joel A. Carpenter and Wilbert R. Shenk (Grand Rapids, Mich.: Eerdmans, 1990), 92–132 and especially 117–30.

29. George T. B. Davis, *When The Fire Fell* (Philadelphia: Million Testaments Campaign, 1945), 10.

30. Examples of Old Testament–based revival messages are Smith, *The Glorious Revival under King Hezekiah;* and Vance Havner, *Amos: The Prophet with a Modern Message* (Grand Rapids, Mich.: Zondervan, 1937).

31. Noteworthy by their absence were the two most recent phenomena: the pentecostal revivals, which is easily understandable, given fundamentalists' opposition to pentecostalism; and more curious, the great urban campaigns of Billy Sunday's heyday from 1910–1920. I suspect that Sunday's revivalism, viewed from so recent a perspective, had not acquired a supernatural aura and appeared very much "worked up" and mechanical.

32. Grace W. Woods, *The Half Can Never Be Told* (Atlantic City, N.J.: World Wide Revival Prayer Movement, 1927), Foreword, 19–21, 26–27, 69; Wadsworth, *Will Revival Come?,* 7–8, 11–12; H. M. and G. W. Woods, "Letter No. 9," in *By Way of Remembrance,* 77–80, 109; Davis, *When The Fire Fell,* 7–24; Frank G. Beardsley, *Religious Progress through Religious Revivals* (New York: American Tract Society, 1943), 39–51. According to historian Kathryn T. Long, the 1857–1858 revival was a perennial favorite because it had been interpreted in predominantly Reformed categories of revival theory and history, which stressed a wave-and-trough pattern of revival and declension. See Long, "The Power of Interpretation: The Revival of 1857–58 and the Historiography of Revivalism in America," *Religion and American Culture* 4 (Winter 1994): 77–106.

33. Wadsworth, *Will Revival Come?,* 15–16.

34. "The Year Closes," 171. See also Grant Wacker, "Uneasy in Zion: Evangelicals in Postmodern Society," in *Evangelicalism and Modern America,* ed. George Marsden (Grand Rapids, Mich.: Eerdmans, 1984), 17–28, for an illuminating discussion of evangelicals' sense of "cultural custodianship," as Wacker puts it.

35. Quoted in Edmund S. Morgan, *The Puritan Dilemma: The Story of John Winthrop* (Boston: Little, Brown, 1958), 93.

36. The definitive work on this subject is Richard J. Carwardine, *Evangelicals and Politics in Ante-bellum America* (New Haven, Conn.: Yale University Press, 1993). See also Carwardine's "Evangelicals, Politics and the Coming of the American Civil War: A Transatlantic Perspective," in *Evangelicalism: Comparative Studies of Popular Protestantism in North America, The British Isles, and Beyond, 1700–1990,* ed. Mark A. Noll, David W. Bebbington, and George A. Rawlyk (New York: Oxford University Press, 1994), 198–218. Several essays in Mark A. Noll, ed., *Religion and American Politics: From the Colonial Period to the 1980s* (New York: Oxford University Press, 1990), are helpful as well, especially Ruth H. Bloch, "Religion and Ideological Change in the American Revolution," 44–61; Daniel Walker Howe, "Religion and Politics in the Antebellum North," 121–45; and Bertram Wyatt-Brown, "Religion and the 'Civilizing Process' in the early American South, 1600–1860," 172–95. The enduring counterpoint or opposition to this "evangelical Whig" ideology was often centered in immigrant, religiously liturgical communities, as shown in Robert P. Swierenga's chapter, "Ethnoreligious Political Behavior in the Mid-Nineteenth Century: Voting, Values, Cultures," 146–71. Among the classics on this subject are Perry Miller, *The Life of the Mind in America: From the Revolution to the Civil War* (New York: Harcourt, Brace & World, 1965); and Ralph Henry Gabriel, *The Course of American Democratic Thought,* 2d ed. (New York: Ronald Press, 1956), Pt. I.

37. Howe, "Religion and Politics"; Wyatt-Brown, "Religion and the 'Civilizing Process'"; and Timothy L. Smith, *Revivalism and Social Reform in Mid-Nineteenth-Century America* (New York: Abingdon Press, 1957).

38. Moody, "The Return of Our Lord," in *The American Evangelicals, 1800–1900,* ed. William G. McLoughlin (New York: Harper Torchbooks, 1968), 185.

39. Quoted in James M. Gray, "The Christian and Civic Government," *Alliance Weekly,* 31 October 1936, 696.

40. This is the point made by Sandra Sizer, "Politics and Apolitical Religion: The Great Urban Revivals of the Late Nineteenth Century," *Church History* 48 (March 1979): 81–98.

41. On Moody's handling of these dual—and often contending—duties, see Marsden, *Fundamentalism and American Culture,* 32–39.

42. "Human Interests," *MM* 35 (August 1935): 553.

43. Judson E. Conant, *The Growing Menace of the Social Gospel* (Chicago: Bible Institute Colportage Association, 1937), 60.

44. Henry C. Wingblade, "B.Y.P.U. Topics: Building A Better World," *Baptist Evangel,* 15 September 1936, 5.

45. The complex world of fundamentalist social and political ideas and activity is still in need of exploration and analysis, despite the flood of literature on the religious New Right in the 1980s. The best treatments of this subject have come from George Marsden. His masterwork, *Fundamentalism and American Culture,* discusses the range of fundamentalist cultural and political stances in chapter 15, and fundamentalism and politics more generally in chapter 23. In two more recent essays, Marsden elaborates further on this subject; see his "Understanding Fundamentalist Views of Society," in *Reformed Faith and Politics,* ed. Ronald H. Stone (Washington, D.C.: University Press of America, 1983), 65–76; and his "Preachers of Paradox: The Religious New Right in Historical Perspective," in *Religion and America: Spiritual Life in a Secular Age* (Boston: Beacon Press, 1983), 150–68. Marsden's main point is that there is a paradoxical tension in fundamentalism between millenarian alienation and a Puritan heritage of covenantal social custodianship. He concludes that some sort of political conservatism was usually the outcome, a point that has rarely been disputed. But see Robert E. Wenger, "Social Thought in American Fundamentalism, 1918–1933" (Ph.D. diss., University of Nebraska, 1974), which highlights, perhaps to the point of distortion, some fundamentalists' views that sound rather liberal at points.

There was a spectrum of political views, however. Recent studies of William Aberhart, the fundamentalist radio preacher who became premier of Alberta and leader of the Social Credit movement in the 1930s and 1940s, explore his odd marriage of fundamentalism and collectivist political experimentation. See David R. Elliott, "The Devil and William Aberhart: The Nature and Function of His Eschatology," *Studies in Religion* 9 (1980): 325–37; Joseph A. Boudreau, "The Medium and the Message of William Aberhart," *American Review of Canadian Studies* 8 (1978): 18–30; and especially David R. Elliott and Iris Miller, *Bible Bill: A Biography of William Aberhart* (Edmonton, Can.: Reidmore Books, 1987). C. Allyn Russell, "Mark Allison Matthews: Seattle Fundamentalist and Civic Reformer," *Journal of Presbyterian History* 57 (Winter 1979): 447–66; and the chapter on William Bell Riley in Russell, *Voices of American Fundamentalism: Seven Biographical Studies* (Philadelphia: Westminster, 1976), 79–106, chart the extent to which Progressive and Populist commitments informed the work of important fundamentalist leaders. The best examination of the far right fringe of fundamentalism is Leo P. Ribuffo's portrait of Gerald Winrod in his *The Old*

Christian Right: The Protestant Far Right from the Great Depression to the Cold War (Philadelphia: Temple University Press, 1983).

46. Oswald J. Smith, "Building A Better World," *Revelation* 10 (February 1940), 79–80.

47. "The World's Redemption," *Alliance Weekly,* 5 September 1936, 566–67.

48. Perhaps the most striking illustration of this hope was a cartoon that portrayed a figure of Uncle Sam kneeling at the altar rail and praying for forgiveness. "Where He Belongs," a cartoon by E. J. Pace, *SST,* 20 October 1934, 662.

49. See, for example, Havner, *Amos: The Prophet with a Modern Message,* 6–13; Harold L. Lundquist, "Can America Be Saved?" *MM* 40 (November 1939): 120–21; Paul S. Rees, *America, Awake or Perish!* (Grand Rapids, Mich.: Zondervan, 1940), 6–14.

50. Orr, *The Church Must First Repent,* 14.

51. Grace W. Woods, *Revival in Romance and Realism* (New York: Revell, 1936), 24–42. For further information on the Bible Union of China, see M. Searle Bates, "The Theology of American Missionaries in China, 1900–1950," in *The Missionary Enterprise in China and America,* ed. John K. Fairbank (Cambridge, Mass.: Harvard University Press, 1974), 150–54; Paul Hutchinson, "The Conservative Reaction in China," *Journal of Religion* 2 (July 1922): 337–61; and W. H. Griffith Thomas, "Modernism in China," *Princeton Theological Review* 19 (October 1921): 630–71.

52. Woods, *Revival in Romance and Realism,* 41–50, 77–78, 110–13, 162–63, 213–14, 225–26; Woods, *Preparing The Way,* 9, 12; and Woods, *By Way of Remembrance,* 77–80 provide the sources for the above three paragraphs.

53. Wadsworth, *Will Revival Come?,* 3–4; Davis, *When The Fire Fell,* back page notices.

54. Orr, *This Is The Victory!,* 37–39, 90, 113–28. For Orr's many travels in these years, see his other books: *Can God—? 10,000 Miles of Miracle in Britain* (London: Marshall, Morgan & Scott, 1934); *The Promise Is to You: 10,000 Miles of Miracle—to Palestine* (London: Marshall, Morgan & Scott, 1935); *Times of Refreshing: 10,000 Miles of Miracle—through Canada* (Grand Rapids, Mich.: Zondervan, 1936); *If Ye Abide—10,000 Miles of Miracle in South Africa* (London: Marshall, Morgan & Scott, 1936); *All Your Need: 10,000 Miles of Miracle through Australia and New Zealand* (London: Marshall, Morgan & Scott, 1936); *Prove Me Now!—Saith the Lord: 10,000 Miles of Miracles to Moscow* (London: Marshall, Morgan & Scott, 1936); *Through Blood and Fire in China* (London: Marshall, Morgan & Scott, 1939).

55. Orr, "Notes on the Beginnings of the Mid-Twentieth-Century Awakening," Apps. A–D in J. Edwin Orr, *The Second Great Awakening in America* (London: Marshall, Morgan & Scott, 1952), 160–201.

56. "Are We in a Revival?" *Revelation* 4 (April 1934): 135.

57. J. Elwin Wright, "Bible Demonstration Day," *New England Fellowship Monthly* 33 (May 1935): 9. Wright quoted the discouraged prophet Elijah's lament (I Kings 19:10) during the reign of the wicked tyrants Ahab and Jezebel.

58. David R. Enlow, *Men Aflame: The Story of Christian Business Men's Committees* (Grand Rapids, Mich.: Zondervan, 1962), 5, 13–14, 17–21, 24, 35, 38–39, 47–48, 55.

59. J. Elwin Wright, "Observations of the President," *New England Fellowship Monthly* 43 (April 1945): 8–9.

Chapter 7

1. William G. McLoughlin, *Modern Revivalism: Charles Grandison Finney to Billy Graham* (New York: Ronald Press, 1959), 444–54; McLoughlin, *Billy Sunday Was His*

Real Name (Chicago: University of Chicago Press, 1955), 286–88. Lyle W. Dorsett, *Billy Sunday and the Redemption of Urban America* (Grand Rapids, Mich.: Eerdmans, 1991), suggests another reason for decline. As Sunday grew wealthy off revivalism and allied himself with the rich and the powerful, he began to alienate the ordinary people who had been the backbone of his mass appeal.

2. Quoted in Robert S. and Helen M. Lynd, *Middletown in Transition: A Study in Cultural Conflicts* (New York: Harcourt Brace, 1937), 302.

3. Ibid., 303.

4. "Billy Sunday, The Last of His Line," *Christian Century,* 20 November 1935, 1476.

5. Havner, "Come and See—The Road to Certainty," *MM* 34 (January 1934): 211–12.

6. One of the earliest acknowledgements of this paradox in fundamentalism is in Paul A. Carter's superb essay "The Fundamentalist Defense of the Faith," in *Change and Continuity in Twentieth-Century America,* ed. John Braeman et al. (Columbus: Ohio State University Press, 1968), 179–224.

7. Harry S. Stout, *The Divine Dramatist: George Whitefield and the Rise of American Evangelicalism* (Grand Rapids, Mich.: Eerdmans, 1993).

8. Nathan O. Hatch, *The Democratization of American Christianity* (New Haven, Conn.: Yale University Press, 1989), 127.

9. Ibid., 125–61.

10. Quoted in William McLoughlin, *Revivals, Awakenings and Reform: An Essay on Religion and Social Change in America, 1607–1977* (Chicago: University of Chicago Press, 1978), 126.

11. Charles Grandison Finney, *Lectures on Revivals of Religion,* ed. William G. McLoughlin (Cambridge, Mass.: Harvard University Press, 1960), 181, quoted in Hatch, *The Democratization of American Christianity,* 199.

12. McLoughlin, *Modern Revivalism,* 217–28.

13. James F. Findlay, *Dwight L. Moody, American Evangelist, 1837–1899* (Chicago: University of Chicago Press, 1969), 233–44; Sandra Sizer, *Gospel Hymns and Social Religion: The Rhetoric of Nineteenth Century Revivalism* (Philadelphia: Temple University Press, 1978), 149–59.

14. The two paragraphs above and those following draw almost exclusively on the excellent study of Rader by Larry K. Eskridge, "Only Believe: Paul Rader and the Chicago Gospel Tabernacle" (M.A. thesis, University of Maryland, 1985). On Rader's early career, see pp. 6–29; on his sojourn at Moody Church, pp. 30–41; on the beginning, structure and character of the Chicago Gospel Tabernacle, pp. 58–77.

15. Ibid., 81–83, 75, 76 (quote).

16. Ibid., 38, 66, 76–81.

17. Ibid., 59.

18. Ibid., 116–23.

19. Ibid., 116–46.

20. Ibid., 123–25.

21. Ibid., 127.

22. Ibid., 129.

23. Accounts of working in broadcasting with Rader appear in Lois Neely's biography of Clarence Jones, *Come Up To This Mountain* (Wheaton, Ill.: Tyndale House, 1980); Jones' own unpublished reminiscence, "Paul Rader—Pioneer of Gospel Broadcasting," (ca. 1960), Paul Rader Papers (Collection 38, Box 1, Folder 12), Archives of

the Billy Graham Center, Wheaton College, Wheaton, Illinois; and Dave Breese's biography of Lance Latham, *Lance: A Testament of Grace* (Rolling Meadows, Ill.: Awana Youth Association, 1978). See also the illustrated exhibit catalog, *Jazz Age Evangelism: Paul Rader and the Chicago Gospel Tabernacle, 1922–1933* (Wheaton, Ill.: Archives of the Billy Graham Center, 1984).

24. See Neely, *Come Up To This Mountain;* and Clarence W. Jones, *Radio: The New Missionary* (Chicago: Moody Press, 1946).

25. For further discussion of the differences between first- and second-generation fundamentalism, see the introductions to several documentary anthologies I edited: *Missionary Innovation and Expansion* (New York: Garland Publishing, 1988); *Sacrificial Lives: Young Martyrs and Fundamentalist Idealism* (New York: Garland Publishing, 1988); *Enterprising Fundamentalism: Two Second-Generation Leaders* (New York: Garland Publishing, 1988); and *The Youth for Christ Movement and Its Pioneers* (New York: Garland Publishing, 1988).

26. Barry C. Siedell, *Gospel Radio* (Lincoln, Neb.: Back to the Bible Broadcast, 1969), 56–57, 61–64; note in *Radio World*, 17 March 1923, 1; William R. DePlata, *Tell It From Calvary* (New York: Calvary Baptist Church, 1972), 46–47; Daniel P. Fuller, *Give the Winds A Mighty Voice: The Story of Charles E. Fuller* (Waco, Tex.: Word Books, 1972), 75–76; "Salvation by Radio," *MBI Bull* 10 (November 1930): 4; Robert L. Sumner, *A Man Sent from God: A Biography of Dr. John R. Rice* (Grand Rapids, Mich.: Eerdmans, 1959), 76; "Berachah Broadcasting Plant," *Serving and Waiting* 16 (July 1926): 108; Renald E. Showers, "A History of the Philadelphia College of the Bible" (Th.D. diss., Dallas Theological Seminary, 1962), 81; "Dr. Barnhouse and Radio," *Eternity* 12 (March 1961): 28.

27. Quentin Schultze, "Evangelical Radio and the Rise of the Electronic Church, 1921–1948," *Journal of Broadcasting and Electronic Media* 32 (Summer 1988): 294–95.

28. "The *Sunday School Times* Radio Directory," *SST,* 30 May 1931, 313; "A Directory of Evangelical Radio Broadcasts," *SST,* 23 January 1932, 44–45; "Notes on Open Letters: Do People Want Gospel Radio Broadcasts?" ibid., 42.

29. Herman S. Hettinger, "Broadcasting in the United States," *Annals of the American Academy of Political and Social Sciences* 177 (January 1935): 6; Alice Goldfarb Marquis, "Written on the Wind: The Impact of Radio during the 1930s," *Journal of Contemporary History* 19 (July 1984): 388–95, 405.

30. H. W. Ferrin, "Musings at the Microphone," *Radio Caroller Announcer* 1 (March 1930): 2; "'Uncle John' to Address Hinsdale Group," *Covenant Companion,* 1 April 1933, 6; *Jimmy's Boat* (Chicago: Moody Bible Institute Radio Department, n.d.), a story told on the *Morning Glory Club;* "Notes on Open Letters: Do People Want Gospel Radio Broadcasts?," 42; James R. Adair, *M. R. DeHaan: The Man and His Ministry* (Grand Rapids, Mich.: Zondervan, 1969); Bob Bahr, *Man with a Vision: The Story of Percy Crawford* (Chicago: Moody Press, n.d.), 36–38.

31. Schultze, "Evangelical Radio," 291.

32. Spencer J. Miller, "Radio and Religion," *Annals of the American Academy of Political and Social Sciences* 177 (January 1935): 136–40; Fuller, *Give the Winds A Mighty Voice,* 101–3; Schultze, "Evangelical Radio," 292–302; Dennis N. Voskuil, "Reaching Out: Mainline Protestantism and the Media," in *Between the Times: The Travail of the Protestant Establishment in America, 1900–1960,* ed. William R. Hutchison (New York: Cambridge University Press, 1989), 81–86; and especially Voskuil, "The Power of the Air: Evangelicals and the Rise of Religious Broadcasting," in *Amer-*

ican Evangelicals and the Mass Media, ed. Quentin J. Schultze (Grand Rapids, Mich.: Zondervan, 1990), 69–95, which is an instructive overview of this subject. The Fosdick quote comes from Robert Moats Miller, *Harry Emerson Fosdick: Preacher, Pastor, Prophet* (New York: Oxford University Press, 1985), 214.

33. The rest of the programs were sponsored by Roman Catholics, Jewish organizations, the Christian Scientists, and a large number of "unclassified Protestant" organizations, presumably evangelicals mostly. Schultze, "Evangelical Radio," 296–97.

34. Fuller, *Give the Winds A Mighty Voice,* 151–57; and Schultze, "Evangelical Radio," 296–99. See Voskuil, "The Power of the Air," 91–92, for the "blessing in disguise" interpretation.

35. "The Dudley Bible Institute," *Radio Caroller Announcer* 1 (April 1929): 11; Lillie F. Oliver, *Richard Weber Oliver: A Challenge to American Youth* (Providence, R.I.: Challenge Publishing Co., 1932), 108–68; "Providence Institute Has Risen Above Obstacles in Past 50 Years," *Providence Journal Bulletin,* 26 October 1950, clipping in historical files of Barrington College, now located at Gordon College; notice, *Radio Caroller Announcer* 1 (April 1929): 9; George Pophin, "Fathers and Sons," *The Rhode Islander,* 25 June 1976, 35.

36. Howard W. Ferrin, "Greater Providence: A Great Opportunity," *Radio Caroller Announcer* 1 (April 1929): 19. On the growing work in the city, see Briggs P. Dingman, "The Providence Gospel Center," *Announcer* 1 (March 1930): 8–9; "The Providence Gospel Center," *Announcer* 1 (January 1930): 8; "Providence Bible Institute," *Radio Caroller Announcer* 1 (July–August 1929): 11–12; Howard W. Ferrin, "The New School," *Radio Caroller Announcer* 1 (October 1929): 7.

37. R. W. Oliver, "The Providence Gospel Center," *Sheaf of the First Fruits* 28 (May 1930): 18; Dingman, "The Providence Gospel Center"; "Meet Mr. Oliver," *Radio Caroller Announcer* 1 (May 1929): 9; Lillie F. Oliver, *Richard Weber Oliver,* 169–93; "At Home with the Institute Family," *Victory* 1 (February 1934): 15; "At Home with the Institute Family," *Victory* 1 (April–May, 1934): 11; notices, *Institute Life* 1 (March 1934): 11, and *Institute Life* 5 (June 1938): 1–2.

38. Notice, *Institute Life* 4 (November 1937): 1; "Coming Events of Interest," *New England Fellowship Monthly* 31 (April 1933): 14; "Radio Carollers in Boston Arena," *New England Fellowship Monthly* 31 (May 1933): 6; *Bulletin of Providence Bible Institute,* 1950–51, abbrev. ed. (Providence, R.I.: Providence Bible Institute, 1950), 21.

39. *Brief Facts about the Moody Bible Institute* (Chicago: Bible Institute Colportage Association, 1928), n.p.; "Enrollments," File drawer G, Moodyana Room, Moody Bible Institute, Chicago, Illinois; "Report of the President of the Moody Bible Institute," *MBI Bull* 10 (September 1930): 11–12; "Report of the President," *MBI Bull* 12 (November 1932): 14; "Report of the President," *MBI Bull* 15 (November 1936): 13; "The President Reports," *MBI Bull* 22 (November 1942): 4; *These Forty Years, 1894–1934* (Chicago: Bible Institute Colportage Association, n.d.), 2–3; *A Brief Story of the Bible Institute Colportage Association of Chicago: Forty-five Years of Printed Page Ministry* (Chicago: B.I.C.A., n.d.), 4–6; Eileen Fleeton, "Fifty Years of Colporting," *Sunday* 6 (December 1944): 19–20, 54.

40. "Salvation by Radio"; "Annual Report of the Broadcasting Station of the Moody Bible Institute of Chicago for Year Ending April 30, 1927," 19, Files of the station manager, WMBI, Moody Bible Institute, Chicago, Illinois (this and other such annual reports will be cited hereinafter by the short title, "Annual Report, [date]"); "Annual Report, 1928" and "Annual Report, 1929," passim.

41. "Annual Report, 1930," 6–7, 13, 15, 21; *WMBI Song Favorites No. 1, WMBI Song Favorites No. 2,* and *WMBI Song Favorites No. 3,* sheet music published by the Moody Bible Institute Radio Department, File drawer G, Moodyana Room, Moody Bible Institute, Chicago, Illinois; "Radio Station WMBI," *MM* 31 (May 1931): 80; "Monthly Program of Station WMBI," *MM* 35 (June 1935): 502; *MM* 35 (July 1935): 550; *MM* 35 (August 1935): 595; "Monthly Program of Station WMBI," *MM* 40 (April 1940): 468; "Annual Report, 1940," 8, 10.

42. "Annual Report, 1932," 7; "Annual Report, 1934," 6–7; "Annual Report, 1935," 7; "Annual Report, 1937," 6; "Annual Report, 1939," 31; "Annual Report, 1938," 28; data on meetings in churches compiled from WMBI annual reports for the years 1929–1942.

43. Wilbur M. Smith, *A Watchman on the Wall: The Life Story of Will H. Houghton* (Grand Rapids, Mich.: Eerdmans, 1951), 101–13, 112 (quote).

44. William M. Runyan, "Fifty Years—And Pushing Ahead," *MM* 36 (March 1936): 354–56; "To Newspaper Editors," *MM* 37 (June 1937): 503; C. B. Nordlund, "The Moody Centenary Celebrations," *MM* 38 (February 1938): 309–10; "Our Daily Meditations and the Moody Centenary: A Letter from Richard Ellsworth Day, and an Announcement," *Revelation* 6 (December 1936): 499; "Report of the President for the Business Division," *MBI Bull* 19 (March 1939): 3, 8; Smith, *Watchman on the Wall,* 128-35; "Great Revival Due Soon, Moody Successor Certain," *Toronto Daily Star,* 13 February 1937, cited in Smith, *Watchman on the Wall,* 191. A friend of the Institute claimed that she had seen a well-thumbed copy of *Let's Go Back to the Bible* on President Roosevelt's desk in the Oval Office (Smith, *Watchman on the Wall,* 130).

45. See Smith, *Watchman on the Wall,* 142–48; "How Moody Bible Institute Serves in Wartime," *MBI Bull* 22 (February 1943): 2–13; John R. Riebe, "Founder's Week Conference Report," *MM* 42 (March 1942): 407–10; and, to illustrate a frequent emphasis in the *Moody Monthly,* the three consecutive editorials on revival in the October 1941 issue (vol. 42, 67–68).

46. "Hear WMBI Favorites over Your Station," *MM* 41 (September 1940): 31; "Miracles and Melodies," *MM* 42 (April 1942): 487.

47. Riebe, "Founder's Week Conference Report," 409.

48. The following paragraphs on the Fullers and their radio ministry draw extensively upon the information presented in three books: J. Elwin Wright, *The Old Fashioned Revival Hour and the Broadcasters* (Boston: Fellowship Press, 1940); Wilbur M. Smith, *A Voice for God: The Life of Charles E. Fuller, Originator of the Old Fashioned Revival Hour* (Boston: W. A. Wilde, 1949); and Fuller, *Give the Winds A Mighty Voice.* This last book is a thoroughly documented and very detailed biography and discussion of the Fuller's ministries written by their son.

49. The succession of Bible and prophetic conferences, evangelistic meetings, and visiting speakers at Calvary Church is documented in a scrapbook of newspaper clippings located in the Charles E. and Grace Payton Fuller Papers, DuPlessis Center Archives, Fuller Theological Seminary, Pasadena, California.

50. Charles M. Crowe, "Religion on the Air," *Christian Century,* 23 August 1944, 973–75; "Big Churches Learn Radio 'Savvy' to Counter Revivalist Air Racket," *Newsweek,* 22 January 1945, 74–75; "Notes on Open Letters: The Financial Integrity of the Old Fashioned Revival Hour," *SST,* 27 May 1944, 378, 381.

51. *Heart to Heart Talks,* 21 September 1935, 2; *Heart to Heart Talks,* 28 December 1935, 2; *Heart to Heart Talks,* 22 February 1936, 2.

52. Wright, *Old Fashioned Revival Hour,* 24–25.

53. See, for example, *Heart to Heart Talks,* 5 September 1936, 2, where Fuller states: "I cannot tell you now what bitter opposition there is, but we know that Satan is doing all he can to stop the Radio Revival Hour, for through this means the Word of God is going out in his—Satan's, realm."

54. See for example, the *Heart to Heart Talks* for 17 April 1937, 24 July 1937, 30 October 1937, and 19 August 1939.

55. For detailed descriptions of the broadcast, see Wright, *Old Fashioned Revival Hour,* 100–9; Smith, *A Voice for God,* 127–39, and Fuller, *Give the Winds A Mighty Voice,* 162–66. Recordings of the *Old Fashioned Revival Hour,* however, are indispensable to understanding its content, character and appeal. Unfortunately, very few of the recordings of the pre–World War II years have survived. Two notable survivals are the programs for March 10, 1940, and for October 12, 1941, located in the Charles E. and Grace Payton Fuller Papers, DuPlessis Center Archives, Fuller Theological Seminary, Pasadena, California.

56. See Wright, *Old Fashioned Revival Hour,* 125–240, for a large selection of letters, and listen to the recordings of the broadcast for March 10, 1940 and October 12, 1941 in the Charles E. and Grace Payton Fuller Papers to hear Grace Fuller reading letters on the air. A very large collection of letters she selected are on file at the DuPlessis Center Archives.

57. There are two large files of Charles Fuller's sermons at the DuPlessis Center Archives. They cover the years 1936–1966. Refer also to the audio recordings of Fuller preaching on the *Old Fashioned Revival Hour* on March 10, 1940 and December 12, 1941. For Fuller and the Southern Baptists, see Fuller, *Give the Winds A Mighty Voice,* 171.

58. Quoted in Wright, *Old Fashioned Revival Hour,* 241–42.

59. Ibid., 18.

60. Schultze, "Evangelical Radio," 301.

61. Fuller, *Give the Winds A Mighty Voice,* 135.

62. R. Laurence Moore, *Religious Outsiders and the Making of Americans* (New York: Oxford University Press, 1986), 165–72, is very convincing on this point.

63. Quentin Schultze, *Televangelism and American Culture: The Business of Popular Religion* (Grand Rapids, Mich.: Baker Book House, 1991), 196.

Chapter 8

1. Harold John Ockenga, "The Unvoiced Multitudes," in *Evangelical Action! A Report of the Organization of the National Association of Evangelicals for United Action* (Boston: United Action Press, 1942), 19. Wright's speech and a full report of the proceedings are found in this same volume.

2. Wright was a member of Park Street Congregational Church in Boston, where Harold John Ockenga was the pastor.

3. A roster of delegates and observers is included in *Evangelical Action!,* 92–100.

4. These themes are expounded in the three principal histories of the NAE, James DeForest Murch, *Cooperation without Compromise: A History of the National Association of Evangelicals* (Grand Rapids, Mich.: Eerdmans, 1956), an early, apologetic history by an NAE official; Bruce Shelley, *Evangelicalism in America* (Grand Rapids, Mich.: Eerdmans, 1967), an NAE-commissioned work by a professional historian; and Arthur H. Mathews, *A Voice for the Unvoiced Multitudes: Fifty Years of the National Association of Evangelicals* (Carol Stream, Ill.: National Association of Evangelicals, 1992), which is

also an officially sponsored treatment. Cf. John A. Hutchison, *We Are Not Divided: A Critical and Historical Study of the Federal Council of the Churches of Christ in America* (New York: Round Table Press, 1941).

5. Elizabeth M. Evans, who worked with Wright for many years in the New England Fellowship, became the principal chronicler of this remarkable but relatively unknown story. See her book, *The Wright Vision: The Story of the New England Fellowship* (Lanham, Md.: University Press of America, 1990); and Muriel Wright Evans and Elizabeth M. Evans, *Incidents and Information of the First 48 Years: Rumney Conference's 75th Anniversary* (Rumney, N.H.: New England Fellowship, 1978).

6. Evans, *The Wright Vision*, 1–8.

7. Ibid., 8–9; Evans and Evans, *Incidents and Information*, 8–9; J. Elwin Wright, "God's Program for Us," *The Sheaf of the First Fruits* 22 (October 1924): 2.

8. Evans, *The Wright Vision*, 7–9, 66–67. Houghton's sojourn in the South and his relationship to Torrey are documented in Wilbur M. Smith, *A Watchman on the Wall: The Life Story of Will H. Houghton* (Grand Rapids, Mich.: Eerdmans, 1951), 69–80.

9. Evans and Evans, *Incidents and Information*, 9; J. Elwin Wright, "The 1931 Program," *The Sheaf of the First Fruits* 28 (October 1930): 12.

10. Minutes of the director's report to the annual meeting of the Advisory Council, New England Fellowship, 30 September 1931, in the possession of Kathryn Evans, Bradenton, Florida; Evans and Evans, *Incidents and Information*, 20–22; "Summary of Work in 1933," *New England Fellowship Monthly* 32 (January 1934): 4; *New England Fellowship Official Report for 1934* (Boston: New England Fellowship, 1934), 5; *New England Fellowship Official Report for 1935* (Boston: New England Fellowship, 1935), 3; J. E. Wright, "We Are Sorry," *New England Fellowship Monthly* 34 (July–August 1936): 10 (quotation); *Annual Report of the New England Fellowship for 1939* (Boston: New England Fellowship, 1939), 9; *A Quick Glance Back over the 1941 Trail: Annual Report of the New England Fellowship* (Boston: Fellowship Press, 1941), 3; tape recording of *Old Fashioned Revival Hour* broadcast from Boston, Massachusetts, 12 October 1941, DuPlessis Center, Fuller Theological Seminary, Pasadena, California.

11. The only significant blind spot in the Fellowship's evangelical ecumenicity was its failure to cross the color line. I found no evidence that black congregations ever participated in Fellowship events.

12. Wright, "A Few Observations," *New England Fellowship Monthly* 35 (April 1937): 8–9; Evans, *The Wright Vision*, 103.

13. See R. T. Davis' circular letter, originally sent to Will H. Houghton, J. Davis Adams, Howard W. Ferrin, and Louis T. Talbot, 11 December 1940, Ralph T. Davis correspondence, Africa Inland Mission Records (Collection 81, Box 14, Folder 27), Archives of the Billy Graham Center, Wheaton College, Wheaton, Illinois (hereinafter cited as AIM Records). Will H. Houghton to Ralph T. Davis, 23 December 1940, AIM Records. See also J. Davis Adams to Ralph T. Davis, 13 December 1940, and Howard W. Ferrin to Ralph T. Davis, 13 December 1940, both in AIM Records.

14. The Bible Protestant Church was formed in 1939 by a number of the more fundamentalistic congregations of the Methodist Protestant Church who refused to go along with their denomination's merger with the Methodist Episcopal Church and the Methodist Episcopal Church, South. The Bible Presbyterian Church was formed in 1937 by a faction of those who followed J. Gresham Machen out of Princeton Seminary and the Presbyterian Church of the U.S.A. Carl McIntire was this group's chief spokesman and organizer. McIntire's weekly paper, the *Christian Beacon*, was the group's principal sounding board. Bible Presbyterians' opposition to the Federal Council is expressed in the following articles in the *Beacon*: Alexander Fraser, "A Protest and

a Plea," 28 March 1940, 2, 5; and these editorials: "A National Council," 11 April 1940, 4; "Federal Council," 15 August 1940, 4; "Council," 31 October 1940, 4; and "Federal Council," 21 August 1941, 4. Two detailed early accounts of these events are Carl McIntire, "History of the American Council of Christian Churches," *Christian Beacon*, 16 April 1942, 2, 7; and Robert T. Ketcham, "Facing the Facts: Facts Concerning the Federal Council, the American Council, and the National Association," *Christian Beacon*, 26 November 1942, 1–2, 4, 6–8, reprinted from the *Baptist Bulletin*, November 1942.

15. McIntire, "History," 2; "American Council of Christian Churches Organized; Headquarters in New York," *Christian Beacon*, 18 September 1941, 1; "National Association of Evangelicals," *Revelation* 12 (October 1942): 445.

16. "National Association of Evangelicals," *Revelation* 12 (October 1942).

17. Out of the group assembled, only Stephen Paine, president of the Wesleyan Methodists' Houghton College, represented an evangelical tradition other than fundamentalism. Rounding out the list was Horace Dean of the Philadelphia School of the Bible, T. J. Bach of the Scandinavian Alliance Mission, Moody's vice president H. C. Crowell, Ironside's associate pastor, Charles Porter, and Ernest Wadsworth of the Great Commission Prayer League. McIntire brought along the American Council officers H. McAllister Griffiths and Harold S. Laird.

18. McIntire, "History"; Ketcham, "Facing the Facts," 2; J. Elwin Wright, "An Historical Statement of Events Leading up to the National Conference at St. Louis," *Evangelical Action!*, 5–7.

19. "Minutes, Meeting of the Committee for United Action Among Evangelicals," 27–28 October 1941, Chicago, Illinois, AIM Records; Wright, "An Historical Statement," 5–8. The committee consisted for the most part of prominent East Coast fundamentalists. Among them were Ayer, Bradbury, Horace F. Dean of the Philadelphia School of the Bible, and Harold J. Ockenga. Others on the committee were Bishop William Culbertson of the Reformed Episcopal Church; Richard Ellsworth Day, a freelance religious author; Howard W. Ferrin of the Providence Bible Institute; Clarence Roddy, a prominent Baptist pastor in Brooklyn; Alex Sauerwein, a Presbyterian pastor in Flushing, New York; Jacob Stam, superintendent of the Star of Hope Mission in Paterson, New Jersey; Thomas E. Whiteman, an executive with the Woolworth company; and Stephen W. Paine, president of Houghton College. Again, Paine, as a Wesleyan Methodist, was the only one in the group who was not fully identified with the fundamentalist movement. The committee seems to have been regionally focused in order to facilitate its frequent meetings.

20. "Minutes of the Committee for United Action among Evangelicals," 19 January 1942, New York, N.Y., AIM Records.

21. The text of Davis's letter is in the Minutes of the Committee for United Action among Evangelicals, 10 November 1941, New York, N.Y.; see also Minutes of the Committee, 22 December 1941, New York, N.Y.; and Minutes of the Committee, 19 January 1942, New York, N.Y., all in AIM Records.

22. Wright includes the text of the call and the list of signers in "An Historical Statement," *Evangelical Action!*, 8–13. A copy is also in the Davis Correspondence, AIM Records.

23. Cary N. Weisiger III, "The National Association of Evangelicals," *The Southern Presbyterian Journal* 2 (September 1943): 15. Form letter from the Temporary Committee for United Action among Evangelicals, per R. T. Davis, Secretary, 2 March 1942, Papers of Herbert John Taylor (Collection 20, Box 65, Folder 16), Archives of the Billy Graham Center (hereinafter cited as H. J. Taylor Papers); form letter, signed

by Ralph T. Davis, 27 March 1942, H. J. Taylor Papers; J. Elwin Wright, "National Conference for United Action at St. Louis," *New England Fellowship Monthly* 40 (February 1942): 9. Shortly before the meeting, Davis informed Wright that he had shipped some copies of the *Christian Beacon* to the hotel, which could be distributed if the need arose. Davis cautioned him not to open the boxes "unless we have to do so." It is not known which issue of the *Beacon* was in these boxes, or what was to be highlighted in it. Nevertheless, nearly every issue of the paper contained attacks on the Federal Council and the mainline denominations, and several recent issues contained the platform and bylaws of the American Council. R. T. Davis to Rev. J. Elwin Wright, 4 April 1942, AIM Records.

24. Ockenga, "The Unvoiced Multitudes," *Evangelical Action!,* 19–46; 29, 38 (quotations).

25. Stephen W. Paine, "The Possibility of United Action," *United Action!,* 49–61, 59–60 (quote).

26. McIntire's pamphlet, *History of the American Council of Christian Churches,* and a report in the *St. Louis Post-Dispatch* (8 April 1942, 3C) of its being distributed at the meeting are reprinted in the *Christian Beacon,* 16 April 1942, 2, 6. The NAE's official report of the meeting's business sessions, "The Conference Sessions," *Evangelical Action!,* 64–71, does not report on any of the floor debates or other conflicts at the convention. McIntire and his colleagues, however, were not at all reluctant to give blow-by-blow accounts. See Carl McIntire, "The Attack upon the American Council by the National Association of Evangelicals," *Christian Beacon,* 29 October 1942, 1–2, 5; Robert T. Ketcham, "Shadow of the Federal Council," *Christian Beacon,* 14 May 1942, 2, reprinted from the *Baptist Bulletin;* Ketcham, "And Still They Ride The Fence"; Newton C. Conant, "A Personal Observation of the St. Louis Meeting"; and Harold T. Commons, "St. Louis 'Blues,'" all in *Christian Beacon,* 16 April 1942, 1ff.; William McCarrell, "'Stand Fast in the Faith, Quit You Like Men, Be Strong': St. Louis Report," *Christian Beacon,* 23 April 1942, 1.

27. J. Elwin Wright, "Report of the Promotional Director," *United We Stand: A Report of the Constitutional Convention of the National Association of Evangelicals,* La Salle, Hotel, Chicago, Illinois, 3–6 May 1943, 5–6. For examples of the promotional efforts see two handbills, "New York Mobilization Day for United Action, June 8, 1942" and "New England Mobilization Day for United Action, June 9, 1942," in H. J. Taylor Papers; and two news stories, "Fall Series of Regional Conferences Under Way September 21" and "Fall Series of Regional Conferences Under Way September 21," both in *United Evangelical Action,* 1 September 1942, 1, 4.

28. Wright, "Report of the Promotional Director, *United We Stand,* 7–8.

29. Harold J. Ockenga, "Christ for America," in *United We Stand,* 10–12, 15–16.

30. "Christ for America," in *United We Stand,* 29–38, provides the text of the constitution, by-laws, statement of faith, and resolutions and reports emanating from the Chicago convention. See the plates between pp. 32–33 for a full and illustrated roster of the NAE's officers. Note again the absence of black church leaders. One small black pentecostal denomination, the United Holy Church of America, did eventually join the NAE. Lutherans were few and far between also. Another group that was largely absent was the Disciples of Christ–Christian Church and the antimodernist group that had separated from the Disciples, the Churches of Christ. Among the delegates, I can identify only one who represented this tradition: James DeForest Murch of Cincinnati, the editor of the *Christian Standard,* which was the principal voice of the more evangelical wing within the Disciples–Christian denomination. Murch eventually became editor of the NAE's periodical, *United Evangelical Action.*

31. J. Elwin Wright, "Growth of NAE is Modern Evangelical Miracle," *United Evangelical Action,* 15 April 1945, 5; Murch, *Cooperation without Compromise,* 196, 202–3. The figures cited by Murch are inflated. For a more accurate accounting, see Robert Patterson, "The History of the National Association of Evangelicals," paper presented to the NAE staff c. 1991; and Mathews, *A Voice for the Unvoiced Multitudes,* Apps. A–E, 164–71.

32. Ockenga, "Christ for America," 15. J. Elwin Wright, "Growth of NAE is Modern Evangelical Miracle," *United Evangelical Action,* 15 April 1945, 5; Murch, *Cooperation Without Compromise,* passim.

33. Carl McIntire, "Discussing 'An Issue of the Present Hour': An Analysis," *Christian Beacon,* 11 February 1943, 8. On McIntire's and Ockenga's friendship and estrangement, see George M. Marsden, *Reforming Fundamentalism: Fuller Seminary and the New Evangelicalism* (Grand Rapids, Mich.: Eerdmans, 1987), 41–44, 48–50; cf. Carl McIntire, "N.A.E., Fuller Seminary, Championed by Ockenga," *Christian Beacon,* 10 May 1951, 1, 4–5, 8.

34. Harold J. Ockenga, "Contentious Versus Evangelical Christianity," *United Evangelical Action,* 1 August 1942, 2.

35. See, for examples, the flurry of articles in the *Christian Beacon* following the April 1942 meeting in St. Louis, cited in n. 26 above, as well as the editorial "Appeasement," *Christian Beacon,* 9 July 1942, 4; and Carl McIntire, "Analysis of National Association of Evangelicals and Answer to the Question, 'Has the N.A.E. Compromised on the Federal Council Issue?'" *Christian Beacon,* 11 November 1943, 1, 4, 5, 8.

36. Ockenga, "Contentious Versus Evangelical Christianity"; "An Issue of the Present Hour," *United Evangelical Action* 2 (January 1943), 2; J. Elwin Wright, "An Appraisal of Our Situation," *United Evangelical Action* 2 (August 1943), 2; "National Association," *Christian Beacon,* 29 October 1942, 4; Ketcham, "Shadow of the Federal Council"; Carl McIntire, "Discussing 'An Issue of the Present Hour,'" 1–2, 5, 8; "Shall Heresy Go Unnoticed? Positive Not Negative," Christian Beacon 8 July 1943, 1, 4.

37. Ralph T. Davis to Hobart S. Geer, 26 May 1942, and Ralph T. Davis to Harold J. Ockenga, 26 May 1942 (quoting Geer), both in AIM Records; "Appeasement"; "National Association of Evangelicals," *Christian Beacon,* 1 July 1943, 4.

38. Michael S. Hamilton, "Wheaton College and the Fundamentalist Network of Voluntary Associations, 1919–1965," paper presented at a conference, "Evangelicals, Voluntary Associations, and American Public Life," Wheaton College, Wheaton, Illinois, 13–15 June 1991, 23; *Evangelical Action!,* 93, 144–45; Lewis Sperry Chafer, "United Action of Evangelicals," *Bibliotheca Sacra* 99 (1942): 385–86.

39. Moody Bible Institute never did join the NAE, and the *Moody Monthly* made no direct reference to either it or the American Council during the 1940s. See Will H. Houghton, "America's Spiritual Responsibility in the War and After," *MM* 44 (October 1943): 69; "In A World of Tragic Need," *MM* 45 (May 1945): 472; Herbert L. Lundquist, "Contending for the Faith," *MM* 46 (August 1946): 728. But see "Moody's Founder's Week Conference Largest Yet," *United Evangelical Action* 5 (March 1946): 11, which mentions that several of the keynote speakers were NAE leaders.

40. Carl McIntire, "Pentecostal Group Overwhelms N.A.E. Denominations," *Christian Beacon,* 20 April 1944, 8.

41. J. Elwin Wright, "An Appraisal of Our Situation," *United Evangelical Action* 2 (August 1944): 2.

42. "An Issue of the Present Hour," *United Evangelical Action,* January 1943, 2.

43. For arguments that such distinctions were not commonly made, see Marsden, *Reforming Fundamentalism,* 47–50; and Marsden, "Unity and Diversity in the Evan-

gelical Resurgence," in *Altered Landscapes: Christianity in America, 1935–1985,* ed. David W. Lotz (Grand Rapids, Mich.: Eerdmans, 1989), 64–68. For examples of *fundamentalist* and *evangelical* being used interchangeably, see Harold Ockenga's introduction to Carl F. H. Henry, *The Uneasy Conscience of Modern Fundamentalism* (Grand Rapids, Mich.: Eerdmans, 1947), and indeed a similar usage throughout Henry's text. But note Henry's recollection that while "'in the 1930s we were all fundamentalists, . . . the term "evangelical" became a significant option when the NAE was organized'" (quoted in Marsden, *Reforming Fundamentalism,* 10).

44. J. E. Wright, "The Federal Council Prepares the Way for Coming World Church," *United Evangelical Action* 2 (March 1943): 1–4. Wright's articles were later compiled and published as *How Modern Is The Federal Council?* (Boston: Fellowship Press, 1943); and *Death in the Pot* (Boston: Fellowship Press, 1944). See, for example of other NAE-sanctioned attacks, Ernest Gordon, *An Ecclesiastical Octopus: A Factual Report on the Federal Council of the Churches of Christ in America* (Boston: Fellowship Press, 1948), which had been published first as a series of articles in *United Evangelical Action.*

45. Robert Patterson, "The History of the National Association of Evangelicals," paper presented to the NAE staff (c. 1991), p. 10. In 1948 the Reformed Church of America, the United Presbyterian Church of North America, and the Presbyterian Church, U.S. (southern) each considered—and defeated—proposals to join the NAE. Certainly other factors were behind their decisions, but being forced to choose between the NAE and the Federal Council certainly did not strengthen the case for joining the NAE (Mark Silk, "The Rise of the 'New Evangelicalism': Shock and Readjustment," *Between the Times: The Travail of the Protestant Establishment in America, 1900–1960,* ed. William R. Hutchison [New York: Cambridge University Press, 1989], 280–81).

46. "Sectarianism Receives New Lease on Life," *Christian Century,* 19 May 1943, 596, 614. This insight on the problem of trying to distinguish separatism and independency comes from Marsden, *Reforming Fundamentalism,* 45–47, 63–65, 94–95.

47. Robert A. Schneider, "Voice of Many Waters: Church Federation in the Twentieth Century," in Hutchison, *Between The Times,* 93–121; Fosdick, c. 1927, quoted in Robert Moats Miller, *Harry Emerson Fosdick: Preacher, Pastor, Prophet* (New York: Oxford University Press, 1985), 214; Silk, "The Rise of the 'New Evangelicalism,'" 278–99.

48. Roger Finke and Rodney Stark, "How the Upstart Sects Won America: 1776–1850," *Journal for the Scientific Study of Religion* 28 (1989): 27–44. The search for legitimacy is a major theme in David Edwin Harrell, Jr's, analysis of the postwar pentecostal/charismatic movement. It pervades each of his works on this topic: *All Things Are Possible: The Healing and Charismatic Revivals in Modern America* (Bloomington: Indiana University Press, 1975); *Oral Roberts: An American Life* (Bloomington: Indiana University Press, 1985); and *Pat Robertson: A Personal, Political and Religious Portrait* (San Francisco: Harper & Row, 1987).

49. Wuthnow, *The Restructuring of American Religion: Society and Faith since World War II* (Princeton, N.J.: Princeton University Press, 1988), 71–131.

50. George M. Marsden, *Fundamentalism in American Culture: The Shaping of Twentieth-Century Evangelicalism, 1870–1925* (New York: Oxford University Press, 1980), 194–95, 204–5.

51. "One Dutch Immigrant Plus One New Testament," *Revelation* 1 (December 1931): 405, 428–30. Another example of this attraction of Northern European ethnic Protestants to fundamentalist congregations is found in Everett L. Perry's dissertation chapter on the Midwest Bible Church, located in northwest Chicago, which Perry

had studied during 1943. Some twenty percent of the congregation's members had once been Lutheran. See Perry, "The Role of Socio-Economic Factors in the Rise and Development of American Fundamentalism" (Ph.D. diss., University of Chicago, 1959), 441–51.

52. For the Reformed and Christian Reformed leaders' response, see James D. Bratt, *Dutch Calvinism in Modern America: A History of a Conservative Subculture* (Grand Rapids, Mich.: Eerdmans, 1984), 93–104. Thomas Boslooper, *Grace and Glory Days* (Clearwater, Fla.: Woodswalker Books, 1990), is a lively and detailed popular account of the fundamentalist-inspired turbulence in Dutch West Michigan during the 1920s and 1930s. For a more theological approach, see Joseph H. Hall, "The Controversy over Fundamentalism in the Christian Reformed Church, 1915–1966" (Th.D. diss., Concordia Theological Seminary, 1974). William A. Bevier, "A History of the I.F.C.A. [Independent Fundamental Churches of America]" (Th.D. diss., Dallas Theological Seminary, 1958), 68–69, 87, 109, 168, documents the defection of a number of Reformed and Christian Reformed congregations; while James R. Adair, *M. R. DeHaan: The Man and His Ministry* (Grand Rapids, Mich.: Zondervan, 1969), tells the story of the most famous of the defecters, M. R. DeHaan, who left the pulpit of Calvary Reformed Church in Grand Rapids in 1929 and founded Calvary Undenominational Church, the largest and most influential fundamentalist tabernacle in the city. Nine years later DeHaan founded the *Radio Bible Class,* which gained a national audience for its weekly broadcasts.

53. Letter quoted in the "Annual Report of the Broadcasting Station of the Moody Bible Institute for the Year Ending March 31, 1936," on file in the offices of station WMBI, p. 22.

54. The Christian Reformed Church left the NAE in 1951, citing a fundamental disagreement with the more "Methodistic" NAE constituents over the proper doctrine and practice of evangelism. In 1988 the denomination joined the NAE once again. The two preceding paragraphs owe much to James Bratt's *Dutch Calvinism in Modern America,* chs. 9 and 10, which offer the best analysis and coverage available of the Christian Reformed Church's relationship with fundamentalism in the 1930s and 1940s.

55. Throughout the scholarly literature on these varied traditions one finds occurrences of such "leavening." See, for example, Paul Merritt Bassett, "The Fundamentalist Leavening of the Holiness Movement, 1914–1940: The Church of the Nazarene, A Case Study," *Wesleyan Theological Journal* 13 (Spring 1978): 65–91; G. Everett Arden, *Augustana Heritage: A History of the Augustana Lutheran Church* (Rock Island, Ill.: Augustana Press, 1963), 311–19; Karl A. Olsson, *By One Spirit: A History of the Evangelical Covenant Church of America* (Chicago: Covenant Press, 1962), 526–46, 618–20; Rodney J. Sawatsky, "History and Ideology: Mennonite Identity Definition through History" (Ph.D. diss., Princeton University, 1977), chs. 6–8; Bratt, *Dutch Calvinism in Modern America,* 95–97, 127–34; Ernest Trice Thompson, *Presbyterians in the South, Volume Three: 1890–1972* (Richmond, Va.: John Knox Press, 1973), 266–73, 468–90, 552–53; and William R. Glass, "The Development of Northern Patterns of Fundamentalism in the South, 1900–1950" (Ph.D. diss., Emory University, 1991).

56. Grant Wacker, "Twentieth-Century Evangelicalism: A Guide to the Sources," *Evangelical Studies Bulletin* 7 (Fall 1990): 8; see also Wacker, "Uneasy in Zion: Evangelicals in Postmodern Society," in *Evangelicalism and Modern America,* ed. George Marsden (Grand Rapids, Mich.: Eerdmans, 1984), 22–25.

57. An exposition and critique of this motive among post-1945 evangelicals (and their scholarly interpreters) appears in Donald W. Dayton, "Yet Another Layer of the Onion, or Opening the Ecumenical Door to Let the Riffraff In," *Ecumenical Review*

40 (January 1988): 87–110; and Dayton, "An Analysis of the Self-Understanding of American Evangelicalism with a Critique of Its Correlated Historiography," paper presented at the Wesleyan/Holiness Study Project Fellows Seminar, Asbury Theological Seminary, Wilmore, Kentucky, 28–30 January 1988. For an example of this yearning for respectability and the fundamentalist-evangelicals' role in satisfying it, see Harrell, Jr., *Oral Roberts*, 178–80, which recounts Roberts's first meeting with Billy Graham, during Graham's crusade in Portland, Oregon, in 1950. Graham graciously invited Roberts to the platform and had him offer the evening's prayer. Says Harrell of this occasion: "for Oral it was loaded with meaning. . . . Graham's personal kindness, his glad and wholesome embrace of a fellow Christian, placed Oral momentarily in a larger, more respectable, world than he had ever imagined he could be a part of" (p. 180).

58. "Meeting of Evangelicals in St. Louis," *Baptist and Reflector*, 7 May 1942, 3.

[59.] For a fuller discussion of the rather complex relationship between fundamentalists and Southern Baptists, see my chapter "Is 'Evangelical' A Yankee Word? Relations between Northern Evangelicals and the Southern Baptist Convention in the Twentieth Century," in *Southern Baptists and American Evangelicals: The Conversation Continues*, ed. David S. Dockery (Nashville, Tenn.: Broadman-Holman, 1993), 78–99.

60. Wright, "Report of the Promotional Director," 7, and "Work Plan for 1943–44," 41, both in *United We Stand*; "Association Plans Nation-Wide Revival," *United Evangelical Action* 2 (May 1943): 1.

61. Horace F. Dean, "Christ for America," *SST*, 1 May 1943, 351–52; Philip E. Howard, Jr., "A Jew Preaches Christ in Philadelphia," *SST*, 28 February 1942, 159–61, 164; "City-Wide Revival in Buffalo: Dr. John R. Rice and J. Straton Shufelt Lead Great Meeting," *United Evangelical Action* 4 (May 1944): 7; "The Appelman Meetings in Grand Rapids," *SST*, 16 December 1944, 944–45; "'Christ for America' Plans Two February City-Wide Drives," *United Evangelical Action*, 15 January 1945, 5: 1, 3.

62. J. Elwin Wright to H. J. Taylor, 25 May 1943; J. Elwin Wright to H. J. Taylor, 29 June 1943; both in H. J. Taylor Papers.

Chapter 9

1. Forrest Forbes, *God Hath Chosen: The Story of Jack Wyrtzen and the Word of Life Hour* (Grand Rapids, Mich.: Zondervan, 1948), 54–55.

2. "Bobby Sox Hit Sawdust Trail," *News-Views: The Chicago Daily News Pictorial Section*, 3 February 1945, 2. Accounts of the movement's rapid expansion and spectacular rallies in 1944–1946 appear in Mel Larson, *Youth for Christ: Twentieth Century Wonder* (Grand Rapids, Mich.: Zondervan, 1947), 51–59, 84–95; J. Elwin Wright, "Youth for Christ," *United Evangelical Action*, 15 February 1945, 8; and James Hefley, *God Goes to High School* (Waco, Tex.: Word, 1970), 38–499, 69. The Youth for Christ movement included organizations other than Youth for Christ International, which was founded in the summer of 1945. Other significant groups included Percy Crawford's *Young People's Church of the Air*, based in Philadelphia; Jim Rayburn's Young Life Campaign, first headquartered in Dallas; Jack Wyrtzen's Word of Life, emanating from greater New York; and many smaller groups. Additional youth-related ministries participated in this evangelistic surge; most notable were Dawson Trotman's Navigators Fellowship among servicemen and the Inter-Varsity Christian Fellowship, which began in the United States in 1941. For a brief overview of this phenomenon, see Bruce Shelley, "The Rise of Evangelical Youth Movements," *Fides et Historia* 18 (January 1986): 47–63.

3. Hillyer Straton is quoted here from an interview with Granville Hicks, "The Son of a Fundamentalist Prophet," *Christian Register*, 10 March 1927, 197–98, reprinted

in *The Uncertain World of Normalcy: The 1920's,* ed. Paul A. Carter (New York: Pitman, 1971), 143–44. The younger aggregate profile of fundamentalist factions is documented in Walter E. Ellis, "Social and Religious Factors in the Fundamentalist–Modernist Schisms among Baptists in North America, 1895–1934" (Ph.D. diss., University of Pittsburgh, 1974), 30, 110, 175.

4. "World's Christian Fundamentals Association," *The King's Business* 27 (March 1936): 94; "Young People to the Front," *New England Fellowship Monthly* 33 (November 1935): 9.

5. See, e.g., Mel Larson, *Young Man On Fire: The Story of Torrey Johnson and Youth for Christ* (Chicago: Youth Publications, 1945).

6. William R. De Plata, *Tell It from Calvary* (New York: Calvary Baptist Church, 1972), 61–62; Larson, *Youth for Christ,* 36–37; Rachel K. McDowell, "Churches to Begin Mobilization Week," *New York Times,* 24 October 1936, 20.

7. Larson, *Youth for Christ,* 37–41.

8. Bob Bahr, *Man with a Vision: The Story of Percy Crawford* (Chicago: Moody Press, n.d.), 17–29, 39–41, 50–51, 58.

9. Percy Crawford, "A Modern Revival," *Revelation* 2 (August 1932): 325, 349; Bahr, *Man with a Vision,* 31–34, 45–56.

10. Larson, *Youth for Christ,* 35; Bahr, *Man with a Vision,* 38–49. See Bahr, 51–56, and Appendix for examples of Crawford's sermons.

11. Forbes, *God Hath Chosen,* 9–27, 31–32, 40–41; Clarence Woodbury, "Bobby-Soxers Sing Hallelujah," *American Magazine* 141 (March 1946): 26–27, 123; Frank S. Mead, "Apostle to Youth," *Christian Herald* 68 (September 1945): 15–16; De Plata, *Tell It from Calvary,* 63–64; Larson, *Youth for Christ,* 45; Torrey Johnson and Robert Cook, *Reaching Youth for Christ* (Chicago: Moody Press, 1944), 9–10.

12. Forbes, *God Hath Chosen,* 47–60, 61–65; Mead, "Apostle to Youth," 15, 17; Woodbury, "Bobby-Soxers Sing Hallelujah," 123; "20,000 Pack Garden for Youth Rally," *United Evangelical Action,* 15 October 1944, 1, 4, reprinted from the *New York Times,* 1 October 1944.

13. "Indiana Birthplace of 'Youth for Christ,'" *United Evangelical Action,* 1 August 1945, 18; Larson, *Youth for Christ,* 48–55; "6,000 At Minneapolis Rally," *United Evangelical Action,* 19 March 1945, 3.

14. Larson, *Young Man on Fire,* 22–33, 45–66, 73–76, 79–81; Johnson and Cook, *Reaching Youth for Christ,* 9–24.

15. A Modern Miracle in 1944," *United Evangelical Action,* 1 September 1944, 11–12; Larson, *Young Man on Fire,* 83, 86–89; Mel Larson, "Reaching Youth for Christ," *The King's Business* 35 (December 1944): 400–1, 432; Mel Larson, "28,000 Jam Chicago Stadium for Rally," *Evangelical Beacon,* 31 October 1944, 1, 3.

16. Johnson and Cook, *Reaching Youth for Christ,* 37, 36, 41–42, 44–45, 49–52.

17. "Youth for Christ," *Time,* 4 February 1946, 46–47; "Wanted: A Miracle of Good Weather, and the 'Youth for Christ' Rally Got It," *Newsweek,* 11 June 1945, 84; Woodbury, "Bobby Soxers Sing Hallelujah," 27; Marshall Frady, *Billy Graham: A Parable of American Righteousness* (Boston: Little, Brown, 1979), 162; John Pollack, *Billy Graham: The Authorized Biography* (New York: McGraw-Hill, 1965), 85.

18. Forbes, *God Hath Chosen,* 93 (quotation), 94–96; William F. McDermott, "Bobby-Soxers Find the Sawdust Trail," *Colliers,* 26 May 1945, 22; "Bobby Sox Hit Sawdust Trail," 2; Woodbury, "Bobby-Soxers Sing Hallelujah," 27. See also George Beverly Shea with Fred Bauer, *Then Sings My Soul* (Old Tappan, N.J.: Revell, 1968).

19. Larson, *Youth for Christ,* 55, 68, 86; Larson, *Young Man on Fire,* 74, 76; Theodore W. Engstrom, "Publicizing Your Church," *MM* 45 (June 1945): 272; Hefley,

God Goes to High School, 34; *Minutes of the First Annual Convention,* Youth for Christ International, 22–29 July 1945, 23–24, Youth for Christ Records (Collection 48, Box 13, Folder 36), Archives of the Billy Graham Center, Wheaton College, Wheaton, Illinois.

20. Wright, "Youth for Christ," 8; "Youth for Christ Expands in Continent," *United Evangelical Action,* 1 January 1946, 9; Larson, *Youth for Christ,* 60–63, 69–71; Hefley, *God Goes to High School,* 29–30; "G.I. Missionaries to Manila," *Sunday* 7 (February 1946): 26–29, 49–52.

21. "Wanted: A Miracle of Good Weather," 84; Mel Larson, "70,000 Attend Chicago Youth for Christ Rally Held on Memorial Day," *United Evangelical Action,* 15 June 1945, 1, 8.

22. "Wanted: A Miracle of Good Weather"; Larson, "70,000 Attend Chicago Youth for Christ Rally," 1, 8; "Youth's New Crusade," editorial reprinted from the Hearst papers as "William Randolph Heart's Editorial Endorsement of 'Youth for Christ,'" *United Evangelical Action,* 16 July 1945, 13; "Hearst Papers Now Boost Youth for Christ," *United Evangelical Action,* 2 July 1945, 1; *Minutes of the First Annual Convention,* 6, 23–24. Torrey M. Johnson to Herbert J. Taylor, 25 October 1945, H. J. Taylor Papers; "Youth for Christ Expands in Continent," 9.

23. Richard H. Pells, *Radical Visions and American Dreams: Culture and Social Thought in the Depression Years* (New York: Harper & Row, 1973), 362; Geoffrey Perrett, *Days of Sadness, Years of Triumph: The American People, 1939–1945* (Baltimore: Penguin Books, 1974), 443.

24. Perrett, *Days of Sadness,* 196–99, 325–42, 350–56, 407–9, 441–43; Charles M. Alexander, *Nationalism in American Thought, 1930–1945* (Chicago: Rand McNally, 1969), 190–201; Pells, *Radical Visions,* 116–50, 358–64; Allan Nevins, "How We Felt about the War," in *While You Were Gone: A Report of Wartime Life in the United States,* ed. Jack Goodman (New York: Simon & Schuster, 1946), 3–27; Philip Gleason, "Americans All: World War II and the Shaping of American Identity," *American Quarterly* 36 (Fall 1984): 342–58.

25. Pells, *Radical Visions,* 141–50, 358–61; Alexander, *Nationalism,* 155–56, 223–24, 229; Nathan Glazer, *American Judaism,* rev. ed. (Chicago: University of Chicago Press, 1972), 108.

26. Perrett, *Days of Sadness,* 384–85; Lewis Gannett, "Books," and Bosley Crowther, "The Movies," in Goodman, ed., *While You Were Gone,* 455, 516.

27. Perrett, *Days of Sadness,* 384 (quotation), 238–40, 385–87, 394–95.

28. Donald Barnhouse, "God Bless America," *Revelation* 12 (September 1942): 396, 426; Hyman Appelman, "America's First Line of Defense," *MM* 43 (July 1943): 615. See also two editorials (among many) in the *Moody Monthly:* "The Statesmen and God," 42 (March 1942): 392; and "What Is Wrong?" 43 (March 1943): 395.

29. Perrett, *Days of Sadness,* 347–50; Anna W. M. Wolf and Irma Simonton Black, "What Happened to the Younger People," in Goodman, ed., *While You Were Gone,* 78–85; Agnes E. Meyer, *Journey through Chaos* (New York: Harcourt Brace, 1944), 6, 60–65, 209–13, 250. For fundamentalists' reaction, see "Sinning Children—An Editorial," *MM* 44 (March 1944): 372; A. W. Tozer, "What's Behind Juvenile Delinquency?" *MM* 45 (September 1944): 10–11, 21.

30. Johnson quoted in Larson, *Young Man on Fire,* 112.

31. Woodbury, "Bobby-Soxers Sing Hallelujah," 121.

32. Ibid., 27, 121 (quotation).

33. Woodbury, "Bobby-Soxers Sing Hallelujah," 27; McDermott, "Bobby-Soxers

find the Sawdust Trail," 23. For accounts of how many responded to evangelists' invitations to receive Christ, see Billy Graham, "Report of the Vice-President at Large," *Minutes of the Second Annual Convention,* Youth for Christ International, 22–29 July 1946, Minneapolis, Minnesota, 38–39, Youth for Christ Records (Collection 48, Box 13, Folder 37),.

34. "Youth's New Crusade," reprinted from the Hearst newspapers as "William Randolph Hearst's Editorial Endorsement of 'Youth for Christ,'" *United Evangelical Action,* 15 July 1945, 13; Larson, *Youth for Christ,* 111; Willard M. Aldrich, "Young People Are A Crop," *MM* 45 (November 1944): 138, 140; Larson, *Young Man on Fire,* 91; *Minutes of the First Annual Convention,* 6, 16, 23–24.

35. Leo P. Ribuffo, *The Old Christian Right: The Protestant Far Right from the Depression to the Cold War* (Philadelphia: Temple University Press, 1983), 178–81; "Anti-Semitism Is Denied," *New York Times,* 16 December 1945, 31.

36. "Has Youth for Christ Gone Fascist?" *Christian Century,* 14 November 1945, 1243–44; Harold E. Fey, "What About 'Youth for Christ'?" ibid., 1243–44.

37. "Youth for Christ," *Time,* 46–47.

38. Examples of the genre include the editorial "Between War and Peace," *Catholic Action* 27 (December 1945): 27–28; Charles Clayton Morrison, *Can Protestantism Win America?* (New York: Harper & Brothers, 1948); and Willard L. Sperry, *Religion in America* (New York: Macmillan, 1946), 258–63. Insights on the postwar civil-religious climate are to be found in Robert S. Alley, *So Help Me God: Religion and the Presidency, Wilson to Nixon* (Richmond, Va.: John Knox, 1972), 69–81; John F. Wilson, *Public Religion in American Culture* (Philadelphia: Temple University Press, 1979), 15, 50–51, 54–55; and Robert T. Handy, *A Christian America: Protestant Hopes and Historical Realities,* 2d ed. (New York: Oxford University Press, 1984), 186–87.

39. Torrey Johnson, "God Is In It!," *Minutes of the First Annual Convention,* Youth for Christ International, 22–29 July 1945, 30.

40. Harry S. Truman, "The Need for Moral Analyzing," *New York Times,* 6 March 1946, 11; "Honoring Evangelical Chaplains of the Armed Forces," *New York Times,* 25 April 1946, 5, describes General Eisenhower's speech. Billy Graham, "Report of the Vice President at Large," *Minutes of the Second Annual Convention,* 36, 41; Larson, *Youth for Christ,* 29; and Hefley, *God Goes to High School,* 13, each quote politicians' calls for revival.

41. J. Elwin Wright, "Post-War Opportunity Requires Action Now," *New England Fellowship Monthly* 43 (March 1945): 8–9; James DeForest Murch, "The Church's Post-War Program," *United Evangelical Action,* 1 September 1945, 12; "The Trouble Lies Deep," *United Evangelical Action,* 15 September 1945, 12–13.

42. Johnson, "God Is In It!," 27, 30. This sermon is also published in a polished version as "Almighty Challenge," *Winona Echoes* 51 (1945): 157–65.

43. Larson, *Youth for Christ,* 98; Johnson and Cook, *Reaching Youth for Christ,* 36.

44. Larson, *Youth for Christ,* 75.

45. Larson, "Youth for Christ Movements," *MM* 45 (December 1944): 205, 245 (Chicago Rally); Shelley, "The Rise of Evangelical Youth Movements," 47–63 (H. J. Taylor's pervasive role). Larson, *Youth for Christ,* 53; "6,000 at Minneapolis Rally," 3; and *Minutes of the Second Annual Convention,* 33, 49 document LeTourneau's frequent participation.

46. For examples of the perspectives of evangelical businessmen, see Richard Schmeberger, "Postwar Planning for the Churches," *MM* 44 (February 1944): 825 (quotation); Theodore W. Engstrom, "Publicizing Your Church," *MM* 45 (January 1945):

272, 294; and C. Davis Weyerhaeuser, "A Layman Asks A Question," *MM* 46 (October 1945): 59–60.

47. Torrey M. Johnson to Herbert J. Taylor, 25 October 1945, H. J. Taylor Papers; Billy Graham, "Report of the Vice President at Large," *Minutes of the Second Annual Convention*, 38–39.

48. *Christianity Today*, 8 November 1985, ran a series of articles on the parachurch phenomenon. See especially Bruce Shelley, "The Parachurch Vision: The Pioneers at Fifty," 41–43; and Joel Carpenter, "Impatient to Do God's Work," 27. See also J. Alan Youngren, "Parachurch Proliferation: The Frontier Spirit Caught in Traffic," *Christianity Today*, 6 November 1981, 38–39; and Richard G. Hutcheson, Jr., *Mainline Churches and the Evangelicals: A Challenging Crisis?* (Atlanta, Ga.: John Knox, 1981), 62–79.

49. Larson, "The Challenge of the Future for Youth for Christ," sermon delivered at Orchestra Hall, Chicago, 16 June 1945, reprinted in Larson, *Young Man on Fire*, 111–14, 112 (quotation); "Rallying 'Youth for Christ' in Greater Oklahoma City," program brochure of the Oklahoma City Youth for Christ Rally for December 1945–January 1946, Youth for Christ Records.

50. "Organize YFC in Little Rock," *United Evangelical Action*, 15 March 1945, 14. There is no indication in this account that Little Rock YFC crossed the color line.

51. Vance Havner, "*Come and See*—The Road to Certainty," *MM* 34 (January 1934): 211.

52. "Youth for Christ," *Revelation* 16 (April 1946): 151; "Breadth or Depth," *Revelation* 15 (July 1945): 285; anon., "Today's Youth Evangelism—Is It Shallow?" *The King's Business* 36 (July 1945): 251.

53. Mead, "Apostle to Youth," 51; John Ray Evers, "'Youth for Christ' Meets Pittsburgh," *Christian Century*, 10 October 1945, 1171–72. See also Daniel A. Poling, "The New Evangelism," *Christian Herald* 69 (January 1946): 18–19, 58–61; Fey, "What About 'Youth for Christ'?" 1243–44.

54. R. Laurence Moore, *Religious Outsiders and the Making of Americans* (New York: Oxford University Press, 1986), 165–72, is very convincing, and exactly right, I think, on this point.

55. Quentin Schultze, *Televangelism and American Culture: The Business of Popular Religion* (Grand Rapids, Mich.: Baker Book House, 1991), 196, notes this enduring drive for self-promotion.

56. Shelley, "Rise of Evangelical Youth Movements," 47–63. See also Joel Carpenter, "'Geared to the Times but Anchored to the Rock': How Contemporary Techniques and Exuberant Nationalism Helped Create an Evangelical Resurgence," *Christianity Today*, 8 November 1985, 44–47.

Chapter 10

1. Torrey Johnson, "God Is In It!" *Minutes of the First Annual Convention*, Youth for Christ International, 22–29 July 1945, 32, Youth for Christ Records (Collection 48, Box 13, Folder 36), Archives of the Billy Graham Center, Wheaton College, Wheaton, Illinois.

2. Two works that do assess this development are Denton Lotz, "'The Evangelization of the World in This Generation': The Resurgence of a Missionary Idea among the Conservative Evangelicals" (Ph.D. diss., University of Hamburg, 1970); and Ralph D. Winter, *The Twenty-five Unbelievable Years, 1945 to 1969* (South Pasadena, Calif.: William Carey Library, 1970), 47–51.

3. This foregoing section reflects both the facts and the insights to be found in Richard V. Pierard's excellent essay "Pax Americana and the Evangelical Missionary Advance," in *Earthen Vessels: American Evangelicals and Foreign Missions, 1880–1920,* ed. Joel A. Carpenter and Wilbert R. Shenk (Grand Rapids, Mich.: Eerdmans, 1990), 155–79.

4. Rowland V. Bingham, *Seven Sevens of Years and a Jubilee: The Story of the Sudan Interior Mission* (Toronto: Evangelical Publishers, 1943), 116; Robert Hall Glover, "What Should Be Our Post-War Evangelical Missionary Strategy?" *United Evangelical Action,* 15 September 1945, 6, 19; Clarence W. Jones, *Radio: The New Missionary* (Chicago: Moody Press, 1946), 112, 113 (quotation).

5. For examples of military jargon, see Torrey M. Johnson, "Almighty Challenge," *Winona Echoes* 51 (1945): 164; and Mervin E. Rosell, "God's Global 'Go'," ibid., 260–65. David Bosch, "The Vulnerability of Mission," *Baptist Quarterly* 34 (October 1992): 351–63, offers an important critical view of the crusading mentality evident in European missions since the sixteenth century.

6. Rosell, "God's Global 'Go'," 264.

7. Interview of Donald Arthur Cook (Collection 259), Archives of the Billy Graham Center.

8. My father's experience provides a case in point. Raised in a rural community in southwestern Michigan, Allan Carpenter had no travel experience outside the Upper Midwest until he was drafted into the army in 1942. He served with a railroad battalion in India and what is now Bangladesh. While never volunteering for missionary service himself, he became an avid supporter of missions in the decades to come. He took a particular interest in the work of some Regular Baptist missionaries who were establishing a medical ministry in Bangladesh.

9. Sam Tamashiro, "GI Missionaries to Manila," *Sunday* 7 (February 1946): 26–29, 49–52; J. Herbert Kane, *Faith, Mighty Faith: A Handbook of the Interdenominational Foreign Missions Association* (New York: IFMA, 1956), 64–65; Pierard, *"Pax Americana,"* 172–73.

10. Glover, "Post-War Evangelical Missionary Strategy," 19; Bingham, *Seven Sevens of Years and a Jubilee,* 116.

11. For a suggestive overview of American cultural traits in modern missions, including a faith in technology's power to advance the reign of God, see Andrew F. Walls, "The American Dimension in the History of the Missionary Movement," in Carpenter and Shenk, eds., *Earthen Vessels,* 1–25.

12. J. B. Knutson, "New Tribes Mission," *Encyclopedia of Modern Foreign Missions,* ed. Burton L. Goddard (Camden, N.J.: T. Y. Nelson, 1967), 428–31; Roy Ostreicher, "Post War Plans," *Brown Gold* 3 (June 1945): 4; financial report, *Brown Gold* 3 (January 1946): 2.

13. Kane, *Faith, Mighty Faith,* 93–97; Pierard, *"Pax Americana,"* 177.

14. "The Story of EFMA: Evangelical Foreign Missions Association," typescript dated 31 October 1950, Records of the Evangelical Foreign Missions Association (Collection 165, Box 2, Folder 16), Archives of the Billy Graham Center; William W. Menzies, *Anointed to Serve: The Story of the Assemblies of God* (Springfield, Mo.: Gospel Publishing House, 1971), 206.

15. William C. Ringenberg, *The Christian College: A History of Protestant Higher Education in America* (Grand Rapids, Mich.: Christian University Press, 1984), 208–9; Ringenberg, *Taylor University: The First 125 Years* (Grand Rapids, Mich.: Eerdmans, 1973), 160, 169.

16. Interview of Donald Arthur Cook.

17. Interview of George Murray Winston (Collection 306), Archives of the Billy Graham Center. The Navigators was an organization begun in San Pedro, California in the early 1930s by a young evangelist, Dawson Trotman, as a ministry to sailors. It featured small-group Bible study, the memorization of Scripture and intensive, one-on-one spiritual mentoring called "discipleship." By the end of the war, the Navigators movement had spread throughout the armed forces and reported cadres in more than 450 army camps and at least 350 navy vessels. D. G. Buss, "The Navigators," *Dictionary of Christianity in America,* ed. Daniel G. Reid et al. (Downers Grove, Ill.: InterVarsity Press, 1990), 803.

18. Paul M. Bechtel, *Wheaton College: A Heritage Remembered, 1860–1984* (Wheaton, Ill.: Harold Shaw, 1984), 194.

19. R. Arthur Mathews, *Towers Pointing Upward* (Columbia, S.C.: Columbia Bible College, 1973), 143–45. The school's enrollment was also surging, from 203 in 1941–1942 to 450 in 1950–1951.

20. Pierard, *"Pax Americana,"* 171; Forrest Forbes, *God Hath Chosen: The Story of Jack Wyrtzen and the Word of Life Hour* (Grand Rapids, Mich.: Zondervan, 1948), 44, 76, 120; Knutson, "New Tribes Mission," 429–30; masthead of *Brown Gold* 2 (May 1944): 2; Mel Larson, *Youth For Christ: Twentieth-Century Wonder* (Grand Rapids, Mich.: Zondervan, 1947), 59; Mel Larson, *Young Man on Fire: The Story of Torrey Johnson and Youth for Christ* (Chicago: Youth Publications, 1945), 84.

21. James Hefley, *God Goes to High School* (Waco, Tex.: Word Books, 1970), 34–44; Larson, *Youth for Christ,* 22–23, 79–81, 92–93, 128; "Five YFC Leaders Will Fly to Europe," *United Evangelical Action,* 4 April 1945, 2; Torrey Johnson, "Pressing On in Youth for Christ," *Minutes of the Second Annual Convention,* Youth for Christ International, 22–29 July 1946, 7–8, Youth for Christ Records (Collection 48, Box 13, Folder 37, Archives of the Billy Graham Center.

22. Kane, *Faith, Mighty Faith,* 76–78; Hefley, *God Goes to High School,* 67–68; Paul W. Freed, *Towers to Eternity: The Story of Trans World Radio* (Cherry Hill, N.J.: Trans World Radio, 1968).

23. Hefley, *God Goes to High School,* 66–67.

24. Keith and Gladys Hunt, *For Christ and the University: The Story of InterVarsity Christian Fellowship of the U.S.A./1940–1990* (Downers Grove, Ill.: InterVarsity Press, 1991), 56–73.

25. Ibid., 86–120; see also Lawrence Neale Jones, "The Inter-Varsity Christian Fellowship in the United States: A Study of Its History, Theology and Relations with Other Groups" (Ph.D. diss., Yale University, 1961), 95–184.

26. H. Wilbert Norton, *To Stir The Church: A Brief History of the Student Foreign Missions Fellowships, 1936–1986* (Madison, Wis.: Student Foreign Mission Fellowship, 1986), 1–33; and Norton, "The Student Foreign Missions Fellowship over Fifty-five Years," *International Bulletin of Missionary Research* 17 (January 1993): 17–21.

27. Hunt & Hunt, *For Christ and the University,* 125–28; Norton, *To Stir The Church,* 32–34.

28. The most rapid rate of increase occurred during the 1950s and early 1960s. See Robert T. Coote, "The Uneven Growth of Conservative Evangelical Missions," *International Bulletin of Missionary Research* 6 (July 1982): 118–23.

29. All statistics for 1952 cited in this paragraph and those below are from R. Pierce Beaver, "The Protestant Foreign Missionary Enterprise of the United States," *Occasional Bulletin of the Missionary Research Library* 4:7 (8 May 1953), 1–15. "1933–

1943," *Translation* 1:1 (1943): 9–10; "Four Typical Bible Translators," *Translation* 1:3 (1943): 1; "Three Years' Advance for CBFMS," *Conservative Baptist Foreign Mission Society News & Views* 3 (January 1947): 1.

30. Vernon Mortenson, "The Evangelical Alliance Mission," *Encyclopedia of Modern Foreign Missions,* 248; statistical report in the *Missionary Broadcaster* 17:2 (1941): 11; "Africa Inland Mission," *Encyclopedia of Modern Foreign Missions,* 5; statistical report in *Inland Africa* 29 (September–October 1945): back cover.

31. Statistics for 1935 in this paragraph and the one below are drawn from *Interpretative Statistical Survey of the World Mission of the Christian Church,* ed. Joseph I. Parker (New York: International Missionary Council, 1938), 40–45.

32. Pierard, *"Pax Americana,"* 158, n. 4; also see Joel A. Carpenter, "Propagating the Faith Once Delivered: The Fundamentalist Missionary Enterprise," in Carpenter and Shenk, eds., *Earthen Vessels,* 93; and Carpenter, "Appendix: The Evangelical Missionary Force in the 1930s," in *Earthen Vessels,* 335–42, for a more detailed look at these trends.

33. Walls, "The American Dimension," 18.

34. Pierard, *"Pax Americana,"* 160–65; Charles E. Van Engen, "A Broadening Vision: Forty Years of Evangelical Theology of Mission, 1946–1986," in Carpenter and Shenk, eds., *Earthen Vessels,* 206–11; and Arthur Glasser, "The Evolution of Mission Theology since World War II," *International Bulletin of Missionary Research* 9 (January 1985): 9–13. After the communist takeover in China in 1949 and the advent of the Korean War in 1950, the "closing doors" imagery took on a new meaning and urgency. But that is another story.

35. Johnson is quoted in "Youth for Christ," *Time,* 4 February 1946, 46–47.

36. R. Laurence Moore, *Religious Outsiders and the Making of Americans* (New York: Oxford University Press, 1986), 169–73.

Chapter 11

1. Harold J. Ockenga, "Can Fundamentalism Win America?" *Christian Life and Times,* June 1947, 13–15.

2. G. Bromley Oxnam, *The Church and Contemporary Change* (New York: Macmillan, 1950), 29–30, quoted in Robert Wuthnow, *The Restructuring of American Religion: Society and Faith since World War II* (Princeton, N.J.: Princeton University Press, 1988), 60.

3. Charles Clayton Morrison, *Can Protestantism Win America?* (New York: Harper & Brothers, 1948), 1, 2.

4. Perhaps the most suggestive of Harold Fey's articles in portraying a sense of threat to the "American Way of Life" is "Catholicism Comes To Middletown," *Christian Century,* 6 December 1944, 1409–11. On the Catholic resurgence in America, see Jay P. Dolan, *The American Catholic Experience: A History from Colonial Times to the Present* (Garden City, N.Y.: Doubleday, 1985), 352, and esp. 384–417; William M. Halsey, *The Survival of American Innocence* (Notre Dame, Ind.: University of Notre Dame Press, 1980); and Edward R. Kantowicz, *Corporation Sole: Cardinal Mundelein and Chicago Catholicism* (Notre Dame, Ind.: University of Notre Dame Press, 1983), especially chs. 12 and 13, for examples of how the Catholic renewal was expressed in one of its centers.

5. These articles were compiled and published as *Can Protestantism Win America?* The above paragraph refers to pp. 88–89, 219.

6. Relatively little has been written about Ockenga. Two important sources of information are Harold Lindsell, *Park Street Prophet: A Life of Harold John Ockenga* (Wheaton, Ill.: Van Kampen Press, 1951), a fawning biography written by one of his protégés; and John M. Adams, "The Making of a Neo-Evangelical Statesman: The Case of Harold John Ockenga" (Ph.D. diss., Baylor University, 1994), which is particularly well documented and insightful on Ockenga's formative years. See also George M. Marsden, *Reforming Fundamentalism: Fuller Seminary and the New Evangelicalism* (Grand Rapids, Mich.: Eerdmans, 1987), a story in which Ockenga plays an important role.

7. Ockenga, "Christ for America," *United We Stand: A Report of the Constitutional Convention of the National Association of Evangelicals, La Salle Hotel, Chicago, Illinois, May 3–6, 1943* (Boston: National Association of Evangelicals, 1943), 11.

8. Lindsell, *Park Street Prophet,* 89; Elizabeth Evans, *The Wright Vision: The Story of the New England Fellowship* (Lanham, Md.: University Press of America, 1991), 109–11.

9. The Gordon incident is recounted in Ernest B. Gordon, *Adoniram Judson Gordon: A Biography* (New York: F. H. Revell, 1896), 117–19.

10. Lindsell, *Park Street Prophet,* 75–76.

11. Ibid., 142–44; Ockenga, "Can Fundamentalism Win America?", 14.

12. Wilbur M. Smith, *Therefore Stand: A Plea for a Vigorous Apologetic in the Present Crisis of Evangelical Christianity* (Chicago: Moody Press, 1945), 483, 506.

13. The three Asbury scholars were Harold Kuhn, J. Harold Greenlee, and George Turner. The students from the Churches of Christ were Jack P. Lewis of Harding College and Lemoine Lewis of Abilene Christian University. The pentecostal was Stanley Horton, who went on to teach at the Central Bible College of the Assemblies of God. Three sources in particular have informed the following paragraphs about the "Harvard fundamentalists": Carl F. H. Henry, *Confessions of a Theologian: An Autobiography* (Waco, Tex.: Word, 1986), 110–11, 114–15, 120–23; Kenneth S. Kantzer, "Carl Ferdinand Howard Henry: An Appreciation," in *God and Culture: Essays in Honor of Carl F. H. Henry,* ed. D. A. Carson and John D. Woodbridge (Grand Rapids, Mich.: Eerdmans, 1993), 369–73; and Rudolph Nelson, *The Making and Unmaking of an Evangelical Mind: The Case of Edward Carnell* (New York: Cambridge University Press, 1987), 54–63.

14. This list combines the persons named in Nelson, *The Making and Unmaking of an Evangelical Mind,* 54–56; and in Kantzer, "Carl Ferdinand Howard Henry: An Appreciation," 369.

15. Nelson, *Making and Unmaking,* 52, 56–57.

16. Marsden, *Reforming Fundamentalism,* 43–45, 76–79; Nelson, *Making and Unmaking,* 36–49. George M. Marsden, *Fundamentalism and American Culture: The Shaping of Twentieth-Century Evangelicalism, 1870–1925* (New York: Oxford University Press, 1980), 136–38, gives an overview of J. Gresham Machen's vision of Christianity transforming culture. Machen's most compelling statement of this cultural mandate is "Christianity and Culture," *Princeton Theological Review* 11 (January 1913): 1–15. But see D. G. Hart, *Defending The Faith: J. Gresham Machen and the Crisis of Conservative Protestantism in Modern America* (Baltimore: Johns Hopkins University Press, 1994), 133–70, which argues that Machen was much more reluctant than the Dutch Reformed philosophers—or mainstream fundamentalists, for that matter—to prescribe a major interventionist role for organized Christianity in public affairs. It is possible the fundamentalist progressives made Machen into more of a cultural reformer than he would have allowed had he stayed on the scene.

17. Adams, "Making of a Neo-Evangelical Statesman," 139–49; Marsden, *Reforming Fundamentalism,* 32–34; Nelson, *Making and Unmaking,* 37–41.

18. Nelson, *Making and Unmaking,* 58; Kantzer, "Carl Henry," 371.

19. Henry, *Confessions,* 122–23; Nelson, *Making and Unmaking,* 58–60.

20. Kantzer, "Carl Henry," 371; Nelson, 58–69.

21. Kantzer, "Carl Henry," 371; Henry, letter to the author (n.d.), received 24 May 1993.

22. Henry, *Confessions,* 111–13, 120–22; J. C. Brown, "Brightman, Edgar Sheffield (1884–1953)," *Dictionary of Christianity in America,* ed. Daniel G. Reid et al. (Downers Grove, Ill.: InterVarsity Press, 1990), 189; Taylor Branch, *Parting The Waters: America in the King Years, 1954–63* (New York: Simon & Schuster, 1988), 90–94.

23. Henry to the author, 24 May 1993; Henry, *Confessions,* 121; Kantzer to the author, 18 June 1993; Kantzer, "Carl Henry," 370–71.

24. Henry, *Confessions,* 106–7; Nathan R. Wood, *A School of Christ* (Boston: Gordon College of Theology and Missions, 1953), 195–200; *The Gordon* 1:1 (February 1946), n.p.; Nelson, *Making and Unmaking,* 61–63.

25. Henry to the author; Kantzer to the author; Nelson, *Making and Unmaking,* 69–70.

26. Marsden, *Reforming Fundamentalism,* 24; Henry to the author; Kantzer to the author; "An Evangelical Manifesto, Issued by the Plymouth Conference for the Advancement of Evangelical Scholarship, Plymouth, Mass., August 18," *United Evangelical Action,* 15 September 1945, 4.

27. Marsden, *Reforming Fundamentalism,* 19–20; Lindsell, *Park Street Prophet,* 128–29.

28. Smith, *Therefore Stand,* 498–99; Marsden, *Reforming Fundamentalism,* 24–25, 70; Lindsell, *Park Street Prophet,* 129–30.

29. Nelson, 69–78; Marsden, *Reforming Fundamentalism,* 26–28, 97–98, 105, 120.

30. Marsden, *Reforming Fundamentalism,* 61 (quote), 60–63; Harold J. Ockenga, "The Challenge to the Christian Culture of the West," typescript summary of convocation address, inauguration of Fuller Theological Seminary, 1 October 1947, p. 10, Archives of Fuller Theological Seminary.

31. Henry, *Confessions,* 127. See also Nelson, 73–78.

32. Marsden, *Reforming Fundamentalism,* 35 (quote), 36, 69–75; J. A. Carpenter, "Smith, Wilbur (M)oorehead (1894–1976)," *Dictionary of Christianity in America,* 1099–1100. Smith's memoirs, *Before I Forget* (Chicago: Moody Press, 1971), remain the most comprehensive published record of his long and distinguished career.

33. Marsden, *Reforming Fundamentalism,* 25; Smith, *Before I Forget,* 135; Smith, *Therefore Stand,* xvii (quote), 498–99.

34. Smith's early career is documented in *Before I Forget,* 11–68, 71, 75–79, 124–25, 238–45; see also Marsden, *Reforming Fundamentalism,* 25–26, 36, 69–70.

35. Smith, *Before I Forget,* 65–68, 133–34; Marsden, Reforming Fundamentalism, 58.

36. Smith, *Before I Forget,* 83–88, 106–24; Marsden, *Reforming Fundamentalism,* 35–36, 41–44; Marsden, "Perspectives on the Division of 1937," in *Pressing Toward The Mark: Essays Commemorating Fifty Years of the Orthodox Presbyterian Church,* ed. Charles G. Dennison and Richard C. Gamble (Philadelphia: Orthodox Presbyterian Church, 1986), 295–328.

37. Smith, *Therefore Stand,* 480, 483.

38. Ibid., 478, 498, 502, 504, 506.

39. Henry discussed these problems in detail in "Twenty Years a Baptist," *Foundations* 1 (1957): 46–54.

40. Henry, *Confessions,* 42–76, 89–113.

41. Ibid., 101–2, 106, 111. Carl F. H. Henry, *Successful Church Publicity: A Guidebook for Christian Publicists* (Grand Rapids, Mich.: Zondervan, 1943).

42. Henry, *Confessions,* 105–13.

43. Carl F. H. Henry, *Remaking The Modern Mind* (Grand Rapids, Mich.: Eerdmans, 1946), 7.

44. Carl F. H. Henry, *The Uneasy Conscience of Modern Fundamentalism* (Grand Rapids, Mich.: Eerdmans, 1947), 16–23.

45. Henry, *Uneasy Conscience,* 65, 89.

46. Carl F. H. Henry, "The Vigor of the New Evangelicalism," *Christian Life* 1 (January 1948): 30, 31, 32.

47. Ibid., 36, 37, 38, 85.

48. Henry, "The Vigor of the New Evangelicalism" [part three], *Christian Life* 1 (April 1948): 32–33.

49. Ibid., 34.

50. Ibid., 34–35, 65–67.

51. Ibid., 67–68.

52. Ibid., 69.

53. Henry, *Uneasy Conscience,* 65, 69, 70, 71–72, 76, 79, 84, 88, 89.

54. Donald W. Dayton, "'The Search for the Historical Evangelicalism': George Marsden's History of Fuller Seminary as a Case Study," *Christian Scholar's Review* 23 (September 1993): 30–31, argues that a critique of dispensationalism was central to the "new evangelicalism." There is much to commend that argument, but it is also true that the early Fuller had about equal numbers of dispensationalists and nondispensationalists on its faculty. So it seems that the new evangelicalism, as Henry and Ockenga saw it, could accommodate dispensationalism in some of its less starkly sectarian forms. Nevertheless, hanging onto or jettisoning dispensationalism was a key sign of whether one merely wished to reform fundamentalism or substantially change it.

55. Marsden, *Reforming Fundamentalism,* 76, 150–52.

56. Henry, *Confessions,* 95, 107–8, 116, 26–27. See also Nelson, *Making and Unmaking,* 16–27, as well as 51–53, 60–62, 71–74. Carnell also acquired a new house and a new Buick as he moved to Fuller.

57. Marsden, *Reforming Fundamentalism,* 64–67; Ockenga, "The Challenge to the Christian Culture of the West," 10–11.

58. "Blue Network Grants Free Radio Time to American Council of Christian Churches: 'Christ and Him Crucified' to be Preached," *Christian Beacon,* 2 December 1943, 1; Edward Heerema, *R.B.: A Prophet in the Land: Rienk Bouke Kuiper, Preacher–Theologian–Churchman* (Jordan Station, Ontario: Paideia Press, 1986), 146–49; "Dr. Buswell Joins Faith Theological Seminary," *SST,* 17 February 1940, 137; Edward A. Steele III, "Buswell, The Man," *Presbyterion: Covenant Seminary Review* 2 (Spring–Fall 1976): 10–11; Edwin H. Rian, *The Presbyterian Conflict* (Grand Rapids, Mich.: Eerdmans, 1940), 102–3.

59. "Fellowshipping Churches of the G.A.R.B.C., 1948," *Baptist Bulletin* 14 (August 1948): 5–18; William A. Bevier, "A History of the I.F.C.A." (Th.D. thesis, Dallas Theological Seminary, 1958), 373.

60. Bruce L. Shelley, *Conservative Baptists: A Story of Twentieth-Century Dissent,* 3d ed. (Wheaton, Ill.: Conservative Baptist Press, 1981), is the best account of this struggle; see also the accounts of the controversies at the state level, where much of the

conflict actually took place, e.g., William Vance Trollinger, Jr., *God's Empire: William Bell Riley and Midwestern Fundamentalism* (Madison: University of Wisconsin Press, 1990), 133–50, on the Conservative Baptist "revolt" in Minnesota; and Albert Wardin, Jr., *Baptists in Oregon* (Portland: Judson College, 1969), 455–73, on the split in the Oregon Baptist state convention.

61. Bill J. Leonard, "Southern Baptist Relationships with Independent Baptists," *Baptist History and Heritage* 25 (July 1990): 43–51; William Robert Glass, "The Development of Northern Patterns of Fundamentalism in the South, 1900–1950" (Ph.D. diss., Emory University, 1991); Joel A. Carpenter, "Is 'Evangelical' a Yankee Word? Relations Between Northern Evangelicals and the Southern Baptist Convention in the Twentieth Century," in *Southern Baptists and American Evangelicals: The Conversation Continues,* ed. David S. Dockery (Nashville, Tenn.: Broadman & Holman, 1993), 78–99.

62. Michael S. Hamilton, "The Fundamentalist Harvard: Wheaton College and the Enduring Vitality of American Evangelicalism, 1919–1965" (Ph.D. diss., University of Notre Dame, 1994), 222–26, documents the tensions at Wheaton College prompted by the rise of "new evangelical" perspectives in the late 1940s.

63. Henry, *Confessions,* 117, recounts the story of Jones's chapel address; on the opening up of a definite split between separatist fundamentalism and the new evangelicals, see Marsden, *Reforming Fundamentalism,* 162–71.

64. Henry, *Confessions,* 105–6; James DeForest Murch, *Cooperation without Compromise: A History of the National Association of Evangelicals* (Grand Rapids, Mich.: Eerdmans, 1956), 87–89, 172–73.

65. Murch, *Cooperation without Compromise,* 92–93; Henry, *Confessions,* 123. In the passage cited, Henry notes that the speaking assignment originally was Wilbur M. Smith's.

66. Keith and Gladys Hunt, *For Christ and the University: The Story of InterVarsity Christian Fellowship of the U.S.A., 1940–1990* (Downers Grove, Ill.: InterVarsity Press, 1991), 111, 114–15; Mark A. Noll, *Between Faith and Criticism: Evangelicals, Scholarship, and the Bible in America* (San Francisco: Harper & Row, 1986), 83–84, 101–3.

67. Hunt and Hunt, *For Christ and the University,* 66–82, offers an insightful character study of C. Stacey Woods. On Ockenga's involvement, see Hunt & Hunt, 126–28; and Lindsell, *Park Street Prophet,* 91. Wilbur Smith's Inter-Varsity work is mentioned in: Hunt and Hunt, 87, 113–14; H. Wilbert Norton, *To Stir The Church: A Brief History of the Student Foreign Missions Fellowship, 1936–1986* (Madison, Wis.: Student Foreign Mission Fellowship, 1986), 32, 34; Smith, *Before I Forget,* 246; and Marsden, *Reforming Fundamentalism,* 71. For Henry's participation, see his *Confessions,* 105, 126.

68. A classic expression of this pragmatic, task-oriented ecumenical spirit for the sake of revival is an article by C. Davis Weyerhaeuser, a prominent business executive in Tacoma, Washington, and a trustee of the Moody Bible Institute: "A Layman Asks A Question," *MM* 46 (October 1945): 59–60.

69. Smith, *Before I Forget,* 241–42; 246–47; Henry, *Confessions,* 119–20.

70. Lindsell, *Park Street Prophet,* 141–44; Billy Graham, "Harold John Ockenga: A Man Who Walked with God," *Christianity Today,* 15 March 1985, 35.

Chapter 12

1. J. Edwin Orr, *Good News in Bad Times: Signs of Revival* (Grand Rapids, Mich.: Zondervan, 1953), 1–3, 5; "Round the World for Revival," *The Christian,* 9 December 1937, 17.

2. Orr, *Good News in Bad Times,* 5–7.

3. *Good News In Bad Times* is Orr's most systematic treatment of the postwar resurgence of revivalism. James Edwin Orr, *The Second Evangelical Awakening in America: An Account of the Second Worldwide Evangelical Revival Beginning in the Mid-Nineteenth Century, with Appendices Dealing with the Beginning of the Mid-Twentieth Century Movement* (London: Marshall, Morgan & Scott, 1952), Apps. A, B, C, and D, contains narratives Orr wrote or compiled on this phenomenon. Another brief early assessment is Orr, "Preparing for Revival," in *Revival In Our Time: the Story of the Billy Graham Evangelistic Campaigns, Including Six of His Sermons* (Wheaton, Ill.: Van Kampen Press, 1950), 32–37. Orr is obviously both chronicler and advocate, but his vantage point as a participant is extremely valuable.

4. For a variety of interpretations of the postwar revival, see William G. McLoughlin, Jr., "Is There A Third Force in Christendom?" *Daedalus* (Winter 1967): 43–68; McLoughlin, *Modern Revivalism: Charles Grandison Finney to Billy Graham* (New York: Ronald Press, 1959), 505–12; Martin E. Marty, *The New Shape of American Religion* (New York: Harper & Brothers, 1959), 21–27; A. Roy Eckhardt, *The Surge of Piety in America: An Appraisal* (New York: Association Press, 1958), 42–77; Winthrop Hudson, *Religion in America,* 2d ed. (New York: Charles Scribner's Sons, 1973), 382–85; Sydney Ahlstrom, *A Religious History of the American People* (New Haven, Conn.: Yale University Press, 1972), 949–63; and Will Herberg, *Protestant–Catholic–Jew: An Essay in American Religious Sociology,* 2d ed. (Garden City, N.Y.: Doubleday Anchor Books, 1960), 56–64. Varying interpretations of Billy Graham's career and role in the postwar revival include William G. McLoughlin, *Billy Graham: Revivalist in a Secular Age* (New York: Ronald Press, 1960); Marshall Frady, *Billy Graham: A Parable of American Righteousness* (Boston: Little Brown, 1979); Stanley High, *Billy Graham: The Personal Story of the Man, His Message, and His Mission* (New York: McGraw-Hill, 1956); and John Pollock, *Billy Graham, The Authorized Biography* (New York: McGraw-Hill, 1965). William Martin, *A Prophet with Honor: The Billy Graham Story* (New York: William Morrow, 1991), is by far the best of these. As subsequent notes will show, this chapter owes much by way of facts and interpretation to Martin's excellent work.

5. Roger Finke, "The Illusion of Shifting Demand: Supply-Side Interpretations of American Religious History," in *Narrating American Religious History,* ed. Thomas Tweed (Berkeley and Los Angeles: University of California Press, 1997), 108–126.

6. Two authors in particular are insightful on this theme. See James Gilbert, *Another Chance: Postwar America, 1945–1968* (Philadelphia: Temple University Press, 1981), Introduction; and Robert Wuthnow, *The Restructuring of American Religion: Society and Faith since World War II* (Princeton, N.J.: Princeton University Press, 1988), 35–53.

7. Wuthnow, *The Restructuring of American Religion,* 35–37; Herberg, *Protestant–Catholic–Jew,* 46–51; Douglas T. Miller, "Popular Religion of the 1950's: Norman Vincent Peale and Billy Graham," *Journal of Popular Culture* 9:1 (1975): 66–67. Hudson, *Religion in America,* 382–91, provides a helpful overview, and Eckhardt, *The Surge of Piety in America* is a provocative contemporary account.

8. John R. Rice, *We Can Have Revival Now* (Wheaton, Ill.: Sword of the Lord, 1950), 173–77; Horace F. Dean, *Christ for America: A Nationwide Campaign for Union Evangelistic Meetings by Cities* (New York: Revell, 1943); Dean, "Introductory Word," in Oswald J. Smith, *The Fire of God* (Philadelphia: Christ for America, 1948), front flyleaf; Harold Lindsell, *Park Street Prophet: A Life of Harold John Ockenga* (Wheaton, Ill.: Van Kampen Press, 1951), 91, 153; Mel Larson, *God's Man in Manhat-*

tan: The Biography of Dr. William Ward Ayer (Grand Rapids, Mich.: Zondervan, 1950), 165–68.

9. Martin, *A Prophet with Honor,* 106–7; Rice, *We Can Have Revival Now,* 163–65; David Edwin Harrell, Jr., *All Things Are Possible: The Healing and Charismatic Revivals in Modern America* (Bloomington: Indiana University Press, 1975), 10–52; Harrell, *Oral Roberts: An American Life* (Bloomington: Indiana University Press, 1985), 62–69, 80–110; Paul L. Maier, *A Man Spoke, A World Listened: The Story of Walter A. Maier and the Lutheran Hour* (New York: McGraw-Hill, 1963), 325–32.

10. Bruce Shelley, "The Rise of Evangelical Youth Movements," *Fides et Historia* 18 (January 1986): 50–52; Orr, *Good News in Bad Times,* 175–85; Martin, *A Prophet With Honor,* 94, 104, 110–13.

11. "May We Hope for Revival Today?" *SST,* 22 March 1941, 225; George T. B. Davis, "How Prayer Brings Revival," in Dean, *Christ for America,* 27–34; and Ernest M. Wadsworth, *Will Revival Come?* (Chicago: Great Commission Prayer League, 1937), 3–4; David Enlow, *Men Aflame: The Story of Christian Business Men's Committee International* (Grand Rapids, Mich.: Zondervan, 1962), 63.

12. Orr, *Good News in Bad Times,* 33–36; Armin Gesswein, "How Does a Revival Begin?," *MM* 44 (October 1943): 61–62, 86; Gesswein, "Gear Your Thinking to Revival," *Youth for Christ Magazine,* May 1950, 20–22, 88–91.

13. Orr, *The Second Evangelical Awakening in America,* 160–65, 166–68; Orr, *Good News in Bad Times,* 36–41.

14. Norman Grubb, quoted from *Life of Faith,* 16 February 1949, in Orr, *The Second Evangelical Awakening,* 161–62.

15. Claude C. Jenkins, brief report reprinted from *Life of Faith,* 25 May 1949, in Orr, *The Second Evangelical Awakening,* 162.

16. Orr, *The Second Evangelical Awakening,* 163, 188; Orr, "Preparing for Revival," 34–35.

17. Ruth A. Tucker, "Mears, Henrietta Cornella (1890–1963)," *Dictionary of Christianity in America,* ed. Daniel G. Reid et al. (Downers Grove, Ill.: InterVarsity Press, 1990), 722; Ethel May Baldwin and David V. Benson, *Henrietta Mears and How She Did It* (Glendale, Calif.: Regal Books, 1966), 60–72.

18. Orr, "Preparing for Revival," 34.

19. Ibid., 33–35 (quotation); George M. Marsden, *Reforming Fundamentalism: Fuller Seminary and the New Evangelicalism* (Grand Rapids, Mich.: Eerdmans, 1987), 89–90; Orr, *The Second Evangelical Awakening,* 184–85, 188.

20. Martin, *Prophet with Honor,* 112–13.

21. Ibid., 92, 110; Frady, *Billy Graham,* 162–63; Pollock, *Billy Graham,* 85; Torrey Johnson and Robert Cook, *Reaching Youth for Christ* (Chicago: Moody Press, 1944), 23–24.

22. Martin, *Prophet with Honor,* 96–99; Pollock, *Billy Graham,* 36–41.

23. To cite one example, William Ward Ayer, the fiery radio broadcaster and pastor of Calvary Baptist Church in New York, made an extensive preaching tour of the British Isles for Youth for Christ in 1948. See Mel Larson, *God's Man in Manhattan: The Biography of Dr. William Ward Ayer* (Grand Rapids, Mich.: Zondervan, 1950), 113–14; and William Ward Ayer, *Six Decades of Gospel Preaching, 1918–1978* (St. Petersburg, Fla.: Ayerow Publications, 1978), 17.

24. Martin, *Prophet with Honor,* 98–99; Pollock, *Billy Graham,* 38–39; Frady, *Billy Graham,* 170–73. Graham does not recall that his time together with Olford was all that highly charged as a spiritual experience.

25. Orr, "Preparing for Revival," 32; Bill Bright, "Los Angeles Echoes," reprinted in Orr, *The Second Evangelical Awakening*, 190; Orr, *Good News in Bad Times*, 7, 36, 46, 53.

26. For further reflection on fundamentalist spirituality and its appeal to religious heroism, see the introduction to *Sacrificial Lives: Young Martyrs and Fundamentalist Idealism*, ed. Joel A. Carpenter (New York: Garland Publishing, 1988), [vii–xv].

27. Vance Havner, *Road to Revival* (New York: Revell, 1940), 11–14; pp. 49–50 and 57–60 contain similar rhetorical riffs. See also Havner, "Why Not Revival?" *MM* 46 (May 1946): 540–41; and Havner, *It Is Time* (New York: Revell, 1943), 16–19.

28. Ernest M. Wadsworth, *Will Revival Come?*, 2d enl. ed. (Chicago: Moody Press, 1945), 125.

29. William Vance Trollinger, Jr., "Riley's Empire: Northwestern Bible School and Fundamentalism in the Upper Midwest," *Church History* 57 (June 1988): 197–212.

30. Martin, *Prophet with Honor*, 101–2. Riley approached at least one other bright young fundamentalist about the job. Henry Morris, an engineering instructor from Rice University who was then studying for his doctorate at the University of Minnesota, was a committed creationist whose book, *That You Might Believe* (Chicago: Good Books, 1946), convinced Riley that he might make a good president for Northwestern College. See Ronald L. Numbers, *The Creationists* (New York: Alfred A. Knopf, 1992), 196.

31. William Vance Trollinger, Jr., *God's Empire: William Bell Riley and Midwestern Fundamentalism* (Madison: University of Wisconsin Press, 1990), 152–53; Martin, 101–3.

32. Pollock, *Billy Graham*, 42–43; C. Allyn Russell, *Voices of American Fundamentalism: Seven Biographical Studies* (Philadelphia: Westminster Press, 1976), 79; Martin, *Prophet with Honor*, 103.

33. Martin, *Prophet with Honor*, 100–1, 104; Frady, *Billy Graham*, 173–75.

34. Martin, *Prophet with Honor*, 106–8; Frady, *Billy Graham*, 177, 191. A definitive list of the dates and locations of the Graham evangelistic team's engagements in these early days is available from the Archives of the Billy Graham Center, Wheaton College, Wheaton, Illinois.

35. Orr, *Good News in Bad Times*, 151, 155.

36. Frady, *Billy Graham*, 178–82.

37. Martin, *Prophet with Honor*, 109; Frady, *Billy Graham*, 177–78; Pollock, *Billy Graham*, 52.

38. Martin, *Prophet with Honor*, 108–9.

39. Martin, *Prophet with Honor*, 113–14.

40. Frady, *Billy Graham*, 182.

41. Orr, *Good News in Bad Times*, 152–54.

42. Pollock, *Billy Graham*, 52–53; Frady, *Billy Graham*, 183–84; Martin, *Prophet with Honor*, 112.

43. Orr, *Good News in Bad Times*, 154. Orr's account adds a holiness experiential dimension, the fresh anointing by the Spirit, which the other storytellers leave out.

44. Martin, *Prophet with Honor*, 114; see also the film footage of Graham preaching in Los Angeles on file at the Archives of the Billy Graham Center.

45. Graham, "We Need Revival!" in *Revival In Our Time*, 51, 52 (quotation).

46. Ibid., 53.

47. Ibid., 53–57.

48. Graham, "Prepare to Meet Thy God," *Revival in Our Time*, 98.

49. Martin, *Prophet with Honor*, 116.

50. Orr, "Preparing for Revival," 36.

51. Hamblen's conversion is discussed in every account of the Los Angeles campaign, but the most detailed narrative comes from Edwin Orr, who participated in the efforts of the Hollywood Christian Group to bring Hamblen back to God. See Orr, *Good News in Bad Times,* 114–24.

52. Martin, *Prophet with Honor,* 116–18; Mel Larson, "Tasting Revival—at Los Angeles," *Revival in Our Time,* 13–15. Martin reminds the reader that a few years earlier Hearst had also given the order to puff Youth for Christ, and reveals that because of those earlier contacts with the Hearst papers, the Graham crusade had friends inside the newsroom of the *Los Angeles Examiner* who alerted Hearst to this story's possibilities.

53. Orr, *Good News in Bad Times,* 156–57; "Ripples of the Revival," *Youth for Christ Magazine,* January 1950, 22, 24.

54. Orr, *Good News in Bad Times,* 157; Larson, "Tasting Revival—at Los Angeles," 13–16; "Ripples of the Revival," 25; "A Sickle for the Harvest," *Time,* 14 November 1949, 63–64; "A New Evangelist Arises," *Life,* 21 November 1949, 97–98, 100.

55. Martin, *Prophet with Honor,* 123; Harold Lindsell, *Park Street Prophet: A Life of Harold John Ockenga* (Wheaton, Ill.: Van Kampen Press, 1951), 141–44, chronicles Ockenga's yearning for revival.

56. McLoughlin, *Modern Revivalism,* 62–63, 491; Martin, *Prophet with Honor,* 123; Lindsell, *Park Street Prophet,* 91, 145–46, 153; Harold J. Ockenga, "Is America's Revival Breaking?" *Evangelical Beacon,* 18 July 1950, 5.

57. Lindsell, *Park Street Prophet,* 146–51; "3,000 Decide for Christ in 18 Days," *Youth for Christ Magazine,* March 1950, 48–52.

58. Lindsell, *Park Street Prophet,* 149, 152; "3,000 Decide," 52.

59. Lindsell, *Park Street Prophet,* 152; "Garden Packed for Big Revival Rally," *Boston Post* 17 January 1950, 1ff.

60. Quoted in "3,000 Decide," 51.

61. Harold Ockenga, "Revival Is Here!" *Youth for Christ Magazine,* April 1950, 10.

62. Harold John Ockenga, "Afterthoughts on Boston," in *The Second Evangelical Awakening,* 192–93; "3,000 Decide," 52–53; Martin, *Prophet with Honor,* 128.

63. Lindsell, *Park Street Prophet,* 146–47.

64. Ibid., 51–52; Orr, *Good News in Bad Times,* 189.

65. Ockenga, "Afterthoughts on Boston," 192; Orr, *Good News in Bad Times,* 187–88; Lindsell, *Park Street Prophet,* 154–58; "3,995 Decide for Christ as Graham Team Reaches 65,300 in 13 New England Cities," *Youth for Christ Magazine,* May 1950, 45, 91.

66. Graham's next stop after his New England tour would be Washington, D.C., where he was to lead in prayer on April 27 at the U.S. House of Representatives and then speak at a congressional prayer breakfast the following day.

67. Ockenga, "Is America's Revival Breaking?" *Evangelical Beacon,* 18 July 1950, 5.

68. Ibid., 6.

69. *Youth for Christ Magazine* printed enthusiastic accounts of the new revivalists' meetings in dozens of American cities in 1950. For accounts of Billy Graham's meetings see "7,000 Decisions in 22 Days in Columbia, S.C.; 40,000 at Final Service in Graham Campaign," April 1950, 30–33; "Throngs Up to 21,500 Attend Graham Campaign in Portland, Oregon," September 1950, 28–29; "Graham Portland Crusade Second Largest in American History as 632,000 Attend; 9,000 Converts," October 1950, 34–39; "275,000 Attend 22-day Minneapolis Crusade, Greatest in City's History;

4,500 Decisions, 1350 for Salvation," November 1950, 26–29; "20,000 Gather in Rain at Chattanooga, Tenn., to Hear Graham; 700 Raise Hands for Prayer," December 1950, 53–55; "25,000 Converge on Atlanta, Ga., for Opening of Graham Southern Crusade," December 1950, 55.

Merv Rosell's remarkable meetings in 1950 are also reported: "Thousands Accept Christ as More than 100,000 Attend Long Beach Crusade," September 1950, 30–32; "26,000 Throng Kansas City Arena as Rosell, Fuller Open Campaign," September 1950, 34–36; "1468 Decisions among 150,000 at Iowa Crusade," November 1950, 32–33; "300 First Decisions in Chicago United Youth Crusade," November 1950, 35; "1700 First Time Decisions in Kansas City as 5300 Flock to Altar; 225,000 in Attendance," October 1950, 53–55; "As Troops Fight in Korea, 30,000 Revival Goers Pray on Iowa Statehouse Steps," October 1950, 44–50. For an account of Rosell's meetings in Phoenix and Denver, see Orr, *Good News in Bad Times,* 183–85.

Youth for Christ Magazine covered other evangelists from the youth rally circuit as well, notably: *Jack Shuler:* "Shuler at Zollner Stadium in Ft. Wayne Triumph," September 1950, 59; "12,000 at Final Rally in Ft. Wayne Six-Week Campaign," September 1950, 33; Campaign in Louisville Greatest in City's History," September 1950, 32; "Sioux Falls, S.D., Feels Revival Pulsebeat in Jack Shuler Campaign," December 1950, 55–56; *Bob Cook:* Nettie Castle, "200 Converts in San Diego Campaign," April 1950, 39; *Torrey Johnson:* "Oakland Tent Crowded in Mid-Century Revival Campaign," May 1950, 42; "1,000 Converts in Oakland Campaign," July 1950, 16–17; *Jimmy Johnson:* "Memphis '16 Big Days' Spill Over into 23 Days; 726 Decisions for Christ as 70,000 Attend," November 1950, 36–37.

70. From *Youth for Christ Magazine:* Laura Z. LeFevre, "500 Converted in Lancaster, Pa., Revival," April 1950, 42–43; "God Works in Coon Rapids, Iowa," July 1950, 18; "Tent Erected in Dinuba, Calif., Crusade Goes into Overtime," November 1950, 34. These meetings, which owed so much in their style and personnel to the Youth for Christ movement, demonstrated what D. L. Moody had known about modern revivalism eighty years before: it was not a rural phenomenon nurtured in the South and Midwest but was made in the nation's urban centers and then exported out to the hinterlands.

71. Orr, *The Second Evangelical Awakening,* 169–70; V. R. Edman, "We Felt the Presence and Power of God," *Youth for Christ Magazine,* March 1950, 10, 90; Edwin S. Johnson, "More Powerful than the H-Bomb," Ibid., 91–92; Bud Schaeffer and Arthur S. Brown, "How Revival Came to Wheaton College," Ibid., 92.

72. Kiernan quoted in Orr, *The Second Evangelical Awakening,* 175. For accounts of media coverage and the growing chain of campus revivals see ibid., 174–83; Orr, *Good News in Bad Times,* 54–66; and W. H. Holland, "118-Hour Revival at Asbury College," *Youth for Christ Magazine,* April 1950, 35–37, 41. See also "42 Hours of Repentance," *Time,* 20 February 1950, 56–567; and "College Revival Becomes Confession Marathon," *Life,* 20 February 1950, 40–41.

73. Quoted in Orr, *The Second Evangelical Awakening,* 175.

74. Billy Graham and his associates visited the White House for the first time in July 1950 for an interview with President Truman. According to William Martin, Graham's visit was memorable mostly in that the group greatly offended Truman by telling the press about their time of prayer with the President (Martin, *Prophet with Honor,* 131–32).

75. Enlow, *Men Aflame,* 65; Orr, *Good News in Bad Times,* 105–16, 121, 123, 128–33, 145–47.

76. Orr, *Good News in Bad Times,* 254; Hoffman, *Revival Times in America* (Boston: W. A. Wilde, 1956), 180, 189.

Conclusion

1. Phillip E. Hammond, "In Search of a Protestant Twentieth Century: American Religion and Power since 1900," *Review of Religious Research* 24 (March 1983): 281.

2. Martin E. Marty, "The Revival of Evangelicalism and Southern Religion," in *Varieties of Southern Evangelicalism*, ed. David E. Harrell, Jr. (Macon, Ga.: Mercer University Press, 1981), 9.

3. Ibid., 11–21.

4. Ibid., 11.

5. Ernest Sandeen's two most important works on fundamentalism, *The Roots of Fundamentalism: British and American Millenarianism. 1800–1930* (Chicago: University of Chicago Press, 1970), and "Fundamentalism and American Identity," *Annals of the American Academy of Social and Political Sciences* 387 (January 1970): 56–65, virtually equate latter-day evangelicalism with the earlier fundamentalism. Similar perspectives prevail among the authors of the dozen essays in *The Evangelicals: What They Believe, Who They Are, Where They Are Changing*, ed. David F. Wells and John D. Woodbridge (Nashville: Abingdon Press, 1975).

6. Smith, "The Postfundamentalist Party," a review of *The Evangelicals* in the *Christian Century*, 4–11 February 1976, 125. See also Cullen Murphy, "Protestantism and the Evangelicals," *Wilson Quarterly* 5 (Autumn 1981): 105–16, which was written in consultation with Smith and bears his stamp throughout.

7. Donald W. Dayton, "An Analysis of the Self-Understanding of American Evangelicalism with a Critique of its Correlated Historiography" (paper delivered at the Wesleyan Holiness Study Project's fellows seminar, Asbury Theological Seminary, 28–30 January 1988); and Dayton, "The Search for the Historical Evangelicalism: George Marsden's History of Fuller Seminary as a Case Study," *Christian Scholar's Review* 23 (September 1993): 12–33.

8. In order to become acquainted with the main points of this ongoing debate, see Dayton, "The Search for the Historical Evangelicalism," and the published responses that appeared in the same issue of the *Christian Scholar's Review*, especially George M. Marsden, "Response to Don Dayton," 34–40; Douglas A. Sweeney, "Historiographical Dialectics: On Marsden, Dayton, and the Inner Logic of Evangelical History," 48–52; and Joel A. Carpenter, "The Scope of American Evangelicalism: Some Comments on the Dayton-Marsden Exchange," 53–61.

9. Moore, *Religious Outsiders and the Making of Americans* (New York, Oxford University Press, 1986), 149.

10. James Guth, Corwin Smidt, John C. Green, and Lyman Kellstedt, *National Survey of Religion and Politics: Summary Report*, Ray C. Bliss Institute of Applied Politics (Akron, Ohio: University of Akron, 1992).

11. Grant Wacker, "Uneasy in Zion: Evangelicals in Postmodern Society," in *Evangelicalism and Modern America*, ed. George Marsden (Grand Rapids, Mich.: Eerdmans, 1984), 17–28, 22 (quote).

12. Martin E. Marty, *The New Shape of American Religion* (New York: Harper & Brothers, 1959), 21–27.

13. Bob Jones [Jr.], *Corn Bread and Caviar* (Greenville, S.C.: Bob Jones University Press, 1985), 104.

14. Wallis A. Turner, "How Different Shall We Be?" *MM* 56 (July 1956): 15–16.

15. W. Somerset Maugham, *The Razor's Edge* (New York: Collier, 1944), 343.

16. "Door Interview: Garrison Keillor," *Wittenburg Door* 84 (April–May 1985): 18.

INDEX

Aberhart, William, 287n.45

ABFMS. *See* American Baptist Foreign Mission Society

Abolitionism, 102, 282n.54

Academy Awards, 167

Activism, 28, 106–7

Adams, J. Davis, 294n.13

Advent Christian, 144

Adventists, 125

Aerial Girls (radio program), 129

Africa Inland Mission, 27, 30; as faith mission, 82, 185; and NAE, 144, 151, 277n.34

AIM. *See* African Inland Mission

Albers, Rudy, 137

Albright, William F., 73, 273n.63

Alienation: and martyr's mentality, 14–15, 66–67, 90, 100–101, 186, 241; recovery from, 111, 139, 231–34, 237; and search for legitimacy, 190–94, 198, 203; sense of, felt by fundamentalists, 33–35, 38, 40–43, 52, 56, 86, 107

All-Bible Graded Series, 25, 258n.63

Allenby, General Edmund Henry Hynman, 92

Alliance Tabernacle (New York), 161, 163–64

American Baptist Foreign Mission Society, 43, 46, 48

American Board of Commissioners for Foreign Missions, 185

American Board of Missions to the Jews, 98

American Broadcasting Company, 24, 131

American Conference of Undenominational Churches, 45

American Council of Christian Churches, 48,

145–48, 205, 251n.1 (Intro.), 297n.39; and NAE, 150, 152–54, 160

Ammerman, Nancy Tatom, 268n.4, 270n.34

Amos and Andy (radio program), 130

Anderson, Walter, 169

Angelus Temple (Los Angeles), 130

Announcer, The (Dudley Bible Institute), 132

Announcers Trio (WMBI), 134

Antichrist. *See under* Prophecy

Antielitism, 35–37, 95, 101, 106

Antifeminism, 67–69, 271n.38

Antimodernism, 5–8, 16, 26–29, 120, 125, 157, 162; failure of, 3, 11, 15, 34, 37, 187. *See also* Cultural battles; Great Apostasy; Modernism

Anti-Semitism, 27, 37, 42, 97–99, 102–5, 220, 244, 281n.54, 283n.71. *See also* Jews; Zionism

Apocalypse. *See under* Prophecy

Apostasy. *See* Great Apostasy

Appelman, Hyman, 159–60, 168, 213, 216

Appleby, R. Scott, 252n.4

Archaeology, 73–74

Archer, Gleason, 191, 194–95

Armageddon. *See under* Prophecy

Asbury College and Seminary (Wilmore, Ky.), 191, 230

Assemblies of God, 8, 25, 31, 144, 147, 159, 174, 181, 185, 255n.17

Associated Press, 226–27

Association of Baptists for the Evangelization of the Orient, 23, 28, 68

Association of Christian Youth in America (New York), 163

319